Cambridge Studies in Social and Emotional Development
General editor: Martin L. Hoffman

Measuring emotions in infants and children

The activities of the Council's Committee on Social and Affective Development During Childhood have been supported primarily by the Foundation for Child Development, a private foundation that makes grants to educational and charitable institutions. Its main interests are in research, social and economic indicators of children's lives, advocacy and public information projects, and service experiments that help translate theoretical knowledge about children into policies and practices that affect their daily lives.

Measuring emotions in infants and children

*Based on seminars sponsored by the
Committee on Social and Affective Development During Childhood
of the Social Science Research Council*

Edited by

CARROLL E. IZARD

University of Delaware

CAMBRIDGE UNIVERSITY PRESS

Cambridge
London   New York   New Rochelle
Melbourne   Sydney

Published by the Press Syndicate of the University of Cambridge
The Pitt Building, Trumpington Street, Cambridge CB2 1RP
32 East 57th Street, New York, NY 10022, USA
296 Beaconsfield Parade, Middle Park, Melbourne 3206, Australia

© Cambridge University Press 1982

First published 1982

Printed in the United States of America

Library of Congress Cataloging in Publication Data
Main entry under title:
Measuring emotions in infants and children.
(Cambridge studies in social and emotional development)
Includes index.
1. Emotions in children – Testing – Congresses.
2. Facial expression – Congresses. I. Izard, Carroll E.
II. Social Science Research Council (U.S.).
Committee on Social and Affective
Development During Childhood. III. Series.
[DNLM: 1. Child development – Congresses.
2. Emotions – In infancy and childhood –
Congresses. WS 105.5.E5 M484 1978–79]
BF723.E6M43   155.4'12   81–10032
ISBN 0 521 24171 5   AACR2

Contents

List of contributors   *page* vii

Foreword *Jerome Kagan and Peter B. Read*   ix

Part I Introduction

1 Measuring emotions in human development *Carroll
   E. Izard*   3

Part II Psychobiological functions

2 Developmental psychoendocrinology: an approach to the
   study of emotions *Katherine H. Tennes and John W. Mason*   21

3 Heart rate and heart rate variability as signs of a
   temperamental dimension in infants *Jerome Kagan*   38

4 Psychophysiological patterning and emotion revisited: a
   systems perspective *Gary E. Schwartz*   67

Part III Facial, vocal, and body signals

5 Two complementary systems for measuring facial
   expressions in infants and children *Carroll E. Izard and
   Linda M. Dougherty*   97

6 The assessment of vocal expression in infants and
   children *Klaus R. Scherer*   127

7 Gaze behavior in infants and children: a tool for the study
   of emotions? *Ralph V. Exline*   164

8 The measurement of emotional state *Michael Lewis and
   Linda Michalson*   178

v

9   Measuring the development of sensitivity to nonverbal
     communication *Bella M. DePaulo and Robert Rosenthal*   208

Part IV Subjective experience, empathy, and attachment

10 The construct validity of the Differential Emotions Scale as
     adapted for children and adolescents *William E. Kotsch,
     David W. Gerbing, and Lynne E. Schwartz*   251

11 The measurement of empathy *Martin L. Hoffman*   279

Part V Commentary

12 Emotion and the cardiovascular system: a critical
     perspective *Paul A. Obrist, Kathleen C. Light, and Janice
     L. Hastrup*   299

13 An ethological approach to research on facial
     expressions *William R. Charlesworth*   317

14 The construction of emotion in the child *George Mandler*   335

     Index   345

Contributors

William R. Charlesworth
Institute of Child Development
University of Minnesota

Bella M. DePaulo
Department of Psychology
University of Virginia

Linda M. Dougherty
Department of Psychology
University of Southern California

Ralph V. Exline
Department of Psychology
University of Delaware

David W. Gerbing
Department of Psychology
Baylor University

Janice L. Hastrup
Department of Psychology
University of North Carolina at
Chapel Hill

Martin L. Hoffman
Department of Psychology
University of Michigan

Carroll E. Izard
Department of Psychology
University of Delaware

Jerome Kagan
Department of Psychology and Social
Relations
Harvard University

William E. Kotsch
Department of Psychology
Baylor University

Michael Lewis
Institute for Research in
Human Development
Educational Testing Service

Kathleen C. Light
Department of Psychology
University of North Carolina at
Chapel Hill

George Mandler
Department of Psychology
University of California at San Diego

John W. Mason
Veterans Administration
Medical Center
West Haven, Connecticut

Linda Michalson
Institute for Research in
Human Development
Educational Testing Service

Paul A. Obrist
Department of Psychiatry
School of Medicine
University of North Carolina

Robert Rosenthal
Department of Psychology and Social
Relations
Harvard University

Klaus R. Scherer
Department of Psychology
Justus-Liebig-Universität
Giessen, West Germany

Gary E. Schwartz
Department of Psychology
Yale University

Lynne E. Schwartz
Department of Psychology
Baylor University

Katherine H. Tennes
Department of Psychiatry
University of Colorado
Health Science Center

Foreword

This volume is based upon papers prepared for two conferences sponsored by the Social Science Research Council's Committee on Social and Affective Development During Childhood. Established in 1975 with funds from the Foundation for Child Development and the Bush Foundation, this committee has sponsored numerous activities intended to generate new forms of developmental research and to relate cognitive to what have been regarded as noncognitive forms of development. The members of the committee believe in the inherent connectedness of the emotional, cognitive, and social domains and were concerned that the quantity and quality of developmental research on social and emotional processes did not reflect the magnitude of their contribution to the course of human development.

The Social Science Research Council has a long history of research planning in the social sciences. Since its founding in 1923, it has convened interdisciplinary groups of scholars who, through their joint efforts – sponsorship of conferences, workshops, training institutes, and publications – have given both impetus and substance to emerging areas of the social sciences. The Council has stimulated the development of new ideas, methods, and empirical research in areas of the social sciences as diverse as sociolinguistics and social indicators.

In the early 1970s, several meetings held at the Council's offices explored the reasons for the relative paucity of developmental research in the social and emotional domains and examined some promising new research programs in these areas. Despite the influential theoretical contributions of Freud, Mead, and Erikson, and a prevailing belief among developmental psychologists in the importance of socioemotional development, the study of cognition has dominated the field of child development, and empirical investigations of the sequences in affective display or social behavior have not flourished. The Council's Committee on Social and Affective Development During Childhood was formed in the belief that concerted planning efforts by interested scholars could redress this discrepancy and stimulate new work.

Facing the title page of this volume is a list of those scholars who joined the committee in its early years and began to chart a course of research planning activities. Many of this group's early deliberations focused on obstacles to the generation of new research on emotional development. It was concluded that many difficulties stemmed from the limited measurement techniques available for assessing affective dimensions of human behavior. Although methodological advances were being made in the fields of perception, memory, and reasoning in children, comparable progress in the evaluation of social and emotional variables had not occurred as rapidly or as easily. The committee decided, therefore, to initiate a formal discussion of methods in the study of emotions in children and to consider efforts that would disseminate to interested scholars knowledge of new techniques. The committee held two conferences on the measurement of emotions at the Educational Testing Service's conference center in Princeton, New Jersey, in November 1978 and May 1979. Researchers who had employed techniques for measuring aspects of emotion were asked to present their research and to discuss the applicability of their techniques to the study of child development. Participants in these meetings included William Charlesworth, Ralph Exline, Jeanne Brooks-Gunn, Martin Hoffman, Carroll E. Izard, Jerome Kagan, Michael Lewis, George Mandler, Paul Obrist, Harriet Oster, Peter B. Read, Robert Rosenthal, Klaus Scherer, Gary Schwartz, Katherine Tennes, and Everett Waters.

The chapters composing this volume are only a sample of the conference presentations and discussions. It is impossible to capture completely the complexity and vitality of the discussions, and because of constraints associated with publication, several important contributions could not be represented here. The entire project has benefited from the leadership of Carroll Izard, whose scholarly dedication to the advancement of research on emotions continues to inspire and inform researchers who have become intrigued with the study of affective phenomena. His introductory chapter reviews some of the major themes addressed by conference participants and provides a valuable guide to the articles that follow.

We hope that this is only the first of several volumes that will facilitate the study of affects in children and encourage more scientists to probe a psychological domain that has suffered from empirical neglect for too long.

Jerome Kagan
Peter B. Read

Part I

Introduction

1   Measuring emotions in human development

Carroll E. Izard

This volume does not attempt to represent all measurement procedures relevant to the study of emotions or emotion-related phenomena. Rather, it presents some of the most promising techniques that apply to the different components or levels of emotion. Some omissions could not be avoided in this initial effort to present a significant sample of devices for the measurement of emotion. For example, this volume does not contain a chapter on brain research techniques, nor does it contain one on the measurement of infant–mother attachment, although the latter was a major topic of one of our conferences. We were also unable to include a discussion of the so-called cognitive–ethological approach to the study of emotions, an approach whose central aim is to measure the ongoing stream of cognition and emotions (see Csikszentmihalyi, 1979; Diener & Dweck, 1978; Meichenbaum & Butler, in press).

Conference participants grappled with many difficult themes concerning the nature of emotions and how best to study them in a developmental context. In the following pages, I shall discuss some of these themes and then provide a brief overview of the individual chapters. The themes that were central to our discussions included: (a) the components of emotion and the types of emotion variables; (b) autonomic versus somatic indexes of emotions; (c) emotion–cognition relationships; (d) relationships among biological, behavioral, and experiential indexes; and (e) the relationship among emotion states, traits, and thresholds.

Components of emotion and types of emotion variables

The view that emotion processes fall into three broad classes is gaining acceptance. These are most commonly described as biological, behavioral, and experiential. Each class has a number of divisions.

The biological level. The biological domain includes anatomical, neurophysiological, and biochemical studies of brain mechanisms and neurohumors involved

3

in emotion processes. In turn, the biochemistry of emotions embraces endocrinological studies of neurotransmitters in the limbic system and in limbic–cortical
interconnections. At present there is very little evidence for strong relationships
between specific hormones and specific emotions, but the investigation of profiles or patterns of hormones and neurotransmitters as indicants of emotion began
only recently (e.g., Mason, 1975).

To date, no single brain mechanism seems to be solely responsible for any
particular emotion, but there are promising approaches that consider complex
interconnections between mechanisms and particular emotion processes (e.g.,
Veinstein & Simonov, 1979). Although few neuroscientists are considering discrete emotions and, in particular, their role in development, the neurosciences
have added substantially to our knowledge of the neural substrates of emotion
and emotion-related behavior (for a summary, see Izard & Saxton, in press).

The behavioral–expressive level. There are observable indexes of specific discrete emotions, some signals appearing at birth and most of the others by 7 to 9
months of age (Izard et al., 1980). The past decade has seen the growth of a
robust body of empirical evidence supporting Darwin's (1872) hypothesis of the
innateness and universality of certain emotion expressions. The data indicate that
there are six to nine such universal expressions, under the control of the somatic
nervous system (Ekman, 1968; Izard, 1971). Their universality testifies to the
fact that each of these patterns of facial movement has a biological substrate and
a conscious representation that cut across ethnic and cultural boundaries.

Research in the past decade has also made it clear that these innate/universal
expressions are subject to modification, masking, and even exaggerated distor-
tion through socialization and enculturation (Ekman, 1972; Izard, 1971). Still,
studies of cultural differences in the socialization and regulation of affect expression have hardly begun. Although there can be no doubt that social learning and
the rules and obligations of a given culture influence affect expression, it seems
reasonable to assume that this effect is smallest in infants and young children.
Nevertheless, any investigator using facial behaviors as indicators of specific
emotions needs to be aware that social learning and cultural forces can influence
emotion expression as early as the 2nd year of life and have considerable impact
in the 3rd year. Cultural influence notwithstanding, spontaneous facial patterns
of infants and young children are among the most veridical indicators of specific
emotions.

I do not mean that mastering methods of measuring facial indicators is the
surest procedure. Even the most efficient system of coding facial behaviors requires considerable time to learn, longer to become highly proficient, and even
longer to apply if there are very many data to be analyzed. Furthermore, current

methods (e.g., Ekman & Friesen, 1978; Izard, 1979; Izard & Dougherty, 1980) of analyzing facial behavior require a clear, closeup video record of the face.

The behavioral–expressive sphere also includes signals other than facial ones. Evidence is accumulating to support the notion that at least for some emotions, vocalizations have emotion-specific acoustical properties (Scherer, 1979). Some studies have shown that gaze patterns may be specific to certain emotions, or at least to classes of emotion (Exline et al., 1979). Finally, it is certainly possible that at least in early development, there may be some emotion-specific postural–gestural–locomotor activities.

In discussing the behavioral–expressive component of emotion, I should also note that it is possible to consider responses or functions of the autonomic nervous system as part of emotion expression. In fact, some researchers have contrasted external and internal expressors (Buck et al., 1969, 1972; Jones, 1950). Although there can be little doubt that the autonomic nervous system is frequently involved in emotion processes, there is a paucity of evidence for emotion-specific indexes of functions of the autonomic nervous system. This issue arises in several of the contributions to this volume. See especially the chapters by Kagan, Obrist, Mandler, and G. Schwartz.

The subjective–experiential level. Any complete definition of emotion has to deal with its representation in consciousness – variously called the felt-emotion, experiental, phenomenological, or cognitive component. William James (1890/1950) said that we never really know what emotion an individual is experiencing until he or she tells us. No one has yet proved James wrong, although it is possible to show a strong correlation between thought processes or imagery and emotion-specific electromyographic (EMG) patterns of facial activity (Schwartz et al., 1976).

The method of choice for assessing subjective experiences of emotions is some form of direct self-report. One approach that goes back, at least conceptually, to Spencer and Wundt and that was revived in the 1940s by Schlosberg (1941, 1952, 1954) involves attempts to dimensionalize emotion. The early efforts of Schlosberg and his colleagues sought to predict emotion categories of facial expressions from ratings based on the dimensions of tension–relaxation, pleasantness–unpleasantness and, later, acceptance–rejection. This approach is not represented in the present volume, but the reader can readily find ample reports of empirical studies and reviews (e.g., Bartlett & Izard, 1972; Block, 1957; Izard, 1971, Chapter 4; Mehrabian & Russell, 1974; Royce & McDermott, 1977; Russell, 1978, 1979).

The most frequent approach to measuring the subjective experience of emotion employs affect-adjective rating scales (e.g., Izard, 1972; Nowlis, 1965; Zuckerman, 1960). One of these that has been adapted for children and adolescents and that covers a wide range of emotions is presented in Chapter 10 by Kotsch, Gerbing, and L. Schwartz.

Autonomic versus somatic indicators

Conceptions of the roles of autonomic and somatic factors in emotion activation and emotion experience are quite divergent. I have argued (Izard, 1971, 1977) that the somatic activity in facial behaviors is an integral part of the emotion, not simply an expression of it. Mandler (Chapter 11) has made a similar case for autonomic responses. The investigator who is trying to decide whether to use autonomic or somatic indicators will be particularly interested in the chapters by Kagan, Mandler, Obrist, and G. Schwartz. Current evidence seems to indicate that there are more emotion-specific somatic indicators than autonomic ones, but the choice will depend, in part, on the investigator's hypothesis. Like Schwartz (Chapter 4), I believe it is important to encourage the multivariate approach, using, wherever feasible and appropriate, both classes of indicators. There certainly are important studies to be done that cannot use both types of measures, and in this case I think it is important to seek some kind of independent validation of the presence of emotion or patterns of emotions. Self-report (see the chapter by Kotsch et al.) and measures of gross-motor behaviors in context (see the chapter by Lewis) offer viable possibilities. Similarly, studies using self-report scales can be strengthened by evidence obtained with either somatic or autonomic indexes.

Emotion and cognition

The relationship between emotion and cognition is a complex theoretical issue that has been treated in detail by a number of theorists (Izard, 1977; Lazarus, 1974; Leeper, 1948, 1965; Leventhal, 1980; Mandler, 1975; Plutchik, 1980; Tomkins, 1962). The reader is referred to these sources for various theoretical views, but some parts of the issue are relevant to the topic of this volume, methods of measurement.

Some theorists conceive of emotion and cognition as aspects of a single process, whereas others see emotion and cognition as functions of relatively independent though highly interrelated and interactive systems. Investigators should be aware of the theoretical issues involved and should note that choice of one particular conceptualization of emotion-in-relation-to-cognition will make a difference in choosing and adapting measuring techniques and experimental procedures.

Even if emotion is a function of a separate and relatively independent system, any given index of emotion will probably fall on a continuum with respect to the degree that it reflects cognitive processes or is influenced by them. Perhaps an illustration will help clarify this notion. A pain-released distress expression on the face of a neonate is at one extreme of the continuum, where cognitive processes participate minimally or not at all in the affect index derived from coding the trauma-induced facial movements. On the other hand, a self-report or affect-adjective checklist completed by an adult while imagining a pain experience (or an experience of anger or fear) is at the other extreme, where cognitive processes are highly involved. Neither all facial movement indexes nor all self-report indexes can be lumped together at opposite ends of the continuum. For example, one has to consider whether the facial behaviors are voluntary or involuntary, and in the case of the former, cognitive processes would certainly be more involved. Similarly, self-reports of imagery-induced emotion require more cognitive mediation than self-reports of real pain or fear during the affective experience.

Relationships among biological, behavioral, and experiential indexes

Attempts to find relations among psychophysiological indexes have met with negative or mixed results (Hodges, 1976). The new aspect of this problem is the question of the relationship of the various psychophysiological indexes to a *pattern* of specific emotions (see G. Schwartz's Chapter 4). The older studies were concerned mainly with emotion as arousal or with some general concept of emotionality. These studies, therefore, at least from the standpoint of discrete emotion concepts, lacked specificity. Even those that studied specific emotions did not allow for the fact that emotions, even though specific or discrete, typically occur in patterns or sequences of several different emotions (Izard, 1972; G. Schwartz, Chapter 4).

It is important for investigators launching studies involving cross-level indexes of emotions to keep two things in mind. First, a target emotion should be clearly identified by a set of objective criteria in at least one measurement domain. Second, it is necessary to be aware of differences among the domains on the temporal dimension. For example, autonomic indexes such as changes in heart rate (HR) are much slower than somatic indicators such as facial movements, and some adjustments must be made to allow for the lag.

Emotion traits, states, and thresholds

The concepts of emotion states and emotion traits have been widely discussed. For example, Spielberger (1966, 1972) has marshaled evidence to support Cattell and Scheier's (1961) notion that anxiety can be measured either as a transitory state or as a trait, or stable individual difference, in anxiety proneness. His position is that trait anxiety refers to "differences in the disposition to perceive a wide range of stimulus situations as dangerous or threatening, and in the tendency to respond to such threats with A-State reactions" (Spielberger, 1972, p. 39). The distinction between state and trait has proved useful, particularly in research on anxiety. That there are individual differences in tendency or proneness to experience affect certainly seems to be supported by temperament research and common observations (Thomas & Chess, 1977; Thomas, Chess, & Birch, 1968).

I have discussed traitlike differences in emotion expression and emotion responsiveness in terms of individual differences in emotion thresholds (Izard, 1971, 1977). For example, the notion that individuals differ in their thresholds for anger is similar to the notion of individual differences in tendency or proneness to experience or express anger, but the threshold concept can also explain individual differences in measures of emotion states.

On choosing methods and making inferences

This introductory chapter and the volume as a whole emphasize the importance of viewing emotions as complex phenomena having neurophysiological–biochemical, behavioral–expressive, and subjective–experiential components. One barrier to progress in research on emotions has been the relative isolation of scientists working in different disciplines or specialities, often using indexes of only one component of emotion. This isolation was due in part to the fact that some of the research was not concerned with identifying specific emotions, and the investigators often had aims other than the study of specific emotions. There has also been skepticism about measures in domains outside one's speciality, and some pessimism was created by the seemingly vast differences in techniques from one level to another. Cross-speciality and interdisciplinary interchanges and research efforts should help us surmount these barriers (see Chapter 4).

The investigator's aims and hypotheses ultimately determine the methodology and measurement techniques for a particular study. We believe, however, that consideration of several principles in choosing methods and making inferences from the data will help strengthen the empirical foundation for the scientific study of emotions in human development.

1. An emotion is defined by neurophysiological–biochemical, behavioral–expressive, and experiential–conscious processes, and thus data from any one of these three levels may be considered as indicative but not sufficient to identify the specific emotion or even to verify that that emotion or any emotion occurred. Investigators may infer the occurrence of some emotion, but if they seek evidence on specific emotions, or patterns or sequences of specific emotions, they will need convergent data from at least two levels, especially in the absence of instrumental behaviors and ecological conditions consistent with the emotion indexed. Whether or not a self-report of the feeling or experience of the specific emotion in consciousness is a necessary factor in identifying that emotion is debatable, particularly if we add postural–gestural–locomotor and ecological variables to our definitional network. For example, the facial expression of fear on a child running from a snarling dog provides rather convincing data for the occurrence of fear. Note, however, that the flight behavior alone, without some acceptable indicator of fear, is insufficient. The child could have teased the "mean old dog" and then run with excitement and mischievous joy to a well-known point beyond the reach of the dog's leash. Similarly, a facial expression of anger accompanied by aggressive or destructive behavior (tearing up the magazine left by the departed mother in the separation episode of the Strange Situation) in a prelingual 13-month-old toddler is convincing evidence of the occurrence of anger. Again, the situation and destructive behavior are insufficient to identify anger. The child could be playing a game with the magazine and laughing uproariously. In the case of the child in the ecological condition (EC), territory of the mean old dog, we can set up a hierarchical table of data sets that go from least to most convincing with respect to their contribution to the identification of a specific emotion.

a. Escape-avoidant behavior (child fleeing) (Br), alone
b. Vocal expression or scream (V-ex), alone
c. Facial expression (F-ex), alone
d. Br + V-ex
e. Br + F-ex
f. V-ex + F-ex
g. Br + V-ex + F-ex

The ranking of F-ex as a more important index than V-ex reflects, at this point, the weight of the empirical evidence – there is currently more evidence for fear-specific facial indicators than for voice-specific ones.

The identification of specific emotions in preverbal, prelocomotor infants presents a special problem. There is substantial evidence that young infants (birth to 9 months) can produce the facial expressions of seven discrete emotions and that of the affect of pain or physical distress (Izard et al., 1980). Still, we cannot assume that such infants can appraise the ecological conditions or exhibit much in the way of instrumental behaviors. It is reasonable to suppose that they can and do exhibit an age-related and increasingly organized set of emotion-related vocal and postural–gestural behaviors, but these have not been the subject of systematic investigation.

2. *Emotions tend to occur in patterns or sequences, sometimes with rapid shifts in emotion signals and emotion-related behaviors.* Further, emotions, at least their facial expressions, often occur in combinations, or blends (e.g., sig-

nals of sadness in the brow region and those of anger in the mouth region). This serves as a caution in the use of stimulus situations or incentive events in the expectation of observing indicators of only one emotion. An adult bias such that a person sees only sadness or only anger in a toddler on departure of the mother runs counter to the little empirical data that is available (Gaensbauer, Mrazek, & Emde, 1979; Shiller & Izard, 1981; Young & Décarie, 1977).

3. Emotion-related variables can show traitlike consistency whether or not they are known functions of identifiable discrete emotions. Measures of sensitivity to nonverbal affect signals, empathy, and temperament factors are examples. An important point here is that excellent research on emotion-related phenomena can be done without identification of specific emotions or emotion patterns. See the chapters by Hoffman and Kagan.

4. Emotion-related phenomena, such as fear-related behaviors, can be identified and studied by the ethological approach. It is useful to distinguish between an emotion (e.g., fear), and emotion-related behaviors (e.g., fear-related behaviors) that accompany or follow the emotion. Staying with the broad definition given earlier, observable expressive or display behaviors (like the facial expression of fear) that occur as reflexlike accompaniments of the internal processes are integral to the emotion and can be distinguished from emotion-related instrumental, manipulatory, or locomotor behaviors. Emotion-related behaviors (which include perceptual–cognitive processes) can be viewed as emotion-motivated activities, but this is not a position that all observers would accept. Emotion-related behaviors may also become skills or a coping style that attenuates or inhibits the emotions they once accompanied. Thus a pattern of coping responses that are now triggered by interest and anticipation may be a modification of an original set of responses that were generated by fear. The interest-activated coping pattern in a previously threatening situation now serves to attenuate or completely inhibit the fear that the situation once engendered.

The ethological approach asks us to consider the cognitive and behavioral capacities of the infant or child, lest adult biases lead to misattributions or unacceptable inferences. Results from this approach are more convincingly related to specific emotions when the ecological conditions have been previously shown to produce specific emotion signals in the age group being investigated and when the behaviors have been previously shown to be associated with specific emotion indexes. If we assume that these conditions are met, the study of fear-related or anger-related behaviors, for example, can have importance in its own right, whether or not these behaviors are accompanied by negative emotion. Indeed, in the absence of negative emotion, these actions can provide evidence that the individual is behaving very adaptively – for example, escaping from a dangerous situation without the toxic experience of fear, which is costly to the person at best; in extreme conditions, escape behaviors reduce or eliminate fear before it becomes terror and leads to behavioral freezing or panic.

Overview of the volume

This volume contains contributions on methodology, research strategies, and measurement procedures and techniques for each of the three components of emotion. There are chapters on psychoendocrinology and psychophysiology (neurophysiological component), facial, vocal, and gaze behavior (behavioral-expressive component), and self-report scales (subjective–experiential component). The final section of the book consists of commentaries by three experts, each of whom focuses on a major issue in one or more of the three sections of the volume.

In their chapter on psychoendocrinology (Chapter 2), Tennes and Mason consider emotion as "a primary determinant of endocrine activity in human adults," but they acknowledge the scarcity of information about the ontogeny of emotion–endocrine relationships. Their review focuses on the hypothalamic–pituitary–adrenocortical system, with special attention to studies of infants and young children in stressful situations. They suggest that individual differences in hormone production correspond to different personality traits that can be interpreted as emotion-related characteristics such as *reserved, intense, openly expressive of affect*. They maintain that developmental studies of hormones and emotions should involve social, psychological, and endocrinological approaches.

Kagan (Chapter 3) reports some exciting evidence for the hypothesis that cardiac functions may provide an index of a temperamental dimension in the developing child. Data supporting this hypothesis were derived from a study that examined heart rate range. Range showed considerable stability across time for different age groups, and a low range was correlated with behavioral inhibition in uncertain situations. Even though heart rate range may not index a specific emotion or an identifiable pattern of specific emotions, the data point to the possibility of developing psychophysiological indexes of temperament, a concept rooted in affective phenomena.

In Chapter 4, G. Schwartz adopts a systems perspective that places the psychophysiology of emotions in a broad interdisciplinary framework. The result is an exciting conceptual synthesis that may become a watershed in this domain of theory and research. His theoretical stance and his empirical data raise challenging questions for discipline-specific minitheories and for single-variable research paradigms. A systems view calls for defining and hence measuring emotions at different levels, a position quite consistent with the "first principle" discussed in Chapter 1. Schwartz's cogent analysis of the emotion domain underscores the fact that the basic components of an emotion are themselves systems within systems, each of which operates on its own level and requires a different level of analysis. For example, the neurophysiological component of an emotion is a system (set of neural structures, pathways, and transmitters) within a larger system or network of interacting systems that comprise the brain and nervous system.

Does a systems perspective call for changes in approaches to measurement? Yes, argues Schwartz, we should look for *patterns* of subjective experience, skeletal muscle activity, autonomic nervous system activity, and central nervous system activity, and for patterns of interactions across these levels of functioning. The theoretical framework and data presented in Chapter 4 suggest that the search for emotion-specific intersystem patterns of functioning should continue.

In Chapter 5, Izard and Dougherty present a summary of the evidence for the innateness and universality of the expressions of certain basic, or fundamental, emotions. They also discuss the individual–motivational and social–communicative functions of emotion-specific facial signals.

The chapter describes two systems for measuring the facial–expressive signals of emotions. The Maximally Discriminative Facial Movement Coding System (Max) is an objective, anatomically based movement coding system. The movements or appearance changes that are coded are those that have been shown to be involved in the expression or signal configuration of one of the fundamental emotions as defined in differential emotions theory. Coders observe each facial area (brow, eye, mouth) separately and simply judge the presence or absence of a particular movement. An independent coder examines the coded data in relation to a priori formulas, or combinations of appearance changes, that identify the fundamental emotions and blends of two emotions.

The second system is based on the same appearance changes as the first, but coders observe the whole face and make an integrative judgment as to the presence of a particular emotion or blend. In learning this system coders become knowledgeable about the appearance changes for each discrete emotion, and a pattern of appearance changes is directly labeled as a particular emotion, according to preestablished criteria. The chapter includes data on the reliability and validity of the two systems of measuring emotion signals.

In Chapter 6, Scherer reviews the evidence for the relationship between vocal expression and emotion. He makes a strong case for the universality of certain vocalizations and for the existence of emotion-specific vocal signals. Methods for the objective measurement of the acoustic properties of vocal expression are discussed, and reports of detailed descriptions of procedures are referenced.

Scherer divides the parameters of voice analysis into the temporal, frequency, and amplitude domains. He shows that one of the most informative parameters for studying the vocal expression of emotions is fundamental frequency. He identifies the limitations of subjective ratings of vocalizations but recognizes their usefulness in determining how lay persons make inferences about emotions from perceived changes in voice and speech.

In discussing acoustic analysis of infant vocalizations, Scherer concludes that all of the parameters are applicable, with the possible exception of formants. His review of the previous research reveals a paucity of developmental research with infants and children.

In Chapter 7, Exline presents a selective review of the research on emotions and gaze behavior. He shows that under some circumstances there is substantial correspondence between specific emotions and gaze patterns. He draws on his own extensive gaze research with adults and that of others in indicating what strategies should be applicable in studies of infants and children. He also identifies a number of developmental problems that can be addressed with gaze research techniques.

Chapter 8, by Lewis, presents an ethological approach to measuring emotion-related phenomena that contrasts with the microanalytic methods presented in other chapters of this section. The different methods serve different aims. Microanalysis of facial behaviors identifies specific emotion expressions such as joy, sadness, anger, and fear according to criteria established on the basis of both theory and empirical data. Lewis's ethological method defines emotion, or the phenomena to which observers attribute emotion, in terms of selected, specified situations and specified target behaviors that may occur in these situations. Drawing upon previous research and certain theoretical considerations, he specifies a number of anger situations, fear situations, and so forth and reports new data showing that although context influences emotion attribution in various situations, individual infants show characteristic differences in emotion-related behaviors across specified situations. This finding leads to a discussion of enduring emotional dispositions, or emotion traits.

Rosenthal and his colleagues have devised a set of items for measuring sensitivity to nonverbal expressions of emotion signals and have subjected these items to rigorous test-development procedures. The result is a comprehensive and psychometrically sophisticated measure of the emotion-related aspects of "social intelligence" – the Profile of Nonverbal Sensitivity (PONS). In Chapter 9, DePaulo and Rosenthal review evidence of the importance of social intelligence in human service professions and in everyone's day-to-day social interactions. This measure and two related tests derived from it are described, and a summary of the evidence of their reliability, validity, and usefulness is presented. Rosenthal and his colleagues have amassed a substantial body of evidence indicating that the PONS is a reliable measure of a stable characteristic, or trait, defined in terms of sensitivity to nonverbal affect signals and the ability to decode them accurately.

The stimulus material for the PONS is a 45-minute film presenting 220 auditory and visual segments that represent 11 channels of nonverbal communication. The affective phenomena represented in the items range from fundamental emotion signals to affective–cognitive structures like admiration and sympathy, but the test does not have subscales for specific fundamental emotions. DePaulo and Rosenthal summarize or cite numerous studies that support the validity of the PONS as a measure of sensitivity to nonverbal signals. They discuss the development of various aspects of the process of nonverbal decoding and the possible applications of PONS and its derivatives in studies of developmental processes in the perceptual–social–affective sphere.

Chapter 10, by Kotsch, Gerbing, and L. Schwartz, describes the Differential Emotions Scale (DES; Izard, 1972; Izard et al., 1974), a self-report technique for measuring the subjective experience of each of 10 fundamental emotions. The scale was originally developed as a state (DES) or trait (DES II) measure for young adults. Early work with the scale showed that emotion-eliciting situations (and indeed the events of daily life) typically give rise to patterns of discrete emotions.

The set of verbal descriptors for each DES emotion scale was derived from cross-culturally common free-response labels given to photographs of facial expressions of the corresponding emotion. A recent revision (vocabulary simplification) of the DES, the DES III, was designed for use with children, adolescents, and adults of low educational status. Kotsch, Gerbing, and L. Schwartz present an extensive psychometric evaluation of the DES III based on large samples of young people ranging in age from 8 to 18 years. The instructions requested the subjects to describe their emotion states, or emotion experiences, "during the past week." In general the psychometric properties of the DES III subscales were quite satisfactory and were comparable across age levels. The authors concluded that the DES III provides a psychometrically sound instrument for studying the emotion experiences of children and adolescents from 8 to 18 years of age.

Some of the problems involved in conceptualizing and measuring empathy are presented in Chapter 11. Hoffman focuses on empathy not as a cognitive awareness of another's feelings but rather as a vicarious affective response to others. He recognizes that this broad conception leaves a number of definitional problems unresolved, and he suggests ways of resolving them. For example, must the observer's (empathic) emotion match the emotion of the person who elicits the empathic response? Is the father who gets angry when his child cries in pain from the blow of a bully equally as empathic as the one who shows sadness?

Hoffman discusses those aspects of his theory of empathy that have direct implications for measurement. The theory suggests that the first problem in planning research on empathy is to decide whether the study of different modes of empathic arousal requires different methods and strategies. This appears to be the case, particularly if the investigator is interested in the antecedents and consequences of empathic behaviors. Modes of empathic arousal vary from learning (or conditioning) of an association between one's own emotion experience and another's observable expression of emotions to the cognitive process of imagining oneself in another's place.

Hoffman delineates four levels of empathic response that can be seen as a joint function of the empathic affect and the level of development of the cognitive sense of the other. The levels vary primarily in terms of the degree to which the growing child differentiates self and other.

In viewing empathy as vicarious affect, Hoffman recognizes that it must be studied on several levels. He discusses the pros and cons of autonomic, somatic, and verbal indexes, favoring somatic indexes, particularly facial patterns, as the most promising single approach.

The three chapters (12, 13, 14) of commentary represent the views of experts in three different specialities that relate to emotions, emotion arousal, or emotion expression. Chapter 12 gives us the benefit of two decades of research on cardiovascular functions by Obrist and his colleagues. Obrist, Light, and Hastrup review a wealth of data to support their conclusion that no single index of cardiovascular functions can be used as the sole criterion of the presence of a pure affect. To examine the issue a bit further, I raised the question (Kagan raised it independently) as to whether the often observed HR deceleration in anticipation or in response to a stimulus might reflect *interest,* a state that has not always been widely regarded as an emotion. Obrist and his colleagues gave the expected and, I believe, correct answer in the Addendum to their chapter – in effect, the answer is: It may do so, but you will not know for sure without independent validational data such as observable facial patterns, facial EMG, and self-report. This appears to be consistent with Schwartz's systems approach that suggests the possible fruitfulness of searching for patterns of substrates for patterns of emotions.

Obrist and his colleagues indicate that cardiovascular measures may well serve as indexes of arousal and hence as convergent data on emotion processes. Further, as Obrist, Light, and Hastrup show, research on the behavioral effects of cardiovascular functions may throw new light on the problem of hypertension, a condition in which emotions have been implicated.

Chapter 13 provides an ethological psychologist's view of issues involved in studying the behavioral–expressive component of emotion in natural settings. The perspective in this chapter is enriched by the confluence in Charlesworth's background of ethology, developmental psychology, and emotion research. His chapter, as well as that of Lewis, raises some challenging questions. For example, how complete and veridical is a definition of emotion based on a description of a situation, or ecological niche, and the behaviors that are exhibited within it?

Charlesworth focuses not on the relation of expression to internal state but rather on the social-regulatory functions of facial expressions. The ethological literature on nonhuman animals is rich with illustrations of the power of display behaviors of various species to regulate behaviors of observing conspecifics. Charlesworth presents data and cogent arguments supporting the proposition that human facial displays (emotion expressions) serve the same function. A dominant child, like the dominant rhesus macaque or baboon, uses facial expressions or threat gestures to ward off challengers and settle squabbles between lower ranking members of the group. A full consideration of the adaptive communicative aspects of emotions reveals "multiple links between emotions and basic behavioral survival processes."

Building on a background of research in emotions and cognitive psychology, Mandler, in Chapter 14, presents an information-processing approach to the study of emotions and development. He holds that emotion experience is a function of "global autonomic (visceral) arousal" and "cognitive evaluation." He indicates that his position is readily testable, with indexes of autonomic functions reflecting the intensity of an emotion and measures of evaluative cognitions its quality. He elaborates his concept of *autonomic perception* as the mediator of the effects of visceral arousal, and he suggests that *autonomic imagery* can operate as such a mediator in the absence of physiological arousal.

He sees arousal as primarily a function of interruption, noting that interruptions can be either positive or negative. Cognitive evaluation is defined broadly as the mental system that perceives, evaluates, and constructs its internal and external environment. Among the things the child constructs, according to Mandler, are a sense of good and bad or some knowledge of a good/bad dimension and the emotional states that we label with such terms as anger and fear. Mandler's view that the emotions are constructed in the course of development has a number of implications for methodology and measurement. These implications are elaborated in his discussion of the development of cognitive–evaluative and autonomic/visceral processes.

Concluding remarks

At the present time a volume representing such a diversity of theoretical orientations and research approaches as this one cannot possibly maintain total consistency with respect to terminological, definitional, or other issues. Having discussed these difficulties at the outset, we hope that our readers will be prepared to recognize and appraise the differences themselves.

References

Bartlett, E. S., & Izard, C. E. A dimensional and discrete emotions investigation of the subjective experience of emotion. In C. E. Izard (Ed.), *Patterns of emotions: A new analysis of anxiety and depression*. New York: Academic Press, 1972.

Block, J. Studies in the phenomenology of emotions. *Journal of Abnormal and Social Psychology,* 1957, *54,* 358–63.

Buck, R., Savin, V. J., Miller, R. E., & Caul, W. F. Nonverbal communication of affect in humans. *Proceedings of the 77th Annual Convention of the American Psychological Association,* 1969, *4,* 367–8.

Buck, R., Savin, V. J., Miller, R. E., & Caul, W. F. Nonverbal communication of affect in humans. *Journal of Personality and Social Psychology,* 1972, *23,* 362–71.

Cattell, R. B., & Scheier, I. H. *The meaning and measurement of neuroticism and anxiety.* New York: Ronald Press, 1961.

Csikszentmihalyi, M. *Attention and the holistic approach to behavior.* Paper presented at the Social Science Research Council's Seminar on Emotion and Cognition, San Francisco, November 1979.

Darwin, C. R. *The expression of the emotions in man and animals.* London: John Murray, 1872.

Diener, C., & Dweck, C. An analysis of learned helplessness: Continuous changes in performance, strategy, and achievement cognitions following failure. *Journal of Personality and Social Psychology,* 1978, *36,* 461–82.

Ekman, P. Universal and cultural differences in facial expressions of emotion. In J. K. Cole (Ed.), *Nebraska Symposium on Motivation* (Vol. 19). Lincoln: University of Nebraska Press, 1972.

Ekman, P., & Friesen, W. V. *The Facial Action Coding System (FACS).* Palo Alto, Calif.: Consulting Psychologists Press, 1978.

Exline, R., Paredes, A., Gottheil, E., & Winkelmayer, R. Gaze patterns of normals and schizophrenics retelling happy, sad, and angry experiences. In C. E. Izard (Ed.), *Emotions in personality and psychopathology.* New York: Plenum Press, 1979.

Gaensbauer, T. J., Mrazek, D., & Emde, R. N. Patterning of emotional response in a playroom situation. *Infant Behavior and Development,* 1979, *2,* 93–187.

Hodges, W. F. The psychophysiology of anxiety. In M. Zuckerman & C. D. Spielberger (Eds.), *Stress and anxiety.* Hillsdale, N.J.: Erlbaum, 1976.

Izard, C. E. *The face of emotion.* New York: Appleton-Century-Crofts, 1971.

Izard, C. E. *Patterns of emotions: A new analysis of anxiety and depression.* New York: Academic Press, 1972.

Izard, C. E. *Human emotions.* New York: Plenum Press, 1977.

Izard, C. E. *The Maximally Discriminative Facial Movement Coding System (Max).* Newark, Del.: University of Delaware, Instructional Resources Center, 1979.

Izard, C. E., & Dougherty, L. M. *System for Identifying Affect Expressions by Holistic Judgments (Affex).* Newark, Del.: University of Delaware, Instructional Resources Center, 1980.

Izard, C. E., Dougherty, F. E., Bloxom, B. M., & Kotsch, W. E. *The Differential Emotions Scale: A method of measuring the subjective experience of discrete emotions.* Unpublished manuscript, University of Delaware, 1974.

Izard, C. E., Huebner, R. R., Risser, D., McGinnes, G. C., & Dougherty, L. M. The young infant's ability to produce discrete emotion expressions. *Developmental Psychology,* 1980, *16*(2), 132–40.

Izard, C. E., & Saxton, P. M. *Emotions.* Unpublished manuscript, 1980.

James, W. *The principles of psychology.* New York: Dover, 1950. (Originally published, 1890.)

Jones, H. E. The study of patterns of emotional expression. In L. Reymert (Eds.), *Feelings and emotions.* New York: McGraw-Hill, 1950.

Lazarus, R. S. Cognitive and coping processes in emotion. In B. Weiner (Ed.), *Cognitive views of human motivation.* New York: Academic Press, 1974.

Leeper, R. W. A motivational theory of emotion to replace "emotion as disorganized response." *Psychological Review,* 1948, *55,* 5–21.

Leeper, R. W. Some needed developments in the motivational theory of emotions. In D. Levine (Ed.), *Nebraska Symposium on Motivation* (Vol. 13). Lincoln: University of Nebraska Press, 1966.

Leventhal, H. Toward a comprehensive theory of emotion. In L. Berkowitz (Ed.), *Advances in experimental social psychology*. Vol. 13. New York: Academic Press, 1980.

Mandler, G. *Mind and emotions*. New York: Wiley, 1975.

Mason, J. W. Emotion as reflected in patterns of endocrine integration. In L. Levi (Ed.), *Emotions – Their parameters and meaurement*. New York: Raven Press, 1975.

Mehrabian, A., & Russell, J. *An approach to environmental psychology*. Cambridge, Mass.: MIT Press, 1974.

Meichenbaum, D., & Butler, L. Cognitive ethology: Assessing the streams of cognition and emotion. In K. Blankstein, P. Pliner, & J. Powly (Eds.), *Advances in the study of communication and affect: Assessment and modification of emotional behavior* (Vol. 6). New York: Plenum Press, in press.

Nowlis, V. Research with the mood adjective check list. In S. S. Tomkins & C. E. Izard (Eds.), *Affect, cognition, and personality*. New York: Springer, 1965.

Plutchik, R. *Emotion: A psychoevolutionary synthesis*. New York: Harper & Row, 1980.

Royce, J. R., & McDermott, J. R. A multidimensional system dynamics. *Motivation and Emotion*, 1977, *1*, 193–224.

Russell, J. A. Evidence of convergent validity on the dimensions of affect. *Journal of Personality and Social Psychology*, 1978, *36*, 1152–68.

Russell, J. A. Affective space is bipolar. *Journal of Personality and Social Psychology*, 1979, *37*, 345–56.

Scherer, K. R. Nonlinguistic vocal indicators of emotion and psychopathology. In C. E. Izard (Ed.), *Emotions in personality and psychopathology*. New York: Plenum Press, 1979.

Schlosberg, H. S. A scale for the judgment of facial expressions. *Journal of Experimental Psychology*, 1941, *29*, 497–510.

Schlosberg, H. S. The description of facial expressions in terms of two dimensions. *Journal of Experimental Psychology*, 1952, *44*, 229–37.

Schlosberg, H. S. Three dimensions of emotion. *Psychological Review*, 1954, *61*, 81–8.

Schwartz, G. E., Fair, P. L, Salt, P., Mandel, M. R., & Klerman, J. L. Facial muscle patterning to affective imagery in depressed and non-depressed subjects. *Science*, 1976, *192*, 489–91.

Shiller, V. M., & Izard, C. E. Patterns of emotion expressions during separation. Unpublished paper, 1981.

Spielberger, C. D. Theory and research on anxiety. In C. D. Spielberger (Ed.), *Anxiety and behavior*. New York: Academic Press, 1966.

Spielberger, C. D. (Ed.). *Anxiety: Contemporary theory and research*. New York: Academic Press, 1972.

Thomas, A., & Chess, S. *Temperament and development*. New York: Brunner/Mazel, 1977.

Thomas, A., Chess, S., & Birch, H. G. *Temperament and behavior disorders in children*. New York: New York University Press, 1968.

Tomkins, S. S. *Affect, imagery, consciousness: Vol. 1. The positive affects*. New York: Springer, 1962.

Veinstein, I. I., & Simonov, P. V. [Emotional structures in the brain and heart]. Moscow: Nauka, 1979. (In Russian.)

Young, G., & Décarie, T. G. An ethology-based catalogue of facial–vocal behaviour in infancy. *Animal Behavior*, 1977, *25*, 95–107.

Zuckerman, M. The development of an affect adjective check list for the measurement of anxiety. *Journal of Consulting Psychology*, 1960, *24*, 457–62.

Part II

Psychobiological functions

2   Developmental psychoendocrinology: an approach to the study of emotions

Katherine H. Tennes and John W. Mason

Over the past 20 years psychiatrists and physiologists have carried out numerous interdisciplinary studies of the effects of psychological influences upon endocrine systems. As a result of such efforts, emotions have been established as a primary determinant of endocrine activity in human adults. Still, we have very little information about the origin of these relationships in infancy and childhood. Only recently have investigators in the field of child development begun to consider the contribution of hormones to individual and group differences in psychosocial behavior. Progress in psychoendocrine studies of adults was made possible by the rapid advances in techniques for assaying hormones that occurred in the 1950s and 1960s. The study of psychoendocrine relationships in infants and children was hampered by the lack of micromethods for hormone assay. With the development of radioimmunoassay, this problem was solved. Radioimmunoassay methods require very small amounts of blood and are precise, specific, economical, and technically less difficult than earlier methods. A second impetus to interdisciplinary studies of developmental psychology and endocrinology at present is the availability of a body of knowledge about the development of behavior that has expanded over the past 20 years. We have many paradigms to draw upon for interdisciplinary investigations, including observations of infants and preverbal children.

The purposes of this chapter are (a) to review selected studies of adults that have been important in contributing evidence of a causal relationship between hormones and emotions and (b) to report on the psychoendocrine studies of infants and children, including our own, that have been carried out to date. The review is intended to provide a background of guiding principles from the psychoendocrine field that can be applied to developmental studies of emotions. We also intend to encourage innovative developmental investigations combining psychological and biological approaches.

21

Limitations of this review

As a means of limiting the scope of the discussion and retaining the focus upon the development of emotions, we have restricted our review mainly to the pituitary–adrenocortical axis and to studies of normal humans. The important contributions of animal studies, a subject worthy in its own right and of immense importance in determining long-term developmental effects, will not be included. A review of endocrinological aspects of adult psychopathology is also excluded from this review, because despite the highly useful information produced by such studies, they have not, to our knowledge, generated specific developmental hypotheses. Studies of normal human adults have provided research models applicable to studies of children. (For reviews of animal studies and psychopathology, see Carroll, 1976; Levine, 1975; Mason, 1968a; Sachar, 1967.)

Theoretical background

Historically, the systematic investigation of psychoendocrine relationships can be divided into three major phases. In the first phase, during the early part of the century, Walter B. Cannon introduced the first scientific evidence of the effects of emotions upon hormones (Cannon, 1936). He postulated that activation of the sympathetic–adrenal–medullary system served to mobilize energy for coping with fear-eliciting stimuli. The influence of his formulation was far-reaching and enduring. The second phase of research was generated by Selye's proposal, first advanced in 1936 (Selye, 1936), that a second endocrine system, the pituitary–adrenal cortex, also released hormones in response to psychological stimuli as well as to disturbance of the metabolic equilibrium of the body. The remarkable technological advances in methods for assaying adrenocorticosteroids from 1950 to 1970 resulted in abundant and illuminating investigations of the effects of psychological influences upon the hypothalamic–pituitary–adrenocortical axis (Mason 1968a, 1975a). Selye introduced the term *stressors* to include all of the physical and psychological stimuli capable of activating the adrenocortical axis. He defined *stress* as the "nonspecific bodily responses to such stimuli" (Selye, 1950). Some questions have been raised regarding Selye's concept *nonspecificity* and his formulation of a *general adaptation syndrome* (Mason, 1971). Nevertheless, as a result of his hypothesis, the sensitivity of the pituitary–adrenocortical axis to psychological influences was firmly established.

In the third and current phase, psychoendocrine research has moved to a new level of complexity. Interest is changing from investigations of a single hormone to investigations of multiple endocrine systems interacting in patterns, an approach advocated by Mason in 1968 (Mason, 1968a, 1975a). Intricate patterns

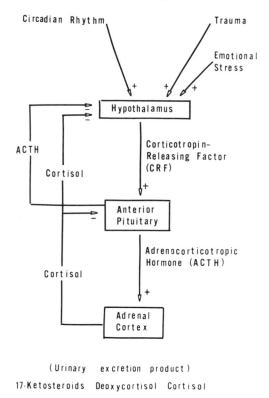

Figure 2.1. Schematic diagram of the hypothalamic–pituitary–adrenocortical axis in normal adults

of endocrine interactions including pituitary–adrenal, sympathetic–adrenal–medullary, pituitary–gonadal, and thyroid are being examined simultaneously for their impact upon psychological phenomena. As yet, multiple endocrine systems have not been examined in the developing child.

It is research from the second phase, that is, the effects of stress upon the pituitary–adrenocortical axis, that provides the background for developmental investigations and forms the main subject of this review. We will discuss the studies involving adults' and children's corticosteroid responses to stress and will then briefly present studies of the emotions and other endocrine systems.

The hypothalamic–pituitary–adrenocortical axis

The hypothalamic–pituitary–adrenocortical axis is a complex system that has been only partially explained (Sayers & Portanova, 1975). As is shown in Figure 2.1, stimuli reaching the hypothalamus release a neural hormone called the corticotropin-releasing factor (CRF). The chemical structure of this hormone has not been identified, although the hormone is known to exist. When CRF is released from the medial basal hypothalamus into the hypothyseal portal vessels, it stimulates release of adrenocorticotropic hormone (ACTH) from the pituitary. ACTH, reaching the adrenal cortex through the circulation, stimulates the secretion of cortisol. Cortisol enters the circulatory system, where approximately 96% is bound to transcortin and the remaining, free cortisol becomes the biologically active component.

Feedback regulation

The level of plasma cortisol is regulated by a negative feedback loop. High levels of cortisol in circulation inhibit the secretion of ACTH at the pituitary and may have a suppressing effect at the hypothalamus. There appear to be two separate feedback responses, one sensitive to the rate of secretion of cortisol and the other to the level of cortisol in circulation (Sayers & Portanova, 1975; Yates & Maran, 1974). The inhibition of ACTH in response to a rapid rise in cortisol secretion occurs within 15 minutes of the rise, whereas the inhibitory effect of maintaining a high level of circulating cortisol is delayed for 1 to 2 hours (Kreiger & Liotta, 1979).

Circadian regulation

The normal release of hormones in the hypothalamic–pituitary–adrenocortical axis is controlled by a circadian rhythm driven by the central nervous system. The circadian pattern has a 24-hour cycle that reaches a peak at roughly 4:00 to 8:00 A.M., with the nadir lasting from about 10:00 P.M. to midnight (Bliss et al., 1953). The diurnal pattern is associated with an individual's habitual sleep–activity pattern and, as jet-age travelers know well, requires several days to adjust if the habitual sleep–activity cycle is changed. ACTH and plasma corticosteroids are secreted in bursts that occur most frequently in the early morning hours of sleep (Hellman et al., 1970). In the evening the bursts are more widely spaced and include quiescent periods when output may reach zero (Gallagher et al., 1973). There is also some evidence that the rhythm is entrained by light–dark transitions in concert with, or superimposed upon, the sleep–wake pattern (Kreiger, 1975).

   Physical traumas or emotion-arousing stimuli increase the secretory activity of the adrenal cortex within the dynamics of the normal circadian pattern and the negative feedback controls. The responsivity of the system to stress may vary with the phase of the 24-hour circadian rhythm. Furthermore, an extremely intense stimulus, such as surgery or psychopathology, may override both the circadian control and the negative feedback, so that the secretion of cortisol remains high throughout a 24-hour period (Cope, 1972; Sachar, 1975).

The regulatory influence of the circadian rhythm and the feedback mechanism are necessary considerations in designing research aimed at assessing the impact of an emotional state upon the endocrine response.

Adrenocortical activity in infancy

Neonatal adrenocortex

There is good evidence that the adrenocortical system is active but immature at birth. The biosynthesis and metabolism of steroids in the newborn differ markedly from those in the adult (Hall et al., 1971; Kenny, Richard, & Taylor, 1970). Although neonatal production rates are somewhat elevated for these ages in comparison with later ages, it is possible to assess variability of adrenocortical activity from plasma cortisol levels at birth (Cathro, Forsyth, & Cameron, 1969). Neonates respond to a physical stress such as circumcision with an increase in adrenocortical activity as early as 6 hours after birth (Talbert, Draybill, & Potter, 1975). Kenny found excreted 17-hydroxycorticosteroids (17-OHCS), a metabolite of cortisol, to be in a relatively constant relationship to cortisol production rate in infants after 5 days of age (Kenny, Malvaux & Migeon, 1963). Urinary free-cortisol excretion is considered to be a reliable index of secretion rate only after 4 months of age (Juselius & Kenny, 1972).

Response to behavior states

In the neonatal period, evidence of an infant's emotional state is limited largely to observing whether he is awake or asleep, quiet or crying. Yet even these primitive precursors of differentiated emotions are reflected in changes of plasma cortisol levels. Anders et al. (1970) in a study of four infants between 1 and 15 weeks found significantly higher cortisol levels associated with 20 minutes of crying than with the same length of time in sleep. Ninety percent of the variance in plasma cortisol was accounted for by the elevations associated with crying. We confirmed Anders's finding in a study of 3-day-old infants (Tennes & Carter, 1973). Plasma cortisol levels, taken at 7:00 A.M., were lowest if the infant had been asleep for the previous 20 minutes, moderate after alert-awake states, and highest after crying.

These relatively simple exploratory studies of psychoendocrine relationships in neonates did not differentiate among causes of crying nor among individual differences in the threshold of emotional arousal. The only conclusion that can be drawn is that the adrenocortical response is aroused by a negative emotion manifest as crying.

Circadian sleep regulation

Relatively little is known about the circadian rhythm associated with sleep in infancy and childhood. Franks (1967) reported that the adult pattern of elevated 17-OHCS in the morning and depressed levels in the evening did not occur before 3 years of age. In a study of 1-year-old children, we measured excreted cortisol for each voiding during 8 daytime hours, including a 1- to 2-hour nap (Tennes & Vernadakis, 1977). Cortisol production was significantly reduced during the nap, and the second voiding after a nap showed a rebound above the mean. Still, there was no significant difference in the suppression of cortisol between naps taken in the morning and naps taken in the afternoon. These findings suggest a direct entrainment by sleep but an absence of a circadian effect at 1 year of age.

Adults: adrenocortical activity and stress

Widely diverse situations have been utilized to examine the effect of psychological influences upon the pituitary–adrenocortical axis. Subjects most frequently studied have been athletes, men in the military service, students, and hospitalized patients. As a result of well over 200 studies, the effectiveness of psychological stress in activating the adrenocortical system to levels elevated above normal, but less extreme than the levels associated with physical trauma, has been well established (Mason, 1968b). We will briefly review some of the factors that contribute to variability in the adrenocortical response to psychological stress in adults. These factors have been selected for their relevance to developmental studies of early psychoendocrine relationships.

Influence of novelty

Novelty or uncertainty stimulates the activity of the pituitary–adrenocortical axis. A first-time effect has been observed in normal subjects upon admission to a research ward (Mason et al., 1965), upon being brought into an unfamiliar laboratory (Davis et al., 1962), or upon being faced with an unknown experimental procedure (Sabshin et al., 1957).

Recently Czeisler et al. (1976), using indwelling catheters to measure continuous production of cortisol for 24 hours, compared four presurgery patients with five normal hospitalized controls. The only event associated with a significant deviation from the normal circadian pattern in the two groups was the response to preoperative procedures that the patients, but not the controls, experienced on the evening before surgery. Although the increased secretion always began during preoperative preparation, it was not possible to separate the psychological impact from the physical manipulation. Still, the patient showing the smallest peak of cortisol secretion during the preoperative preparation had undergone the same operation a year earlier. It is particularly important to control for novelty in studies involving infants or children when procedures necessary for obtaining a biological specimen may in themselves change adrenocortical activity.

Coping

Several studies of adults have suggested that elevation or suppression of corticosteroids does not occur in response to recurrent stress if the individuals have learned to cope with a particular situation. Trained parachutists do not respond to routine jumps with increased production of cortisol (Daniel, Mikulaj, Vrazda, 1973). Helicopter medics in action in the Vietnam War showed no difference in excreted 17-OHCS when days of combat were compared with days at base camp (Bourne, Rose, Mason, 1967). In a recent study of Norwegian paratroopers in training, the absence of an elevation of corticosteroids over base levels was regarded as evidence of coping (Levine, Weinberg, & Ursin, 1978). These findings suggest that the individual history of exposure to stress is an important consideration in evaluating the impact of an event that may appear to involve extremely stressful circumstances.

Individual differences

An issue that has emerged as one of central importance in psychoendocrine research concerns the wide range of differences in the hormone response among individuals exposed to the same stressful life experience. Some individuals respond with a marked increase in cortisol production; others with little increase or even a lower level of hormone production. This diversity has confounded attempts to use the assessment of hormone activity as an index of a single emotion such as fear or anxiety.

A study that was particularly informative in regard to individual differences involved the parents of children fatally ill with leukemia (Wolff, Friedman, Hofer, & Mason, 1964). In response to acutely stressful occasions associated with the child's illness, some of the parents showed elevated corticosteroid levels, others had low levels, and some appeared to suppress production (Mason, 1975a). Study of the suppressors revealed that a high percentage of these subjects used mechanisms of psychological defense, particularly denial, that were effective in maintaining low levels of emotional distress. A systematic study was then carried out in which the effectiveness of psychological defenses, as rated by a psychiatric team, was found to be predictive of the parent's mean chronic urinary corticosteroid level (Wolff, Hofer, & Mason, 1964). One to two years after the death of the child, the parents' psychoendocrine status was reevaluated (Hofer et al. 1972a, 1972b). The rank order of the parents' corticosteroid levels before their loss was unrelated to the rank order at the time of the follow-up. Comparison of parents in the highest and lowest quartiles for cortisol secretion rates at the return visit indicated that the activity and intensity of the mourning process at the time of the follow-up visit tended to distinguish the two extreme endocrine groups and to account, in part, for the lack of stability in corticosteroid values under the two conditions (Hofer et al., 1972b). It was also hypothesized that parents whose values before the child's death were lower than their values on two return visits had actively suppressed adrenocortical function by highly effective defenses against the chronic threat of the child's demise. Studies involving army recruits (Rose, Poe, & Mason, 1968) and women anticipating breast biopsy (Katz et al., 1970), which used the same criteria for assessing effectiveness of defense as those used in the study of parents of fatally ill children, confirmed the relationship between defense mechanism and corticosteroid activity.

Children: adrenocortical activity and stress

Hospitalization has frequently been used to represent a situation expected to arouse emotional perturbations and also as a setting conducive to obtaining biological specimens for hormone assay. Three studies involving children's adjustment to hospitalization report somewhat contradictory results. The studies illustrate some of the difficulties in appraising children's adaptation to stress.

Barnes et al. (1972) investigating manifest anxiety in 11 children aged 5 to 14 found urinary 17-OHCS on the day before cardiac surgery significantly elevated above values on the day of discharge and at follow-up clinic visits. They found no difference in adrenocortical levels between the 7 most anxious and the 4 least anxious children (anxiety was estimated by a psychiatrist and a pediatric nurse). The study depended upon evaluation of a single emotion. Even though children may express emotions more openly than adults, assessment of more complex psychological phenomena might be necessary to understand associations with hormones.

Knight et al. (1979) modeled their study after the adult study of parents of fatally ill children. Twenty-five children aged 7 to 11 who were hospitalized for minor elective surgery showed no significant difference in mean cortisol production rates on a presurgery clinic outpatient day and on the day after admission to the hospital. Furthermore, there was a significant inverse relationship between the children's cortisol production and their adjustment on the ward. In addition, in contrast with effective defense styles in adults, for these children denial was ineffective in reducing distress and was associated with high rather than low levels of adrenocortical activity.

In the third study of hospitalized children, Mattson, Gross, & Hall (1971) examined the psychosocial adaptation and corticosteroid response of 10 hemophiliac boys aged 6 to 14 at home, in a research center, and during hospitalization for a bleeding episode. Home, the research center, and the hospital ward were each associated with increasingly elevated excreted corticosteroids for all the boys. Psychosocial adaptation was significantly correlated with adrenal cortical activity but in a direction contrary to expectation. The coping behavior of good adapters (high cortisol excretors) was described as "extensive use of cognitive functions; reasonable motor activity; controlled yet flexible emotional expression; and psychological defenses such as adaptive use of denial and isolation of distressing affects, control through thinking and identification with other bleeders and the medical staff " (p. 223). The coping behavior of poor adapters (low cortisol excretors) was described as "intense often careless motor activity, much irritability and occasional periods of uncontrolled emotional expression" (p. 221), "denial of any risks associated with being a hemophiliac and dramatic affect expression as a defense against recognition of their serious physical condition" (pp. 223–4).

It was not surprising to find that hospitalization for the hemophiliac boys represented a greater stress than hospitalization for minor surgery in the group studied by Knight. The evidence of these two thoughtfully designed and psychologically sensitive studies is conflicting; Knight found that children who coped more successfully during hospitalization were *low* excretors of cortisol, whereas Mattson et al. found that hemophiliac boys who were well adapted to management of their illness and cooperative on the ward were *high* excretors. Mattson suggested that for the poorly adapting hemophiliacs, affect expression served a defensive purpose, moderating their state of tension so that corticosteroid levels remained low. Speculation and hypotheses about such a discrepancy need to be tested by further research.

In summary, the preponderance of evidence from the studies of adults supports three conditions relative to the cortisol response to stress: (a) Stress experiences as such tend to increase corticosteroid activity, (b) adequate coping behavior maintains normal levels, and (c) effective defense mechanisms may suppress activity. The evidence from studies of children aged 5 to 14 is sufficiently controversial to suggest that evaluations of children's emotional response to stress may require innovative conceptualization and modes of assessment different from those used in adult studies.

Infancy: adrenocortical activity and separation distress

The 1-year-old's distress at brief separations from the mother provides the researcher with an emotion-arousing situation in children that is comparable to some of the stressful situations investigated in adults (Tennes, Downy, & Vernadakis, 1977). We observed 1-year-old infants at home during an hour-long separation from the mother in accord with the common practice in our culture of leaving children with a baby-sitter for brief separations. We found a modest but consistent linear relationship between cortisol excretion levels and our ratings of the infants' manifest anxiety. Infants who cried at the mother's departure and remained agitated during her absence excreted highest levels of cortisol. Infants who protested mildly but only briefly or had no manifest anxiety had lower levels. A third classification of distress response also emerged from the data. Infants who were distressed at the separation but after the mother's departure became quiet and inactive, refusing social contact with the caretakers, had significantly lower levels of cortisol than the distressed and agitated infants. We speculated that those infants who responded with passivity and a blunting of emotions might be the individuals who would later use defense mechanisms effectively in maintaining low levels of corticosteroids.

A second post hoc observation in the study suggested that the nature of the mother–child relationship might influence the hormonal response to separations. Ainsworth (1979) described three patterns of infant's response to the mother's return after a brief separation. The greeting was indicative of the mother–child relationship. Using a modification of Ainsworth's categories, we classified the infants' responses to reunions as (a) responsive, (b) ambivalent, or (c) avoidant. There was a significant difference in mean cortisol excretion levels among the three groups ($p > .01$) (unpublished data). The infants who greeted the mother with eager pleasure had highest levels, the ambivalent were moderate, and those who ignored her return or turned away were lowest excretors. We did not study the quality of the mother–child relationship independently of the separation. According to Ainsworth's findings the infants who responded with greatest pleasure would be expected to have the most positive attachment to the mother. In our study, the highest excretors of cortisol responded most emotionally to both separations and reunion. If the mother's relationship to the child is a factor in arousing the hormone, the questions raised are: How does the mother's attitude become linked to the child's physiology? Is the interaction between mother and infant throughout the 1st year of life a crucial factor in determining the child's chronic hormonal response pattern? Or does the child have a constitutionally determined level of endocrine production that is a factor in determining the nature of the mother's reaction to the child? If the first possibility is correct, a study of corticosteroid levels in infants cared for by different mother-surrogates in series might be revealing. If the second is correct, the stability of the infant's hormone responsivity needs to be examined from birth, ideally in a longitudinal study. A third possibility is that the two named alternatives are not isolated effects but operate in combination.

Studies of adults do not generally include retrospective data from childhood. One exception to this rule was an intensive study of 91 army recruits during the 1st month of basic training. Examination of childhood events revealed that 12 of 14 men who had experienced the death of a parent during childhood had chronic mean corticosteroid levels in either the top or the bottom quartile of the total population. Of those in the top quartile, 5 of the 6 men had lost mothers, whereas 5 of the 6 men in the lowest quartile had lost fathers (Poe, Rose, & Mason, 1970). The findings suggest that extreme levels of corticosteroid activity, either high or low, may be associated with severe childhood emotional trauma. A prospective study of the relationship between stress and corticosteroid activity requires evaluations of constitutional factors, stable environmental influences, and traumatic events as well.

Young children: corticosteroid rhythms and behavior profiles

Using ethological methods, Montagner et al. (1978) observed children 1 to 6 years of age in day-care centers and kindergartens and collected urine samples at regular intervals during the day on three to five occasions. Behavioral profiles that categorized the children as leaders, dominant, aggressive, dominated, or isolated were found to be associated with differing daily patterns of excreted corticosteroids. Circadian curves of leaders were more regular and significantly lower than of dominant-aggressive children. This study represents a promising approach to investigating interactions between hormones and psychosocial behaviors.

Personality correlates of corticosteroid activity

Stability of chronic cortisol levels

A number of investigators have shown that interindividual differences are greater than intraindividual differences in excreted corticosteroids if measurements are made at regular intervals over periods of weeks or months. Fox et al. (1961) examined individual day-to-day variations in 17-OHCS output in healthy young college males over a 5-week period and found no significant change in the same subject during the 5-week interval; individual differences in chronic levels were highly significant ($p > .001$). Rose et al. (1968) confirmed the finding in 50 military trainees.

The parents of children fatally ill with leukemia, in the study referred to earlier, were observed for periods ranging from 1 week to 8 months. Most of the observations revealed a remarkable stability of individual adrenocortical levels during the period of the child's final illness, with little overlapping of values between subjects who had highest and lowest mean values (Friedman, Mason, & Hamburg, 1963).

There is also some evidence that stable individual differences in adrenocortical production levels begins in childhood. Mattson's study of hemophiliac boys, carried out over a 3-year period, reported significant correlations ranging from .66 to .88 in 17-OHCS levels excreted in three different settings. In our study of the 1-year-old infants' response to separations, we found a significant correlation between cortisol excretion levels on control and experimental days ($r = .69$, $p > .001$) (Tennes et al., 1977). In a follow-up study 3 years later, we found a correlation of .44 between the 1-year-olds' and the 3-year-olds' levels of cortisol which, however, did not reach statistical significance (unpublished data).

The studies suggest that individuals may be characterized as high or low responders and that response to psychological stress and the ability to defend or to cope may be imposed upon a basic level of physiologic functioning typical for the individual.

Personality traits

A number of investigators have attempted to describe the personality traits of individuals who have extremely high or extremely low chronic levels of cortisol or to contrast personality traits common to individuals above and below the mean. Despite the anecdotal nature of some of the reports, and the small numbers of subjects frequently involved, the evidence tends to support a modest but positive relationship between emotionality and chronically high corticosteroid levels. High responders are more intense in their personal relationships (Fox et al., 1961), more involved with people (Price et al., 1957) and more openly expressive of affect (Bloch & Brackenridge, 1972; Hofer et al., 1972b; Wolff, Friedman, Hofer, & Mason, 1964). Low responders have been more often described as reserved, controlled, bland (Fox et al., 1961; Hofer et al., 1972b; Price et al., 1957) or pleasant but detached (Rahe, Rubin, & Arthur, 1974). There are exceptions to the general tendency that include, for example, a report of high responders who, more frequently than low responders, described themselves as disinterested in socialization (Poe et al., 1970) or the description of hemophiliac boys by Mattson et al. (1971).

The resolution of such discrepancies in personality descriptions may require investigation of more than one endocrine system. For example, an elevation in growth hormone in response to psychologically stressful stimuli is observed in about one-third of normal adult subjects (Brown & Heninger, 1976; Mason, 1975b). In a study of both cortisol and growth hormone in response to stress, Greene et al. (1970) determined plasma cortisol and growth hormone levels every 30 minutes for 3 hours while patients were undergoing cardiac catheterization. They found that calm and depressed patients showed no elevation of either the growth hormone or cortisol, patients who were anxious and interacted socially with medical personnel had elevated levels of cortisol only, and patients who were anxious but not socially engaged had elevated levels of both cortisol and growth hormone.

If individual differences in chronic levels of endocrine production are stable over time, questions regarding the ontogenesis of the relationships are again raised. Are the individual differences in temperament associated with endocrine function determined constitutionally, or do differential early experiences influence the responsiveness of the endocrine system?

Multiple endocrine systems

Although much attention has been devoted to the pituitary–adrenocortical axis, there is a need to explore other endocrine systems more fully. The remarkable advances in radioimmunoassay methods for measurement of many hormones have made it possible to extend our view of the scope of psychoendocrine mechanisms to include cortisol, epinephrine, norepinephrine, growth hormone, prolactin, thyrotropin, thyroxine, testosterone, estone, estradiol, and insulin (Mason, 1975a). The most commonly observed multiple endocrine pattern in response to emotionally stressful stimuli so far has been an elevation of cortisol, epinephrine, norepinephrine, thyroxine, and growth hormone with suppression of testosterone and insulin (Mason, 1975b). We would expect the pattern to be different in infants and children because of differences in production rates of the individual hormones during immaturity, but to our knowledge no integrated data relating multiple hormones to behaviors at various developmental states is available.

Another endocrine system of considerable interest in the study of emotional behavior is the pituitary–gonadal axis. Evidence from studies of human adults supports a relationship between gonadal hormones and emotional stimuli associated with the increase in cortisol (Kreuz, Rose, & Jennings, 1972; Mason, 1975a), with aggression (Kling, 1975) and in sexual behavior (Rose, 1972). Because of the immaturity of sexual function during infancy and childhood, androgens and estrogens may be regarded as having a limited role in the study of the development of emotions. Still, an exception to this general inactivity of the system occurs during two brief periods of prenatal and postnatal development. Significantly higher levels of testosterone are produced by the male fetus than by the female between the 12th and the 16th week of gestation, the prenatal period of gonadal differentiation (Warne et al., 1977). A second resurgence of testosterone production occurs in the male postnatally beginning at 2 weeks, reaching a peak at about 3 months, and then dropping off by 7 months to the same levels as in the female (Winter et al., 1976). The role of testosterone in differentiating behavior in male and female infants between birth and 6 months, or the impact of testosterone on the developing central nervous system, has not yet been investigated. Maccoby et al. (1979) in a study designed to examine the relationship between levels of testosterone in cord blood with later developing rough-and-tumble play reported that the child's ordinal position was an important factor in determining testosterone level of cord blood. Erhardt (Erhardt & Baker, 1974; Erhardt & Money, 1968) found an increase in masculine activities and interests associated with prenatal exposure to elevated levels of androgens. These two studies represent isolated efforts to examine the effects that early exposure to sex hormones exerts upon later developing behaviors in the human. If circulating androgens have a prepotent effect upon later developing emotions, the 1st year of life may be critical in determining sex differences as well as variation among males. Furthermore, as the psychoendocrine field develops, it appears likely that the investigation of patterns or integrated multiple hormonal responses may provide further insight into the organization of the psychological processes involved in the development of emotions.

Concluding remarks

Psychoendocrine studies are a potentially powerful adjunct to investigations of the development of emotions in infancy and childhood.

The following conclusions stem from our evaluation of the studies of adults and children reviewed here.

1. In designing research involving interactions between endocrine systems and emotions, it is necessary to recognize the complex regulatory processes involved in endocrine physiology.
2. Studies of adults have established that emotions are a significant variable in endocrine activity. They have also demonstrated that dynamic psychological processes or styles of adaptation may alter hormone production.
3. Too few studies of children have been conducted to permit conclusions about developing relationships between emotions and endocrine activity.
4. A study of the corticosteroid response to separation distress in infants suggested that early experiences with the mother may contribute to individual differences in endocrine responses. The alternate hypothesis was that the infant's endocrine responsivity may be a factor in determining the mother's response to the child. The effect of congenital predisposition needs to be separated from the impact of the environment. It has yet to be determined whether postnatal experiences, either stable or traumatic, affect the chronic physiological functioning of endocrine systems.
5. A promising direction for future research involves assessment of multiple endocrine systems in interaction with complex psychological processes.
6. Technical developments in assay of hormones together with advances in psychosocial methodology suggest rich potential for exciting and innovative work on psychoendocrinology in human infants.

References

Ainsworth, M. *Attachment: Retrospect and prospect*. Presidential address at the meeting of the Society for Research in Child Development, San Francisco, April 1979.

Anders, T. F., Sachar, E. J., Kream, J., Roffwarg, H., & Hellman, L. Behavioral state and plasma cortisol response in the human newborn. *Pediatrics*, 1970, *46*, 532–7

Barnes, C. M., Kenny, F. M., Call, T., & Reinhart, J. Measurement in management of anxiety in children for open heart surgery. *Pediatrics*, 1972, *49*, 250–9.

Bliss, E. L., Sandberg, A. A., Nelson, D. H., & Eikness, K. The normal levels of 17-hydrocorti-costeroids in the peripheral blood in man. *Journal of Clinical Investigation*, 1953, *32*, 818.

Bloch, S., & Brackenridge, C. Psychological performance and biochemical factors in medical students under examination stress. *Journal of Psychiatric Research*, 1972, *16*, 25–33.

Bourne, R., Rose, R., & Mason, J. Urinary 17OHCS levels: Data on seven helicopter ambulance medics in combat. *Archives of General Psychiatry*, 1967, *17*, 104–10.

Brown, W., & Heninger, G. Stress induced growth hormone release: Psychologic and physiologic correlates. *Psychosomatic Medicine*, 1976, *38*, 145–7.

Cannon, W. B. *Bodily changes in pain, hunger, fear and rage* (2nd ed.). New York: Appleton-Century-Crofts, 1936.

Carroll, B. Limbic system–adrenal cortex regulation in depression and schizophrenia. *Psychosomatic Medicine*, 1976, *38*, 106–20.

Cathro, D. M., Forsyth, C. C., & Cameron, J. Adrenocortical responses to stress in newborn infants. *Archives of Diseases in Childhood*, 1969, *44*, 88–95.

Cope, C. L., *Adrenal steroids and disease*. London: Pitman Medical, 1972.

Czeisler, C. A., Moore, E. M., Regestein, Q., Kisch, E. S., Fang, V. S., & Ehrlich, E. N. Episodic 24 hour cortisol secretory patterns in patients awaiting elective cardiac surgery. *Journal of Clinical Endocrinology and Metabolism*, 1976, *42*, 273–82.

Daniel, J., Mikulaj, L., & Vrazda, L. Mental and endocrine factors in repeated stress in man. *Studia Psychologica*, 1973, *15*, 273–81.

Davis, J., Morrell, R., Fawcett, J., Upton, V., Bondy, P. K., & Spiro, H. M. Apprehension and elevated serum cortisol levels. *Journal of Psychosomatic Research*, 1962, *6*, 83–6.

Erhardt, A., & Baker, S. Fetal androgens, human central nervous system differentiation and behavior sex differences. In R. Freedman, R. Richart, & R. Vande Wiele (Eds)., *Sex difference in behavior*. New York: Wiley, 1974.

Erhardt, A., & Money, J. Prenatal hormone exposure: Possible effects on behavior in man. In R. Michael (Ed.), *Endocrinology and human behavior*. London, Oxford University Press, 1968.

Fox, J. M., Murawski, B. J., Bartholomay, A. F., & Gifford, S. Adrenal steroid excretion patterns in eighteen healthy subjects. *Psychosomatic Medicine*, 1961, *28*, 33–40.

Franks, R. C. Diurnal variation of 17-hydroxy-corticosteroids in children. *Journal of Clinical Endocrinology and Metabolism*, 1967, *27*, 75–8.

Friedman, S. B., Mason, J. W., & Hamburg, D. A. Urinary 17-hydroxycorticosteroid levels in parents of children with neoplastic disease. *Psychosomatic Medicine*, 1963, *25*, 364–76.

Gallagher, T. F., Yoshida, K., Roffwarg, H. D., Fukushima, D. F., Weitzman, E. D., & Hellman, L. ACTH and cortisol secretory patterns in man. *Journal of Clinical Endocrinology and Metabolism*, 1973, *30*, 1058–68.

Greene, W. A., Conron, G., Schalch, D. S., & Schriner, B. F. Psychologic correlates of growth hormone and adrenal secretory responses of patients undergoing cardiac catherization. *Psychosomatic Medicine*, 1970, *32*, 599–612.

Hall, C. St-C., Branchaud, C., Klein, G., Loras, B., Rothman, S., Stern, L., & Girous, C. Secretion rate and metabolism of the sulfates of cortisol and corticosterone in new born infants. *Journal of Clinical Endocrinology and Metabolism*, 1971, *33*, 98–104.

Hellman, L., Nakada, F., Curtis, J., Weitzman, E. D., Kream, J., Roffwarg, H., Ellmon, S., Fukushima, K., & Gallagher, T. F. Cortisol is secreted episodically by normal man. *Journal of Clinical Endocrinology and Metabolism*, 1970, *30*, 411–22.

Hofer, M. A., Wolff, C. T., Friedman, S. B., & Mason, J. W. A psychoendocrine study of bereavement: Part 1. 17-hydroxycorticosteroid excretion rates of parents following death of their children from leukemia. *Psychosomatic Medicine*, 1972, *34*, 481–91. (a)

Hofer, M. A., Wolff, C. T., Friedman, S. B., & Mason, J. W. A psychoendocrine study of bereavement: Part 2. Observations on the process of mourning in relation to adrenocortical function. *Psychosomatic Medicine*, 1972, *34*, 492–504. (b)

Juselius, R., & Kenny, F. Urinary free cortisol excretion during growth and aging: Correlation with cortisol production rate and 17-hydroxycorticosteroid excretion. *Metabolism*, 1972, *23*, 847–52.

Katz, J. J., Achman, P., Roffwarg, Y., Sachar, E. J., Weiner, H., Hellman, L., & Gallagher, T. F. Psychoendocrine aspects of cancer of the breast. *Psychosomatic Medicine*, 1970, *32*, 1–18.

Kenny, F., Malvaux, P., & Migeon, C. Cortisol production in newborn babies, older infants and children. *Pediatrics*, 1963, *31*, 360–73.

Kenny, F., Richard, C., & Taylor, F. Reference standards for cortisol production and 17-hydroxycorticosteroid excretion during growth: Variation in the pattern of excretion of radiolabeled cortisol metabolites. *Metabolism*, 1970, *19*, 280.

Kling A. Testosterone and aggressive behavior in man and non-human primates. In B. E. Eleftherious & R. I. Sprott (Eds.), *Hormonal correlates of behavior* (Vol. 1). New York: Plenum Press, 1975.

Knight, R., Atkins, A., Eagle, C., Evans, N., Finkelstein, J., Fukushima, D., Katz, J., & Weiner, H. Psychological stress, ego defenses and cortisol production in children hospitalized for elective surgery. *Psychosomatic Medicine*, 1979, *41*, 40–1.

Kreiger D. Circadian pituitary adrenal rhythms. In L. Hedlund, J. Fanz, & A. Kenny (Eds.), *Biological rhythms and endocrine function*. Advances in Experimental Medicine and Biology (Vol. 54). New York: Plenum Press, 1975.

Kreiger, D., & Liotta, A. Pituitary hormones in brain: Where, how and why? *Science*, 1979, *205*, 366–72.

Kreuz, L., Rose, R., & Jennings, J. Suppression of plasma testosterone levels and psychological stress: A longitudinal study of young men in officer candidate school. *Archives of General Psychiatry*, 1972, *26*, 479–82.

Levine, S. Developmental psychobiology. In S. Arieti (Ed.), *American handbook of psychiatry*. New York: Basic Books, 1975.

Levine, S., Weinberg, J., & Ursin, H. Definition of the coping process and statement of the problem. In H. Ursin, E. Baade, & S. Levine (Eds.), *Psychobiology of stress: A study of coping men*. New York: Academic Press, 1978.

Maccoby, E., Doering, C., Jacklin, C., & Karemer, H. Concentrations of sex hormones in umbilical-cord blood: Their relation to sex and birth order of infants. *Child Development*, 1979, *50*, 632–42.

Mason, J. W. Organization of psychoendocrine mechanisms. *Psychosomatic Medicine*, 1968, *30*, 565–791. (a)

Mason, J. W. A review of psychoendocrine research on the pituitary-adrenal corticol system. *Psychosomatic Medicine*, 1968, *30*, 576–607. (b)

Mason, J. W. A re-evaluation of the concept of nonspecificity in stress theory. *Journal of Psychiatric Research*, 1971, *8*, 323–333.

Mason, J. W. Emotion as reflected in patterns of endocrine integration. In L. Levi (Ed.), *Emotions – Their parameters and measurement*. New York: Raven Press, 1975. (a)

Mason, J. W. Clinical psychophysiology: Psychoendocrine mechanisms. In M. Reiser (Ed.), *American handbook of psychiatry* (Vol. 4). New York: Basic Books, 1975. (b)

Mason, J. W., Sachar, E., Fishman, J., Hamburg, D., & Handlon, J. Corticosteroid responses to hospital admission. *Archives of General Psychiatry*, 1965, *13*, 1.

Mattson, A., Gross, S., & Hall, T. Psychoendocrine study of adaptation in young hemophiliacs. *Psychosomatic Medicine*, 1971, *33*, 215–25.

Montagner, H., Henry, J., Lombardst, M., Restoin, A., Bolzoni, D., Durand, M., Humbert, Y., and Moyse, A. Behavioral profiles and corticosteroid excretion rhythms in young children. Parts 1 and 2. In V. Reynolds and N. Blurton Jones (Eds.), *Human behavior and adaptation*. London: Francis and Taylor, 1978.

Poe, R., Rose, R., & Mason, J. Multiple determinants of 17-hydroxycorticosteroid excretion in recruits during basic training. *Psychosomatic Medicine*, 1970, *32*, 369–78.

Price, D. B., Thaler, M., & Mason, J. W. Preoperative emotional states and adrenal cortical activity. *Archives of Neurology and Psychiatry*, 1957, *77*, 646–56.

Rahe, R. H., Rubin, R. T., & Arthur, R. J. The three investigators study: Serum uric acid, cholesterol and cortisol variability during stresses of everyday life. *Psychosomatic Medicine*, 1974, *36*, 258–68.

Rose, R. M. The psychological effects of androgens and estrogens – A review. In R. Shader (Ed.), *Psychiatric complications of medical drugs*. New York: Raven Press, 1972.

Rose, R. M., Poe, R. D., & Mason, J. W. Psychological state and body size as determinants of 17OHCS excretion. *Archives of Internal Medicine*, 1968, *121*, 406–13.

Sabshin, M., Hamburg, D. A., Grinker, R. R., Persky, H., Basowitz, H., Korchin, S. J., & Chevalier, J. A. Significance of preexperimental studies in the psychosomatic laboratory. *Archives of Neurology and Psychiatry*, 1957, *78*, 207–19.

Sachar, E. J. Corticosteroids in depressive illness: 1. A re-evaluation of control issues and of the literature. *Archives of General Psychiatry*, 1967, *17*, 544–53.

Sachar, E. J. Neuroendocrine abnormalities in depressive illness. In E. J. Sachar (Ed.), *Topics in psychoendocrinology*. New York: Grune & Stratton, 1975.

Sayers, G., & Portanova, R. Regulation of the secretory activity of the adrenal cortex: Cortisol and corticosterone. In H. Blaschko, G. Sayers, & A. D. Smith (Eds.), *Handbook of physiology: Section 7, Endocrinology: Vol. 6. Adrenal Gland*. Washington, D.C.: American Physiological Society, 1975.

Selye, H. A syndrome produced by diverse nocuous agents. *Nature*, 1936, *138*, p. 32.

Selye, H. *Stress*. Montreal: Acta, 1950.

Talbert, L. M., Draybill, E. N., & Potter, H. D. Adrenal cortical response to circumcision in the neonate. *Obstetrics and Gynecology*, 1975, *48*, 208–10.

Tennes, K., & Carter, D. Plasma cortisol levels and behavioral states in early infancy. *Psychosomatic Medicine*, 1973, *35*, 121–8.

Tennes, K., Downey, K., & Vernadakis, A. Urinary cortisol excretion rates and anxiety in normal one-year-old infants. *Psychosomatic Medicine*, 1977, *39*, 178–87.

Tennes, K., & Vernadakis, A. Cortisol excretion levels and daytime sleep in one-year-old infants. *Journal of Clinical Endocrinology and Metabolism*, 1977, *44*, 175–9.

Ursin, H., Baade, E., & Levine, S. *Psychobiology of stress: A study of coping men*. New York: Academic Press, 1978.

Warne, G., Faiman, C., Reyes, F., & Winter, J. Studies in human sexual development: V. Concentrations of testosterone, 17-hydroxyprogesterone and progesterone in human amniotic fluid throughout gestation. *Journal of Clinical Endocrinology and Metabolism*, 1977, *44*, 934–38.

Winter, J., Hughes, I., Reyes, F., & Faiman, C. Pituitary–gonadal relations in infancy: 2. Patterns of serum gonadal steroid concentrations in man from birth to two years of age. *Journal of Clinical Endocrinology and Metabolism*, 1976, *42*, 679–86.

Wolff, C., Friedman, S., Hofer, M., & Mason, J. Relationship between psychobiological defenses and mean urinary 17-hydroxycorticosteroid excretion rates: 1. A predictive study of parents of fatally ill children. *Psychosomatic Medicine*, 1964, *26*, 576.

Wolff, C., Hofer, M., & Mason, J. Relationship between psychological defenses and mean urinary 17-hydroxycorticosteroid excretion rates: 2. Methodologic and theoretical considerations. *Psychosomatic Medicine*, 1964, *26*, 592.

Yates, F. E., & Maran, J. D. Stimulation and inhibition of adrenocorticotropin release. In E. Knobil & W. Sawyer (Eds.), *Handbook of physiology: Section 7, Endocrinology: Vol. 4. The Pituitary Gland, Part 2*. Washington, D.C.: American Physiological Society, 1974.

3 Heart rate and heart rate variability as signs of a temperamental dimension in infants

Jerome Kagan

A great deal of progress has been made since investigators first used absolute heart rate or increases in heart rate as indexes of the psychological construct of arousal. At one time affect was treated as an undifferentiated state of internal excitation that could be indexed by changes in almost any autonomic reaction. This assumption, and its accompanying measurement strategy, were altered when the Laceys (1967, 1970) reported that adults showed a slowing of heart rate when they were attending to an external event but a speeding of heart rate when they were asked to perform difficult cognitive operations, such as memory or reasoning. In both cases the adults were in a greater state of arousal than they were before the experimental intervention, but the direction of change in cardiac rate depended on the psychological requirements imposed on the subject.

After the Laceys had demonstrated with adult subjects that a cardiac deceleration was likely to accompany attention to visual and auditory events and acceleration to problems requiring mental work, developmental psychologists began to observe infants in a similar way, hoping that the combination of the cardiac response and the behavioral posture of attention would provide a more sensitive index of the infant's state of attentiveness than the behavioral variable alone (Graham & Clifton, 1966). The first studies were promising. Kagan and his colleagues found that the probability of a cardiac deceleration increased when an infant or child was oriented toward a visual or auditory event (Kagan & Rosman, 1964; Lewis et al. 1966; McCall & Kagan, 1967). The relation was far from perfect, however, since the deceleration did not always occur when the infant appeared to be attending to the stimulus event. Subsequent research suggested that a deceleration was most likely to occur with the initial presentation of a new event and that the deceleration response habituated more rapidly than the behavioral response. It appeared, therefore, that the deceleration reflected a surprise reaction.

Two different classes of events can surprise the infant. First, a totally unex-

This research was supported in part by research grant HD 10094 from National Institute of Child Health and Human Development, U.S. Public Health Service.

38

pected stimulus, such as that which occurs in the beginning of each new series, surprises the child, and typically decelerations are largest to the first stimulus in every series. Second, an event that is a moderate departure from a schema is likely to surprise the infant. But in both cases the child is likely to quiet motorically, adopt an attentive posture, and display a deceleration of 6 to 10 beats over a 4- to 6-second interval. These decelerations occur within the first 3 seconds of the onset of attention to an event and usually reach a trough within 3 to 7 seconds (Kagan, Kearsley, & Zelazo, 1978). Subsequent investigations affirmed that events that are discrepant from the child's immediate past experience often, but not always, elicit a cardiac deceleration (Lewis & Goldberg, 1969; McCall & Kagan, 1967; McCall & Melson, 1969). In addition, 27-month-old children showed larger initial decelerations to the presentation of difficult perceptual problems than they did to easier ones, although there were no obvious differences in behavioral orientation, suggesting that the cardiac response was providing additional information regarding the attentional state of the child (Kagan, 1971).

A longitudinal study of Caucasian infants exposed to both visual and auditory events at 4, 8, 13, and 27 months revealed good cross-episode generality for the magnitude of the cardiac deceleration but only short-term interindividual stability across ages. That is, the infants did not preserve their ranks for magnitude of deceleration to the stimulus events from 4 or 8 to 27 months (Kagan, 1971). This fact suggests that the magnitude of the deceleration response is primarily a function of the information value of the stimulus and that the value changes as the child grows.

There are two interpretations of the cardiac deceleration response. Lacey (1967) has suggested that the cardiac deceleration is the organism's way of increasing its receptivity to external events. Lacey views the deceleration as a quasi-instrumental response and bases this hypothesis on the fact that a change in rate of sensory afferents from the heart stimulates the carotid sinus to discharge. These signals are passed to the reticular formation and thence to the cortex. It is assumed that the bombardment of cortex decreases the organism's sensitivity to inputs from eye, ear, and skin. A low and steady heart rate minimizes these noisy signals from the carotid sinus and leads to increased sensitivity.

Obrist offers an alternative hypothesis, suggesting that a decrease in heart rate is a result of vagal excitation and is accompanied by a decrease in somatomotor activity. Obrist argues that heart rate decreases as the organism becomes quiet and that both cardiac and somatic affects are different biological manifestations of the same process (Obrist, 1976; Obrist et al., 1970).

Although the relation of cardiac acceleration to mental work in schoolchildren and adults is reliable, it has proven extremely difficult to demonstrate this phenomenon in infants, perhaps because preverbal children are not capable of engaging in the operations that accompany cardiac acceleration in 10-year-olds and adults (see van Hover, 1974).

Investigators have also tried to use cardiac acceleration as an index of the emotion of fear because some 9-month-old infants will display an increase in heart rate when placed on the deep side of the visual cliff (Campos, 1976). But this methodological assumption is flawed somewhat by the fact that 7- to 12-month-old infants will decelerate, not accelerate, when a stranger approaches them and before they begin to cry. Most child psychologists have assumed that the infants are afraid of the stranger, but it is difficult to reconcile this assumption with the absence of cardiac acceleration. At present the relation between cardiac deceleration or acceleration and specific cognitive functions in adults is relatively hardy and represents an important advance in our knowledge (see Campos, 1976, for a review of this information in young children).

More recently scientists have begun to study the correlates of variability in heart rate during well-structured stimulus presentations. Porges and Raskin (1969) have reported a decrease in heart rate variability in adults who were sustaining attention to a variety of events (see Porges, 1972; Porges & Humphrey, 1977; Walter & Porges, 1976, for similar results). And as might be expected, there are marked individual differences in the variability of cardiac rate displayed to problem situations.

My colleagues and I have gathered data on infants that suggest a relation between variability in heart rate and a temperamental dimension in the child. The temperamental dimension in question is the disposition to become vigilant and subsequently to display inhibition and even distress in situations of uncertainty. These are the behaviors that parents might call timidity in contrast to fearless exuberance.

During resting conditions the heart rate is typically under parasympathetic influence; vagal tone tends to keep the heart rate low, and the variability of the heart cycle is yoked to the inspiration–expiration cycles of respiration. This phenomenon is called *sinus arrhythmia*. Katona and Jih (1975) suggest that heart rate variability is a sensitive index of the degree of parasympathetic control of the heart. After blocking the vagi of dogs by cooling, investigators computed the difference between the average heart period before and after cooling and found that the correlation between the difference score and the peak-to-peak variation in heart rate caused by spontaneous respiration (the vagi were not cooled) was .97 (Katona & Jih, 1975).

But under conditions when sympathetic tone is increased (e.g., when the subject is trying to cope with a noxious stimulus or solve a difficult problem), vagal influence on the heart is inhibited, respiratory control of the cardiac cycle diminished, and heart rate rises and tends to become less variable. There are a great many studies indicating that heart rate rises when adults are attempting to cope with difficult problems. If the idealized consequence of the increase in sympathetic tone always occurred, there would always be a negative relation between absolute heart rate and heart rate variability, but this is not the case (Kagan et al., 1978).

Let us consider briefly some relevant studies. Several investigators have shown that when adults are given a period of 10 to 20 seconds during which to anticipate a signal associated with high response uncertainty, cardiac rates rise during this period, but only if the problem is relatively difficult and the signal has high response uncertainty. (See Coles & Duncan-Johnson, 1977; Lawler, Obrist, & Lawler, 1976; Petry & Desiderato, 1978; Porges, 1972; Porges & Humphrey, 1977; Porges & Raskin, 1969.) One of the important studies in this area was reported by Obrist and his colleagues (see Obrist et al., 1978). When adults were placed in a situation in which they could not control shock, their heart rates did not rise during an experimental interval. If the subjects believed they could control the shock, however, their heart rates were higher, indicating the importance of the subject's belief that he was able to control the noxious event. The authors conclude, "Sympathetic effects are more consistently and appreciably evoked under conditions in which the individual is attempting to exert some control over the stressors" (p. 321).

These considerations lead one to expect a greater inverse correlation between heart rate and heart rate variability under relaxed conditions than under conditions of arousal or difficult mental work. This prediction is in accord with the fact that heart rate and respiration in kittens are not correlated during active sleep but do covary in quiet sleep. The hypothesis also accords with the data summarized, which suggest that when a subject is psychologically vigilant – prepared to deal with an event – he or she should show a slightly higher heart rate and more restricted range (see Cheung & Porges, 1977). If infants differ temperamentally in the tendency to become cognitively vigilant and to try to cope with stimulus events in moderately uncertain situations, we might expect a correlation between a lower threshold for displaying signs of apprehension (if the child was unable to deal with the event) and a tendency to show higher and more stable heart rates in contexts where a vigilant set might be produced. We now consider some recent studies that implicate individual differences in heart rate and variability as potential indexes of a disposition to inhibition in uncertain contexts.

Study 1: The day care—home control study

The first source of evidence comes from a longitudinal study of children half-Caucasian, half-Chinese, who were followed from $3\frac{1}{2}$ to 29 months of age and were assessed at $3\frac{1}{2}$, $5\frac{1}{2}$, $7\frac{1}{2}$, $9\frac{1}{2}$, $11\frac{1}{2}$, $13\frac{1}{2}$, 20, and 29 months of age. The description of the procedures and the major results appear elsewhere (Kagan et al.,

1978). We will only summarize that study. The heart rate data to be reported came from Chinese and Caucasian children who either were attending a day-care center or were being reared totally at home. Continuous heart rate data were gathered during the habituation phase of several visual episodes and an auditory episode. In one visual episode, called *block,* the child saw an adult hand lift a 2-inch orange wooden block from a blue box, move it in front of the child several times, and then replace it in the box. This procedure was repeated six or eight times, depending on the age of the child, each trial lasting 10.5 seconds with an interstimulus interval of 4.5 seconds. This episode was administered five times across the interval $3\frac{1}{2}$ to $11\frac{1}{2}$ months.

In a second episode the child was shown a series of four different masks in a fixed order on two separate occasions for a 20-second period. The masks were shown to the children 3, 5, 9, and 11 months old.

In a third episode, called *light,* the child was shown 10 identical repetitions of an 11-second sequence in which the examiner's hand moved an orange rod in a circular arc until it contacted a bank of three light bulbs that lit upon contact. This event was shown at every age from $3\frac{1}{2}$ through 29 months.

In a fourth visual episode, called *car,* the child saw a small wooden car resting on top of a wooden ramp. After a few seconds the car rolled down an incline and struck a styrofoam form, which fell upon contact. This procedure was repeated for eight trials and was shown to children 9, 11, 13, 20, and 29 months of age. At $9\frac{1}{2}$ and $11\frac{1}{2}$ months the child saw a set of five chromatic slides projected on a screen. In each set an object or a background gradually became transformed into a second object or background. Each slide was shown for 6 seconds with no interstimulus interval. In the final visual episode, shown to individuals at 20 and 29 months, the child saw a series of 14 chromatic slides, 1 at a time, each illuminated for $14\frac{1}{2}$ seconds. In this series 5 of the slides depicted discrepant events, and 9 were ecologically valid events. In the auditory episode the child heard 12 repetitions of a particularly meaningful phrase 4.5 seconds in duration. This event was administered at every age from $3\frac{1}{2}$ through 29 months.

We coded the range of each child's rate during each stimulus presentation as an index of cardiac variability. Heart range was defined as the difference between the highest and lowest heart rate on those trials during the familiarization period when the child was highly attentive and not irritable. Trials when fixation time was less than 80 percent or when more than 1 second of fretting occurred were omitted from analysis. Thus the child's absolute heart rate levels were not near the upper limit of the child's cardiac range.

Results reveal that the Caucasians displayed larger heart rate ranges on most trials of all episodes at almost every age, and there were no social class or rearing differences in heart rate variability. The consistent difference between Chinese and Caucasian infants was not solely a function of larger or more frequent cardiac decelerations or accelerations among the Caucasians. In a separate analysis we compared the heart rate ranges of the two groups for those trials in which neither an acceleration nor a deceleration occurred (i.e. when the child showed no obvious change in heart rate on the stimulus trial compared with the 3 seconds prior to the onset of that trial). The Chinese continued to show smaller average heart rate values than the Caucasians at most ages and during most episodes. Even when we eliminated all trials in which a vocalization, smile, or motor action occurred, as well as all trials in which a deceleration or acceleration occurred, the Chinese continued to have smaller heart rate range values.

Because the Chinese children had less variable heart rates at every age, we evaluated the stability of cardiac range. The correlations were computed separately for the two ethnic groups for the mean of the two lowest ranges for each episode. The data revealed remarkable stability for the Chinese and moderate stability for the Caucasians. Among the Chinese heart rate range at 5 months predicted range during the 1st year and range at 7 months predicted range at all future ages. For example, the values at 7 months correlated with the two lowest ranges at every succeeding age (e.g., .80 at 9 months, .52 at 29 months). Among the Caucasians, stability was present but less consistent. The magnitudes of these stability correlations for range exceeded those found for any behavioral variable quantified in this study, including fixation time, crying, vocalization, and smiling.

It is of interest, therefore, that the Chinese children showed more inhibition in unfamiliar social situations and more distress at separation from the mother than did the Caucasians. Because the Chinese children also had less variable heart rates, it is possible that children with a disposition to be inhibited in uncertain situations might also be more vigilant in a laboratory situation. The greatest ethnic difference occurred following separation from the mother – the Chinese children showed more frequent distress at separation than the Caucasians.

The remarkably high cross-age stability of heart rate range and the consistently lower ranges displayed by the Chinese children provoked us to examine this corpus of data in more detail. We now report results that were not present in the original monograph. Because the Chinese and Caucasian children differed most in the occurrence of separation distress and inhibition in unfamiliar situations, we concentrated on those behaviors in these new additional analyses. The analysis to be described was restricted to 30 Chinese and 25 Caucasian children who had good records for most of the sessions from $3\frac{1}{2}$ through 29 months of age. The child's heart rate range was based on the mean of the two lowest range values for the familiarization trials for block, light, car, and auditory episodes at each age. Heart rate was based on the mean of the high and low values for all familiarization trials across all the episodes at a particular age. There was no correlation between heart rate and heart rate range for this sample of children.

For each child we computed an index of his or her tendency to show consistently high or low heart rates and consistently high or low ranges on the four episodes (block, light, car, and auditory) over the 2 years of assessment. Each child was given a standard score for heart rate and a standard score for range for each episode at each age, based on all the data for all subjects administered that episode at that age. We chose as a criterion for consistently high/low rate and high/low range a standard score of plus or minus .5. We determined, for each of the four episodes, for how many test sessions the child's standard score met or exceeded the criterion of .5 or −.5. Each child had a maximum of 26 occasions to meet the criterion (the auditory procedure contributed 8 occasions, *block* contributed 5 occasions, *light* contributed 8 occasions, and *car* contributed 5 occasions). After examining the distribution of scores we decided that those children who met the criterion 60% or more of the time would be classified as either high or low rate and high or low range.

Children who did not meet the 60% criterion were eliminated from further analyses because we wanted to deal with children who had consistently high or low cardiac scores. There were 9 children who had consistently high heart rates, 10 had consistently low heart rates, 7 had consistently high ranges, and 8 had consistently low ranges (34 from the original sample of 55 children).

Relation of cardiac pattern to behavioral inhibition

Two behavioral indexes of vulnerability to uncertainty were used. The first was the number of occasions when the child cried when a brief separation from the mother occurred in a laboratory setting. The reader will recall that the separations occurred at 3, 5, 7, 9, 11, 13, 20, and 29 months (the actual range was 1 to 6). The second variable, called the *behavioral inhibition index,* was an average score based on behavior in a variety of situations, which a priori should have generated some uncertainty. The inhibition index was derived for each child by computing an average standard score (all scores were standardized within ethnic group and age) for 11 variables that were indicative of inhibition in response to uncertainty. The 11 variables were: (a) proximity to the mother during a 45-minute session when the child was with a female stranger, a familiar woman, and the mother; (b) proximity to the mother during a play session when the child was with the mother, an unfamiliar peer, and the unfamiliar peer's mother at 13, 20, and 29 months (6 variables); (c) the magnitude of decrease in time playing during the period when child was with the unfamiliar peer as compared with the time playing when the child was alone with the mother at 13, 20, and 29 months (3 variables); and (d) proximity to the mother during a visit to an unfamiliar daycare center when the child was 29 months old.

There was no relation between the frequency of separation anxiety and the inhibition index; there was no general apprehensiveness dimension. Second, the patterns of heart rate and heart rate range for the entire sample did not predict either the inhibition index or frequency of distress in response to separation. Rather, a combination of ethnicity, form of care, and sex were the best predictors of separation distress and inhibition. For example, of the 13 children with the most frequent occasions of separation (five of six occasions), 7 were Chinese girls in day care. But although Chinese girls in day care were vulnerable to separation distress, Caucasian girls or boys in day care were not. Similarly, of 14 children high on the inhibition index (the standard score was equal to or greater than .5), 6 were Caucasian boys or girls in day care. These data imply that a combination of rearing experience, ethnicity, and sex were subduing any potential temperamental disposition to behavioral inhibition that might have been indexed by cardiac rate and range.

It was necessary, therefore, to locate pairs of children who were matched by type of care, ethnicity, and sex but who varied on behavioral signs of anxiety or inhibition in order to determine whether patterns of heart rate might index a temperamental vulnerability to anxiety and inhibition. When the matching had been performed, some support for this hypothesis emerged.

Two Caucasian girls attending the day-care center had consistently high heart rates and low ranges. Both girls showed separation distress on *three* occasions. The two Caucasian girls attending the day-care center who had consistently low heart rates and high ranges displayed separation distress on only *one* occasion. Similarly, two Chinese girls attending the day-care center with high rates and low ranges showed separation distress on *five* occasions; the two Chinese girls in the day-care center who had low rates and high ranges showed separation anxiety on *two* and *five* occasions, respectively. The two Chinese boys in day care with high rates and low ranges showed separation distress *three* times; the two Chinese boys in day care with low rates and high ranges showed separation anxiety only *twice*. Finally, one Caucasian home control boy with high rate and low range showed separation anxiety four times, whereas three Caucasian home control boys who had low rate and high range showed separation anxiety twice, twice, and once, respectively.

Thus of seven pairs of children matched on form of care, ethnicity, and sex, the six children with consistently high rates and low ranges showed separation distress more frequently than their matched counterparts who consistently displayed low rates and high ranges ($p < .05$). These data, although the sample was small, imply that heart rate and range may correlate with the disposition to separation distress when sex, form of care, and ethnicity are strictly controlled.

In a separate but obviously related analysis, we selected eight pairs of children matched on ethnicity, sex, and form of care (three Caucasian pairs and five Chinese pairs) who differed in separation distress, and we examined their heart rate records for the four episodes (*car* at 9, 11, and 13 months; auditory at 3, 5, 7, 9, 11, and 13 months; *light* at 3, 5, 7, 9, 11, and 13 months; and *block* at 3, 5, 7, 9, and 11 months). These children differed with respect to the number of occasions of separation distress – either five or six occasions versus one or two occasions (only eight pairs of children differed so dramatically in frequency of separation distress and could be matched for the three background dimensions).

We reanalyzed the cardiac data for these 16 children and computed three new cardiac variables for each trial of the habituation series when the children were attentive to the stimulus. One variable was the median rate for the five heartbeats prior to the onset of the stimulus, the second was the median rate for the first five beats after stimulus onset, and the third variable was the highest heart rate during the trial. Recall that the original index of rate was the mean of the high and low values for that trial. Because these three variables were highly correlated, we averaged the three values across the habituation trials. In addition, these values showed good intraindividual consistency across the four procedures, so we averaged the values across the four episodes. For six of the eight pairs, the children who showed more frequent separation distress had higher heart rates at 7, 9, and 11 months of age, but not earlier, for all three cardiac variables.

In a complementary analysis we examined the heart rate values from $3\frac{1}{2}$ to $13\frac{1}{2}$ months for 19 children who showed separation distress on five or six occasions versus one, two, or three occasions. The results matched those described above. Of the 9 children who showed separation anxiety on five or six occasions, 5 showed an increase in heart rate at age of 7 to 11 months *compared with their values at $3\frac{1}{2}$ and $5\frac{1}{2}$ months*. By contrast, only 1 of 10 children who showed infrequent separation distress showed an increase in heart rate during the period 7 to 11 months ($p = .05$ by the exact test).

It is important to note that the children who were high or low on separation distress did not differ in heart rate at $3\frac{1}{2}$ and $5\frac{1}{2}$ months; the differences in rate only emerged from $7\frac{1}{2}$ to $11\frac{1}{2}$ months. Previous work (Kagan et al., 1978) has indicated a major increase in fearfulness among most infants between $7\frac{1}{2}$ and $11\frac{1}{2}$ months of age – the time when anxiety in response to strangers and separation appear. These data suggest that the higher heart rates displayed by the anxious children during this interval are not due to an inherent tendency to have a higher heart rate. Rather, it seems that when the hypothetical maturational change in cognitive functioning occurs at 7 to 9 months of age, some infants become more vigilant to discrepant events than others do. As a result of the change in psychological state, their heart rates are higher when uncertain events are encountered.

The temperamental variable is psychological in nature but will not be expressed until the child has matured to a point where he or she attempts to cope with the unexpected. This generalization is in line with the work reported by

Skarin (1977) and Campos et al. (1975). Skarin has reported that 11-month-old boys and girls showed a much greater increase in heart rate when they encountered a stranger than 6-month-olds did. He argued that these results reflect the cognitive developmental changes that take place at about 7 to 9 months of age. Campos and his colleagues reported that when a stranger approached a child, 5-month-olds showed deceleration, whereas 9-month-olds tended to show cardiac acceleration. These investigators also note an important psychological change – which we attribute to cognitive maturation – that leads to both different behaviors and different autonomic patterns when events associated with uncertainty occur at about 7 to 8 months of age.

A final analysis of the data for this sample is suggested by the hypothesis summarized earlier (see Obrist et al., 1978), that sympathetic influences on the heart should decrease the probability of the expected cardiac deceleration in response to the initial presentations of unexpected events. It will be recalled that at 5 and 7 months the children saw the block and light episodes and heard the auditory sequence. At 9 and 11 months the car episode was added to the battery; at 13, 20, and 29 months the block was dropped, leaving three episodes administered at the three oldest ages. Typically, the children showed a cardiac deceleration to some of the initial presentations of the standard, after which deceleration became less frequent. Cardiac deceleration when a new event is initially presented is usually interpreted as reflecting a special psychological state that some have labeled surprise and others view as reflecting a comparison with past experience. According to physiological theory, the deceleration is due to an increase in vagal influence on the heart. But as many investigators have noted, all children do not show frequent decelerations or decelerations of large magnitude in response to unexpected stimuli.

We analyzed the data for 31 Chinese and 29 Caucasian children who had good cardiac data across the period 5 to 20 months. We computed the proportion of the first 4 trials of each episode during which each child displayed a deceleration (12 trials at 5, 7, 13, and 20 months and 16 trials at 9 and 13 months). Decelerations were only coded when the children were attentive and not irritable. Independent coders evaluated the child's cardiac rate, determining increase, decrease, or stability during the initial fixation of each visual event by comparing the direction of the heart rate during the first fixation of the stimulus (or the onset of the stimulus event for the auditory episode) with the rate during the 3-second base period prior to the onset of the first visual fixation (2 seconds for the auditory event). A deceleration was coded if the heart rate began to decrease with the onset of fixation and the cardiac rate at the trough of that decline was lower than the lowest rate during the base period prior to the onset of the stimulus. Reliability for the judgment was .95. The magnitudes of deceleration were also computed by taking the difference between the trough or peak rate during the first fixation and the trough or peak during each base period. Trials during which the child looked at the stimulus less than 80% of the time or during which more than 1 second of fretting occurred were not scored.

The Caucasian children had slightly larger average decelerations than the Chinese at some ages but not all. The ethnic difference in magnitude of deceleration was greatest for the auditory episode. A variable of major interest was the proportion of trials during which decelerations occurred. The Caucasian children had only a slightly higher mean proportion of deceleration trials; the difference was not statistically significant. But examination of the individual scores revealed that more Chinese than Caucasians showed deceleration on less than 40% of their trials at the three early ages (5, 7, and 9 months); 8 Chinese but only 2 Caucasians had scores this low. Although this ethnic difference is not statistically significant, the Chinese with these low deceleration scores were more prone to separation anxiety. The Chinese children who showed less than 40% of their trials deceleratory had more frequent occasions of separation anxiety than the Chinese children with more frequent decelerations. The number of occasions of separation distress ranged from one to six, with 11 Chinese children showing separation anxiety five or six times and 7 children showing separation distress on only one or two occasions. Of the 11 children who had frequent separation distress, 5 decelerated less than 40% of the time; only 1 Chinese child with low separation anxiety had a deceleration score that low at 5, 7, and 9 months ($p < .05$ by the exact test). Comparable analyses of the Caucasian data revealed no relation between the occurrence of separation anxiety and occurrence of deceleration.

The fact that the Chinese sample contained more children who showed deceleration scores of less than 40% at 5, 7, and 9 months implies that some of the young Chinese infants were more aroused sympathetically during the opening trials of the episodes. The Chinese infants who were sympathetically aroused at these early ages were more likely to cry following separation throughout the period 5 to 29 months, suggesting that there may be a temperamental tendency for some children to be more vulnerable to apprehension in uncertain situations and that heart rate range, absolute heart rate and, perhaps, the absence of cardiac deceleration when unexpected events occur might index this psychological tendency.

In sum, the first set of data yielded four possible facts. First, heart rate range was a remarkably stable attribute, more stable than any behavioral variable. Second, Chinese children, who were typically more inhibited than Caucasians in uncertain situations, had less variable heart rates at almost every age. Third, when we matched children by sex, ethnicity, and form of rearing, the children with the higher heart rates and lower ranges showed more frequent separation anxiety than the children with the opposite pattern. Finally, absence of cardiac deceleration in response to the initial presentation of interesting events seemed to be more characteristic of the more fearful Chinese children.

Study 2: Heart rate range and behavioral inhibition

We now summarize some additional data on another sample of children that support these findings. The main hypothesis being explored is that a higher heart rate and/or a more restricted heart rate range to events that require some effort to assimilate will be characteristic of behaviorally inhibited children who are prone to display behavioral signs of anxiety in uncertain situations.

Method

Sample. The sample consisted of two longitudinal cohorts. The younger cohort consisted of 14 Caucasian children who were seen every month from 13 to 22 months of age. Of the children in this group, 2 would not accept electrodes for the recording of heart rate, hence the data to be reported come from 12 children. The older cohort consisted of 16 children seen monthly from 20 to 26 months of age and at 29 months of age. Heart rate data are available for only 15 children because 1 refused to accept the electrodes.

Procedures. The heart rate data were gathered in two separate but closely spaced sessions each month while the child was viewing a set of chromatic slides illustrating familiar and moderately unfamiliar objects (animals, spoons, faces, dogs, blocks). The visual information belonged to one of 13 categories. Of the 13 categories 12 formed 6 complementary pairs. Each month one member of the pair was shown (six members per month). The category that did not have a complementary pair was shown every month as the first presentation on the first of the two monthly sessions. The format of the presentation was the same for all categories. For each conceptual category the infant saw 10 pairs of stimuli belonging to a particular category during the initial familiarization phase. Each pair was exposed for $7\frac{1}{2}$ seconds with a 1-second interstimulus interval. On any 1 trial the pair of pictures was identical, but each of the 10 pairs in the category illustrated different objects or scenes. For example, when the conceptual category was "dog," the child saw a pair of identical dogs on Trial 1, a different pair of identical dogs on Trial 2, and so forth. Although we shall only be concerned here with the child's heart rate reactivity to the habituation phase, we should note that on the 11th trial the child saw two different stimuli. One was a new exemplar of the category to which the child had been habituated; the other stimulus was a member of a different category. The complementary categories were:

men's faces / dogs; array of four different objects / array of four identical objects; a pair of identical objects / four identical objects; photographs of unfamiliar infants / photographs of the child being tested; arrays of four objects seriated with respect to the length of the vertical dimension / array of four objects in a nonseriated pattern; and finally an array of four objects arranged in a symmetrical pattern / array of four objects arranged in an asymmetrical pattern. The category with no complement illustrated scenes of a particular girl who was standing and performing an action affecting a woman who was seated (the girl might be feeding the woman, offering her an object, or touching her). The woman and the girl were the same individuals on all trials, but their interaction varied. Two coders independently recorded each infant's fixation time for each of the two stimuli without knowledge of the pictures being projected; the intercoder reliability was .9. In addition, the child's heart rate was monitored throughout the episodes.

At the first session of each monthly visit the child was always shown the category "girl acting on the woman" as the first episode. The six complementary categories were varied in order of presentation, and the child saw one category on one month and its complement the next month. Thus each month the child was exposed to seven categories, or a total of 70 habituation trials in all (10 habituation trials per category).

Variables coded. During the stimulus-exposures fixation time, fretting, and vocalization were being coded by observers, and the child's heart rate was being monitored continually. This report concentrates primarily on the heart rate data. The child's absolute heart rate during the habituation phase for each category was based on the average of the single high and single low heart beats for each of the 10 habituation trials computed for each of the concepts separately. Heart rate was not coded on any trial on which the child looked for less than 4 of the $7\frac{1}{2}$ seconds of exposure or fretted for more than 1 second. Each child had a maximum of 10 trials per concept and therefore a maximum of 70 heart rate values each month. Because of occasional lapses of attention, fretting, or technical difficulties, the number of values contributing to a child's heart rate values on any month was typically between 50 and 60.

The computation of heart rate range was also restricted to the 10 habituation trials prior to the transformation and, as with the coding of heart rate, was only computed when fixation time was at least 4 seconds in duration and less than 1 second of fretting occurred. Heart rate range was defined as the difference between the highest and lowest heart rates during the stimulus trial. The average range for all 10 habituation trials was highly correlated with the mean of the two lowest ranges for those 10 trials (correlations ranged from .8 to .9), so we used the mean of the two lowest ranges as the index of cardiac variability. This was the variable used in the analysis of the original day care–home control study; it gives greater emphasis to the lowest values the child achieved and is not spuriously influenced by the values obtained on 1 or 2 trials when range was unusually high due to a large deceleration or acceleration that accompanied a yawn, cough, or major motor movement.

Results

Growth function for fixation time. Although the focus of this report is on heart rate and heart rate range, it is useful to consider first the growth function for attentiveness to the stimuli. We examined the average total fixation time across the 10 standards (prior to the dishabituation trial) for each category for each of the two cohorts. The data for fixation time were remarkably orderly. There was an increase in fixation time with age for every category. Typically fixation time displayed a sharp increase between ages 14 and 17 months, followed by a plateau from age 18 months through 29 months, during which the children looked at the pair of slides about 75% to 80% of total exposure time. As we shall see, heart rate decreased sharply during the 4 to 5 months when fixation time was increasing. The complementary categories had equal absolute fixation times, with the exception of symmetry–asymmetry, which had a slightly lower average fixation time (4.8 seconds). The other categories had average fixation times of about 5.6 seconds. Thus total fixation time values did not differentiate among the pairs of complementary categories. Furthermore, for three of the complementary categories, there was no difference in attentiveness between each of the complements (two vs. four objects; seriation vs. nonseriation; and symmetry vs. asymmetry). Still, there was a difference (not statistically significant) in attentiveness for self–peer, same–different, and dog–man. Photographs of the self were studied longer than photographs of the unfamiliar child; the sets of four different objects were looked at more than the sets of four identical objects, and the pictures of the dogs were studied more than the male faces. It appears that both familiarity and variety were incentives for attention. Finally, there was minimal cross-age stability for fixation time from month to month. The median stability coefficient was .2, and no concept showed better stability than any other. The data from the earlier study (Kagan et al., 1978) also revealed minimal interindividual stability of fixation time to a set of varied visual episodes across the period 5 to 29 months.

Growth functions for heart rate and heart rate range

Younger cohort. Average heart rate (based on the mean across all categories) showed a steady decrease over the period 13 to 22 months from a mean of 135

J. KAGAN

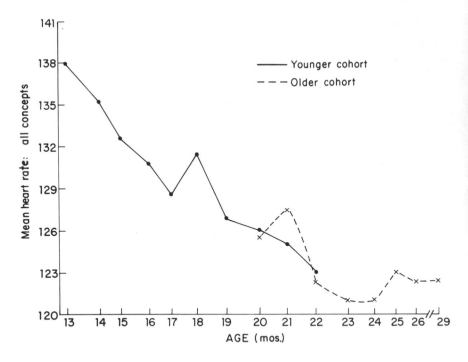

Figure 3.1. Mean heart rate to visual stimuli by age for younger and older cohorts

beats per minute to about 125 beats per minute (see Figure 3.1). Only the man–dog category showed a consistent difference in rate between the paired complements; dog was associated with the higher heart rate (the difference was about 4 beats).

Heart rate range produced a U-shaped function with a trough at 17 months (see Figure 3.2). This function for the group was replicated for 12 of the 13 categories. The only exception was the 10 paired photographs of self; for this set of stimuli, the lowest range occurred at 20 months of age. Pictures of self produced the lowest ranges of any of the categories. Within each pair of complementary categories, the only pair to yield a difference in range was dog–man, with dog eliciting a smaller range than man. (It may not be coincidence that the pattern of higher heart rate and more restricted range in response to the photographs of the dogs is the one we hypothesized would reflect apprehension.)

Older cohort. Cardiac rate and range changed less dramatically for the older cohort than for the younger across the period of testing. Heart rate decreased very gradually from 20 to 23 months and then remained steady for the subsequent months. Heart rate range remained relatively constant across the period 20 to 29

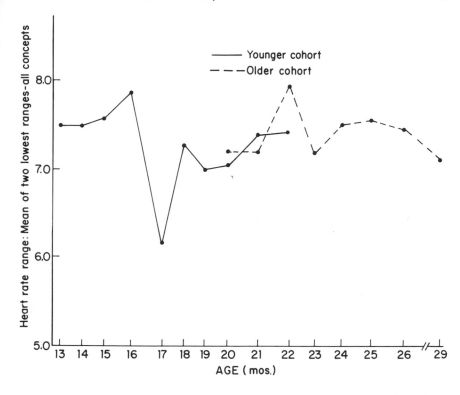

Figure 3.2. Mean heart rate range to visual stimuli by age for younger and older cohorts

months. Two categories had their lowest ranges at 23 months, two at 24 months, and one each at 21, 25, and 29 months. As with the younger children, pictures of the self produced the lowest ranges, suggesting that the more meaningful the stimulus, the lower the heart rate range. It is important to note that the rate and range values were similar for both cohorts during the 3 months of overlap at 20, 21, and 22 months. This fact suggests that the child's age, rather than the number of prior exposures to the stimuli, was the major determinant of heart rate and range values.

Stability of rate and range: older cohort. Table 3.1 contains the stability coefficients for range and rate averaged across all concepts for the older cohort across the period 20 to 29 months (range to the right and above the diagonal, rate to the left and below the diagonal). Unlike fixation time, both absolute heart rate and heart rate range showed good cross-age stability, although rate was more stable. Absolute heart rate was stable across the entire 9-month interval from 20 to 29 months ($r = .77$); the median coefficient for the 28 correlations was .68, and the

Table 3.1. *Cross-age stability correlations for heart rate range and heart rate, older cohort*

Age	20	21	22	23	24	25	26	29
20	—	71	68	65	70	37	50	08
21	60	—	86	87	72	60	74	30
22	59	75	—	87	85	62	75	60
23	78	68	68	—	83	61	63	42
24	80	66	75	76	—	46	71	55
25	69	70	75	70	66	—	53	19
26	64	58	68	74	75	80	—	64
29	77	85	65	68	62	65	66	—

Note: Heart rate range is the mean of the two lowest ranges across all categories. Heart rate given is across all concepts. Range is to the right and above the diagonal; rate is to the left and below the diagonal.

coefficients ranged from .58 to .85. Heart rate range was stable from 20 to 26 months, but there was no stability from 20 to 29 months. The median coefficient was .63, and the coefficients ranged from 0.8 to .87.

Unlike the data from the earlier study of the day-care and home control children (Kagan et al., 1978), rate was more stable than range, and rate and range were negatively correlated. The median correlation between rate and range was −.56, and the magnitudes of the negative correlations increased with age from −.46 at 20 months to −.67 at 29 months (see Table 3.2).

Heart rate and range were not only negatively correlated on the same visit but were also negatively correlated on different visits. For example, heart rate at 22 months was negatively correlated with heart rate range at 24 and 26 months (r = −.6). Indeed, the relation between heart rate at 22 months and range at 26 months was as high as the relation between rate and range at the same age. A total of 61 of the maximum of 64 correlations (95%) between rate and range across the eight sessions was negative, and 13 of the 64 correlations (20%) were statistically significant (at $p < .05$ or better). Thus for this sample of 15 children, high heart rate was associated with a more restricted range.

Stability for individual categories. Although rate and range were stable when the values were averaged across all 13 categories, it is of interest to determine the degree of stability by category (see Table 3.3).

Rate was stable over age for most concepts; only symmetry was a little less stable than the remaining six concepts. Even for symmetry, however, 18 of the 20 coefficients were equal to or greater than .5, and the median coefficient was .55. It seems reasonable, therefore, to pool all the concepts to arrive at a mean

Table 3.2. *Correlation between mean heart rate range and absolute heart rate across all concepts, older cohort*

Absolute heart rate M	Range M							
	20	21	22	23	24	25	26	29
20	−46	−45	−47	−36	−51	−30	−21	−43
21	13	−34	−17	−02	−30	−34	−42	−53
22	−08	−47	−54*	−35	−59*	−48	−64*	−45
23	−27	−66**	−50	−58*	−68*	−47	−53*	−54
24	−05	−30	−38	−35	−53*	−39	−37	−46
25	−36	−63*	−48	−46	−53*	−61*	−51	−31
26	−11	−44	−27	−29	−39	−36	−60*	−32
29	05	−44	−21	03	−27	−06	−54	−67*

$*p < .05. **p < .01.$

Table 3.3. *Range of stability coefficients, median coefficient, and number of significant stability coefficients for absolute heart rate and heart rate range by concept, older cohort*

Concept	Range of stability coefficients	Median Coefficient	Number of significant coefficients
Heart rate			
Girl–woman	.39–.82	.50	15
Man–dog	.39–.79	.57	16
Same–different	.20–.72	.54	15
Number: 2–4	.25–.98	.59	16
Self–peer	.28–.88	.55	15
Seriation–nonseriation	.34–.84	.67	16
Symmetry–asymmetry	.15–.74	.55	7
Heart rate range			
Girl–woman	−.08–+.78	.53	14
Man–dog	−.33–+.82	.45	7
Same–different	−.13–+.70	.36	8
Number: 2–4	−.31–+.71	.42	7
Self–peer	+.15–+.82	.51	12
Seriation–nonseriation	−.03–+.69	.28	7
Symmetry–asymmetry	−.46–+.88	.15	2

Note: The maximum number of correlations is 28.

Table 3.4. *The cross-concept stability of rate at each age: number of significant correlations*

	Age (months)							
Category	20	21	22	23	24	25	26	29
1. Child–woman	6	5	6	6	6	6	5	6
2. Man–dog	5	6	3	6	6	5	2	6
3. Same–different	5	4	5	6	5	6	4	6
4. Two–four	6	5	6	6	4	6	3	6
5. Child–self	6	6	5	6	6	6	4	6
6. Seriation–nonseriation	6	5	6	6	5	5	6	6
7. Symmetry–asymmetry	6	6	5	6	4	3	4	6

Note: Data shown are for the older cohort. The maximum possible number of significant correlations is six.

heart rate for each child. But the stability of heart rate range was more selective and was only acceptable for the category girl–woman and child–self. For the other five complementary categories, fewer than half of the correlations were greater than .5 and the median coefficient was .36. Heart rate range was more seriously influenced by the familiarity of the information than absolute heart rate was. These data indicate the importance of specifying the class of events associated with a stable range. It is inappropriate to talk of intraindividual stability of heart rate or range without specifying the relevant classes of events. Dispositions are tied to stimulus contexts.

The generality of rate and range across concepts at each age. We also examined the correlations for rate and range among the concepts administered each month. As with cross-age stability, there was greater consistency for heart rate than for range across the categories. Table 3.4 presents the number of statistically significant correlations that each category showed with the other categories for the same age (the maximum number of coefficients is six). All seven categories showed acceptable generality, although symmetry was a little less consistent than the other six categories. The consistent stability of heart rate across age and concept is surprising, considering the fact that the average rate for a particular child often showed a complex age function and different growth functions for different concepts. But despite the occasionally complex age changes in rate, subjects seemed to retain their relative rank on this variable at each age. For example, the heart rate of one girl showed an inverted U-function across age for the girl–woman category with a peak heart rate at 25 months, whereas for the category different–same, this girl showed a much different growth function, with a peak rate at 24 months.

Table 3.5. *Cross-concept stability of range at each age: number of significant correlations, older cohort*

Category	Age (months)							
	20	21	22	23	24	25	26	29
Child–woman	3	2	4	3	1	3	3	2
Man–dog	4	1	3	1	2	1	2	3
Same–different	5	0	3	4	1	3	1	3
Two–four	3	3	2	2	1	3	2	1
Child–self	3	4	4	4	2	3	1	4
Seriation– nonseriation	1	2	5	5	1	2	1	2
Symmetry– asymmetry	3	0	3	3	2	1	2	1

Note: The maximum possible number of significant correlations is six.

In contrast to the generality of absolute heart rate, range was selective (as it was for the stability across months; see Table 3.5). The concepts child–self and girl–woman had the largest number of significant correlations with other concepts at most ages whereas symmetry had the poorest cross-category generality. The best consistency across categories occurred during the first four monthly visits and dropped during the last four visits. With the exception of man–dog, the least meaningful concepts generated the poorest cross-concept stability, suggesting that the familiarity of the stimulus affected the consistency of range as seriously as it influenced cross-age stability.

Younger cohort. Both heart rate and range failed to show intraindividual stability across age or consistency across categories for the younger cohort. There was some cross-age stability for rate and range across very short periods; typically the stability coefficients were about .6 and were significant for 2- to 3-month periods. The lack of stability could be due to a number of factors. A favored explanation rests on the fact that unlike the older cohort, there was a sharper developmental function for rate and range (as there was for fixation time) among the younger children. Range showed an obvious U-shaped function with a trough at 17 months, and heart rate showed a large decrease across the period 13 to 20 months. (See Figures 3.1 and 3.2).

Although consistency of rate and range across concepts at any one age improved slightly with age, it varied by concept. From 17 to 22 months consistency of range was a little better for the more familiar information, but especially poor for number and symmetry, which were minimally meaningful for the children.

The greater stability of rate and range among the older subjects coupled with the deep trough in range at 17 months among the younger children suggest, albeit tentatively, that an important transition in mental set may occur around 17 months. It is possible that prior to this age the average child approached our stimulus materials with a nonsymbolic framework. The child did not ask about the meaning or name of the objects illustrated but processed the perceptual pattern nonsymbolically. As the child crossed the hypothetical transition line, a symbolic framework became ascendant, and the child asked about the names of the objects on the screen. Initially, the child was puzzled as he or she searched for the relevant name; as a consequence, heart rate stabilized. With succeeding months the puzzle became partially resolved, and as a result, range increased.

An alternative interpretation is that a few exposures to the pictures, were needed to sensitize the child to the information. No matter what ages were sampled, we would have found the U-shaped function with a trough 2 to 4 months after the first exposure to the stimulus set. This explanation would suggest a trough in range for the older cohort at 24 months, however. As no such trough occurred, the explanation is flawed.

It is to be noted that 17 to 18 months is the time when meaningful speech first appeared for most children in our sample and the time when Lewis and Brooks-Gunn (1979) found that middle-class American children whose noses had been painted with rouge touched their noses when they looked in a mirror and saw the reflection of their faces. The middle of the second year may be the time when the average child inquires as to the meaning of a discrepant event; the time when the child asks, "What is it?" and suppresses a primarily perceptual mode of processing. Lewis's result can be interpreted as indicating that at 17 to 18 months the children who see the rouge on their noses in the mirror privately inquire, "What does that event mean?" The child attempts to determine the significance of the event and as part of the problem-solving process touches his or her nose. Still, the child must know that his or her nose does not ordinarily have a red spot in order to wonder about the spot's significance. Thus, asking the question first demands knowledge of how faces normally appear.

The relation of rate and range to signs of behavioral inhibition, older cohort

Inhibition to a model. Additional data gathered on these children suggest a possible relation between behavioral inhibition in situations of uncertainty and a restricted heart rate range. One situation that produced considerable variation in inhibition occurred when the child watched a familiar woman display three discrete acts with some toys. For the younger cohort this procedure was administered on 2 separate days each month. On the 1st day, the acts were always demonstrated with realistic toys (dolls, animals, beds). On the 2nd day the acts involved less realistic toys (wooden balls, pieces of cloth). Among the older cohort the same regimen held from 20 to 26 months; at 27, 28, and 29 months, the modeling procedure was administered only once with a combination of realistic and less realistic toys (for a total of 17 sessions).

In this procedure each child first played with age-appropriate toys for 10 minutes while the mother and female examiner sat on a couch. After 10 minutes of play, the woman sat on the floor near the child and modeled three actions while the child sat on the mother's lap. The actions and the age of their administration appear below.

Age of administration	*Younger cohort*
13–16 months	Feed bottle to zebra
	Place doll in a bed
	Wash doll's face with a washcloth
17–21 months	Make a doll talk on a telephone
	Make a doll ride on a horse
	Place a hat on a pig
22 months	Make a doll talk on a telephone
	Make a doll cook a banana in a pan and have two dolls eat dinner on two plates
	Make three animals walk
	Simulate rain with hand motions and have the animals hide under a cloth to avoid getting wet
20–21 months	Same acts used for younger cohort at 13 to 16 months
22–26 months	Same acts used for younger cohort at 22 months
27–29 months	Make three dolls throw a ball of yarn back and forth among them

After modeling the acts the woman said, "Now it's your turn to play," and returned with the mother to the couch where both had been sitting. During the 1st minute following the model's return to the couch, some children showed signs of inhibition and, on occasion, obvious distress. Some children cried, some remained close to their mother, many stopped playing. The age function for these signs of inhibition during the first minute after the model displayed these acts with the realistic toys was an inverted U with little or no signs of inhibition until 20 months of age, a peak at 21 to 23 months, and decline in inhibition through 29 months. (This growth function has now been replicated with a cross-sectional sample of children seen in the same laboratory, an independent longitudinal sample observed at home, and a cross-sectional sample of Fijian children.)

Each child's average heart rate range across all 10 administrations of the slides was computed and the distribution divided at the median. Of the eight older children with the lowest heart rate ranges, five showed inhibition on 6 or more of the 17 occasions ($M = 5.8$). Among the seven older children with the highest heart rate ranges, none showed inhibition on 6 or more occasions ($M = 3.0, p <$ .05 by the exact test). The children with the consistently low ranges became more anxious after the model's behavior.

A similar analysis using absolute heart rate as the predictor of inhibition revealed a similar but nonsignificant relation. Children with a higher average heart rate showed a mean of 4.8 inhibitions versus a mean of 4.1 for the children of lower heart rates. But when absolute heart rate and heart rate range were examined together, six children showed a combination of consistently low range and consistently high rate, whereas five children showed the opposite combination of consistently high range and consistently low rate (four children were eliminated from this analysis). The former group had an average of 5.1 occurrences of inhibition as compared with 2.8 for the latter group. Four of the six children with a combination of high rate–low range showed inhibition on five or more occasions. By contrast, only one of five children with the combination of low rate–high range showed signs of anxiety on five or more occasions.

Inhibition of vocalization to discrepant events. We also examined the older child's tendency to display an increase or a decrease in vocalization to the dishabituation trial (Trial 11) following exposure to the 10 pairs of slides for each of the categories shown each month. The variable of interest was the difference between the number of times the child vocalized during each of the three consecutive $7\frac{1}{2}$-second periods of the dishabituation trial subtracted from the number of times a child vocalized in response to the last three standards during the habituation series (across all 13 categories and all ages). A positive score indicated that the child showed a decrease in vocalization and, therefore, inhibition to the discrepant event. A negative score meant the child showed an increase in vocalization, and, therefore, excitability to the unfamiliar event. Seven of the eight children with the lowest heart rate ranges showed a greater tendency to grow quiet than to vocalize in response to the dishabituation trial. Only two of the seven children with the largest heart rate ranges showed a greater tendency to become quiet than to vocalize in response to the discrepant trial ($p < .05$ by the exact test, see Table 3.6).

As with anxiety to the model, heart rate range was a much better predictor of behavioral inhibition than absolute heart rate.

Inhibition with a familiar peer. On each monthly visit the same pair of children were allowed to play together for 20 minutes in a room that was familiar to them

Table 3.6. *Increases or decreases in vocalization in response to the transformation trial*

Heart rate range	Heart rate		
	Low	Medium	High
Low	16	4	14
	7		9
			−9
			6
			1
High	7	−1	no cases
	−8	9	
	0	0	
		−6	

Note: Data shown are the sum of vocalization inhibition trials minus the sum of vocalization excitatory trials for the older cohort. $\chi^2(2) = 7.00.$ $p < .05$.

while the mother sat on a couch nearby. The 16 children in the older cohort were divided into eight same-sex pairs and the same pair of children interacted each month. One pair of coders noted the discrete occurrence of a small set of behaviors while a third dictated into a tape recorder a running nonevaluative description of the behaviors of the 2 children. These narrative data were analyzed by the fourth coder, who was not familiar with the children. There was no relation between the heart rate values and most of the behaviors coded (e.g., time playing with the toys, time playing with the peer, or time near the mother). Heart rate range did correlate with the tendency to imitate a behavior displayed by the other child ($r = .78$, $p < .01$). The greater the range, the more likely that the child imitated the peer during the period 23 to 26 months of age, when imitation of a peer begins to appear with some frequency. Again, range, not rate, was the best predictor of this variable.

This small sample of 2-year-olds with consistently low ranges were more likely to show behavioral signs of anxiety when confronted with the model, were more likely to inhibit vocalization when a discrepant event occurred, and were less likely to imitate a familiar peer, variables that reflect inhibition in time of uncertainty.

Correlates of rate and range for the younger cohort. It will be recalled that among the younger cohort, rate and range were not correlated and were not very stable over age. Moreover, as indicated earlier, the younger children did not display much behavioral inhibition in response to the model. Therefore, we could not use inhibition following the model's action as an index of disposition

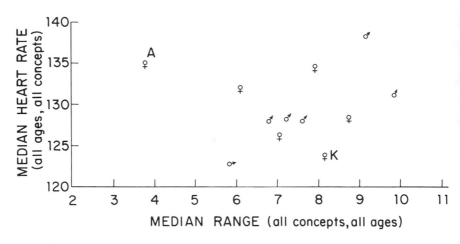

Figure 3.3. Scatter plot for heart rate by heart rate range for younger cohort. A and K designate two different subjects.

to uncertainty. In addition, inhibition of vocalization to the dishabituation trial was not related to rate or range. But the younger children with lower heart rate ranges across the period 13 to 22 months did become more inhibited with the peer. These children made fewer offers of toys to the other child ($r = -.72$, $p < .01$) and were less likely to engage in parallel play with the other child ($r = -.59$, $p < .05$) across the period of observation from 13 to 22 months.

When one examines the two younger children at the extremes of the heart rate distribution, the differences are compelling. Figure 3.3 shows the scatter plot for the 12 younger children for rate and range. Note that Subject A – a girl – showed a combination of low range and high rate, whereas Subject K – also a girl – showed a combination of high range and low heart rate. Subject A was more inhibited than Subject K from 13 through 21 months. For example, at 14 and 15 months of age, Subject A stayed near her mother through most of the peer play sessions and screamed when Subject K approached her. At 16 months Subject A was fretful and clung to the mother; Subject K showed neither of these behaviors. The greatest differences between the two girls occurred at 19 months, when Subject A showed extreme distress after the model's action and remained inhibited and close to the mother during the entire peer play session. At 22 months, however, the behavioral differences between the two girls were minimal. And at 26 months, when the girls returned after a 3-month lapse during which neither had visited the laboratory, there were no obvious differences in behavioral inhibition between the two children, even though the differences in heart rate patterns had not changed.

Although these data are based on small samples, they accord with the original results and suggest that infants in the 2nd year who are behaviorally prone to inhibition in uncertain situations are likely to display more restricted heart rate ranges and a slight tendency for higher heart rates while studying moderately discrepant events.

Discussion

Although these data are based on small samples and lack commanding coherence, we believe that they point to the potential importance of a temperamental dimension and an autonomic variable that seems to covary with that dimension.

We suggest that individual differences in heart rate range are due in part to differences in the degree to which the child is actively working on the unfamiliar stimulus events in order to assimilate them. We might call this state *attentive vigilance*. A child is not disposed to have a stable or a variable range or a high versus a low heart rate in all situations. All children are capable of both patterns. The important determinant of rate and range is the child's psychological state in the situation in which the cardiac data are being gathered. We are suggesting that young children, like adults, differ in their proneness to attentive vigilance when they encounter unexpected events. The children who were more vigilant when viewing the slides (and therefore had more stable ranges) apparently were also more vigilant with the model and with the peer, and as a result they were a little more likely to be anxious when they could not understand or perform the model's actions or deal with the behavior of another child. This state will be influenced, of course, by the child's knowledge. As children gain information about a situation they also gain mastery of it, and the vigilance should subside. And with age the anxiety in response to the model and inhibition with the peer did vanish.

Our reasons for putting forth this hypothesis rest on three sources. First, in both the day-care–home control children and the older cohort in Study 2, differences in heart rate range were remarkably stable over time, in contradistinction to behavioral variables such as attentiveness, vocalization, smiling, or irritability. Longitudinal studies have revealed minimal preservation of individual variation in most behavioral dimensions during the first 2 or 3 years of life. Yet in two independent samples exposed to different stimulus events, heart rate range showed respectable intraindividual stability.

Second, students of infant behavior hold an informal consensus that of the many temperamental variables shown by young children during the first 2 years, differences in the disposition to timidity, inhibition, and fearfulness are more stable than variation in temperamental dimensions like irritability, activity level, or affectivity (see Bronson, 1970; Kagan, 1971; Kagan & Moss, 1962). Tennes and her colleagues (Tennes, Downey, & Vernadakis, 1977; Tennes & Vernadakis, 1979) report that 1-year-olds who are prone to protest when the mother leaves the home for an hour have higher cortisol levels on a prior control day when the mother remains in the home than do children whose protest is usually less intense. Both Tennes's data and our own indicate that temperament contributes to the disposition to separation distress during the first 2 years of life.

Third, the relation between restricted heart rate range and behavioral signs of apprehension or fearfulness accords with current physiological interpretations of variations in cardiac rate. Thus the data have a coherent quality. Perhaps the most significant finding is the fact that the children in Sample 1 who showed frequent separation anxiety only showed higher heart rates between the ages of 7 and 11 months, not before and not after. A large corpus of data indicates that cognitive changes involving an enhancement of retrieval memory and perhaps a disposition to predict future events emerge at this time. It has been argued that this cognitive advance is one reason for the appearance of stranger and separation anxiety during the last half of the 1st year. We noted this fact earlier in referring to the work of Skarin and Campos and his colleagues.

It is reasonable to suppose that infants will differ in the degree to which they attempt to predict future events; the degree to which they try to generate explanations of events that they might not be able to cope with effectively. It is difficult to find the correct language to apply to this psychological dimension. Vigilance seems to capture the combination of tension, apprehension, and attempted prediction that we are trying to convey. As we indicated earlier, if an adult believes that he can cope with a noxious event, he tends to show heart rate acceleration in response to a signal that precedes the event. If there is nothing the subject can do, the signals are accompanied by deceleration (see Obrist et al., 1978). Perhaps this construct is applicable to young children.

We are viewing the psychological disposition to become vigilant as the central individual-difference construct that leads to changes in cardiac pattern as well as behavioral signs of inhibition and distress. Some children invest more effort in trying to understand the unfamiliar; that effort is accompanied by a change in heart rate and range. Failure to understand a discrepant event despite an attempt to do so makes the child vulnerable to anxiety. As a result, the child may cry following separation from the caretaker, show inhibition following a model's actions, or fail to interact with a peer.

These data and the accompanying argument deal with terms that fill the border between the concepts of *affect* and *mood*. All children are capable of crying as a result of a threat or discrepancy, responding to frustration with a tantrum, or smiling when they master a problem. But mothers and psychologists have noted that some children are more prone to particular affect states than others. We often apply the term *mood* to this dimension of variation. If the cardiac parameters of rate and range can be used as partial indexes of this dimension, psychologists will have another methodological tool to call upon in studies of emotional development.

References

Bronson, G. W. Fear of visual novelty: Developmental patterns in males and females. *Developmental Psychology*, 1970, *2*, 33–40.

Campos, J. J. Heart rate: A sensitive tool for the study of emotional development of the infant. In L. P. Lipsitt (Ed.), *Developmental psychobiology: The significance of infancy*. Hillsdale, N.J.: Erlbaum, 1976.

Campos, J. J., Emde, R. N., Gaensbauer, T., & Henderson, C. Cardiac and behavioral interrelationships in the reactions of infants to strangers. *Developmental Psychology*, 1975, *11*, 589–601.

Cheung, N. N., & Porges, S. W. Respiratory influences on cardiac responses during attention. *Physiological Psychology*, 1977, *5*, 53–7.

Coles, M. G. H., & Duncan-Johnson, C. C. Attention and cardiac activity: Heart rate responses during a variable foreperiod, disjunctive reaction time task. *Biological Psychology*, 1977, *5*, 151–8.

Graham, F. K., & Clifton, R. K. Heart rate change as component of the orienting response. *Psychological Bulletin*, 1966, *65*, 305–20.

Kagan, J. *Change and continuity in infancy*. New York: Wiley, 1971.

Kagan, J., Kearsley, R. B., & Zelazo, P. R. *Infancy: Its place in human development*. Cambridge, Mass.: Harvard University Press, 1978.

Kagan, J., & Moss, H. A. *Birth to maturity*. New York: Wiley, 1962.

Kagan, J., & Rosman, B. L. Cardiac and respiratory correlates of attention and an analytic attitude. *Journal of Experimental Child Psychology*, 1964, *1*, 50–63.

Katona, P. G., & Jih, F. Respiratory sinus arrhythmia: Noninvasive measure of parasympathetic cardiac control. *Journal of Applied Physiology*, 1975, *39*, 801–5.

Lacey, J. I. Somatic response patterning in stress. Some revisions of activation theory. In M. H. Appley & R. Trumbull (Eds.), *Psychological stress: Issues in research*. New York: Appleton-Century-Crofts, 1967, 14–44.

Lacey, J. I., & Lacey, B. C. Some autonomic central nervous system interrelationships. In P. Black (Ed.), *Physiological correlates of emotion*. New York: Academic Press, 1970.

Lawler, K. A., Obrist, P. A., & Lawler, J. E. Cardiac and somatic response patterns during the reaction time task in children and adults. *Psychophysiology*, 1976, *13*, 448–55.

Lewis, M., & Brooks-Gunn, J. *Social cognition and the acquisition of self*. New York: Plenum Press, 1979.

Lewis, M., & Goldberg, S. The acquisition and violation of expectancy: An experimental paradigm. *Journal of Experimental Child Psychology*, 1969, *7*, 70–80.

Lewis, M., Kagan, J., Campbell, H., & Kalafat, J. The cardiac response as a correlate of attention in infants. *Child Development*, 1966, *37*, 63–72.

McCall, R. B., & Kagan, J. Attention in the infant: Effects of complexity, contour, perimeter and familiarity. *Child Development*, 1967, *38*, 939–52.

McCall, R. B., & Melson, W. H. Attention in infants as a function of the magnitude of discrepancy and habituation rate. *Psychonomic Science*, 1969, *17*, 317–9.

Obrist, P. A. The cardiovascular–behavioral interaction – As it appears today. *Psychophysiology*, 1976, *13*, 95–107.

Obrist, P. A., Light, K. C., Langer, A. W., Grignolo, A., & McCubbin, J. A. Behavioral–cardiac interactions: The psychosomatic hypothesis. *Journal of Psychosomatic Research*, 1978, *22*, 301–25.

Obrist, P. A., Webb, R. A., Sutterer, J. R., & Howard, J. L. The cardiac somatic relationship: Some reformulations. *Psychophysiology*, 1970, *6*, 569–87.

Petry, H. M., & Desiderato, O. Changes in heart rate, muscle activity and anxiety level following shock threat. *Psychophysiology*, 1978, *15*, 398–402.

Porges, S. W. Heart rate variability and deceleration as indexes of reaction time. *Journal of Experimental Psychology*, 1972, *92*, 103–10.

Porges, S. W., & Humphrey, M. M. Cardiac and respiratory responses during visual search in non-retarded children and retarded adolescents. *American Journal of Mental Deficiency*, 1977, *82*, 162–9.

Porges, S. W., & Raskin D. C. Respiratory and heart rate components of attention. *Journal of Experimental Psychology*, 1969, *81*, 497–503.

Skarin, K. Cognitive and contextual determinants of stranger-fear in 6 and 11-month old infants. *Child Development*, 1977, *48*, 537–44.

Tennes, K., Downey, K., & Vernadakis, A. Urinary cortisol excretion rates and anxiety in normal 1-year old infants. *Psychosomatic Medicine*, 1977, *39*, 178–87.

Tennes, K., & Vernadakis, A. *Behavioral correlates of cortisol in children*. Paper presented at the meeting of the Society for Research in Child Development, San Francisco, March 1979.

Van Hover, K. I. A developmental study of three components of attention. *Developmental Psychology*, 1974, *10*, 330–9.

Walter, G. F., & Porges, S. W. Heart rate and respiratory responses as a function of task difficulty: The use of discriminant analysis in the selection of psychologically sensitive psychological responses. *Psychophysiology*, 1976, *13*, 563–71.

4   Psychophysiological patterning and emotion revisited: a systems perspective

Gary E. Schwartz

The purpose of this chapter is to examine recent theory and research on the psychophysiology of emotion in adults and to consider some of their implications for the measurement of emotion in infants and children. Whereas previous chapters on the psychophysiology of emotion have been conceptualized and organized using discipline-specific theories of psychology and physiology (e.g., Lang, Rice, & Sternbach, 1972), the present chapter is written from the interdisciplinary perspective of general systems theory (von Bertalanffy, 1968). The writings of Miller (1978) on living systems and deRosnay (1979) on the systemic approach are used as a means of integrating biological, psychological, and social levels of analysis of emotion.

Because the systems perspective is not widely used in psychophysiology or developmental psychology, basic aspects of the approach are explained as the chapter unfolds. We begin with a brief discussion of general systems theory as it applies to the psychology and physiology of emotion. This analysis sets the stage for redescribing and reinterpreting some of the old research as well as new data on patterning of subjective experience, patterning of skeletal muscles, patterning of autonomic responses, and patterning of central-nervous-system processes in emotion.

Patterning and emergent properties in living systems

A fundamental tenet of systems theory is that a system is a whole comprising a set of parts. The parts interact in novel ways to produce unique properties, or behaviors, of the system as a whole. Therefore the behavior of a system emerges from the interaction of its parts. The concept of the behavior of a whole system as qualitatively different from the simple sum of the behavior of its parts yet dependent upon the interaction of its parts for its unique properties as a whole is very general. It can apply to any system, living or nonliving, at a micro level (such as the atom) or a macro level (such as the social group; see von Bertalanffy, 1968).

67

Although the general concept of emergent property, or wholism, is by no means fully understood or free from controversy (Phillips, 1976), it is nonetheless considered by a number of philosophers of science to be fundamentally true. Emergent phenomena are found at all levels in nature, from mathematics and physics through chemistry and biochemistry to biology and psychology, sociology, political science, and beyond (even ecology).

One difficulty in thinking *across* levels of complexity (and therefore across disciplines) is that one discipline's system often turns out to be another discipline's part. For example, for the physiologist the system is physiology, which is itself composed of parts (organs are composed of cells), whereas for the psychologist physiology becomes the parts that make up a person or lower animal (organisms are composed of organ systems). We can apply this issue to the relationship between physiology and emotion. From a systems point of view, emotion at the organism level emerges out of the interaction of biological parts at the physiological level; the behavior of the physiology is not a correlate of the emotion, regardless of how the physiology is measured (peripherally or centrally). Rather, the physiology should be viewed and described as a component of the emotion in the same way that a cell is considered a component (rather than a correlate) of an organ.

Thinking in systems terms can be confusing because words such as behavior and level must be carefully redefined. The systems theorist would argue that it is as reasonable to talk about the behavior of a nerve or the behavior of a muscle as it is to talk about the behavior of a person or a group. Behavior is an abstract concept that applies to any level in any system. Consequently, when a person behaves at a psychological level, he or she is also behaving at a physiological level (and every level below this). In systems terms, tensing the muscles in one's arm is not a correlate of overt movement behavior; it is a component of the overt behavior and furthermore is itself a behaving process! The reason why *Behavioral Science,* the journal of the Society for General Systems Research, will publish selected articles in physics and physiology as well as in psychology and sociology is that it adopts the concept of behavior as being very general, a notion that can be applied to any system at any level. To use the term *behavior,* then, requires that the term be carefully qualified in terms of level.

There is a tricky problem in defining levels, however, because different levels can occur *within* disciplines as well as *across* disciplines. For example, in psychology one can talk about complex cognitive processes as being composed of underlying component cognitive processes (Sternberg, 1977) in the same way that one can talk about complex cardiovascular processes in physiology as being composed of underlying component physiological processes (von Bertalanffy, 1968). Note that specifying such sublevels within a given discipline does not eliminate the concept of unique properties (behaviors) that emerge from components interacting with one another. Rather, the need to specify levels within a discipline (as well as across disciplines) requires that we think more clearly about what is a component of what.

Within the discipline of psychology itself, some theorists equate subjective experience with emotion, implying that the concepts are at the same level, whereas other theorists consider subjective experience to be a component of emotion, implying that emotion is a higher-level process of which subjective experience is a part. Note that in both instances the relationship between subjective experience and emotion are concepts at the organism (psychology) level. It is possible to cut across discipline levels, however, and consider the biological underpinnings of both the subjective experience and the emotion. Whether one equates the concept of subjective experience with emotion or views subjective experience as a component of emotion determines the breadth of the physiological analysis required to describe the underlying biological processes.

It follows that one can talk about patterns of processes occurring within any system and therefore within any discipline. One can speak of patterns of subjective experience or patterns of cardiovascular responses where in these cases each pattern is within a narrow category within a particular discipline. One can also discuss patterns of processes occurring across categories but still within general levels, such as patterns of subjective experience and expressive behavior (in psychology) or patterns of cardiovascular and respiratory activity (in physiology). Or one can talk about patterns of processes occurring across broad levels and disciplines, such as patterns of subjective experience and cardiovascular activity. Doing the latter can be dangerous, however, if one does not carefully acknowledge that levels of analysis and structure have been crossed. Theories that simply describe patterns of data across different levels without recognizing the emergent interactions that occur within and between different levels inadvertently lead to oversimplified and inaccurate models of the complex underlying processes.

Although it is a useful first step to describe emotion as consisting of three basic components (subjective experience, overt behavior, and physiological activity; e.g., Lang, 1978), it is a mistake to think that these three categories are at the same level of analysis and therefore to treat them as if they are relatively independent parts. From a systems point of view, subjective experience and overt behavior are both categories of behavior at the organism level each of which comprises patterns of physiological processes. Physiology is therefore not independent of these two categories. On the contrary, physiological processes are the building blocks of both of these processes and therefore must be conceptualized and researched from this perspective.

It should be mentioned that we use the term *psychophysiology* rather than psychology or physiology in the title of this chapter in order to highlight a particular systems perspective. In systems theory, *psychophysiology* emphasizes the fact that not only does psychology emerge out of physiology but psychology and physiology represent different levels of analysis *of the same, ultimate, whole system.* It should be clear that according to systems theory, analyzing the physiological parts, in relative isolation, will not lead to a complete understanding of emotion as a whole process. Emotion takes on its unique holistic properties as a result of complex interactions and *organizations* of its component processes (cf. Chapter 1). This is why an analysis of emotional processes from a systems point of view requires that the investigator measure patterns of variables and search for unique *interactions* or *emergents* between the variables.

Using this general perspective, we will selectively review past and present research on psychophysiological patterning at four different interrelated levels: (a) patterns of subjective experience, (b) patterns of skeletal muscle activity, (c) patterns of autonomic activity, and (d) patterns of central-nervous-system activity. New methodological, empirical, and conceptual points will be highlighted for later consideration when we discuss implications of the findings for developmental theory and research.

Patterning of subjective experience and emotion

Most theorists of emotion believe that different emotions reflect different organizations or patterns of processes at psychological and biological levels of analysis. Although this point is not often discussed, even the relatively basic framework of Schachter and Singer (1962) requires implicitly that patterning of processes occur in different emotions. Note that in the Schachter and Singer theory, the patterning occurs *across* levels. Schachter and Singer propose that specific cognitions (psychology) interact with general levels of physiological arousal (biology) to determine the specific emotional experiences and overt behavioral responses that are elicited.

Few researchers have systematically examined subjective experience closely to uncover possible distinct patterns within the experience as a function of different emotions. The pioneering work of Izard (1972) is very important in this regard. Not only has Izard assessed multiple emotional experiences in different affective situations using the Differential Emotions Scale (DES; see Chapter 12), but he has proposed that a subset of emotions such as anxiety and depression is actually composed of different combinations of underlying fundamental emotions. In systems terms Izard is proposing that anxiety and depression are unique emotional states that emerge from the interaction of patterns of fundamental emotions. At least six different fundamental emotions (happiness, sadness, anger, fear, surprise, and disgust) have been found to exist cross-culturally and to be linked to specific facial expressions (Ekman, Friesen, & Ellsworth, 1972; Izard, 1971).

As part of an ongoing research program examining affective imagery and the self-regulation of emotion, we decided to determine whether it was possible to obtain standardized situations that college students could imagine and that would evoke consistent patterns of subjective experience. In the process of conducting research on this methodological question, we decided to attempt to replicate and extend Izard's (1972) research on the relationship between anxiety, depression, and patterns of fundamental emotions using an abbreviated DES scale (Schwartz & Weinberger, 1980).

Initially, 55 subjects filled out a questionnaire asking them to "give a one sentence statement or a single phrase about a situation that either happened in the past, or could happen in the future, that would make you feel one of the following: happy, sad, angry, fearful, anxious, depressed." Subjects were further told to note that "for each emotion, three separate situations are requested that reflect three different intensities of emotion: strong, moderate and weak." Each subject was thus required to give 18 responses.

From this sample, 20 of the questionnaires (from 10 males and 10 females), which were complete and did not contain highly idiosyncratic or redundant answers, were chosen to be validated in a second questionnaire. The items were edited into complete sentences. Then the 18 items in each of the 20 questionnaires were combined to create a pool of 360 statements. These statements were randomly sorted into four forms of 90 items each, with each emotional category and intensity represented by 5 items per form. A total of 216 subjects filled out one of the forms of the questionnaire, using the following instructions:

For each of the following statements, *imagine* that they are happening to you, and rate how you *would feel*. Note that each statement has *six* emotions to be *separately* rated – happy, sad, anger, fear, depression and anxiety. Since it is not uncommon for people to experience more than one emotion in a given situation, you should rate each statement on all six emotions. Use the numbers 1–5 for your ratings, with 1 meaning very little, 3 meaning moderate, and 5 meaning very strong. Numbers 2 and 4 should also be used to reflect intermediate categories between very little and moderate, and moderate and very strong, respectively.

The results of this study are described in detail in Schwartz and Weinberger (1980). Still, a few brief comments about the average data on emotion should be discussed before the most interesting and accidental observations in the study regarding individual items. As can be seen in Figure 4.1, the average ratings (across the three intensities of items) yield highly distinct patterns of subjective experience for the four fundamental emotions (Part A of the graph) and similar yet distinct patterns of response comparing sadness with depression and anxiety with fear (Part B of the graph). The richness of these data should not go unno-

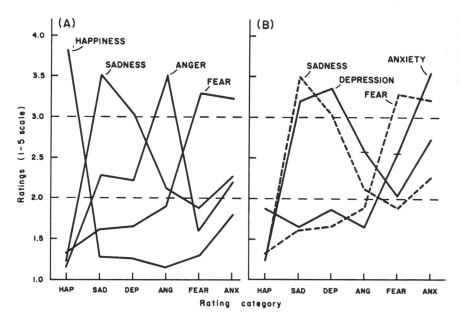

Figure 4.1. Mean ratings of happiness (HAP), sadness (SAD), depression (DEP), anger (ANG), fear (FEAR), and anxiety (ANX) separately (A) for happiness, sadness, anger, and fear situations and (B) for depression and anxiety situations (with sadness and fear situations redrawn for comparison). *Source:* Weinberger & Schwartz (1980).

ticed. For example, it can be seen that anger situations elicit more feelings of depression than either fear or anxiety situations. Also, note that fear situations elicit more feelings of anxiety than anxiety situations elicit feelings of fear.

Figure 4.2 presents the mean ratings for happiness situations subdivided by intensity (high, moderate, low). This figure illustrates that not only do the situations reliably elicit primarily feelings of happiness that vary with intensity, but the *higher* the happiness, the *lower* the sadness, depression, and anger, but *not* fear and anxiety. In fact, high happiness is accompanied by moderately high feelings of anxiety!

These results can be compared with those obtained for the mean ratings for anxiety situations subdivided by intensity. Figure 4.3 shows that not only do the situations reliably evoke primarily feelings of anxiety, but the *higher* the anxiety, the *higher* the fear, depression, and sadness, although the relationship with happiness and anger is less clear. Happiness items and anxiety items clearly differ in the patterns of emotions that they elicit.

Apparently, at least for a sample of college students, specific situations evoke specific patterns of subjective experience that generalize across the population of subjects. This does not mean that all subjects give identical responses to the

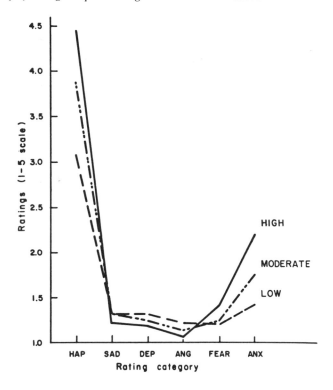

Figure 4.2. Mean ratings for happiness situations subdivided by intensity (high, moderate, low). *Source:* Schwartz & Weinberger (1980).

average items in a given category or to specific items. On the contrary, we believe that individual differences in response to standardized situations are of fundamental importance for basic research and clinical practice and should be assessed carefully. We will return later to the individual difference question when we relate patterns of subjective experience to patterns of physiological activity.

The most surprising and informative aspect of these data are uncovered when patterns of response to individual items are examined (Schwartz, Weinberger, & Brown, 1980). It turns out that specific items pull particular blends or patterns of subjective experience. As shown in Table 4.1, when college students imagine "your dog dies," high ratings occur primarily in sadness and depression (high ratings are italicized in the table), whereas when they imagine "your girlfriend/boyfriend leaves you for another," high ratings now occur in anger and anxiety as well as in sadness and depression. Whereas the former item might be globally labeled a sadness item, the latter item (having the same sadness rating) might be globally labeled either a sadness or a depression item. Note that in response to the question "You realize that your goals are impossible to

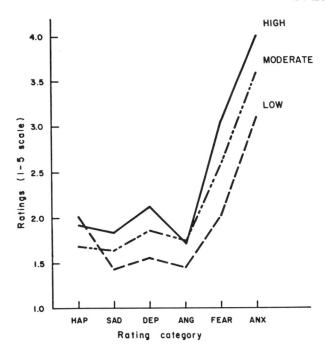

Figure 4.3. Mean ratings for anxiety situations subdivided by intensity (high, moderate, low). *Source:* Weinberger & Schwartz (1980).

reach," college students rate this situation as high in sadness, anger, fear, anxiety, and depression. This is clearly a complex, patterned, highly negative emotional state. Its relevance to problems facing children and adults in modern society (with the increased societal recognition that fundamental limits do exist and that life-style must be limited accordingly if the society is to survive) should be self-evident. It should not be surprising why the general mood today is so negative, because it involves many negative emotions occurring simultaneously.

The value in assessing blends or patterns of subjective experience in the study of emotion should be emphasized for its methodological as well as theoretical implications. Consider the following ratings on two items that might both be globally described as high happiness items for students at Yale: "You are accepted at Yale" and "You have just graduated from Yale." As shown in Table 4.2, the first item evokes high ratings in happiness and also in anxiety. In contrast, the second item evokes moderate to high ratings in sadness, fear, and depression as well as in happiness and anxiety. Clearly both situations evoke high happiness in the average Yale student, but the patterning of emotions is more complex than "pure" happiness in both situations. Furthermore, the patterns differ from each other in important respects.

Table 4.1. *Ratings on an abbreviated differential emotions scale*

Item	HAP	SAD	ANG	Fear	DEP	ANX
Your dog dies	1.09	*4.08*	2.08	1.38	*3.34*	1.93
Your girlfriend/boyfriend leaves you for another	1.13	*4.13*	*3.41*	2.11	*4.09*	*2.72*
You realize that your goals are impossible to reach	1.15	*3.64*	*3.00*	2.48	*3.67*	*3.08*

Note: HAP = happiness. SAD = sadness. ANG = anger. DEP = depression. ANX = anxiety. Italics indicate high ratings.

Table 4.2. *Ratings on an abbreviated differential emotions scale*

Item	HAP	SAD	ANG	Fear	DEP	ANX
You are accepted at Yale	*4.18*	1.14	1.04	1.96	1.09	*3.04*
You have just graduated from Yale	*4.09*	2.74	1.38	2.57	2.36	*3.40*

Note: HAP = happiness. SAD = sadness. ANG = anger. DEP = depression. ANX = anxiety. Italics indicate high ratings.

It is fascinating to see how what at first glance might appear to be minor differences in wording can dramatically change the pattern of subjective experience elicited by an item. As can be seen in Table 4.3, in response to the item "You feel loved," a pure emotion of happiness is generated, whereas in response to the item "You meet someone with whom you fall in love," the more complex pattern of happiness and anxiety is elicited.

There are numerous lessons to be learned from data such as these. Different situations can evoke different combinations of emotions. Therefore, if only one emotion is assessed by itself, this common research practice will lead to an incomplete and therefore erroneous description of the emotional state of the person. The fact that combinations of emotions can be reliably elicited by affective imagery and can be reliably assessed using a simple self-report DES procedure indicates that future research should adopt an approach that draws on the concept of patterns to assess and interpret the subjective dimension of emotion.

Are different patterns of subjective experience associated with different patterns of physiological responses? Are the weak and often inconsistent findings in the literature linking subjective experience to patterns of physiological activity due, at least in part, to the fact that patterns of subjective experience were not

Table 4.3. *Ratings on an abbreviated differential emotions scale*

Item	HAP	SAD	ANG	Fear	DEP	ANX
You feel loved	*4.78*	1.28	1.13	1.19	1.19	1.57
You meet someone with whom you fall in love	*4.58*	1.20	1.04	2.00	1.33	*3.06*

Note: HAP = happiness. SAD = sadness. ANG = anger. DEP = depression. ANX = anxiety. Italics indicate high ratings.

assessed? If patterns of subjective experience are assessed, will we find that certain situations are better than others in eliciting relatively pure emotions? Do emotions actually occur simultaneously in patterns, or do fundamental emotions shift from one to another, whereas the average subjective impression is that they occur concurrently? These questions and many others arise when one begins to adopt a systems perspective and brings it to the study of patterns of subjective experience of emotion.

Skeletal muscle patterning and emotion

If any one physiological system is designed to express different emotions, it is the skeletal muscle system. The skeletal muscles can be finely regulated by the brain to produce delicate, precise, and highly complex patterns of activity. The face, with its high ratio of single motor units to muscle mass and its rich neural innervation is a muscular system structurally capable of reflecting different fundamental emotions and patterns of emotions.

Whether one chooses to label facial expression as psychological behavior or as physiological behavior is more a reflection of the bias of the observer than a true psychophysiological distinction (Schwartz, 1978). In systems terms, what we observe overtly as facial expression *is* an indirect indicator of complex patterns of muscle activity. Subtle and fast-acting changes in muscle activity can be readily quantified by attaching electrodes to the surface of the skin over relative muscle regions (Schwartz et al., 1976b; see Figure 4.4). More precise measurements can be made using fine-wire needle electrodes that pierce the skin to monitor the activity of single motor units (Basmajian, 1974). Both electromyographic (EMG) methods are relatively obtrusive. EMG methods restrict the subject's freedom of movement and often increase the subject's attention to his or her facial behavior. Consequently, EMG recordings can influence the affective processes being measured. Despite these complications, important basic and clinical information can be obtained using EMG as long as the limitations of the method are kept firmly in mind.

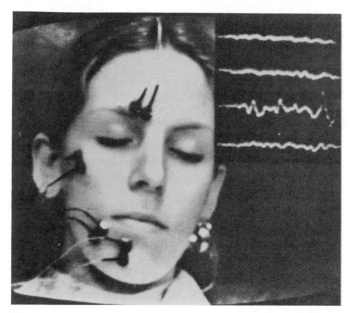

Figure 4.4. Photograph of a videoscreen showing the placement of four pairs of electromyograph electrodes and, superimposed electronically next to the face, the oscilloscope tracings of the amplified electromyographic activity from the four facial regions. *Source:* Schwartz et al. (1976b).

It should be noted that research on patterns of facial muscle activity (and other skeletal muscle activity) has not been restricted to the study of emotion. For example, in the program of research conducted by McGuigan and colleagues (reviewed in McGuigan, 1978), different patterns of facial EMG have been associated with different cognitive tasks.

We have conducted a program of research over the past 5 years measuring facial muscle patterning during affective imagery and other cognitive tasks that elicit different emotions (Schwartz, Ahern, & Brown, 1979; Schwartz, Brown, & Ahern, 1980; Schwartz et al., 1976a, 1976b, 1978). Some of the major results of these studies can be briefly summarized as follows.

1. Different patterns of facial muscle activity accompany the generation of happy, sad, and angry imagery, and these patterns are not typically noticeable in the overt face.

2. Instructions to reexperience, or feel, the specific emotions result in greater EMG changes in relevant muscles than instructions simply to think about the situations (see Figure 4.5).

3. Depressed patients show a selective attenuation in the generation of facial EMG patterns accompanying happy imagery but a slight accentuation in the facial EMG response to sad imagery (see Figure 4.5).

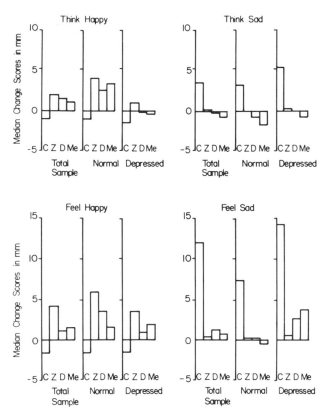

Figure 4.5. Change from resting baseline for muscle activity from the corrugator (C), zygomatic (Z), depressor anuli oris (D), and mentalis (Me) regions during two affective imagery (happy, sad) and two instructional (think, feel) conditions. Data are displayed separately for the total sample ($N = 24$), the normal subgroup ($N = 12$), and a depressed subgroup ($N = 12$). A 1-millimeter change score equals 45 millivolts/30 seconds. *Source:* Schwartz et al. (1976b).

4. Changes in clinical depression following treatment with active drug medication or placebo are accompanied by relevant changes in facial EMG.
5. Females (when compared with males) show a greater tendency to:
   a. generate facial EMG patterns of greater magnitude (relative to rest) during affective imagery and report a corresponding stronger subjective experience to the affective imagery
   b. show greater within-subjects correlations between the experience of particular emotions and relevant facial muscles
   c. show somewhat higher corrugator levels during rest (possibly reflecting more sadness and/or concern) and lower masseter levels during rest (possibly reflecting less anger)

    d. generate larger facial EMG patterns when instructed voluntarily to produce overt expressions reflecting different emotions.

Taken together, these data strongly support the hypothesis that not only does affective imagery result in reliable self-reports of different patterns of subjective experience, but these self-reports are *preceded* by the generation of unique patterns of facial muscle activity that vary both in pattern and intensity with the subsequent self-reports. Because the facial EMG responses are typically not visible to an observer, nor are they typically perceived by the subject (whose attention during imagery is largely focused on the image and the associated feeling states rather than his or her face per se), it is possible that the self-reports and the facial patterns are reflecting two different aspects of the same, underlying neuropsychological system. We are not proposing that self-report and facial activity need always be coupled or synonymous. On the contrary, self-report is determined by many factors in addition to possible feedback (both central and peripheral) involving the face, as is facial behavior determined by many other factors in addition to the expression of emotion. In systems terms, the concept of a single response is an oversimplification, for any behavior involves a composite or pattern of underlying processes. This point is directly related to the whole/part/emergent issue discussed in the beginning of the chapter.

Until discrete patterns of facial EMG are discovered that reflect relatively pure fundamental emotions, it is not possible to address the more complex and intriguing question regarding blends or combinations of different emotions and their relationship to complex patterns of facial EMG. In a recent experiment (Polonsky & Schwartz, 1981) we attempted to determine whether images designed to evoke a combination of happiness and sadness would elicit a combination of facial muscle responses previously found to be reliably associated with happiness and sadness. Our prior research (e.g., Schwartz, Brown, & Ahern, 1980) has documented that zygomatic activity increases reliably during happiness, whereas corrugator activity often decreases *below resting level* during happiness. The pattern is virtually opposite for sadness; corrugator activity increases reliably in sadness, but zygomatic activity typically remains at baseline. We therefore predicted that items selected to elicit a combination of happiness and sadness would be accompanied by relative increases in *both* zygomatic and corrugator activity, though the magnitude of each increase would be less than that found in response to relatively pure emotion items reflecting happiness or sadness.

In the experiment, a standard pure happy item was "You feel loved," a standard pure sad item was "Someone close to you dies," and a standard mixed happy–sad item was "You feel that you are finally separated from your family and are really feeling a tremendous sense of freedom about that, but at the same time you miss the closeness that you had or potential closeness that you could have had." The data indicated that as predicted, the mixed happy–sad item generated moderate increases in both zygomatic and corrugator activity. These EMG levels corresponded to moderate levels of happiness and sadness reported in response to the mixed happy–sad items. As expected, the pure items replicated the previous findings.

These are the first data documenting the hypothesis that discrete blends of affective experience can be associated with discrete blends of physiological activity (i.e., facial EMG). Whether or not more complex blends of affective experience can be mapped onto more complex blends of skeletal muscle activity remains to be demonstrated in future research. Still, the potential for addressing this question now exists as a result of advances in the measurement of patterns of self-report and of EMG.

A systems approach to data of this sort requires that more complex statistical analyses be performed. Fridlund and Schwartz (1980) have recently demonstrated how multivariate pattern-classification strategies can be applied to facial EMG data. The approach includes transduction, feature extraction, and classification. Using this strategy, the data can be analyzed within a single subject. The data from Fridlund and Schwartz document the superiority of analytic strategies that are sensitive to patterns of multiple physiological responses over traditional univariate methods. Figure 4.6 shows a single subject's data comparing anger and fear items for four separate muscles and the composite results of a linear discriminant analysis based on the data. This figure illustrates how the multivariate analysis pulls out an anger–fear difference that is not readily apparent in any single muscle (in this study, subjects imagined 12 standardized anger scenes and 12 standardized fear scenes).

Multivariate pattern analysis procedures can be applied to subjective reports, facial EMG, patterns of facial and other body EMG, autonomic activity, and so forth. The integration of these procedures with research on the psychophysiology of emotion promises to resolve prior confusions and reveal new discoveries. Unfortunately, it requires that we learn new statistical skills and new ways of looking at (and therefore thinking about) data in systems terms; it requires that we develop the difficult skill of being able to think in terms of patterns of processes and interactions of the component parts.

One conclusion seems justified from the EMG data and statistics performed thus far. The face is a system that is uniquely sensitive to affective processes. It therefore provides an excellent means of examining the relationship between subjective experience and physiological activity, because reliable patterns of EMG activity accompany different emotional states.

Autonomic patterning and emotion

At one time it was believed that responses innervated by the autonomic nervous system were highly intercorrelated and involuntary and were therefore only ca-

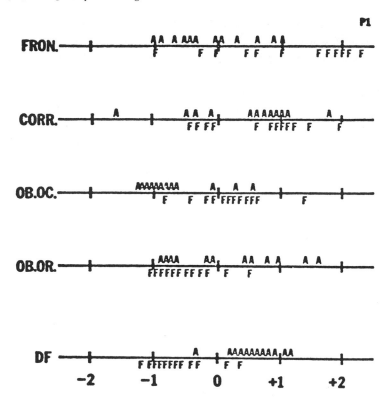

Figure 4.6. Plots of standard electromyograph scores for 12 anger and 12 fear responses of subject P_1 mapped itemwise on each of four muscle regions and on a linear composite of the four regions derived from linear discriminant analysis. It can be seen that the composite function affords better separation of anger and fear items than any of the individual muscle regions. This figure demonstrates that consideration of variable conformations/patterns provides information that cannot be gleaned from any of the univariate analyses alone. Item codes: A, anger; F, fear; FRON., frontalis; CORR., corrugator; OB.OC., obicularis oculi; OB.OR., obicularis oris; DF, discriminant function. *Source:* Fridlund & Schwartz (1980).

pable of reflecting overall levels of arousal and/or alertness (from deep sleep to states of awake excitement). It is now well known, however, that the sympathetic and parasympathetic branches of the autonomic nervous system are each capable of very fine regulation of specific peripheral organs. Moreover, this regulation is quite selective and can be brought under voluntary control using techniques such as biofeedback (reviewed in Schwartz, 1977b).

All physiological responses, to varying degrees, seem to be influenced by both voluntary and involuntary processes. Skeletal muscles are strongly influenced by voluntary processes, but they are also controlled by involuntary reflex patterns elicited by particular stimuli (e.g., in response to localized pain). It now appears that visceral and glandular responses are influenced by voluntary processes more strongly than was previously recognized, though the extent of such control relative to their involuntary reflex patterns is just beginning to be determined.

There has been a paucity of studies examining autonomic patterning accompanying different emotional states. There are many reasons for this lack of research. They include methodological problems in recording and analyzing the data, theoretical biases that discouraged investigators from looking for patterns or accepting serendipitous evidence of patterning in the data, and problems at a psychological level in eliciting and assessing the emotional states. Still, the few studies that have attempted to address this question have come up with a surprisingly consistent pattern of results. These studies have focused on the comparison between anger and fear, two emotions that Ax (1953) claimed were "most often described as being identical physiological states" (p. 433). The studies prior to 1957 are reviewed in Schachter (1957). A recent study was reported by Weerts and Roberts (1976).

Drawing on neuropsychological and neuroendocrine findings, Ax proposed that anger involved a *mixed* epinephrine and norepinephrine pattern, whereas fear involved a relatively pure epinephrine pattern. Schachter added that pain involved a relatively pure norepinephrine pattern, though his pain stimulus (the cold pressor test) may have pulled for this particular pattern because of its local vasoconstrictive effects.

Unfortunately, no single autonomic response is a "pure" reflector of patterns suggestive of epinephrine or norepinephrine. Most autonomic responses are dually innervated by the sympathetic and parasympathetic branches of the autonomic nervous system as well as by hormones. For example, an increase in heart rate can be mediated by (a) an increase in local sympathetic activity, (b) a decrease in local parasympathetic activity, (c) an increase in circulating epinephrine (to list only one possible heart rate stimulating hormone), or (d) any combination or pattern of these mechanisms. Therefore, not all heart rate increases are the same. Systems theory not only helps us understand this point, it also suggests how we can draw differential conclusions about underlying mechanisms. To do so we should measure patterns of processes, ideally at different levels, so as to make it possible to test different interpretations of the data. It should be recalled that a similar point was made previously with regard to facial EMG (i.e., a corrugator increase should not be viewed in isolation).

Ax (1953) and Schachter (1957) dealt with this problem at the physiological level by (a) recording multiple channels of information and (b) scoring each channel in different ways to tap different component processes embedded in the complex response. For example, from the frontalis muscle region channel, Ax scored the data separately for (a) maximum increase in muscle tension and (b) number of peaks in muscle tension. Ax found that not only were these two aspects of muscle tension uncorrelated, but maximum muscle tension was significantly higher in anger than in fear, whereas the number of muscle tension peaks was significantly higher in fear than in anger.

From the skin conductance channel, Ax scored the data separately for (a) maximum increase in skin conductance and (b) number of rises in skin conductance. Ax found that these two aspects of sweat gland activity were uncorrelated, and maximum increase in skin conductance was significantly higher in fear than anger, whereas the number of skin conductance rises was significantly higher in anger than in fear. It seems likely that this pattern of results reflects some important set of underlying neuropsychological differences between anger and fear. The physiological interpretation of these patterns remains to be established, however. The important discovery from these early studies was that consistent differences, especially within the cardiovascular system, were found for anger and fear. Anger was more associated with increases in peripheral resistance, whereas fear was more associated with increases in cardiac output.

If any one easily recordable physiological parameter could be said to tap peripheral resistance more than cardiac output, it is diastolic blood pressure. Whereas systolic blood pressure tended to be higher in fear then anger (reflecting increased cardiac output), diastolic blood pressure was significantly higher in anger than in fear. In the recent Weerts and Roberts (1976) study, diastolic blood pressure was a major variable distinguishing anger and fear elicited by imagery.

We have recently replicated and extended the anger–fear findings in ways that have important implications for basic research and clinical application (Schwartz, Weinberger, & Singer, 1981). Thirty-two college students with a background in acting were instructed on different trials to imagine, and then express *nonverbally* while exercising, one of six different emotional states (happiness, sadness, anger, fear, normal exercise, and relaxation). The exercise task was a modified version of the Harvard step test, which requires subjects to walk up and down a single step.

We used the simplest of physiological recording procedures in this study. Systolic and diastolic blood pressures were recorded manually with an inexpensive portable electronic sphygmomanometer (Lumi-Tronic, $59.00) that automatically signaled systolic and diastolic blood pressure by the presence and absence of audible beeps. Heart rate was recorded manually by taking and counting the pulse. Two experimenters were used. Both were undergraduate students with no background in physiology. They were naive to the complex pattern hypotheses of the experiment.

Each trial consisted of two baseline readings taken 1 minute apart; one reading taken after the 1-minute imagery period (in which subjects *imagined* walking up and down the step, experiencing and expressing the requested emotion), and three readings spaced over approximately 10 minutes following the 1-minute exercise period (in which subjects silently expressed nonverbally the different emotions while actually walking up and down the step).

The rationale for using only three relatively simple measures of cardiovascular function was (a) to give the subjects maximum freedom to utilize their bodies both to experience and express the emotions (the prior studies attached many electrodes sensitive to movement artifact that restricted the subject's overt behavior in a highly unnatural way, a restraint that may in turn have restricted the magnitude of the cardiovascular patterns evoked) and (b) to determine whether the data would be robust enough to be clinically useful (and whether it could be detected using standard clinical procedures).

The reasons for using self-generated imagery followed by exercise were (a) to increase the likelihood that relatively pure emotions would be generated (in the prior studies complex blends of anger and fear were probably evoked, at least in some subjects; also, these studies did not assess the relative purity of their stimulus conditions) and (b) to determine whether allowing subjects to express their emotions overtly would lead to increased physiological patterns that would be clinically meaningful (e.g., maybe running is not a simple exercise; angry running may provoke heart attacks, whereas relaxed or happy running may reduce them).

Given the relative unreliability of the physiological recording procedures used in this study and the limited number of data points obtained, the magnitude and consistency of the results were especially striking. Following imagery, highly significant anger versus fear differences in diastolic blood pressure were found, fully replicating the prior research. Furthermore, anger and fear both differed from happiness and sadness in relative patterning of the three cardiovascular variables, whereas happiness and sadness were in turn different from control and relaxation.

Following exercise, very large differences in systolic blood pressure and heart rate, but not diastolic blood pressure, were found as a function of the different emotions. Apparently, active exercise leads to vasodilation in the muscles and reduced peripheral resistance, which may have overshadowed the relative differences in diastolic pressure between anger and fear. In addition, subjects expressed their anger overtly in this condition. Had they been instructed to express anger toward themselves to reflect frustration, diastolic pressure would perhaps have increased after the active exercise.

Correlations were run between the physiological measures, self-reports of patterns of subjective experience for the imagery and exercise periods, and ratings by the experimenters of patterns of overt emotional expression for the imagery and exercise periods. It turned out that the physiological measures were more correlated with the observer's judgments than the subject's own self-reports. The total pattern of results did not support the most obvious hypothesis, that the observers might have been using the physiological data unconsciously to make their observational ratings. On the contrary, the findings suggested that the observers were seeing relationships that the subjects themselves did not. For example, observer ratings of fear expression during fear exercise were correlated *negatively* with diastolic blood pressure ($r = -.373, p < .05$), a relationship that is highly counterintuitive unless you know that diastolic typically *decreases* below baseline following isotonic exercise and that fear should potentiate that effect because of enhanced isotonic exercise. On the other hand, observer ratings of anger expression during anger exercise were correlated *positively* with diastolic blood pressure ($r = .413, p < .05$). Interestingly, self-ratings of fear experience during fear exercise were not correlated with diastolic blood pressure ($r < .01$), whereas self-ratings of anger experience during anger exercise were correlated with diastolic blood pressure ($r = .414, p < .05$).

After obtaining these findings, we went back to the original studies to see whether the relationships between self-ratings, observer ratings, and physiological measures had been previously examined. Schachter (1957) did obtain observer ratings (he called them "expressed" ratings) as well as self-reports. Only "mean" blood pressure correlations (using a weighted average of systolic and diastolic indexes) were presented in the paper. Nonetheless, *self-reports* for both fear and anger were not significantly correlated with mean blood pressure increase, whereas *expressed* behavior for both fear and anger was correlated with mean blood pressure.

Our hypothesis, from a systems perspective, is that cardiovascular behavior and skeletal-motor behavior are more intimately interconnected (both at the periphery and at the level of the brain) than they are with the neuropsychological systems involved in monitoring these behaviors and making them available to consciousness. In other words, subjective experience includes the monitoring and interpreting of cardiovascular *and* skeletal-motor processes. It therefore follows that self-report can be more readily dissociated from these two processes than the two processes can be dissociated from themselves. Note that the observer *sees* the manifestations of the skeletal-motor behavior and then tries to *infer* from those observations what the person *might* be feeling. The subject, on the other hand, is not limited in forming and labeling his experience solely on the basis of peripheral cues. In fact, people probably vary (from person to person and situation to situation) in how much they attend to their bodies and how they interpret these cues in forming their affective experience and reports. Because an outside observer is more attentive to overall patterns of overt behavior, an outside observer's ratings will more likely be consistent with underlying cardiovascular patterns than will the subject's own self-reports.

This leads us back to the question of the relationship between subjective experience and physiological activity. This question applies to any physiological response, be it at the periphery (skeletal, visceral, glandular) or within the central nervous system. In a clinical setting, we have found that depressed patients and schizophrenic patients differ from each other and from normal controls in how accurately they remember expressing positive affect with their faces and bodies (Brown, Schwartz, & Sweeney, 1978; Brown, Sweeney, & Schwartz, 1979). Briefly, when their self-reports are compared with observers' ratings of actual overt behavior in a group situation, depressed patients report experiencing more pleasure than they express, whereas schizophrenic patients report experiencing less pleasure than they express.

We believe that dissociations between self-report and behavior/physiology are not only possible but likely. Moreover, these dissociations may reflect the disruption of patterns of underlying neuropsychological processes. Normally, these processes are interconnected, interacting, and therefore self-regulated. In some instances, however, the processes may become functionally and/or anatomically disconnected, noninteracting, and therefore "disregulated" (Schwartz, 1977a, 1979).

A classic example of dissociation between subjective experience and physiological behavior accompanied by physiological disregulation involves repression. Repressors are individuals who have developed the skill of avoiding the experience of certain negative emotions. Simply stated, repressors tend to report (and believe) that they are not anxious, angry, or depressed, even though their overt behavior and underlying physiology may indicate the opposite.

We recently conducted an experiment to determine whether it is possible to distinguish between people who report feeling little anxiety and are accurate (called *true low anxious*) from people who report feeling little anxiety but are self-deceptive (called *repressors*). After splitting subjects according to their scores on a standard anxiety scale, we further split the subjects according to their scores on a second scale that we hypothesized would measure defensiveness (see Weinberger, Schwartz, & Davidson, 1979). Thus subjects reporting low anxiety were further split into low defensive–low anxious (true low anxious) and high defensive–low anxious (repressor) groups.

Subjects were exposed to a moderately stressful sentence completion task. They were instructed to complete phrases that were neutral, sexual, or aggressive in tone. Heart rate, sweat gland activity, and frontalis region EMG from the forehead were recorded, as well as their verbal response latencies and measures of verbal disturbance. Although there were some interesting discrepancies among some of the measures (i.e., patterning of the responses did occur), the overall findings indicated that repressors generated significantly larger physiological and overt behavioral responses indicative of negative emotion than true low anxious subjects did (even though the repressors actually reported experiencing less anxiety than the true low anxious subjects). Furthermore, the magnitude of the repressors' physiological and psychological responses was sometimes equal to, and sometimes larger than, the large responses found in a group of true high anxious subjects!

These data suggest an important reason why it is so difficult to obtain correlations between physiological responses and self-reports across subjects. If a subset of subjects inadvertently gives erroneous self-reports because of factors such as current mood state (e.g., depression) and/or defensive style (e.g., repression), then correlations across a random sample of subjects will be not only low but ultimately uninterpretable. From a systems point of view, we must not only distinguish between observer ratings and self-ratings, but we must further distinguish between different processes that subjects use to label their affective states and the accuracy with which they do so.

It follows that systematic discrepancies between observer ratings, self-ratings, and physiological responses become important data in their own right. In fact, patterns of these discrepancies can have important implications for theory and practice. Future workers exploring physiological/subjective relationships in emotion will be likely to profit from looking closely at individual differences in cross-level patterning of these data.

Emotion and patterning by the central nervous system

The degree of subjective, skeletal, and autonomic patterning that is possible depends on the degree of patterning of central-nervous-system processing that is possible. Unfortunately, difficulty in obtaining direct or even indirect electrophysiological measures of brain activity (through depth electrodes or surface electrodes), coupled with the great difficulty in interpreting overt behavior as being an indirect measure of particular neuropsychological processes, has led most psychophysiologists interested in the study of emotion to restrict their recordings and interpretations to peripheral levels of analysis.

Nevertheless, recent theory and research on hemispheric asymmetry in cognition and emotion has made it possible to raise new questions about cognitive/affective patterning and hemispheric patterning associated with different emotional states. For example, using lateral eye movements as a relative indicator of hemispheric activation, Schwartz et al. (1975) demonstrated that in right-handed subjects (a) emotional questions produced more looks to the left (indicative of right hemispheric involvement) than did questions that were not emotional, (b) verbal questions produced more looks to the right (indicative of left hemispheric involvement) than did spatial questions, and (c) spatial questions produced more stares and blinks than did verbal questions. From these three sets of findings, it became possible to uncover discrete *patterns* of lateral eye movements that could distinguish between all four combinations of cognition and affect: verbal nonemotional, verbal emotional, spatial nonemotional, and spatial emotional. In other words, not only could affective processes be distinguished from cognitive processes in terms of patterns of eye movement activity, but their interactions could be uncovered. It is interesting to note how the concept of patterning of cognitive and affective processes at the level of the brain can become a new neuropsychological framework for reinterpreting and extending the original model proposed by Schachter and Singer (1962).

The use of lateral eye movements for the purpose of assessing central-nervous-system patterning illustrates a changing scientific paradigm regarding the relationship between psychology, physiology, and neurology. As discussed in Schwartz (1978), eye movements can be defined as (a) psychological behavior (if they are simply observed by the naked eye), (b) physiological behavior (if they are written out on polygraph paper), or (c) neurological behavior (if they are interpreted as reflecting underlying neurological processes). The fact that the same data can be published in three different journals reflecting three different disciplines is an indication more of the particular conceptual frameworks and biases of the investigators than of the actual processes being measured. A major advantage in measuring lateralization of overt behavior and interpreting it in neurological terms is that the observations can be made unobtrusively, in individuals of any age. Thus, Sackeim, Gur, and Saucy (1978) have reported that the left side of the face (controlled by the right hemisphere) is more reflective of negative emotion. Their data were based on pictures that were taken of overt faces and were shown to judges who rated composite photographs of the right and left sides.

Only recently have researchers attempted to study the emotion/laterality question more closely in terms of fundamental emotions and patterns of self-report. As reviewed in Schwartz, Ahern, and Brown (1979), it is beginning to appear that the hemispheres may be differentially lateralized for positive and negative emotions, with the left hemisphere (in right-handed subjects) more involved with positive emotions and the right hemisphere more involved with negative emotions. Schwartz et al. (1979) reported evidence for positive/negative lateralization using measures of facial EMG recorded from the right and left sides of the face.

Ahern and Schwartz (1979) have proposed that left–right difference in positive and negative emotions may reflect a basic difference in approach/avoidance behavior and that these processes may be mediated subcortically and therefore may be more fundamental than left–right cortical differences in verbal/spatial processing. This conclusion was suggested by the results of data on lateral eye movement indicating that verbal/spatial effects could be attenuated or eliminated, whereas the positive/negative emotion effects still remained.

The hypothesis of left–right differences in positive/negative emotion is probably oversimplified. Current research is beginning to examine patterns of *intra* as well as *inter*hemispheric processes. We have recently reported data that integrate the two apparently discrepant hypotheses proposing that (a) all emotions are lateralized in the right hemisphere and (b) emotions are differentially lateralized depending upon their valence (Davidson et al., 1979). Using EEG measures recorded from the parietal and frontal regions, we found that parietal EEG showed relatively more activation over the right hemisphere for *both* positive and negative emotions, whereas frontal EEG showed relatively more activation over the left hemisphere for positive emotions and relatively more activation over the right hemisphere for negative emotions. It is possible that the parallel processing of stimuli (a process possibly common to all emotions) is initiated in the right parietal region but is differentially interpreted by the left and right frontal regions, for positive and negative emotions, respectively.

Lateralized indexes of positive versus negative emotion have now been reported using eye movements, facial responses, EEG measures, and even facial skin temperature (Schwartz & Logue, 1981). It seems likely that future research will continue to uncover relationships between underlying processes of the central nervous system and their expression in self-report, overt behavior, and physiological activity. It is possible that new findings will emerge that explain the associations and dissociations of variables when they occur. For example, an intriguing hypothesis suggested by Galin (1974) is that repressors defend against negative affect by producing a functional disconnection syndrome between the two hemispheres: the left hemisphere may think that everything is all right, whereas the right hemisphere knows otherwise. We believe that the bringing together of different methodologies, levels of analysis, and topical areas of theory and research toward the solution of common problems can be aided by taking a systems approach that is common to the various disciplines involved.

Some implications for the measurement of emotion in infants and children

Using systems theory as a means of organizing data from different disciplines, we have emphasized the concept of patterning of psychophysiological processes in the experience and expression of emotion. We have proposed that patterns of processes occur within and across levels and that emergent properties arise out of the interaction of component processes that contribute to organized properties underlying emotional behavior (broadly defined).

There are many implications of this perspective for modern theories of emotion. An excellent chapter by Leventhal (1980) proposes some new aspects of emotion that are consistent with the general perspective outlined here. For example, Leventhal proposes that although patterns of bodily feedback contribute to the emergent experience of emotion, if subjects are instructed to attend voluntarily to specific bodily parts, the emotional experience will be disrupted (if not destroyed). An analogy would be how the experience of a forest can be disrupted or destroyed if one attends specifically to the trees. This disruptive effect is clearly predicted by systems theory. Attending to a subset of parts removes information from certain processes and alters others. Therefore, focused attention can attenuate, if not eliminate, certain emergent properties that depend upon the interaction of the multiple components for their existence.

Clearly, one general recommendation is that researchers interested in the measurement of emotion in infants and children should record combinations of responses reflecting different components at various levels and should then analyze the patterns in terms of multivariate combinations. If discrete emotions do exist, then they should have certain holistic (organizational) properties, and their development should follow a general set of rules. Note that according to systems theory, no one response can serve as a single measure of a single emotion. A response cannot be viewed in isolation, as we have shown throughout this chapter and in our reexamination of Ax's (1953) anger–fear data regarding patterning within a given physiological response as well as across response systems. In fact, one may question whether the self-report of "I feel happy" given when a person is in an anxiety-provoking situation is based on the same set of processes as the self-report of "I feel happy" given when a person is in a situation typically associated with happiness. It is possible that discrepancies between studies may be as much due to the limited number of variables measured and the overly simplistic interpretations made of the data as to differences in the particular stimulus conditions used or the subject populations studied.

From an engineering point of view, physiological recording and data analysis systems have continued to improve. For example, it is now possible to measure patterns of skin temperature over the entire body from a distance, using a procedure similar to a video camera (see Schwartz, 1978, for a brief description of data obtained by Schwartz and Logue using thermography equipment). Like video or audio recording procedures, thermography procedures allow subjects to have some freedom of movement. Furthermore, it is possible to collect the data without the subject's knowledge. Skin temperature is quite sensitive to differences between positive and negative emotions, but it reacts more slowly than other autonomic measures such as sweat gland activity or blood flow.

Techniques for recording physiological variables telemetrically are also improving, and some units now include their own microprocessors (Taylor, 1980). Although one would ideally like to monitor every physiological response from a distance without worrying about movement artifact (as is possible to some extent for temperature and also for eye direction and pupil size), this goal is still in the future.

Still, it is our belief that advances in the technology of psychophysiology have far outstripped our ability to use the technology wisely. An electronic machine for measuring blood pressure that is simple, inexpensive, and portable can, when combined with the taking of pulse by hand, generate rich and complex patterns of cardiovascular data relevant to the experience, expression, and self-regulation of emotion (Schwartz, Weinberger, & Singer, 1981). Data on the direction of a subject's eyes or the side of the face that shows the larger emotional response can be used to provide new sources of information about emotion and the brain that have theoretical as well as practical value (Schwartz, Ahern, & Brown, 1979). One challenge is to use simple procedures in novel ways to assess patterns of processes in emotion.

To assess the synchronization of response systems more systematically, it would be valuable to examine more closely the temporal sequences of responses. For example, rather than averaging data over minutes, it would be useful to look for particular instances when a subject is expressing a particular emotion overtly (e.g., in the face) and then assess anticipatory and recovery changes in relevant physiological variables. A finer grained analysis of response topography that includes temporal patterning could increase the yield of research and might make it possible to differentiate between reflexive and voluntary expressions of emotion more effectively.

The hypothesis that emotions can occur in complex blends (e.g., Izard, 1972) must be underscored. As I noted in the section "Patterning of Subjective Experience and Emotion," it is quite easy to assess patterns of subjective experience in adults and in children who can speak and label emotions (see Chapter 12). Pure emotions, if they occur at all, probably occur only for relatively short periods of time. If we routinely attempt to assess patterns of self-report in research, this effort will continually remind us of the complexity inherent in measuring and interpreting emotions.

To a systems thinker, emotion cannot be equated with a particular behavioral expression, a particular subjective experience, or a particular underlying physiological response. Rather, all of the above are incomplete manifestations, at different levels, of a complex process that can be inferred only from the convergence of the patterns of such responses. Although this perspective makes research more difficult, it also makes the research richer, more informative and, it is to be hoped, more relevant to the actual operation of emotions in everyday life.

References

Ahern, G. L., & Schwartz, G. E. Differential lateralization for positive versus negative emotion. *Neuropsychologia,* 1979, *17,* 693–697.

Ax, A. R. The physiological differentiation between fear and anger in humans. *Psychosomatic Medicine*, 1953, *15*, 433–42.

Basmajian, J. V. *Muscles alive* (3rd ed.). Baltimore, Md: Williams & Wilkins, 1974.

Brown, S. L., Schwartz, G. E., & Sweeney, D. R. Dissociation of self-reported and observed pleasure in depression. *Psychosomatic Medicine*, 1978. *40*, 536–48.

Brown, S. L., Sweeney, D. R., & Schwartz, G. E. Differences between self-reported and observed pleasure in depression and schizophrenia. *Journal of Nervous and Mental Disease*, 1979, *167*, 410–5.

Davidson, R. J., Schwartz, G. E., Saron, C., Bennett, J., & Goleman, D. Frontal versus parietal EEG asymmetry during positive and negative affect. *Psychophysiology*, 1979, *16*, 202–3. (Abstract)

DeRosnay, J. *The macroscope*. New York: Harper & Row, 1979.

Ekman, P., Friesen, W. V., & Ellsworth, P. C. *Emotion in the human face*. New York: Pergamon, 1972.

Fridlund, A. J., & Schwartz, G. E. Optimization of multivariate strategies for the classification of facial EMG patterns during affective imagery. *Psychophysiology*, 1980, *17*, 306. (Abstract)

Galin, D. Implications of left–right cerebral lateralization for psychiatry: A neurophysiological context for unconscious processes. *Archives of General Psychiatry*, 1974, *9*, 412–8.

Izard, C. *The face of emotion*. New York: Appleton-Century-Crofts, 1971.

Izard, C. *Patterns of emotions: A new analysis of anxiety and depression*. New York: Academic Press, 1972.

Lang, P. J. The psychophysiology of anxiety. In H. Akiskal (Ed.), *Psychiatric diagnosis: Exploration of biological criteria*. New York: Spectrum, 1978.

Lang, P. J., Rice, D. G., & Sternbach, R. A. The psychophysiology of emotion. In N. S. Greenfield & R. A. Sternbach (Eds.) *Handbook of psychophysiology*. New York: Holt, Rinehart & Winston, 1972.

Leventhal, H. Toward a comprehensive theory of emotion. In L. Berkowitz (Ed.), *Advances in experimental social psychology* (Vol. 13). New York: Academic Press, 1980.

McGuigan, F. J. Imagery and thinking: Covert functioning of the motor system. In G. E. Schwartz & D. Shapiro (Eds.), *Consciousness and self-regulation: Advances in research and theory* (Vol. 2). New York: Plenum Press, 1978.

Miller, J. G. *Living systems*. New York: McGraw-Hill, 1978.

Phillips, D. C. *Holistic thought in social science*. Stanford, Calif.: Stanford University Press, 1976.

Polonsky, W., & Schwartz, G. E. *Individual differences in the hemispheric lateralization of affect: A facial EMG investigation of the repressive coping style*. Manuscript submitted for publication, 1981.

Sackeim, H. A., Gur, R. C., & Saucy, M. C. Emotions are expressed more intensely on the left side of the face. *Science*, 1978, *202*, 434–5.

Schachter, J. Pain, fear and anger in hypertensives and normotensives. *Psychosomatic Medicine*, 1957, *19*, 17–29.

Schachter, S., & Singer, J. E. Cognitive, social and physiological determinants of emotional state. *Psychological Review*, 1962, *69*, 379–9.

Schwartz, G. E. Psychosomatic disorders and biofeedback: A psychobiological model of disregulation. In J. D. Maser & M. E. P. Seligman (Eds.), *Psychopathology: Experimental models*. San Francisco: Freeman, 1977. (a)

Schwartz, G. E. Biofeedback and patterning of autonomic and central processes: CNS–cardiovascular interactions. In G. E. Schwartz & J. Beatty (Eds.), *Biofeedback: Theory and research*. New York: Academic Press, 1977. (b)

Schwartz, G. E. Psychobiological foundations of psychotherapy and behavior change. In S. L. Garfield & A. E. Bergin (Eds.), *Handbook of psychotherapy and behavior change* (2nd ed.). New York: Wiley, 1978.

Schwartz, G. E. The brain as a health care system. In G. Stone, N. Adler, & F. Cohen (Eds.), *Health psychology*. San Francisco: Jossey-Bass, 1979.

Schwartz, G. E., Ahern, G. L., & Brown, S. L. Lateralized facial muscle response to positive and negative emotional stimuli. *Psychophysiology, 1979, 16,* 561–71.

Schwartz, G. E., Brown, S. L., & Ahern, G. L. Facial muscle patterning and subjective experience during affective imagery: Sex differences. *Psychophysiology, 1980, 17,* 75–82.

Schwartz, G. E., Davidson, R. J., & Maer, F. Right hemisphere lateralization for emotion in the human brain: Interactions with cognition. *Science, 1975, 190,* 286–8.

Schwartz, G. E., Fair, P. L., Mandel, M. R., Salt, P., Mieske, M., & Klerman, G. L. Facial electromyography in the assessment of improvement in depression. *Psychosomatic Medicine, 1978, 40,* 355–60.

Schwartz, G. E., Fair, P. L., Salt, P., Mandel, M. R., & Klerman, G. L. Facial muscle patterning to affective imagery in depressed and non-depressed subjects. *Science, 1976, 192,* 489–91. (a)

Schwartz, G. E., Fair, P. L., Salt, P., Mandel, M. R., & Klerman, G. L. Facial expression and imagery in depression: An electromyographic study. *Psychosomatic Medicine, 1976, 38,* 337–47. (b)

Schwartz, G. E., & Logue, A. Patterns of facial temperature during positive and negative emotions. Unpublished manuscript, 1981.

Schwartz, G. E., & Weinberger, D. A. Patterns of emotional responses to affective situations: Relations among happiness, sadness, anger, fear, depression, and anxiety. *Motivation and Emotion, 1980, 4(2),* 175–91.

Schwartz, G. E., Weinberger, D. A., & Brown, S. L. *Self-report of patterns of emotions in complex imagery situations.* Unpublished manuscript, 1980.

Schwartz, G. E., Weinberger, D. A., & Singer, J. A. Cardiovascular differentiation of happiness, sadness, anger, and fear following imagery and exercise. *Psychosomatic Medicine, 1981, 43,* 343–64.

Sternberg, R. *Intelligence, information processing, and analogical reasoning: The componential analysis of human abilities*. Hillsdale, N.J.: Erlbaum, 1977.

Taylor, B. Personal communication, December, 1980.

Von Bertalanffy, L. *General systems theory*. New York: Braziller, 1968.

Weerts, T. C., & Roberts, R. The physiological effects of imagining anger provoking and fear provoking scenes. *Psychophysiology, 1976, 13,* 174. (Abstract)

Weinberger, D. A., Schwartz, G. E., & Davidson, R. J. Low anxious, high anxious, and repressive coping styles: Psychometric patterns and behavioral and physiological responses to stress. *Journal of Abnormal Psychology, 1979, 88,* 369–80.

Part III

Facial, vocal, and body signals

5   Two complementary systems for measuring facial expressions in infants and children

Carroll E. Izard and Linda M. Dougherty

The introductory chapter emphasized that emotions are complex, multilevel, or multicomponent systems and that their measurement must be concerned with neurophysiological–biochemical, behavioral–expressive, and subjective–experiential variables. In most cases each chapter of this volume has been concerned with variables that index one of these levels or components of emotions. The present chapter focuses on variables at the behavioral–expressive level, in particular facial–expressive signals.

Theoretical background

Except for studies of the semantic–affective dimensions that predict or identify categories of facial expressions (e.g., Schlosberg, 1941, 1952, 1954), research in this domain had a stormy history during the first 70 years of this century. Controversy centered mainly on the verifiability of Darwin's (1872) hypothesis of the innateness and universality of certain facial expressions of emotions. In the late 1960s and 1970s, robust empirical data from studies of a wide array of literate and preliterate cultures, individuals born blind, and certain clinical populations converged to give indisputable support of the great naturalist's hypothesis. The studies that produced these data came largely from small groups of investigators representing two quite different orientations – psychologists following a discrete emotions approach (e.g., Ekman, Friesen, & Ellsworth, 1972; Izard, 1971) and biologists using an ethological approach (Eibl-Eibesfeldt, 1971; Hass, 1970). Ethological conceptions are discussed by Charlesworth in Chapter 13. Differential emotions theory (Izard, 1971, 1977; Tomkins, 1962, 1963) and the studies supporting the innateness and universality of certain emotion expressions have been presented in detail elsewhere. This theory will be briefly summarized here, because it provided the conceptual framework for the measurement systems to be described later as well as the empirical foundation for the cross-cultural research on facial expressions.

Differential emotions theory holds that the human personality is a complex

organization of six relatively independent interactive subsystems: the homeos-
tatic, drive, emotion, perceptual, cognitive, and motor systems. Each subsystem
has motivational properties whose salience varies with different developmental
levels, environmental contexts, and self–other interactions. The emotions constitute the primary motivational system for human beings over the lifespan.

These personality subsystems produce four classes of motivation: drives, emotions, affect–perception and affect–cognition interactions, and affective–cognitive structures and orientations. The term *affect* includes drives and emotions.
Drives arise from physiological needs such as hunger, thirst, elimination, pain,
and sex. The fundamental emotions are interest, joy, surprise, sadness, anger,
disgust, contempt, fear, shame/shyness, and guilt. (Figures 5.1–5.4 show how
infants' faces express some of these emotions.) An affect–cognition interaction
is the interaction of a drive or emotion with perceptual and cognitive processes.
Affective–cognitive structures are symbols, images, or thoughts bonded more or
less permanently to a particular affect or pattern of affects. They have traitlike
characteristics and may form a basic personality orientation.

Each emotion has neurophysiological, expressive, and phenomenological
components. The expressive components, particularly facial expressions, have a
physiological and a social function. Expressive movements provide sensory data
to the brain for the cortical–integrative activity that produces emotion experience. Socially, facial expressions provide a set of signals that are important in
fostering social relationships.

The theory holds that emotion expressions are innate and emerge ontogeneti-
cally as they become adaptive in the life of the infant and particularly in infant–
caregiver communication. For example, the physical distress (or pain) cry is
present from birth to serve the needs of survival, maintain proximity of the
caregiver, and guarantee at least minimal social exchange by fostering caregiver–
infant interaction.

The early work of Darwin (1872, 1877), and that of Eibl-Eibesfeldt (1971),
Ekman, Sorenson, and Friesen (1969), Hass (1970), and Izard (1971) has shown
that certain emotions have the same facial expressions in widely different literate
and preliterate cultures. The data from these investigations provide a sound basis
for inferring that the fundamental emotions are subserved by innate neural programs that are part of the substrates of qualitatively distinct states of consciousness.

Cross-cultural studies of the interpretation or significance of facial expression
provide support for the hypothesized relationship between a particular expression
and a specific emotion experience. For example, both literate and preliterate
people describe the inner experience of joy and sadness or anger and fear in a
similar way. Further, the cross-cultural data indicate that people in widely differing sociocultural settings tend to describe similar action consequences for the

Figure 5.1. Four-and-one-half-month old male expressing interest

Figure 5.2. Seven-month-old male expressing joy

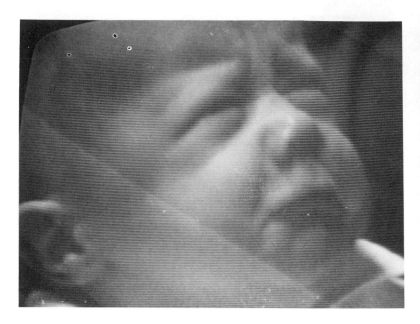

Figure 5.3. One-month-old female expressing sadness

Figure 5.4. Six-month-old female expressing anger

various emotions. It is reasonable to infer that the link between facial expression, neurochemical processes in emotion, and certain actions or action tendencies is the inner emotion experience and its motivational properties.

The study of facial expressions in significant life situations is of importance for several reasons. It is now well established that emotion expressions are communicative and motivational cues for the perceiver (Izard, 1971, 1977). The cross-cultural research already cited suggests that the species-common expressions of fundamental emotions transmit emotion-specific signals to the discerning observer, on whom the signals tend to have a motivational impact.

Nevrovich (1974) showed that photographs of sad children elicited helping behavior in preschoolers. Craig (1978), Prkachin (1978), and Sternbach (1978) have pointed out the significant effects of pain signals on the social environment and interactions with the suffering individual. Hoffman (Chapter 11) and Zahn-Waxler, Radke-Yarrow, and King (1979) have shown that facial affect signals can elicit empathy or vicarious affect in the observer. Charlesworth (Chapter 13) presents a discussion of the effects of affect expression on regulating the behavior of others.

In the past decade a number of developmental psychologists have supported the idea that the emotions and their expressive or social signals play a key role in the growth of the infant and in the organization of the infant's behavioral systems (Emde, Gaensbauer, & Harmon, 1976; Izard, 1978; Spitz, 1965; Sroufe, 1979; Stechler & Carpenter, 1967). Emphasizing the importance of emotions in normal development, Kagan (1978) observed, "The child's growth will not be fully understood until we gain greater insight into those aspects of development we call emotional" (p. 39). One approach to studying the role of emotions in development focuses on the measurement of observable changes in appearance produced by the facial musculature. According to differential emotions theory, combinations of these changes identify the facial expressions of emotions.

Approaches to the measurement of facial behavior

Early studies in this area typically used untrained subjects' global judgments to assess facial expressions of emotions. Current methods for the systematic analysis of facial behavior rely on detailed anatomical knowledge of the movement units or discrete appearance changes that result from actions of the facial musculature. Because the global judgments of untrained subjects simulate judgments made in everyday social interactions, they remain useful in determining social consensus or the social validity of expressions identified by systematic analysis. In interpreting data derived by social consensus, however, it is necessary to consider a number of sources of error, such as context, attributional biases, and cognitive information.

The data from the early research on the identifiability of specific emotion expressions by means of global judgments of untrained subjects proved to be controversial. Both the problem and the procedure fell in disrepute, in part because of conceptual and methodological problems with the early studies (for a summary and critique of these studies, see Ekman et al., 1972; Izard, 1971) and in part because of the limitations associated with the technique of using global judgments of untrained subjects.

During the 1970s several systems for the systematic study of facial behavior were developed. These ranged from ethological (and essentially atheoretical) naturalistic, observational approaches to theory-based microanalytic methods that require closeup video records of the face. Grant (1971) classified emotion reactions into three categories – aggression (behavior associated with attack), flight (behavior associated with retreat), and friendliness (behavior associated with positive approach). He investigated postural behavior in relation to facial behavior. His classifications did not focus on discrete emotions but rather on affective–cognitive structures and affect-related behaviors. Gergerian and Ermiane (1978) have studied facial expressions through the use of *prosopology,* a theoretical framework that holds that each muscular contraction modifies the face in a specific way, producing a characteristic image that has a specific psychological meaning. They maintain that given states of mind (e.g., dominance, strength of will) lead to contractions of particular facial muscles or gaze directions. For example, a feeling of strong will results in the skin of the chin being flattened over the bone. Their system is based on extensive study of the anatomy of the face and provides a definitive map of changes in facial appearance that result from muscular contractions. They used posed photographs of themselves to illustrate the different muscle movements and the facial appearances of such personality characteristics as "tendencies to extraversion and introversion." Although their inferences have not been adequately validated, their manual provides detailed information on facial anatomy and appearance changes. Ekman, Friesen, and Tomkins (1971) developed a measurement system based on components of emotion expressions. The Facial Affect Scoring Technique (FAST) scored appearance changes in three areas of the face for six emotions: joy, surprise, sadness, disgust, anger and fear. Coders code each of three areas of the face separately, with the rest of the face blocked from view. Formulas are then applied to the data to identify emotion expressions.

Ekman and Friesen (1978) later replaced FAST with the Facial Action Coding System (FACS). FACS is an anatomically based, comprehensive system that codes all observable facial actions. FACS contains 24 discrete action units and 20 miscellaneous facial actions. It identifies the same six emotions that FAST does. The illustrative material for FACS consists of (voluntary) muscle contractions modeled by the authors and other adults. FACS measures all behavior on the face regardless of its importance in determining emotion expressions. Thus applying FACS to video records with a high density of facial actions can require as much as 600 minutes or as little as 4 minutes for one minute of behavior, depending on the density of facial actions (Ekman, personal communication, 1981). The FACS manual indicates that it takes approximately 100 hours to learn the system and achieve reliability.

Oster (1978) and Oster and Ekman (1977) have provided information that is useful in adapting FACS for the study of facial expressions of infants. Oster applied FACS to videotaped play sessions between infants and their parents. Although she observed many different expressions, she analyzed her data only in regard to smiling and brow knitting. Results indicated that the adult-based FACS could successfully detect these expressive behaviors in infants.

Young and Décarie (1977) cataloged the global facial and vocal expressions of 75 infants to six different stimulus situations. They identified the expressions of distress, anger, interest, fear, and joy. In a separate analysis they divided the face into four separate regions (brows, eyes, mouth, and other) and coded each region in terms of form, features, lines, or shadows created. They did not look for specific muscle movements. Their catalog included only units of facial–vocal behavior that were observed as part of the affect-expression repertoire possessed by infants in the last quarter of the 1st year of life. They believed that each unit in their system had a social, emotional, or communicative function. Their catalog of expressions identified 42 different facial patterns. Eleven of those patterns were considered positive in hedonic tone (e.g., play face, positive face), 12 were considered negative in hedonic tone (e.g., fear face, tremble face), and the remaining 19 expressions were considered undifferentiated in tone (e.g., surprise face, yawn).

Young and Décarie used two sets of observers in separate rooms to code the infant's behavior individually. One set of three naive observers judged the basic emotions expressed. The other set of two trained observers coded the facial–vocal behavior. No index of interjudge agreement was calculated for the observations. Further, they did not report indexes of agreement between the two measurement systems or indicate which of the undifferentiated facial expressions corresponded to which emotions.

McGrew (1972) developed a behavioral coding system to implement his ethological studies of nursery school children. His system includes 16 facial (as well as 23 head, 29 gestural, 3 leg, 16 body, 9 postural, and 14 locomotor) movements considered to be small behavioral units that can be readily observed. Some of the facial movements have strictly behavioral or functional descriptions (e.g., bared teeth, red face, nose wrinkle), whereas others have descriptions with affective connotation (e.g., play face, pout, smile). Some of the movements are associated with two or more discrete emotions, some with only one emotion, and others are not emotion-specific. Although one could reasonably infer certain emotions from McGrew's movement codes, his system was designed to yield an *ethogram,* or comprehensive repertoire of social behavior, not to identify specific emotions.

Brannigan and Humphries (1972) devised a system for coding facial and postural behavior of children and adults consisting of 136 units. Seventy of these units dealt particularly with facial behavior. Many of their facial units correspond to units of facial behavior in other systems (Ekman & Friesen, 1978; Izard, 1979; Izard & Dougherty, 1980). They made some distinctions within emotion categories that are similar to those made in ethological systems (McGrew, 1972; Young & Décarie, 1977). For example, they identified seven different types of smiles (e.g., simple smile, play face), three different types of angry mouths, and three different types of sad mouths. Like other ethologically oriented investigators, Brannigan and Humphries use labels that have affective connotation for their movement or behavioral units.

Blurton Jones (1971) devised a component facial behavior scoring system based on lines and shadows. He also used muscle contractions in his considerations but depended most heavily on what seemed to be the main positions of facial landmarks. He used his system for rating still photographs of children 2 to 5 years old on 34 categories of facial expression. Each photograph was scored on a 3-point scale of certainty for whether the description of the components applied to the face being coded. Blurton Jones's system contains components that are associated with discrete emotions and some that are not emotion-specific. He was one of the first workers doing research on the measurement of facial behavior to report observer reliability, and he helped to establish standards for acceptable reliability.

A two-system approach to analyzing facial affect signals

Each of the foregoing systems has certain strengths and weaknesses for analyzing the facial behaviors of emotions. Some were designed to measure facial and nonfacial emotion behaviors, whereas others concerned facial behaviors having no known relationship to emotions. None of the systems has focused primarily on infants and young children or has attempted to identify all the fundamental emotions as defined in differential emotions theory. Most of them are microanalytic in nature and require a long learning period and an even longer time for application to substantial amounts of raw data.

Rationale for a two-system approach

Any one of the foregoing systems may be well suited to a particular investigator's needs. Yet there is no system that is both comprehensive and exclusive with respect to facial affect signals and also sufficiently efficient to facilitate research on important developmental and clinical issues that require analysis of relatively extensive amounts of material. This deficiency led us to the development of two complementary systems, a more macroanalytic system for efficiency and a microanalytic system for assuring objectivity and accuracy. The basic assumption underlying the development of the two systems is that emotion includes as an integral component organized patterns of facial muscle activity (appearance changes) that represent or signal the emotions of human experience. The more macroanalytic or holistic system can be used to get an overall map of the sequence and duration of facial expressions. The microanalytic or movement system can be used as a kind of system for quality control to assure the objectivity and accuracy of the sequence of facial expressions identified by the holistic system. The application of the two systems requires a closeup video record of the face, as is the case with other detailed facial behavior coding systems that demand high reliability of the coder.

Overview of the two systems

The two measurement systems to be described below differ from all the foregoing ones in several ways.

1. They attempt to identify the facial expressions of all the emotions defined by differential emotions theory except guilt, for which no specific facial signals have been identified. They also identify the young infant's affect expression of physical distress or pain.
2. Both systems are concerned only with appearance changes that signal the fundamental emotions, blends of two basic emotions, or the affect expression of pain. Appearance changes not associated with affect are disregarded.
3. They were developed specifically for measuring emotions in infants and young children, although they can be readily adapted for use with individuals of any age.
4. All of the illustrative photographs and video segments and the video segments used for training and obtaining reliability come from the spontaneous expressions of emotion by infants and toddlers in a wide range of naturalistic and experimental conditions.

Although either of the two systems is sufficiently reliable and accurate (in relation to each other and to independent criteria) to be used independently to measure emotion-specific facial behaviors, it is suggested that they be used as complementary systems.

The Maximally Discriminative Facial Movement Coding System

The Maximally Discriminative Facial Movement Coding System (Max) (Izard, 1979), a coding system anatomically based on movement units, was developed as an objective system for identifying exclusively the discrete changes in facial appearance necessary for identifying the fundamental emotions.

Max is a refinement of its predecessor, the more detailed Facial Movement Coding System (FMCS) that included 48 movement units in five regions of the face. It required five separate runs of each video segment to code the face. Experience with the FMCS suggested that it could be streamlined by grouping anatomically related facial movements and eliminating those that were not essential in the identification of any of the affect expressions. Thus Max contains only 29 movement units or appearance changes in three regions of the face and requires only three separate runs to code the face. Because it eliminates nonaffect appearance changes and affect signals that are redundant or ineffective in differentiating among affects, it is a more efficient affect-identification system than methods that code all facial behaviors regardless of their relation to affect.

The development of Max (originally FMCS) was initiated by determining the anatomy of facial expressions – determining which muscles are responsible for the movements involved in each of the facial expressions of the fundamental emotions as defined in differential emotions theory (Izard, 1977; Tomkins, 1962, 1963). This was partly accomplished by studying cross-culturally standardized expressions of the fundamental emotions (Ekman & Friesen, 1976; Izard, 1971), and then ascertaining which facial muscles are involved in the movements that constitute the facial patterns of each of the expressions.

Detailed study or knowledge of facial anatomy is not essential for learning and applying Max, but it may facilitate a fuller understanding of some of the finer distinctions between appearance changes. The majority of students who attained reliability on Max in our laboratory had no knowledge of the anatomy of the expressive muscles of the face at the time of their training.

The next step in the development of Max was to generate verbal descriptions of each of the movements or appearance changes in each of the fundamental emotion expressions. The specific vocabulary of these descriptions was dictated by how each movement unit would appear on the young child's face. Each appearance change was illustrated both by artist's drawings and by photographs of children spontaneously exhibiting the desired movement.

The Max videotape presents photographs, artist's drawings, and dynamic video segments of infants' and toddlers' spontaneous facial behaviors illustrating each of the 29 movement codes or appearance changes involved in facial affect expressions. Further, pictorial illustrations were made for each of the anatomically independent appearance changes in isolation. This was done by having an artist draw each Max movement on an otherwise neutral face. The tape also contains 43 precoded training segments of infants' facial behavior from our video library. The illustrative and training video segments that are shown on the videotape were recorded in both natural and laboratory settings. Most were taken at a Delaware well-baby clinic during the visits of the infant and mother for the infant's routine immunizations. Some were obtained in naturalistic and quasi-experimental studies conducted at Vanderbilt University and the Institute of Pediatric Sciences in Moscow, where stimuli included administration of a bitter taste, jack-in-the-box, the approach of a stranger, caregiver–infant play, and other affect-eliciting events.

In the first phase of Max analysis, coders view each video segment three times. During each pass they code a particular facial region and assign each appearance change a unique two-digit number (e.g., brows drawn down and together is Appearance Change 25, eyes narrowed is Appearance Change 32, mouth squarish or rectangular-shaped is Appearance Change 54).

In the second phase of analysis, the sequences of appearance changes coded with Max are compared with combinations (defined a priori) of observable movement units (Max formulas) that identify the discrete emotion expressions or blends of two or more of these expressions (e.g., Appearance Changes 25 + 32 + 54 identify the emotion expression of anger; Appearance Changes 23 + 33 + 56 identify the emotion expression of sadness). Figures 5.5a-d and 5.6a-c present illustrations of these appearance changes. To identify an emotion expression, the appropriate appearance changes must be present on the face simultaneously or within .5 second of each other, which is the allowable error in judging onset and offset times of appearance changes.

The objectivity of Max stems from the fact that coders make judgments only regarding the presence or absence of clearly defined facial appearance changes. Judgments are made independently for each of three regions of the face (brows, eyes/nose/cheeks, and mouth/lips/chin). The coder does not make any judgments of the emotion signal value of the observed appearance changes.

Despite the fact that Max is assumed to be the most efficient of the coding systems based on movement units, it is still quite time-consuming. Video records of infants or young children in situations that elicit frequent changes in facial behavior may require from 20 to 200 minutes of coding time for each minute of facial behavior.

The reliability of Max

A coder's reliability in Max is determined not by the identification of individual appearance changes but by the identification of emotion expressions or blends. Coders are required to achieve at least 80% agreement with the master code on three consecutive sets of three segments of the training material on the Max videotape. The training segments range in duration from 2 to 11 seconds. Once this degree of reliability is achieved on the practice material, coders are deemed skilled enough in the measurement of facial behavior to analyze actual data. Nevertheless, we practice (and recommend) frequent systematic checks on the reliability of all coders, including the most experienced. If reliability falls below

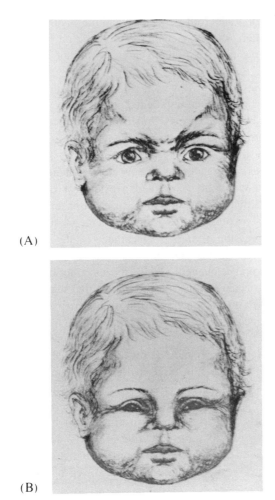

(A)

(B)

Figure 5.5.(A) Max Appearance Change 25: brows lowered and drawn together. (B) Max Appearance Change 33: eyes narrowed or squinted. (C) Max Appearance Change 54:

the accepted standard (75%), recoding and rechecking of reliability should be done.

The first, and most stringent, test of intrasystem reliability is the absolute-time method. Each segment is broken into .1-second increments, and coders' protocols are compared in order to determine the exact amount of time during which they were in agreement on the affects identified. Although agreement of coders

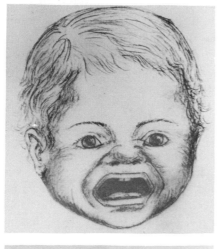

(C)

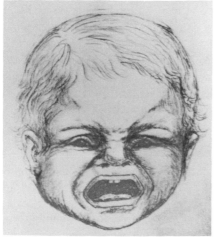

(D)

mouth angular or squarish. (D) Max Appearance Changes 25 + 33 + 54: the emotion expression of anger.

within .5 second is acceptable for coding of movement units, absolute-time reliability may be useful in determining problem areas of coding between two coders and exact reliability for specific purposes.

In the second and most commonly used test of intrasystem reliability, movement codes are counted as agreements if the onset and offset times of the movement codes that identify an expression are within .5 second of each other. We refer to this as the standard method of determining reliability, the one used for computing the reliability reported in this chapter. Both of these methods are discussed in more detail in the Max manual (Izard, 1979).

In using the Max system, onset and offset times are judged to the nearest .1 second. To do time coding the coder proceeds through the video record until an appearance change in one of the facial regions peaks or is clearly visible. Then the coder moves backward until the facial movement stops and notes the estimated onset time. He/she confirms this estimation by moving the tape forward and backward in slow motion across the estimated onset point. The offset time of each appearance change is found in the same manner.

Time coding is necessary for checking reliability between two coders. Once a video segment has been time coded, the absolute-time and standard methods of reliability can be applied. Time coding is also essential to the application of certain techniques for organizing facial expression data. These techniques will be described in a later section.

Ten students in our lab achieved at least 80% reliability on Max independent of coaching by the authors or other experienced coders. Average training time to reach agreement of 80% or better with the master code for the practice material was 11 hours, with a range of 7.5 to 22 hours. The average reliability on reaching criterion was 91.0%. In two studies to be described later, these coders applied Max to a wide variety of video records of infants' spontaneous facial behavior and attained intercoder reliability of 76.9% and 83.0%, respectively.

The validity of Max

Studies with Max have produced some evidence for content, construct, and criterion-related validity. Evidence for each type of validity will be summarized.

Content validity. Content validity, often referred to as sampling validity, involves a systematic analysis of the test content to determine the adequacy of the coverage of the domain being measured. The content universe sampled by Max consists of all the facial appearance changes that signal affect. The content sources are differential emotions theory, which provides definitions of the fundamental emotions, the anatomy of the expressive muscles of the face, and cross-culturally standardized photographs of adult faces showing the appearance changes of the fundamental emotion expressions. The content validity of Max is considered quite adequate, as it includes all facial appearance changes that are not redundant and relate to the fundamental emotions and those involved in the young infant's facial expression of physical distress.

Construct validity. Evidence of the construct validity of Max-determined facial expressions of emotions has been demonstrated in a series of studies using sev-

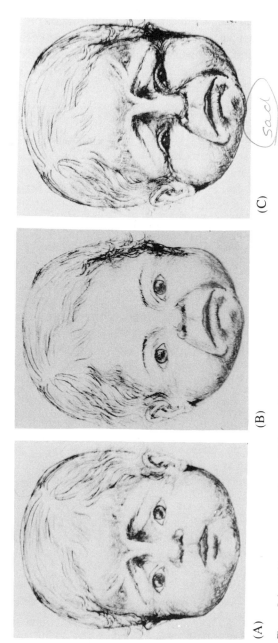

(A)   (B)   (C)

Figure 5.6. (A) Max Appearance Change 23: brows raised at inner corners. (B) Max Appearance Change 56: corners of mouth drawn downward and outward; chin may push up center of lower lip. (C) Max Appearance Changes 23 + 33 + 56: the emotion of sadness.

eral groups of college students and health care professionals (Izard et al., 1980). In this study judges used our Facial Expression Scoring Manual (FESM), to be described later, to select 25 video segments of infants' facial behavior to represent as clearly as possible the discrete expressions of emotion in the repertoire of 1- to 9-month-old infants. These segments were analyzed by two Max coders and two FESM (Affex) coders. They were also presented to groups of untrained subjects who made global judgments of the facial expressions. Both Max coders and the untrained subjects agreed with the FESM coders in identifying the seven emotion expressions – interest, joy, surprise, sadness, anger, disgust, and fear. Construct validity was indicated by Max–FESM agreement of 88.0%.

In a study to be described later, Max and Affex (the revised FESM) were used in complementary fashion to study developmental changes in facial expressions in response to the acute pain of inoculation. Preliminary results indicated that the Max–Affex agreement was 78.2%, a relatively robust index of construct validity.

Criterion-related, or predictive, validity. With respect to criterion-related, or predictive, validity, Max-identified facial expressions can be predictive of three types of behavior – the subjective experience of the expressor, the affect-related behavior of the expressor, and the response of the perceiver. Because it is not possible to predict (or measure) preverbal infants' subjective experiences, the criterion validity of Max for this population can only be evaluated in terms of event–expression–behavior relationships or in terms of the effects on the perceiver. For example, we have hypothesized that inoculation of young infants predicts the facial expressions of pain, anger, and sadness and that separation from mother in the Ainsworth–Wittig Strange Situation predicts anger and sadness expressions in 15- to 18-month-old infants. Preliminary results of ongoing research in our lab support these predictions.

As indicated earlier in the Izard et al. (1980) study, Max analysis predicted untrained subjects' classifications of seven fundamental emotion expressions regardless of whether the stimulus material was presented statically (slides) or dynamically (videotape playback). The subjects included college students and health care professionals. In Table 5.1, the percentages (subjects' consensus in classifying the stimuli into emotion categories) are indexes of criterion-related validity.

Yarczower and Kocs (1980) used Max, FMCS, and FESM (Affex) to predict untrained subjects' judgments of facial expressions of infants. Ninety untrained subjects rated the facial expressions of infants seen on a specially constructed videotape. The investigators assumed that facial movements that were present at least 20% of the time during the segment would provide the basis for a judgment by the subjects. Thus any judgment made by the untrained subjects that matched

Table 5.1. *Criterion-related validity of FESM*

FESM label[a]	Percentage of untrained subjects in agreement with FESM
IE	73.7
EJ	78.8
SS	56.0
SD	53.1
AR[b]	30.3
DR	40.6
CS	54.2
FT	58.2

Note: FESM = Facial Expression Scoring Manual (the earlier version of Affex).
[a] Each emotion category was represented by one to four photographs or video segments. Each stimulus expression was classified by approximately 100 subjects.
[b] Some of the photos and video segments labeled by FESM judges as anger were later correctly coded by Max as discomfort–pain. This probably lowered the percentage in agreement for this category, because the response form for the untrained subjects did not contain a pain category.

Table 5.2. *Three coding systems' agreement with untrained subjects' classifications*

System	N	Agreement M (%)
Max	23	59.1
FMCS	23	61.3
FESM	23	62.7

Note: Max = Maximally Discriminative Facial Movement Coding System. FMCS = Facial Movement Coding System. FESM = Facial Expression Scoring Manual.
Source: Adapted from Yarczower & Kocs (1981).

any of the predicted facial expressions for that segment was considered correct. The mean percentages of correct predictions for Max, FMCS, and FESM were 59.1, 61.3, and 62.7, respectively. For those cases in which Max and FESM agreed on the identification of the emotion, the coding systems predicted the untrained emotion classifications in 73.9% of the cases. This finding suggests that the three systems were equally successful in predicting judgments of untrained subjects and that the combination of Max and Affex substantially improves prediction. Tables 5.1 and 5.2 summarize the results found in the studies by Izard et al. and Yarczower and Kocs.

The System for Identifying Affect Expressions by Holistic Judgments

The Izard et al. (1980) study showed that global judgments, including those of untrained subjects, can be improved with even brief training. Improvement resulted from pointing out and labeling the discrete changes in appearance for each emotion expression in each region of the face, suggesting that with detailed and rigorous training of this sort, the impressionistic, intuitive global judgment could become a more sophisticated, holistic judgment, one that is based on analysis and integration of the information available from the appearance changes in all three of the major regions of the face – brow, eye, and mouth.

Capitalizing on this empirical lead, we incorporated extensive systematic training in the identification of discrete facial affect signals as part of the procedure for learning our System for Identifying Affect Expressions by Holistic Judgments (Affex; Izard & Dougherty, 1980). The system is designed to provide efficiently an overall map of affect expressions, their temporal sequence, and their duration. The efficiency of Affex stems from the fact that judges are trained to observe the whole face and to integrate information from the different regions in a judgment process that labels the observed emotions directly.

Affex also retains any advantages inherent in holistic judgments that are based on simultaneous observation of movement patterns in the whole face. It capitalizes on the mind's capacity to integrate a complex set of signals into a meaningful gestalt that can be reliably identified and labeled.

As with Max, the development of Affex was guided by differential emotions theory (Izard, 1971, 1977; Tomkins, 1962, 1963). The facial criteria for classifying emotion expressions were based on this theory as well as on the empirical research relating to the expressions it defined (Ekman et al., 1972; Ekman & Friesen, 1975; Izard, 1971; Tomkins & McCarter, 1964).

Affex was developed from FESM, which was based on cross-culturally identified emotion expressions of adults. The aim in developing Affex was to devise an efficient system for making direct judgments of the affective meaning of the patterns of facial muscle movements in infants and young children.

The first step in the development of Affex was to substitute illustrative material of infants and young children for the adult exemplars used in FESM and to use Max as a guide in revising the verbal descriptors. Most of the changes in the verbal descriptors follow one rule: When adults show furrows or wrinkles, infants and young children usually show dimples and bulges or lumps, because children have relatively heavy deposits of fatty tissue and highly elastic skin.

In using Affex, judges observe all areas of the face at once while looking for affect-related appearance changes and classifying them directly, according to affect categories. This is the major difference between Max and Affex. Because affect-labeling judgments cannot be said to be totally free of subjective or attributional bias, special steps are taken to minimize misattributions or misjudgments stemming from subjective factors.

First, Affex includes the same appearance changes as those in Max. Use of these established emotion-identification criteria that are pictorially and verbally defined should reduce attributional–interpretive bias to a minimum. Second, Affex judges in our lab typically begin their training by first learning Max, as described above. Because reliability with Max is a prerequisite to training with Affex, judges approach the task with full knowledge of the objectivity required in coding facial behaviors and identifying affects.

The Affex videotape presents photographs, artist's drawings, and dynamic video segments of children's spontaneous facial behaviors illustrating eight emotion expressions as well as the infant's expression of physical distress or pain and several combinations of affect blends. The tape also contains training material consisting of 20 precoded segments ranging in duration from 20 to 95 seconds. The expressions on the videotape are spontaneous, and the expressors are infants and toddlers. The effects of display rules are assumed to be absent or negligible in early infancy and minimal in the 2nd year. Any evidence of their effects should be noted, however, because it could contribute to our understanding of the socialization and self-regulation of emotion expression.

Coders analyze the video records in units organized by appearance changes. They play the video segment to be analyzed in real time until an appearance change is observed. At that point the coder uses the slow-motion mode to determine the onset and offset of the appearance change. Thus Affex requires only one run of the video segment, though forward and backward runs around the appearance changes are necessary to make the final judgment and determine onset and offset times.

The reliability of Affex

Reliability estimates for Affex use the same methods that are used for computing Max reliability – absolute-time and standard method. Coders are required to achieve at least 80% agreement with the master code for the training material on four consecutive training segments. Affex intrasystem reliability in four studies done in our laboratory ranged from 77.0% to 92.0%, with a mean of 86.5%.

Four coders in our laboratory who had already obtained reliability on Max learned Affex using the Affex manual and the Affex videotape. Average training time to achieve at least 80% agreement with the master code for the practice material was 5 hours, with training times ranging from 3 to 11 hours. On their final training segments, the average agreement of these judges with the master code was 92.0%.

Parisi (1977) videotaped the facial expressions of infants at three different ages to 20 emotion-eliciting situations or incentive events. The videotapes were then analyzed by coders using the FESM, the earlier version of Affex. Judges agreed in classifying 411 of the 600 facial responses into discrete categories of emotion. They also agreed on an additional 136 blends. Thus intrasystem reliability was 91% (547 of 600 facial responses).

Shiller & Izard (1980) used Affex to study the emotion expressions of 30 13-month-old toddlers in the Ainsworth–Wittig Strange Situation. Four different discrete emotion expressions of interest, joy, sadness, and anger were reliably identified as well as several blends. Affex intrasystem agreement was 77.0%.

In the Izard et al. (1980) study, Affex intrasystem reliability was 92.0%. In an ongoing study of developmental changes in emotion responses to pain, preliminary analysis yielded a reliability of 85.0%.

The validity of Affex

Evidence for the content, construct, and criterion-related validity of Max generalizes to FESM and Affex, as all three systems are based on the same theory and research. Further, in three studies in our laboratory, intersystem reliability ranged from 73.9% to 88.0%, with a mean of 80.0%.

Content validity. The content universe and the content sources sampled are the same as those for Max. The muscle movements that effect the appearance changes are identical in both systems.

Construct validity. The first test of the construct validity of the system was reported in a study by Izard and his colleagues (1980). As we reported in the section "The Validity of Max," the Max–FESM agreement in this study of selected stimulus material was 88.0%.

Criterion-related, or predictive, validity. The predictive validity of Affex has been examined by testing whether the appearance changes it identifies as affect expressions predict the emotion classification responses of untrained observers (social consensus). The success with which Affex predicts social consensus is summarized in Table 5.1.

In the Parisi (1977) study, the FESM results predicted untrained subjects' classifications of emotion expressions for 73% of the stimulus materials. In the Izard et al. (1980) study, the FESM analysis accurately predicted a wide range of emotion classifications made by untrained subjects. Accuracy of prediction was 55.9%.

The use of Max and Affex as two complementary systems

In order to use Max and Affex as complementary systems for measuring facial behavior, intersystem reliability must be demonstrated. Intersystem reliability is measured by the same two methods used in computing intrasystem reliability. The major difference is that instead of comparing the results of two coders using the same system, affects identified by the appearance changes observed by one coder using Max are compared with the affect expressions identified by another coder using Affex.

Max and Affex can be used as a two-system approach to measuring facial expressions by first applying Affex to the entire video record. Max is then applied to a random or representative sample (10–20%) of the expressions identified by Affex. To obtain intersystem reliability the movement codes of Max are converted into affect expressions through Max movement formulas (Izard, 1979). Max–Affex intersystem reliability is computed using the absolute-time reliability and/or the standard method.

The first test of Max and Affex (then FESM) as complementary systems of measuring infants' affect expressions was in the Izard et al. (1980) study. On the specially selected stimulus material for this study, intersystem agreement was 88.0%.

Izard, Dougherty, Coss, and Hembree (1980) investigated developmental changes in infants' facial responses to pain by using Max and Affex as complementary systems. Ten infants were followed longitudinally through a series of three routine inoculations and 8 infants were followed through two inoculations. Affex was used by five coders to code a 75-second video record for each inoculation episode of each infant (5 seconds prior to inoculation and 70 seconds following inoculation). The Affex analysis produced a continuous sequence of expressions, and time coding divided the video record into segments that showed expressions from onset to offset. The discrete emotion expressions of interest, joy, sadness, anger, and physical discomfort or pain as well as several blends of discrete emotion expressions were identified.

A random sample of the material was drawn from the video record as an internal (Affex) reliability check, with the restrictions that each infant was sampled and all coders were checked equally. Preliminary results indicated that Affex intrasystem reliability was 85.0%.

In order to examine intersystem reliability a sample of the Affex-identified expression segments was drawn for Max coding. The expression segments were sampled randomly with the restriction that each expression category was represented in proportion to its frequency in the video record. This random sample of segments was coded by five coders using Max. Preliminary results indicated that the percentage of agreement between Max and Affex was 78.2%.

A subset of the Max-coded segments was randomly drawn and coded as an internal reliability check on Max. All coders were checked equally. The Max intrasystem reliability was 76.9%.

Organization of the emotion expression data

After the expressions in a video record have been identified by Affex and confirmed by Max coding of a random sample of segments, the data can be organized into meaningful units for studying the emotion expressions of individuals, dyads (e.g., mother–infant), and groups. The data are summarized in expression graphs, or affectograms.

Individual affectograms

An individual affectogram shows the sequence or pattern and duration of emotion expressions exhibited in a given time period (e.g., 70 seconds postinoculation). The affectograms in Figures 5.7 and 5.8 compare the sequence and duration of affects expressed by pairs of same-age, same-sex infants in response to inoculation. Emotion expressions are indicated by type of symbol, with time of the expression's occurrence and duration along the abscissa.

Figure 5.7 presents the expressive responses of two 4-month-old white male infants to the pain of inoculation (DPT 2). Although both infants showed interest before the inoculation and pain or physical distress immediately after, only infant HP-7 displayed brief expressions of sadness in between the pain and anger expressions. HP-7 also showed a brief sign of soothing, an expression of interest, toward the end of the episode. Infant HP-1 never displayed the sadness expression and showed no expression of interest or indication of soothing prior to the end of the episode.

Figure 5.8 presents the expressive responses of two female infants, one 7 and one 8 months of age, to their third DPT inoculation. The differences between the two infants are quite striking. Infant 071 appeared to be minimally affected by the inoculation, as evidenced by the amount of time she spent expressing negative affects. She had a relatively short latency to soothe and show interest and expressed joy at the end of the episode. Infant 079 expressed negative affects throughout the episode, thus showing a relatively long latency to soothe and show interest.

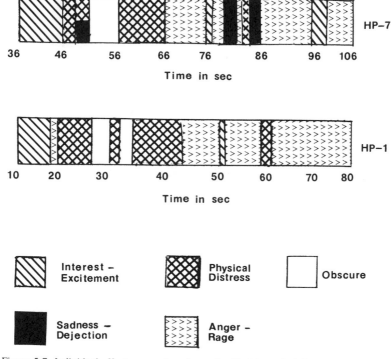

Figure 5.7. Individual affectograms: two 4-month-old white male infants' affect expressions in response to the acute pain of inoculation

Once an affectogram is drawn, an affect index (*AI*) can be easily computed for total positive affect expressed, total negative affect expressed, and each discrete affect expressed.

$$AI = \frac{\text{Time the affect was expressed during the episode}}{\text{Total time in episode that face was codable}}$$

Thus an *AI*, which can range in value from .0 to 1.0, is the proportion of time that a particular affect or pattern of affects is expressed during a given episode. For example, in Figure 5.8 *AI* for negative affect (NA) and the positive emotions of interest (IE) and joy (EJ) was:

Infant 071:

$$AI_{NA} = \frac{31.0}{41.0} = 0.756$$

$$AI_{IE} = \frac{10.0}{41.0} = 0.244$$

$$AI_{EJ} = \frac{0}{41.0} = 0.0$$

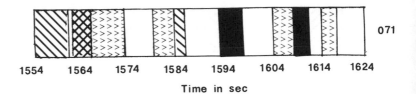

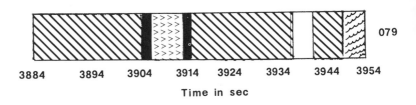

Figure 5.8. Individual affectograms: affect expressions of a 6- and a 7-month-old white female infant in response to the acute pain of inoculation

Infant 079:

$$AI_{NA} = \frac{9.5}{66.0} = 0.144$$

$$AI_{IE} = \frac{51.5}{66.0} = 0.780$$

$$AI_{EJ} = \frac{5.0}{66.0} = 0.076$$

Individual affectograms can aid in exploring the data record for stable relationships between stimulus events and patterns of emotion expressions. The visual format of the affectogram facilitates data analysis during the search for reliable, recurrent patterns of emotion expressions within an individual across events and over time or for similar patterns of facial expressions among a group of infants experiencing similar events. Affectograms can be useful in testing theory-based hypotheses as well as in generating and testing new hypotheses.

Mother

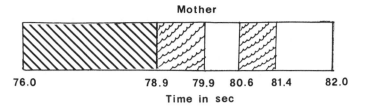

76.0   78.9   79.9 80.6 81.4   82.0

Time in sec

Infant

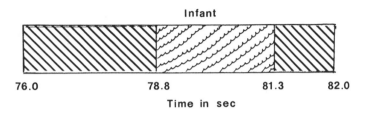

76.0   78.8   81.3   82.0

Time in sec

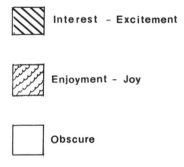

Interest – Excitement

Enjoyment – Joy

Obscure

Figure 5.9. Dyadic affectogram: play episode between a mother and her 9-month-old infant

Dyadic affectograms. The value of constructing a dyadic affectogram (DA) is that it operationalizes the concept of emotion congruence. An emotion congruence index (ECI) that shows the amount of dyadic co-occurrence of the different emotion expressions enables an investigator to study the effects of congruent and incongruent emotion-expressive behavior between mother and infant (or any pair of individuals).

An example of a dyadic affectogram is illustrated in Figure 5.9. During the play episode between the mother and infant in Figure 5.9 the emotion expressions of interest and joy were exhibited. In this dyad an interest expression by the infant was more likely to co-occur with an interest expression by the mother than with a joy expression.

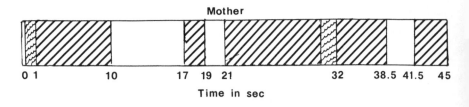

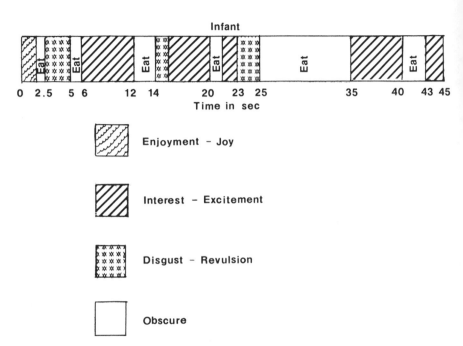

Figure 5.10. Dyadic affectogram: feeding sequence between a mother and her 9-month-old infant.

Figure 5.10 illustrates a feeding episode between the mother and infant. The emotion expressions of interest, joy, and disgust were identified. As in Figure 5.9, an interest expression from the infant was most likely to co-occur with an interest expression from the mother. The infant's expression of disgust also co-occurred with an expression of interest from the mother. The expression of joy from the infant was more likely to co-occur with a joy expression from the mother than with any other expression observed.

Once a DA has been drawn, ECIs can be readily computed:

$$ECI = \frac{\text{Time of emotion expression co-occurrence}}{\text{Total time in episode when faces were codable}}$$

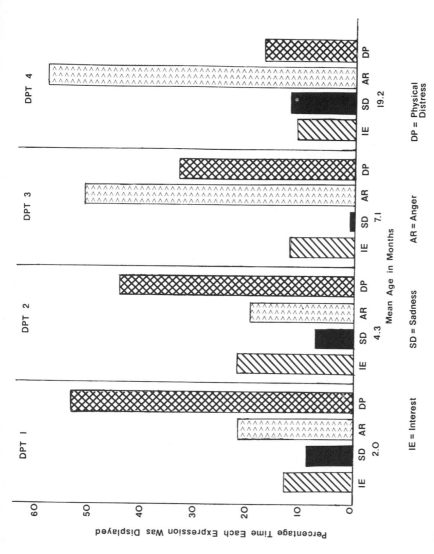

Figure 5.11. Mean percentage of soothing time for the expression of each emotion during period from needle penetration to soothing ($N = 36$, N per group = 9).

Thus *ECI* is expressed as proportions that vary from 0 to 1. In Figure 5.10 the *ECI* for all emotions expressed during the entire episode was .272. This *ECI* represents the proportion of the total time in the episode that the members of the dyad (mother and infant) were expressing the same emotion. *ECI* for each discrete emotion was: interest .255, joy .017, disgust .000.

Group affectograms. Figure 5.11 presents an example of a group affectogram (GA) based on cross-sectional data from four age groups. This affectogram shows developmental changes in facial expressions of emotions in response to trauma (pain of inoculation). Each emotion expression is represented as a mean percentage of total soothing time (defined as period elapsed from needle penetration to 5 consecutive seconds of positive emotion expression). The most striking feature of this graph shows a regular decrease of the physical distress expression with age, and a corresponding increase of anger expression. Sadness decreases with age until the fourth and oldest age group, where it reaches an overall peak. The expression of sadness has been hypothesized to elicit empathy or prosocial behavior (in this case acting as a "help" signal to the caregiver).

Concluding comments

Max and Affex are relatively new systems, and it is still early to judge their ultimate value for studying emotions in human development. In the few studies that have been completed, the reliability and validity of the two systems appear satisfactory.

The two systems were specially developed for research with infants and children, and all the illustrative material consists of spontaneous expressions from these age groups. Judging from the comparability of the facial movement capability of infants and adults and the agreement between results from Max and Affex, the two systems can be used with adolescents and adults, with allowance made for the increasing tendency for furrows and ridges to replace dimples and bulges as age increases. The basic anatomy of the face as it relates to facial patterning capability does not change after birth, and the spontaneous expressions of the fundamental emotions are essentially invariant over the life span.

References

Blurton Jones, N. G. Criteria for use in describing facial expressions of children. *Human Biology*, 1971, *43*, 365–413.

Brannigan, C. R., & Humphries, D. A. Human non-verbal behavior, a means of communication. In N. B. Jones (Ed.), *Ethological studies of child behavior*. Cambridge, England: Cambridge University Press, 1972.

Craig, K. D. Social modeling influences on pain. In R. A. Sternbach (Ed.), *The psychology of pain.* New York: Raven Press, 1978.

Darwin, C. R. *The expression of the emotions in man and animals.* London: John Murray, 1872.

Darwin, C. R. A biographical sketch of an infant. *Mind,* 1877, *2,* 285–294.

Eibl-Eibesfeldt, I. *Love and hate: On the natural history of behavior patterns.* New York: Holt, Rinehart, & Winston, 1971.

Ekman, P. Personal communication, April 27, 1981.

Ekman, P., & Friesen, W. V. *Unmasking the face.* Englewood Cliffs, N.J.: Prentice- Hall, 1975.

Ekman, P., & Friesen, W. V. Measuring facial movement. *Environmental Psychology and Nonverbal Behavior,* 1976, *1*(1), 56–75.

Ekman, P., & Friesen, W. V. *The Facial Action Coding System (FACS).* Palo Alto, Calif.: Consulting Psychologists Press, 1978.

Ekman, P., Friesen, W. V., & Ellsworth, P. *Emotion in the human face: Guidelines for research and an integration of findings.* New York: Pergamon Press, 1972.

Ekman, P., Friesen, W. V., & Tomkins, S. S. *The Facial Affect Scoring Technique (FAST).* Palo Alto, Calif.: Consulting Psychologists Press, 1971.

Ekman, P., Sorenson, E. R., & Friesen, W. V. Pan-cultural elements in facial displays of emotions. *Science,* 1969, *164,* 86–8.

Emde, R. N., Gaensbauer, T., & Harmon, R. J. *Emotional expression in infancy: A biobehavioral study.* New York: International Universities Press, 1976.

Gergerian, E., & Ermiane, R. *Atlas of facial expressions.* Paris: La Pensée Universalle, 1978.

Grant, E. C. Facial expressions and gestures. *Journal of Psychosomatic Research,* 1971, *15,* 391–4.

Hass, H. *The human animal: The mystery of man's behavior.* New York: Putnam, 1970.

Izard, C. E. *The face of emotion.* New York: Appleton-Century-Crofts, 1971.

Izard, C. E. *Human emotions.* New York: Plenum Press, 1977.

Izard, C. E. On the development of emotions and emotion-cognition relationships in infancy. In M. Lewis & L. A. Rosenblum (Eds.), *The development of affect.* New York: Plenum Press, 1978.

Izard, C. E. *The Maximally Discriminative Facial Movement Coding System (Max).* Newark: Instructional Resources Center, University of Delaware, 1979.

Izard, C. E., & Dougherty, L. M. *A System for Identifying Affect Expressions by Holistic Judgments (Affex).* Newark: Instructional Resources Center, University of Delaware, 1980.

Izard, C. E., Dougherty, L. M., Coss, C. L., & Hembree, E. A. *Age-related and individual differences in infants' facial expressions following acute pain.* Unpublished manuscript, 1980.

Izard, C. E., Huebner, R. R., Risser, D., McGinnes, G., & Dougherty, L. M. The young infant's ability to produce discrete emotion expressions. *Developmental Psychology,* 1980, *16*(2), 132–40.

Kagan, J. On emotion and its development: A working paper. In M. Lewis & L. A. Rosenblum (Eds.), *The development of affect.* New York: Plenum Press, 1978.

McGrew, W. C. *An ethological study of children's behavior.* New York: Academic Press, 1972.

Nevrovich, A. Personal communication, November 1974.

Oster, H. Facial expression and affect development. In M. Lewis & L. A. Rosenblum (Eds.), *The development of affect.* New York: Plenum Press, 1978.

Oster, H., & Ekman, P. Facial behavior in child development. In W. A. Collins (Ed.), *Minnesota Symposia on Child Psychology* (Vol. 11). Hillsdale, N.J.: Erlbaum, 1977.

Parisi, S. *Five-, seven-, and nine-month old infants' facial responses to 20 stimulus situations.* Unpublished master's thesis, Vanderbilt University, 1977.

Prkachin, K. M. *Interpersonal influences of pain expressions.* Unpublished doctoral dissertation, University of British Columbia, 1978.

Shiller, V. M. & Izard, C. E. *Patterns of emotion expressions during separation.* Unpublished manuscript, 1980.

Schlosberg, H. S. A scale for the judgment of facial expressions. *Journal of Experimental Psychology*, 1941, *29*, 497–510.

Schlosberg, H. S. The description of facial expressions in terms of two dimensions. *Journal of Experimental Psychology*, 1952, *44*, 229–37.

Schlosberg, H. S. Three dimensions of emotion. *Psychological Review*, 1954, *61*, 81–8.

Spitz, R. A. *The first year of life*. New York: International Universities Press, 1965.

Sroufe, A. L. Socioemotional development. In J. D. Osofsky (Ed.), *Handbook of infant development*. New York: Wiley, 1979, 462–516.

Stechler, G., & Carpenter, G. A viewpoint on early affective development. In J. Hellmuth (Ed.), *The exceptional infant* (Vol. 1). Seattle, Wash.: Special Child Publications, 1967.

Sternbach, R. A. (Ed.), *The psychology of pain*. New York: Raven Press, 1978.

Tomkins, S. S. *Affect, imagery, consciousness: Vol. 1. The positive affects*. New York: Springer, 1962.

Tomkins, S. S. *Affect, imagery, consciousness: Vol. 2. The negative affects*. New York: Springer, 1963.

Tomkins, S. S., & McCarter, R. What and where are the primary affects? Some evidence for a theory. *Perceptual and Motor Skills*, 1964, *18*, 119–58.

Yorczower, M., & Kocs, N. *A comparison of Max and FACS*. Unpublished manuscript, Bryn Mawr College, 1980.

Young, G. & Décarie, T. G. An ethology-based catalogue of facial–vocal behaviour in infancy. *Animal Behavior*, 1977, *25*, 95–107.

Zahn-Waxler, C., Radke-Yarrow, M., & King, R. A. Child rearing and children's prosocial initiations toward victims of distress. *Child Development*, 1979, *50*, 319–30.

6   The assessment of vocal expression in infants and children

Klaus R. Scherer

The phylogeny and ontogeny of affect vocalizations

Charles Darwin, whose detailed descriptions of affective expression in animals and man have pioneered the systematic assessment of emotional states, believed that vocal sounds were originally the results of involuntary and purposeless contractions of the muscles of the chest and glottis accompanying emotional excitement. He held that in the course of evolution these sounds have come to serve a number of different functions, including communication. Darwin concludes: "Hence it follows that the voice, from having been habitually employed as a serviceable aid under certain conditions, inducing pleasure, pain, rage, etc., is commonly used whenever the same sensations or emotions are excited, under quite different conditions, or in a lesser degree" (1872/1965, p. 84).

Our everyday experience of animals and men emoting around us confirms the pervasiveness of affect vocalizations: Emotional expression is rarely silent unless there are strong sociocultural or situational norms prohibiting the emission of affective vocal sounds. This is most conspicuous in nonverbal organisms such as animals and infants, who have not yet learned to turn vocalization on and off in the service of information transmission via speech and who are unaffected by cultural rules regarding display. Darwin claimed that even animals that are usually silent, such as rabbits, use the vocal organs under conditions of extreme arousal, for example, in distress (Darwin, 1872/1965, p. 83). For more vocal species, such as primates, there is evidence that most emotional states expressed in visual displays are also accompanied by vocalizations (Chevalier-Skolnikoff, 1973; Marler & Tenaza, 1977). The frequency and persistence of emotional vocalization of infants is well known to (and not always fondly remembered by) most parents. But even well-socialized adults can be heard to utter affective

The author gratefully acknowledges suggestions by Ursula Scherer, Reiner Standke, and an anonymous reviewer but accepts, of course, responsibility for any shortcomings remaining in the manuscript. Limitations of space make it impossible to deal with many technical issues in acoustics in sufficient detail, and the reader is urged to consult the specialized references given throughout the text.

vocalizations. Green (1975), who studied the vocalizations of Japanese monkeys (*Macaca fuscata*) remarks:

Humans also employ roars, cries, shrieks, screams, screeches and a variety of other sounds. These sounds are not only acoustically homologous with those described here for the Japanese monkey, but they are also used in analogous situations by primates with similar inferred internal states. Roars are used by enraged people, cries by babies abandoned or otherwise distressed, screeches in tantrums of youngsters and whines as they reach the comfort of the mother's embrace. Shrieks and screeches are employed in stressful situations and screams are used by the victims of aggression. [p. 95]

Given the nature of emotion as an emergency reaction of the organism with strong motivational and action preparatory components, it is not surprising that powerful signaling mechanisms have developed in socially living species to allow the prediction of probable behavioral reactions. Because vocal signals carried in the auditory channel of communication are particularly suitable for signal transmission over distances and in conditions of poor visibility, one would expect strong selective pressures to have operated on the vocal expression of emotion to adjust to the needs of impression (perception and inference) in the service of social communication (see Leyhausen, 1967). Consequently, this important communicative function has to be kept in mind during study of the relationships between emotional arousal and vocalization. Yet in spite of evolutionary pressures on the adaptation of emotional vocalization for communicative purposes, affect vocalizations may still serve intraorganismic functions. At least some of our emotional sounds seem to be by-products of adaptive physiological responses, mostly in relation to respiration, such as deep inhalation when we experience surprise or fear. Other vocal effects of emotional arousal may be due to the specific tension level of the musculature in the vocal organs under different emotional states. Finally, the vocal expression of emotion could have important psychological functions in modulating arousal and affecting subjective awareness of an emotion. The vocal expression of affect may be an important mechanism in affect management. Tomkins (1962) states: "To the extent to which speech itself becomes inhibited as a communicator of affect, affect inhibition is radically increased. Dull, lifeless speech is not only a symptom of affect inhibition but also a major cause of the deepening of the disorder" (p. 441).

Thus affect vocalizations can be regarded as concomitants of emotional arousal (particularly in terms of the forceful exhalation and inhalation of air) that have attained important social signaling functions in the course of evolution as well as acquiring, at least in humans, affect modulation and sensory feedback functions. The nature of this vocal affect expression system is not well known at present. We do not know, for example, whether there is a repertoire of discrete vocalization types indicative of a small number of specific emotions, comparable to the call systems in animals. Some of the vocalization labels in the lexicon of our language, such as the roar, gasp, shriek, and scream, seem to suggest that there are distinct types or categories for such vocalizations, and we also seem to have a fairly good idea which emotions they generally represent. Still, we do not know whether sounds labeled by such terms are in fact reliably emitted under certain emotional conditions and whether they share common acoustic parameters. Even the affect vocalization repertoire of monkeys and apes is highly complex, with many intermediate gradations between call types (cf. Green, 1975; Jürgens, 1979; Marler & Tenaza, 1977), so it is unlikely that we would find a small number of discrete types. This is particularly true because one of the major advantages of the nonverbal, or analog, system of communication is that it allows continuous encoding of degrees of intensity or other dimensions (see Scherer, 1980).

Furthermore, the development of language and speech has strongly affected the nature of human vocalizing under conditions of emotional arousal. It has often been pointed out (Kainz, 1962; Wundt, 1900) that with the development of cognition, language, and culture, primitive reflexlike affect vocalizations have come increasingly under conscious control and under the influence of linguistic and social norms. These ritualized and conventionalized interjections or vocal emblems and their role in emotional expression are not yet well explored (see Scherer, 1977). As I have already noted, the development of speech has had the most powerful and pervasive impact on the human use of the vocal organs. Because speech often serves as a vehicle for affect expression, it becomes difficult to disentangle the effects of emotional arousal, linguistic rules, and pragmatic speech norms on the nature of the speech signal.

The effect of emotions on the voice is not restricted to the utterance of such nonverbal exclamations. Emotions seem to act strongly on the vocal organs that are used to produce speech, and so it is not surprising that voice and speech patterns are strongly affected by emotional arousal. Common observation suggests that the manner of speech strongly reflects the emotional state of a speaker unless an extreme effort is made to mask such effects.

Although there has generally been much less work on the vocal correlates than on facial expression of emotion, the evidence presently available shows that many acoustic features of speech seem to be indicators of specific emotional states. In a comprehensive survey of the literature (Scherer, 1979a) evidence was presented to show that general affective arousal, such as that produced by stress or general activation, seems to result in a sizable increase in fundamental frequency (pitch) and in changes of the energy distribution in the spectrum (although there may be strong personality differences in the individual response patterns).

In this survey of the literature Scherer (1979a, pp. 508–16) summarizes 16 relevant studies on vocal correlates of discrete emotions. Despite enormous differences in design, methodology, and analysis techniques in the studies reviewed, the degree of convergence of the results on the patterns of vocal parameters characteristic for particular emotions is quite impressive.

Fundamental frequency, the variability or range of fundamental frequency, loudness, and tempo are important parameters linked to specific emotions. Table 6.1 (reprinted from Scherer, 1979a) shows the emerging pattern of results on the vocal correlates of differential emotions. Apart from the many question marks in the table indicating that the respective relationships have not yet been studied or that the results were inconclusive, it should be noted that only the emotions of anger and grief/sadness have been studied sufficiently often to allow adequate replication of the results. As seen from the table, anger seems to be characterized by high pitch level and wide pitch range, loud voice, and fast tempo, whereas the opposite ends of these vocal dimensions characterize grief/sadness: low pitch and narrow pitch range, downward pitch contour, soft voice, and slow tempo. To some extent these differences may be due to the differential amount of arousal or activation involved in the two emotions. It is unlikely, however, that vocal cues reflect only an underlying activation dimension; the emotional states of a speaker seem to be well communicated to listeners on the basis of vocal cues only.

The pattern of relationships shown in Table 6.1 seems to hold not only for objectively measured correlates of emotional speech but also for inferences of emotional states from content-masked speech samples. Table 6.2 (reprinted from Scherer & Oshinsky, 1977) lists the pattern of emotion inferences from various acoustic cues. This correspondence between externalization and inference (see Scherer, 1978) means that the communication of emotional states via acoustic patterns in speech tends to be quite effective, particularly because the vocal indicators of emotion seem to be very basic and robust (Scherer, Koivumaki, & Rosenthal, 1972). A recent review of the literature on the accuracy of emotion inferences from vocal cues (Scherer, 1981b) shows that judgments of vocally portrayed emotions are much more accurate than one would expect by chance and possibly even more accurate than judgments of emotions from facial expressions. A summary of the results of 28 studies on the accuracy of emotion recognition from the voice yields for accurate judgments an average of 60% (corrected for guessing). In general, negative emotions seem to be judged more accurately than positive emotions.

There is also evidence that more persistent moods may be expressed in vocal parameters. A review by Siegman (1978) on the vocal correlates of anxiety shows fairly strong relationships between anxiety and disfluencies in speech, particularly pausing. As I remarked in a review of personality markers in speech (Scherer, 1979b), it is difficult to judge whether the relationships found are based on biophysical factors, including emotional arousal or, at least to some extent, on self-presentation strategies of speakers.

Table 6.1. *Summary of results on vocal indicators of emotional states*

Emotion	Pitch level	Pitch range	Pitch variability	Loudness	Tempo
Happiness/joy	High	?	Large	Loud	Fast
Confidence	High	?	?	Loud	Fast
Anger	High	Wide	Large	Loud	Fast
Fear	High	Wide	Large	?	Fast
Indifference	Low	Narrow	Small	?	Fast
Contempt	Low	Wide	?	Loud	Slow
Boredom	Low	Narrow	?	Soft	Slow
Grief/sadness	Low	Narrow	Small	Soft	Slow
Evaluation	?	?	?	Loud	?
Activation	High	Wide	?	Loud	Fast
Potency	?	?	?	Loud	?

Source: Reprinted by permission from Scherer, 1979a, p. 513. © 1979 by Plenum Press.

Most work has been restricted to the analysis of speech and has been conducted with adult speakers. There is very little work on nonlinguistic emotional vocalization, which could be compared with infant vocalization, or on emotional speech in children. Even though there is a fairly extensive literature on infant vocalizations, particularly crying (see the section "Past Research and Issues for Investigation") emotional states have rarely been of central interest in this research. Studies on emotional speech in older children and young adolescents are almost nonexistent.

As in adult communication, the study of affect vocalizations has been a distant second to the study of facial expression in the area of emotional development. Apparently, the supposed dominance of the visual system over the auditory system, which is often cited in studies comparing communication channels, has had some impact on research decisions as well. Furthermore, the theory of emotion that has most influenced the study of emotional expression in adults, infants, and children (the differential emotions theory as proposed by Tomkins [1962, 1963] and elaborated by Ekman [1972] and Izard [1971]), has placed primary emphasis on the face as the site for the expression of affect, leaving little room for the voice. In addition, the fleeting nature of sounds, which cannot be captured as easily as facial expressions in photographs, as well as the fact that acoustic gestalts seem to be much less amenable to scientific description, seems to have discouraged the study of affect vocalizations. In addition, facial expression patterns can be directly traced to patterns of muscular innervation under the surface of the skin, whereas physiological structures and processes that determine the acoustic parameters in vocalizations are very complex and much less well known. Finally, whereas the study of human physiognomy and facial expression started as early, with the work of Duchenne (1862) and others, the objective

Table 6.2. *Acoustic parameters of tone sequences significantly contributing to the variance in attributions of emotional states*

Rating scale	Single acoustic parameters (main effects) and configurations (interaction effects) listed in order of predictive strength
Pleasantness	Fast tempo, few harmonics, large pitch variation, sharp envelope, low pitch level, pitch contour down, small amplitude variation (salient configuration: large pitch variation plus pitch contour up)
Activity	Fast tempo, high pitch level, many harmonics, large pitch variation, sharp envelope, small amplitude variation
Potency	Many harmonics, fast tempo, high pitch level, round envelope, pitch contour up (salient configurations: large amplitude variation plus high pitch level, high pitch level plus many harmonics)
Anger	Many harmonics, fast tempo, high pitch level, small pitch variation, pitch contours up (salient configuration: small pitch variation plus pitch contour up)
Boredom	Slow tempo, low pitch level, few harmonics, pitch contour down, round envelope, small pitch variation
Disgust	Many harmonics, small pitch variation, round envelope, slow tempo (salient configuration: small pitch variation plus pitch contour up)
Fear	Pitch contour up, fast sequence, many harmonics, high pitch level, round envelope, small pitch variation (salient configurations: small pitch variation plus pitch contour up, fast tempo plus many harmonics)
Happiness	Fast tempo, large pitch variation, sharp envelope, few harmonics, moderate amplitude variation (salient configurations: large pitch variation plus pitch contour up, fast tempo plus few harmonics)
Sadness	Slow tempo, low pitch level, few harmonics, round envelope, pitch contour down (salient configuration: low pitch level plus slow tempo)
Surprise	Fast tempo, high pitch level, pitch contour up, sharp envelope, many harmonics, large pitch variation (salient configuration: high pitch level plus fast tempo)

Source: Reprinted by permission from Scherer & Oshinsky, 1977, p. 340. © 1977 by Plenum Press.

analysis of vocal sounds has been developed much more recently. Although the study of facial expression is mainly oriented toward anatomy in terms of its underlying concepts and structures, the analysis of sounds depends on a number of disciplines (such as acoustics, mathematics, physiology, phonetics, and electrical engineering) for concepts and methods of study.

In spite of advances in all those disciplines in the first part of the century, the invention and the increasing use of the telephone has had the biggest impact on the development of appropriate methods for the objective analysis of vocal sounds. In the interest of limiting precious channel capacity in telephone lines, electrical engineers have attempted to isolate those parts of the speech signal required for the intelligibility of speech. One of the essential advances in this effort has been the development of equipment to make speech visible, the sound spectrograph, or sonagraph (see Potter, Kopp, & Green, 1947). With the advent of fast digital computers and the growing interest in automatic speech recognition and speech synthesis, further techniques have become available. The purpose of this chapter is to provide an overview of the acoustic parameters that play a major role in the objective analysis of human vocalizations, including speech, and the methods and techniques that are presently available to extract these features from speech signals.

Parameters for the acoustic analysis of human vocalization

The nature of voice production

Before we can turn to a detailed examination of the parameters that are available to describe the characteristics of different human vocalizations, it is necessary to review briefly the processes of voice production and the nature of the resulting sound (a more detailed treatment of this material can be found in Ladefoged, 1962; Lieberman, 1977; Minifie 1973; Zemlin, 1968). The sound waves that compose human vocalizations are produced by interruptions of an air stream that is pushed up and through the vocal tract during exhalation (egressive vocalization) or sucked in during inhalation (ingressive vocalization). The air particles are set in vibration, producing audible sound waves, when they encounter an obstacle that prevents them from freely passing through the tube-shaped vocal tract. The major obstacle for air pushed up from the lungs through the trachea during exhalation is the glottis if the vocal folds are closed (adducted). In this case the pressure of the air column below the glottis (subglottal pressure) rises, forcing the vocal folds to open. After a puff of air has escaped, a number of factors contribute to the closing of the vocal folds. This cycle is repeated, and the series of air puffs released by this vibratory action of the vocal folds (glottal pulses) are passed through the vocal tract and emerge at the mouth opening as a periodic sound wave. Sounds that are produced by the opening and closing of the vocal folds are called *voiced* sounds. If the vocal folds are permanently open during exhalation, the air can pass freely through the glottis but may encounter obstacles farther up in the vocal tract. For example, the air stream can be forced through a very small opening produced by a special configuration of the lip and teeth (as in the production of an /s/) or by the complete closure and sudden opening of the mouth (as in the production of /t/). In this case, the air particles are affected by turbulence, and the resulting sound waves are called *voiceless* or *unvoiced*. Although voiced vocalizations correspond to pure tones, unvoiced vocalizations are noiselike in character.

The characteristics of the sound waves radiated from the mouth opering are not only determined by the nature of the obstacle that interrupts the air stream but also by the general shape of the vocal tract, which changes continuously during speech. This is particularly true for voiced sounds. They are modified by the specific configuration of the vocal tract that serves as an acoustical filter. Thus, the sound waves that represent human vocalization have been shaped by, and thus carry information about, the state of the vocal apparatus and the phonation and articulation processes during this vocalization. To the extent to which emotional arousal affects the structures of the vocal apparatus and the processes involved in vocalization, for example by changing respiration patterns, increasing tension of the musculature, and so forth, such effects are reflected in specific characteristics of the sound waves resulting from emotional vocalizations.

In the following section we shall describe some of those parameters or features of sound waves that can be measured and used to recover information about the nature of the voice production and possible effects of emotional arousal. The acoustic analysis of sound waves required to obtain these parameters can be performed by machines using electroacoustic apparatus or digital computers or by human observers who use their auditory perception as well as their stored knowledge about the nature of sounds and their production. In the case of machine analysis, only objective, physical parameters of the sound waves are determined. From human observers one can obtain not only estimates of these physical characteristics but also direct inferences as to the nature of the voice production processes or even inferences as to the general state of the organism producing the vocalization. This chapter will deal primarily with the objective analysis of physical parameters of sound waves by machine. In addition, however, a short overview of various approaches to the auditory assessment of vocal parameters will be presented.

Objective measurement of acoustic parameters

Sound waves can be completely described by their characteristics in three dimensions or domains: the time domain, the frequency domain, and the amplitude domain. In each of these domains, a number of features, or parameters, can be assessed. In addition, combined parameters, consisting of features from two or more domains, can be constructed. In the following overview (which summarizes a more extensive treatment in Scherer, 1982), I shall describe different parameters for each domain separately. In this section, the parameters are described independent of specific methods for their assessment. Methods and apparatus available for the actual measurement of these parameters receive brief comment in the Appendix.

Time-domain parameters. The first decision to be made is how to segment the stream of events in the time domain into separate units for analysis. A convenient

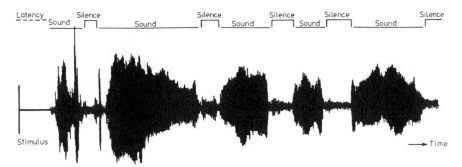

Figure 6.1. Display of the sound and silence sequences in the time signal for a series of infant cries

segmentation procedure for acoustic analysis is to identify units of sound between intervals of silence. (It should be noted, that in some kinds of analyses, e.g., pause extraction, units of silence are identified between intervals of sound. Thus the nature of the analysis determines the kind of unit chosen.) Figure 6.1 shows a plot of the time signal (display of the wave form) of a series of infant cries for which a segmentation into sound units with intervals of silence has been performed. It should be mentioned at this point that although the distinction between sound and silence seems theoretically easy to make, it may be quite difficult in practice. For very low sounds and under conditions of high background noise, it can be rather difficult to define the exact boundaries of a sound burst.

Once sound units have been segmented, a number of parameters can be obtained. The most important of these parameters include the number of occurrences and the duration of units, the duration of intervals between units, and the duration of latency times between a particular stimulus and the occurrence of the first unit. These parameters, displayed in Figure 6.1, are self-explanatory and need little further discussion. If many units are observed over a certain time interval, measures of central tendency and distribution can be obtained (e.g., mean and standard deviation or range of duration, etc.). Often attempts are made to identify higher-order units consisting of a number of lower-order units separated by intervals that are smaller than the intervals between higher-order units (e.g., bouts of crying in infants). In this case, segmentation rules have to be developed on the basis of certain conventions (e.g., Stark, Rose, & McLagen, 1975) or by sequence analysis (e.g., Fagen & Young, 1978).

The segmentation and measurement of units in the time domain becomes complicated when sound/silence events are to be determined for two interacting speakers. In addition to the occurrence, duration, and latency parameters described above, a number of additional categories involving co-occurrence of sounds and particular sequences can be determined (e.g., simultaneous speech, switching pauses, interruptions, etc.; see Feldstein & Welkowitz, 1978).

Occurrence and duration patterns of sound/silence sequences are of course indicative of the general vocalization activity of the organism and may be determined by many causes. In the case of spontaneous, involuntary vocalizations, as in infant cries or adult affect vocalization, the general state of the organism, for example, the degree of distress or exhaustion, may determine the neural control for the production of vocalizations, as well as the breathing and phonation patterns. In the case of purposive speech, vocalization factors such as problems with cognitive speech planning, articulation difficulties, and prosodic patterning may also affect sound/silence sequences. Furthermore, self-presentation and interpersonal accommodation may affect the distribution of a speaker's vocalization bursts in time. Although the mediating factors and mechanisms are largely a matter of conjecture, a large number of studies suggest that such time-dependent parameters of vocalizations seem to be consistently correlated with different emotional states and personality traits (Goldman-Eisler, 1968; Mahl & Schulze, 1964; Rochester, 1973; Siegman, 1978).

Frequency domain. Most sound waves consist of complex wave forms, that is, they are a composite of many simple sinusoidal wave forms. Using the Fourier theorem, each complex wave can be decomposed into its component sinusoidal waves. Each of these sinusoidal waves has a particular frequency, that is, number of complete cycles per time unit (usually measured in cycles per second, or Hertz, which is heard as pitch) and amplitude (which is heard as loudness). The components of a complex wave form are usually displayed in the spectrum, a frequency-by-amplitude plot, which shows the energy for each of the component sinusoidal wave forms at its respective frequency (see Figure 6.2). The spectrum is one of the most important prerequisites for most acoustic analyses, because it allows a comprehensive description of a complex wave form in terms of a relatively small number of energy values plotted against frequency.

Figure 6.2 shows the difference between voiced sounds, as in tonelike cries or vowels, and voiceless sounds, as in consonants. Voiced sounds have a harmonic structure, that is, they have component sinusoidal wave forms at specific multiples of the frequency of the slowest moving wave form, or fundamental frequency (F_0). These energy components are called the *harmonics* of the fundamental frequency. Voiceless sounds on the other hand have component wave forms at all possible frequencies, thus yielding a flat spectrum.

The fundamental frequency of voiced sounds, heard as pitch, is one of the most important acoustic parameters studied so far. It is dependent on a number of factors in the speech production process, but mostly on the tension of the laryngeal musculature and the subglottal pressure (which is a result of breathing).

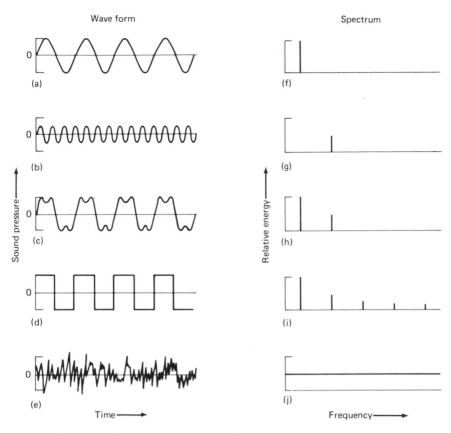

Figure 6.2. Different wave forms and their spectra: (a) low-frequency sine wave; (b) high-frequency sine wave; (c) complex wave form, composite of (a) and (b); (d) square wave; (e) noise (e.g. voiceless consonant) and (f)–(j), the corresponding spectra. *Source:* Scherer (1982).

Because both breathing patterns and muscular tension are heavily affected by emotional arousal, it is not surprising that many studies have found fundamental frequency to be one of the most important indicators of activation or arousal (Scherer, 1979a,b, 1981a).

Fundamental frequency changes continuously and thus can be plotted against time, yielding contours (pitch contours or intonation contours in speech). Figure 6.3 shows intonation contours for a pleading utterance of a small German girl asking for more cake. There is a series of fundamental frequency values for the voiced sections in each word. Linguists and psychologists agree that the shape of these contours carries important information on the emotional state of the speaker. As yet, however, there are no satisfactory procedures to quantify these

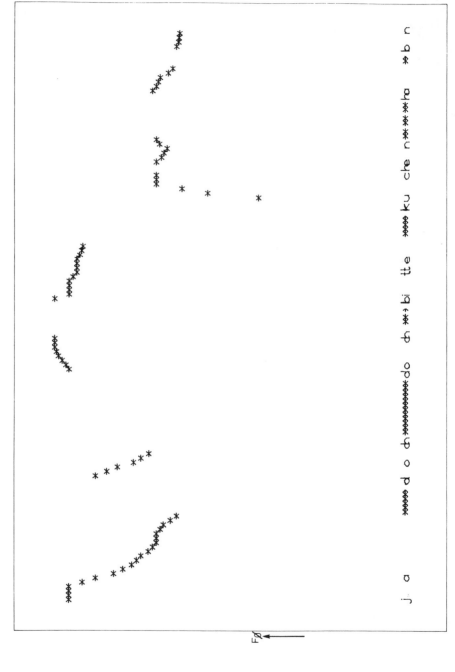

Time →

F∅

shapes to obtain parameters. Often, researchers attempt to determine patterns such as falling, rising, flat, or variable, but as Figure 6.3 shows, this may not be unambiguous, particularly if one attempts to describe contours for lengthy vocalizations. Stern has attempted to use standard types of intonation contours, such as the bell or the sinusoidal (Stern & Wassermann, 1979), but this may only be possible if one deals with fairly stereotypical utterances.

Although intonation contours in speech are fairly smooth and coherent in their change over time, an infant cry, for example, can show much more sudden changes of fundamental frequency. Such sudden changes in fundamental frequency, which cannot be accounted for by changes in the contour, have been called *pitch break, glide,* or *shift* (Stark et al., 1975; Wasz-Höckert et al., 1968). A number of measures of central tendency and variability can be obtained for the fundamental frequency values across a vocalization segment: maximum and minimum value of F_0, F_0 range, and F_0 variability (as standard deviation or percentile measure) have been most popular (for an interesting table of correlations between various different distribution measures, see Laufer & Horii, 1977, p. 176).

Amplitude domain. Although there are many other frequency parameters that can be measured in the spectrum, they cannot be determined without consideration of the energy distribution in the spectrum. Therefore, the amplitude domain will be described before dealing in more detail with parameters that depend on both frequency and amplitude (or energy).[1] Although the intensity of the sound may be an important indicator of the state of the sound producer, reflecting breathing patterns, vocal effort, and muscular tension, it is exceedingly difficult to measure accurately from tape recordings, because the acoustic energy stored on the tape is highly dependent on distance and position of the microphone and the gain setting of the recorder. Consequently, intensity parameters are often used only in terms of changes over time for sounds recorded under comparable conditions for the same speaker. If it can be assumed that recording conditions have been kept absolutely constant, it is possible to obtain measurements of amplitude change over time, which may well reflect information about emotional states. This parameter has not yet been well explored under systematic conditions, however. Of course, the same measures of central tendency and distribution that have been described for fundamental frequency can be used for these parameters.

Parameters based on frequency and amplitude. Most often the relative distribution of energy components in the frequency spectrum rather than the absolute energy of a sound wave is of interest. Such parameters generally consist of en-

Figure 6.3. Intonation contour for a short utterance spoken by a 3-year-old German girl ("Yes . . . I do . . . I do want some cake, please"). *Source:* Scherer (1982).

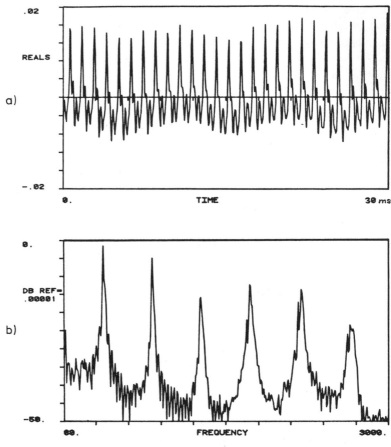

Figure 6.4. Characteristics of an infant cry in the frequency domain: (a) segment of the time signal, (b) fundamental frequency and five harmonics

ergy peaks at particular frequencies. Figure 6.4 shows the harmonics in the spectrum of an infant cry. Although the frequencies of the harmonics are multiples of the fundamental frequency, their respective energy values may be important parameters, because they reflect characteristics of phonation and of the vocal tract conditions, which might be affected by emotional states. For example, if the vocal apparatus is very tense as a result of a high degree of muscular tension, the upper harmonics have much more energy than they would, given a lax setting of the voice production structures. These different voice production settings are often called *tense voice* and *lax voice,* or *tense vs. lax vocalizations* (cf. Laver, 1975, 1980). As it is often impossible or impractical to determine the exact energy of the individual harmonics, it has been suggested that an index consisting of the proportion of energy in the lower part of the spectrum and the energy in the higher part of the spectrum should be computed. Although indexes of this kind have been used with some success as indicators of changes in emotional states (cf. Helfrich & Scherer, 1977; Scherer, 1979a), the location of the cutoff point to be chosen to separate the lower part from the upper part, for example, 500 or 1000 Hertz, has not yet been determined.

In general, the measurement of such proportions, or the measurement of energy values for fixed frequency bands such as half or third-octave bands, is used for long-term spectra. These are average spectra computed over a fairly lengthy vocalization period. This averaging means that characteristics of the individual vocalizations produced, such as specific vowels or consonants, are averaged out, which results in a spectrum that reflects more permanent characteristics of a speaker's voice. On the basis of such assumptions, long-term spectra have been used for speaker recognition purposes. It stands to reason, however, that different long-term spectra may be obtained for different emotional states of a speaker. As yet there has been little systematic research using long-term spectra as indicators of emotional states, although there have been some attempts to link the energy distribution in the spectrum to stress (Scherer, 1981a). Research is hampered by the fact that little is known about useful parameters for such long-term spectra. Except for the low/high frequency ratio or the energy values for frequency bands (see Figure 6.5a), little has been suggested. It may be useful to compute separate long-term spectra for voiced and unvoiced vocalizations.

There is one further set of parameters that can be obtained from spectral analysis of vocalizations, namely resonance characteristics of the vocal tract that serve to filter the glottal pulse produced by phonation. Depending on the particular articulatory setting in the vocal tract, for example, the position of the tongue and the opening of the mouth, the vocal tract will have different filter or transfer characteristics that affect the energy distribution in the spectrum by amplifying particular frequencies and attenuating others. The spectrum for the vowel /a/ is shown in Figure 6.5b displaying the first five formants produced by a particular articulatory setting for this vowel. Parameters that can be obtained are the frequency of the formants, the respective amplitude and the bandwidth, that is, the width of the peak at a particular location (cf. Markel & Gray, 1976). These parameters are dependent on a very complex change in the articulatory configuration during the speech process. Unfortunately, very little is known about the effects of emotions on the articulatory processes and the consequent effects on the formants. Some preliminary results (Scherer & Tolkmitt, 1979; Tolkmitt et al., in press) point to the potential usefulness of formant parameters as indicators of changes in emotional state. By comparison with more frequently used parameters such as fundamental frequency, however, the value of formant parameters is much less established.

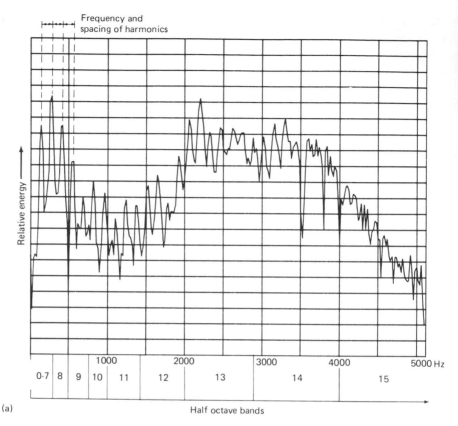

Figure 6.5. Spectra for the vowel [i:]: (a) spectrum showing harmonics and vocal tract resonances as well as half octave bands, (b) smoothed spectrum (vocal tract filter function) showing the formants. *Source:* Scherer (1982).

Auditory assessment

Following this introduction of parameters of the acoustic wave form that can be objectively assessed with the help of electroacoustic equipment or digital computer analysis, a short overview of parameters or variables that are measured with the help of human observers, both expert and lay persons, is appropriate. As in the assessment of objective acoustic parameters, the basis of human observer assessment is the acoustic speech wave form, as this is the input to human auditory perception (even though it may be supplemented at times by the observation of the externally visible correlates of speech production activity). Contrary to the objective measurements, which are restricted to characteristics of the acoustic speech wave form itself, auditory assessment often implies functional categorization of units, subjective evaluation of acoustic parameters, and infer-

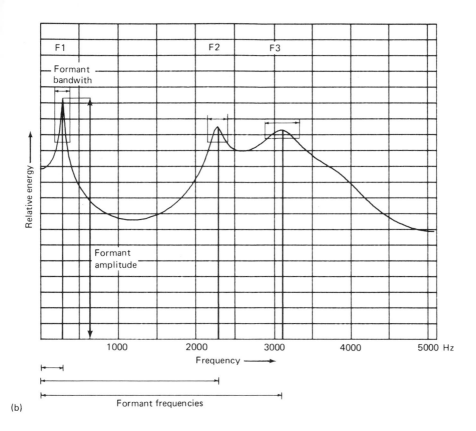

(b)

ences about the production process (phonation and articulation) as well as attributions of speaker states or traits. The variables and analysis procedures used in auditory assessment will now be briefly discussed according to these types.

Auditory assessment of objective acoustic parameters

Almost all of the objective parameters of an acoustic speech wave form that have been discussed above can be "heard" by judges and can consequently be assessed with the help of category systems and rating scales. For a number of reasons, however, these auditorily assessed variables do not necessarily correlate very highly with objectively measured variables of the same acoustic parameters. Reasons include the characteristics of the human hearing system, which does not function like a filter bank analyzer or a digital computer, and expectations and auditory habits, often based on certain aspects of a language and/or cultural norms, which make it difficult to translate an auditory impression into a quantitative judgment on a scale. Thus, both the perception of F_0 (pitch) and intensity (loudness) are affected by the energy distribution in the spectrum (cf. Laver, 1975, p. 258; Lehiste, 1970, pp. 113–20).

Experts trained in acoustics and phonetics are of course able to take such factors into account and to estimate acoustic parameters more accurately than lay persons. Still, even such experts would rarely attempt to make fine-grained distinctions between different levels of acoustic parameters without the help of machine analysis of some kind. The fact that experts can achieve good agreement among themselves in rank ordering a group of speakers on different parameters such as pitch and loudness does not imply that their consensual judgment accurately reflects the parametric value of the feature under investigation (see Scherer, 1974).

Some of the auditory coding schemes that have been proposed for the analysis of paralinguistic or prosodic aspects of speech (e.g. Markel, Meisels, & Houck, 1964; Trager & Smith, 1957) rely on experts or trained coders to determine different levels of pitch, loudness, and other paralinguistic variables. Among the major drawbacks of these schemes (cf. Crystal & Quirk, 1964, pp. 21–23; Dittmann & Wynne, 1961) is the assumption of a standard or modal level for different parameters that can be used to determine deviations (e.g. overhigh, oversoft). Apart from the fact that such modal patterns vary strongly between cultures, dialects, or even subgroups within a speech community, it would be difficult to adjust the expected modal pattern for different age groups of infants and children for whom voice characteristics change very rapidly.

Assessment of speech production via auditory perception

In many cases attempts are made to infer characteristics of the voice and speech production process, in terms of phonation and articulation, on the basis of acoustic characteristics of speech. To some extent, this is implied in some of the rating categories that are sometimes used with naive raters, such as harsh, strident, nasal, throaty, and so forth. In such cases, the labels employed for the rating scales imply particular types of phonation or articulation (e.g., clipped or slurred) that are presumably clearly related to the listener's auditory impression. The assumption that a particular production process can be inferred if a voice sample is consensually placed into a certain category by naive judges may not be realistic, however. For example, even if naive judges agree that a particular voice sounds breathy, this may not correspond to the actual phonation used by the speaker. The impression may be produced by factors other than the incomplete closure of the glottis during phonation (the technical definition of breathiness).

Again, trained experts such as voice scientists and phoneticians are much better able to infer the nature of the production processes on the basis of acoustic patterns. This may be due to the fact that they have frequently attempted to produce certain sound patterns themselves while trying to control the phonation and articulation apparatus and have observed the resulting acoustic patterns. Often, speech scientists use spectrogram recordings to analyze the sounds in addition to auditory evaluation, making use of available research evidence on the effects of particular voice production mechanisms on the energy distribution in the spectrum (cf. Williams & Stevens, 1972). In the analysis of infant vocalizations, satisfactory reliability has been reported for the judgment of vocalization modes such as vocal tenseness, nasality, or breathiness by observers using spectrographic records (Stark et al., 1975; Wasz-Höckert et al., 1968).

Laver (1975, 1980) has developed an extensive descriptive system for different voice qualities in which he specifies different phonatory and articulatory settings and describes the associated acoustic parameters. This system can be used by trained judges to infer the nature of the phonation and articulation processes.

Subjective impressions of voice and speech

Although subjective ratings of lay judges may not be appropriate as a substitute for objective acoustic analysis, they may be important in their own right if one is interested in the perception of voice and speech and the inferences made on this basis by lay persons. Scherer (1978) has proposed a modification of the Brunswikian lens model to study the inferences of emotion and personality from voice and speech. In this model, the proximal cues of the speaker's voice, that is, the perceptual representation of the distal voice cues, play an important role in understanding the nature of the inferences or attributions made on the basis of such impressions. As we have seen above, the relationship between the distal cues of a voice, that is, the objective acoustic parameters, and the proximal cues, that is, the subjectively perceived correlates, may be highly complex. Consequently, in order to understand the process of inferring emotion from voice and speech fully, the nature of the representation of the objective acoustic parameters in the listener has to be studied in detail. For such purposes, it is important to use lay judgments of voice quality, employing acoustic labels as they are used in everyday descriptions of voice and speech. Lists of such labels as well as a discussion of underlying factors and agreement between judges in applying them to voices are presented elsewhere (Scherer, 1982, pp. 171–5).

Attributions of underlying speaker states

One of the most frequent uses of listeners to evaluate speech or other vocalizations is to assess their inferences and attributions concerning the underlying states or traits of the speaker. Generally, these assessments are not used to obtain parameters for the description of speech patterns. In some cases, however, the ability of listeners to make judgments about underlying speaker states or functions of particular vocalization units is used to obtain such parameters. One prime example is the use of trained coders to assess the number of hesitation pauses in speech. Obviously, these coders do not, like an automatic detection device, merely differentiate between sound and silence but have to make functional and inferential assumptions about the significance of a particular silent portion in fluent speech. A comparison of automatically extracted silent portions and coder-counted silent pauses shows that there are large discrepancies (see Scherer, 1979b). This is not surprising, for coders will disregard many silent portions in locations where they would be expected on the basis of speech articulation processes (such as a change in articulatory setting from one consonant to the next) or because of the syntactic structure of a sentence (such as juncture pauses between clauses). Thus coders trying to detect different kinds of pauses make assumptions about the underlying determinants of speaker pausing. Judgments of this sort are very difficult because the interference of speech content is very strong. Very often one coder will hear a hesitation pause preceding a word, whereas another coder will perceive it as following the word. Only after lengthy training and joint listening can agreement on the location and duration of such hesitation pauses be obtained. Consequently it is most important to train coders carefully for coding tasks in which functional interpretations have to be made and to assess their reliability. Both of these procedures are frequently regarded as unnecessary by researchers who tend to think that anyone can recognize a pause.

Analysis of infant vocalizations

Some methodological concerns

Most of the parameters and assessment techniques just discussed have been developed for the analysis of adult speech. It has become evident during this discussion that many of these parameters are strongly linked to the articulation of speech sounds. Consequently, it is not a forgone conclusion that all of these techniques can be profitably and legitimately applied to the analysis of nonspeech infant vocalization. Crystal (1973), in an extensive, well-reasoned discussion of this issue, has rejected the use of phonetic or phonological categories (cf. Irwin & Chen, 1943) for the analysis of prespeech infant vocalizations. He argues that only objective acoustic analysis can provide an unbiased approach to the study of the characteristics of sound making by infants, thus avoiding the danger of imposing linguistic criteria upon nonlinguistic material. This danger seems inherent in many of the auditory assessment procedures used to describe infant sounds, for example, in a segmental approach as in Irwin (1941; Irwin & Chen, 1943), as well as in a highly subjective, impressionistic evaluation, as in Tischler (1957), and possibly even in attempts to infer the phonatory or articulatory bases of infant vocalizations (cf. Partanen et al., 1967; Wasz-Höckert et al., 1968).

The widespread use of the spectrograph in studies on infant vocalization shows the general acceptance of the need for objective acoustic analysis of infant sounds. Although the spectrograph provides an impartial white-gray-and-black record of the energy of various frequency components in vocalizations, the tradition of reading spectrograms is, however, highly influenced by the analysis of speech. In addition, spectrograms are not easily quantified, and consequently the appropriate interpretation of spectrogram records is beginning to seem an art rather than reliable measurement. It is not surprising that spectrograms of infant vocalizations are reproduced in many studies without being properly analyzed. The appeal of a visual representation of fleeting auditory events seems to render quantitative analysis unnecessary. For example, in a classic review of infant vocalizations by Wolff (1969), some of the distinctions made are illustrated by spectrograms, but the features that supposedly differentiate among the cries in terms of their representation in the spectrogram are hardly explained in detail. Somewhat more detailed discussions of relevant parameters in spectrograms can be found in the work of Truby and Lind (1965) and Wasz-Höckert and her collaborators (1968). In many cases, however, the interpretations of these parameters are highly qualitative and are often based on interpretations concerning phonatory and articulatory processes.

In many cases, relying on such interpretations may be dangerous, as the neonatal vocal apparatus is rather different from a fully developed adult human vocal tract. Lieberman et al. (1971) have shown that the vocalizations of infants may be closer to the sounds of nonhuman primates than to human speech. This seems to be due to the fact that newborn infants, just like nonhuman primates, are hardly capable of varying the shape of their vocal tract and produce vocalizations with a fairly uniform vocal tract configuration. Because of this uniformity of the vocal tract shape, resonances or formants are often found only at the natural resonance points of this type of acoustic tube (at 1.1, 3.3, and 5.5 kHz, according to Lieberman et al., 1971, p. 719). Because of the high fundamental frequency of most infant cries (generally between 300 and 400 Hz) their acoustic spectrum often consists mainly of the harmonics of the fundamental (see the section "Objective Measurement of Acoustic Parameters" for discussion of spacing of harmonics and formant location; Figure 6.4 showed an example of an infant's cry spectrum that was dominated by harmonic peaks). Because it is difficult to distinguish between harmonic peaks and formants, it seems advisable to avoid the use of the term *formant* for amplitude peaks in the spectra of infant vocalizations unless it can be safely determined that a peak is not exclusively due to the harmonic structure. Unfortunately, *formant* is used somewhat indiscriminately in the literature (see Sedlackova, 1967).

Even though quite a large number of infant studies use acoustic analysis methods, we still lack normative data on the acoustic nature of infant vocalizations and changes in the course of development. This is particularly true for vocalizations in early infancy that are not cries; these have very rarely been studied (with the exception of the work of Laufer & Horii, 1977; Stark, 1978, and a few others). Furthermore, apart from illustrations with spectrograms, frequency and duration of cries as well as fundamental frequency have been the preferred parameters for study (Delack & Fowlow, 1978; Fairbanks, 1942; Laufer & Horii, 1977; Prechtl et al., 1969; Prescott, 1975). This restriction is partly due to the ease of extraction of certain parameters as well as the availability of certain analysis equipment. It is to be hoped that with the increasingly widespread availability of digital analysis procedures, more parameters will be assessed for more vocalization samples in different age groups for many different infant populations. In general, all of the parameters described above can be used – with some modification – in the analysis of infant vocalization (with the possible exception of formants).

Past research and issues for investigation

Many of the studies on infant vocalizations have been concerned with the stimulus conditions that elicit distress sounds, particularly crying, and have attempted to determine the frequency, duration, and temporal structure (cf. Aldrich et al., 1945; Bayley, 1932; Fisichelli, Karelitz, & Haber, 1969; Irwin & Weiss, 1943; Keitel, Cohn, & Harnish, 1960; Tischler, 1957) as well as the acoustic structure of the cries emitted under these conditions (Fairbanks, 1942; Lester, 1978; Truby & Lind, 1965; Wasz-Höckert et al., 1968; Wolff, 1969). Although it seems reasonable to assume that the conditions studied, such as hunger, pain, and other distress stimuli, are related to the emotional state of the infant, a direct link to an independent assessment of emotional state, such as analysis of facial expression, has not yet been made.

Studies of the ontogenetic development of affect vocalization may help to throw light on the complex interrelationships between physiological, psychological, and cultural functions. As the work on emotional development shows, there seems to be an increasing differentiation of the infant's emotions with progress in physiological and cognitive maturation as well as in the increasing involvement with the environment and the caregiver (Izard, 1978; Lewis & Brooks, 1978; Sroufe, 1979). The study of concomitant changes in affective vocalizations may help to pinpoint the role of undifferentiated arousal and of specific differential emotions as they unfold in determining the nature of emotional sound. In terms of the theories on the differentiation of emotions in the course of development it would seem necessary to attempt to assess the emotional state of the infant independent of particular stimulus conditions, as the cognitive and social development of the infant may strongly affect his or her reaction to outside stimulation. It has been repeatedly pointed out (Crystal, 1973; Wolff, 1969) that the danger of reading something into an infant's cry if one knows something about the situational context (e.g., whether it is feeding time or not) is rather great. A few studies show that observers, and even the mother of the infant herself, cannot reliably judge the infant's state at the time of a particular cry if they are blind to the situation in which it was uttered (cf. Müller, Hollien, & Murry, 1974; Sherman, 1927). The question of whether early infant vocalizations can be differentiated according to different states, such as pain or hunger, as many mothers will have us believe, needs to be further investigated, however. This is not only a question of practical interest; it is also most decisive in terms of the onset of differentiation between different types of emotional states. It would be useful to conduct a systematic study with babies of different ages in which underlying states and vocalizations are assessed as carefully as possible and in which acoustic analyses are combined with judgments by mothers and other persons as to the infant's state.

At present we know very little about the relationship between differential emotional states and acoustic parameters of infant vocalization, except for the very general relationship between distress and crying. It is very difficult to trace the differentiation of emotion in the development of infant vocalizations because there is no direct homology with adult expressions as in facial expression. Still, it is certainly possible to improve the present state of the art. Two approaches seem particularly promising. First, renewed efforts have to be made to get beyond the functional descriptive typologies of different classes of sounds. Such typologies, as proposed by Truby and Lind (1965), Sedlackova (1967), Wolff (1969), and Wasz-Höckert et al. (1968), although based in part on the examination of spectrograms, do not specify critical differences of the major parameters in quantitative terms (although efforts in this direction have been made by Wasz-Höckert and her collaborators, 1968, and others). Consequently, one of the major tasks for the future will be to develop classification procedures based on objectively measured quantitative parameters. It is particularly important to determine whether parameters in infant vocalizations vary with the intensity of the distress or the emotion experienced, whether there are continua along which many of these parameters move or whether there are distinct classes or types of vocalizations associated with specific situations or emotional states. Some of the studies on animal communication may provide interesting models for the approach that could be taken (cf. Marler & Tenaza, 1977; Green, 1975; Jürgens,

1979), particularly if one assumes some degree of evolutionary continuity in affect vocalization (cf. Scherer, 1979a, 1981b; Tembrock, 1977).

Second, by comparing the differentiation of affect vocalization patterns with concomitant developmental changes in other affect expression systems such as facial and postural expression, it may be possible to study the coordination between affect systems and the patterns of mutual influence. For example, to what extent does the ability to produce facial expressions of differential emotions (possibly due to the maturation of innate neuromuscular patterns at certain stages of the development process, cf. Ekman & Oster, 1979; Izard, 1978) influence the acoustic structure of affect vocalizations? The different patterns of muscular tension around the mouth and different degrees of mouth opening in facial expressions can be expected to change the acoustic structure of vocalizations. It would seem most important to engage in studies on the point-by-point correspondence between the facial expression of emotion and the concomitant vocalizations. In addition, the face seems to generate more discrete expressions in terms of the number of discriminable configurations, and as mentioned before, facial expression in children may be more directly comparable to adult emotional expressions. Consequently, information on objective parameters describing the facial expression during the occurrence of a vocalization may be an important aid in the attempt to discover the emotional significance of particular acoustic parameters.

Just as the study of the development of facial expression may prove to be of some value in the diagnosis of mental retardation (Cicchetti & Sroufe, 1978; Emde, Katz, & Thorpe, 1978), it seems well established that the cry patterns of infants with various kinds of genetic abnormalities or other impairments can be reliably distinguished on the basis of acoustic parameters of the vocalizations of these infants (cf. Fisichelli & Karelitz, 1966; Lind et al., 1970; Ostwald, 1974; Vuorenkoski et al., 1971; Wasz-Höckert et al., 1968). Again, it would be intriguing to study the patterns of deviation and retardation in development in both domains of expression. The joint analysis of these two expressive structures may help to further our insight into the nature of the retardation and to improve the diagnostic use of measures of expressive behavior.

Finally, work on early mother–infant interaction (Bateson, 1975; Brazelton, Koslowski, & Main, 1974; Schaffer, Collins, & Parsons, 1977; Stern et al., 1975; Trevarthen, 1977) points to the tremendous importance of facial and vocal signals in the development of mother–infant attachment and the course of emotional and social development. It is most likely that facial and vocal signals are intricately coordinated during the unfolding of reciprocal communication between mother and infant and that each of these may strongly affect the other in terms of their communicative significance. The importance of the human face as a visual stimulus for the infant is well known and does not need to be reviewed here. Similarly, the importance of expressive variations of the human voice has been established early by Hetzer and Tudor-Hart (1927), and there is growing evidence that even very young infants are sensitive to the characteristics of the human voice: Mills and Melhuish (1974) and Mehler and Bertoncini (1979) have shown in experiments involving nonnutritive sucking that a baby will suck more to hear its mother's voice than to hear a stranger's voice. Fourcin (1978) has claimed that the fundamental frequency of the voice is most important for the development of communication between mother and child.

In studying the relationships between vocal and facial signals in mother–infant interaction, it is obviously important not only to focus on the expressive behavior of the infant but to engage in detailed analyses of the facial expression and the acoustic nature of vocalization of the mother. It seems rather likely that imitation of sounds, and possibly facial movements, plays a major role in the acquisition of communicative competence by the child (cf. Crystal, 1978) and may be important for the acquisition of language. As Crystal (1973) has pointed out, there are many interesting questions concerning the acquisition of language sounds. Unfortunately, even more than the study of infant vocalization, research on babbling and other noncry vocalizations in older children has been guided almost exclusively by linguistic or psycholinguistic interest in language acquisition in terms of competence. Very rarely has the expressive or emotional aspect of these vocalizations been considered. A comparison of vocalization patterns during various stages of the language acquisition process in comparison with affect vocalizations by animals and adults may yield some insight into the molding of affect vocalizations by linguistic and cultural norms. The significance of such developmental studies would be even greater if they were conducted in a cross-cultural context, comparing different languages, socialization procedures, and cultural norms. It would be most important to study whether emotional vocalizations are similar for infants in different language communities but change after the acquisition of the first language-specific sounds. There is some intriguing work on the early shaping of the infant vocalization by its mother tongue (Crystal, 1973).

Many more interesting issues could be studied in terms of the relationship between emotional vocalizing and speech acquisition. For example, to what extent is babbling, which seems to be a very important stage in the acquisition of language, similar to the making of emotional sound? What are the earliest aspects of the acquisition of paralinguistic features such as intonation contours? There is some evidence that meaningful intonation contours may be among the earliest semantic devices that the child is able to use (Crystal, 1978). Because intonation is also frequently involved in emotional vocalization, it would be most fruitful to study the relationship between emotional vocalization and the onset of the semantic use of such paralinguistic devices.

It is to be hoped that increasing awareness of the importance of emotional vocalization as affected by cognitive, emotional, and social development will lead to more systematic research on vocalization in infants and children. Evidence obtained in such studies may well throw further light on the nature of the development of affect and communication.

Appendix: Methodological aspects of the acoustical analysis of emotional vocalization

In this section some of the practical aspects of analyzing acoustic parameters of vocalization will be reviewed briefly. The most convenient procedure for acoustic analysis is to record some kind of vocalization sample onto magnetic tape and to apply acoustical analysis to the wave forms stored on the tape. In terms of the details of methodological procedure, then, it is important to consider the selection of vocalization samples, their recording in specific situations, and the apparatus and procedure for the acoustical analysis. Each of these will be discussed in turn.

The selection of vocalizations or speech samples

One of the major handicaps for research on the vocal expression of emotion has been the scarcity of instances in which adults freely express emotions in public, particularly in situations in which psychologists happen to have recording equipment available. Because affect control is one of the major components of civilization (Elias, 1978), most cultures prohibit the overt expression of affect both facially and vocally or channel the expression via display rules (Ekman, 1972). Consequently most of the research on the vocal expression of emotion, like research on facial expression, has been done with emotions portrayed by actors or lay persons. In such cases, standard speech samples, which make certain acoustical analyses more feasible, or fairly controlled content areas have been used to obtain vocalization samples for analysis. With children the use of such procedures is much more difficult, at least until they reach a certain age. On the other hand, infants and younger children, certainly before the onset of shame, use emotional expression much more freely and publicly. Consequently it is not impossible to obtain fairly natural samples of emotional behavior and to record these, if the recording is done fairly unobtrusively.

Even though emotional states occur much more frequently in children than in adults and are much more freely expressed, it is difficult and very time-consuming to rely on the natural occurrence of specific emotional expressions in the presence of the researcher. Typically, research on infants and children is done through repeated visits of the research team to a home, during which time the activities of the children are recorded or observed. If one aims to obtain a fairly comprehensive coverage of vocal expressions for different emotions, it may not be sufficient to record whatever activity occurs during those visits without further provocation on the part of the researcher. There are a number of well-known procedures in developmental research that are equally suited to the eliciting of samples of emotional vocalizing. The following list of examples should suffice to illustrate the various possibilities that exist in this respect.

One possibility involves the systematic selection of standard situations occurring in the home (such as feeding, going to bed, bathing, etc.) that are likely to give rise to particular types of emotion states. If the habits and reaction tendencies of the children are known, it is often easy to provoke a certain emotional reaction. For example, if a child expects certain things, such as a second piece of cake for dessert, distress or anger can be provoked when the second piece is withheld. Similarly, a number of situations can be created that have been shown in the literature to produce certain affective states reliably, such as the foot prick in infants and departure of the mother and the appearance of a stranger during the emergence of fear responses. Games of various sorts can be used to produce certain types of reactions or the imitation of vocal patterns used by adults. With older children, role-playing techniques may be used, or the subjects may be asked to describe slides or films.

Even though some of these techniques will provide fairly natural emotional expressions and vocalizations, it is often highly desirable to obtain vocal expressions of emotional states under conditions when the researcher is not present. Still, this is only possible if the cooperation of the caregiver or a live-in person is obtained or if all of the activity occurring in a certain room of the house is recorded continuously. With children from infancy through an age where they tend to be continuously kept in certain locations such as cribs or playpens, it is possible to install a microphone that is activated by a voice switch, so that the tape recorder is turned on whenever there is vocalizing activity. This procedure is fairly easy to execute (although great care has to be taken to adjust the sensitivity of the voice switch properly), and it is economical in terms of both time and tape, but it has the drawback of providing no information about the conditions under which the vocalization occurred and the state of the infant at the time (which is normally assessed from the total context).

Recording of vocalization samples

Contrary to the conditions under which adult portrayals of emotion can be recorded (in soundproof or anechoic rooms) vocalizations of infants and children have to be recorded under difficult conditions, often with freely moving speakers, in the home or kindergarten. One of the most severe problems is the almost continuous presence of extraneous noise that interferes with and may even mask the vocalization being recorded. Furthermore, due to frequent and fast movement of older children in particular, it becomes very difficult to obtain a tape of quality high enough to permit acoustic analysis. Some of the essential procedures to be followed or to be avoided in recording vocalizations are listed in Table 6.3 (from

Table 6.3. *Prerequisites for high-quality sound recording*

Recommended equipment and procedure	Potential trouble
Basic decisions	
Stereo recording with separate channels when recording two or more speakers whose speech is to be analyzed separately.	Using mono recording, analysis of speech of individual speakers may be impossible. It may even be difficult to transcribe the speakers' utterances.
Open reel recorder for high-quality sound recording and to allow splicing and other manual tape manipulations like localizing events by manually turning the reels.	Splicing will be difficult if not impossible when using cassettes. Because of the tapes used in cassettes are thin and narrow, the sound quality of the recording is generally not acceptable (low crosstalk attenuation, low signal-to-noise ratio).
Half-track recording for higher dynamic range and higher crosstalk attenuation, more protection against dropouts.	$\frac{1}{4}$-track recording has the same disadvantages as cassettes have.
Use the same recorder for all recordings in a study (at least the same type).	Different recorders will show differences in recording characteristics (different phase shifting, etc.) that might prohibit comparisons of speech data (worse if different types of recorders used).
Tape	
Use high-quality low noise tape (standard or double play).	Cheap tapes will show more dropouts, lower abrasion resistance, and lower signal-to-noise ratio. Super long-playing tapes are very thin and will show a high print-through ratio.
Use high tape speed (19 cm/s or 38 cm/s, i.e., $7\frac{1}{2}$ ips or 15 ips).	Lower tape speed will reduce frequency range and makes it difficult to localize segments when splicing.
Do not copy tapes too often.	Every duplication reduces sound quality and increases noise and hum.
Do not store recorded tapes near strong magnetic fields or under high temperature.	Magnetic fields distort the recorded signal; high temperature raises print-through ratio.
Level control	
Use manual level control to obtain high sound quality.	Automatic level control will amplify unwanted sounds and background noise especially in speech pauses. Moreover, sound dynamics are leveled.
Use fixed level. Mark selected level on level control to be sure.	Variable level will not allow comparisons of intensity, etc. between different speakers.
Test the level before starting the recording and constantly check while recording.	Otherwise you may select levels too high or too low, resulting in distorted or weak speech signals. The appropriate level depends on the loudness range you expect. Allow for a margin to comprehend extremely loud sounds.
Video sound	
Use an external microphone for acceptable sound quality on the video tape.	Built-in camera microphones are usually of poor quality. Recordings may be impaired by wind or camera vibrations and sounds. Camera may be too far away from the sound source.

Table 6.3 (*cont.*)

Recommended equipment and procedure	Potential trouble
Video sound (cont.) Separate sound recording on tape recorder.	Frequency range of video–sound recording is sufficient for some purposes (100–10000 Hz), but in any case worse than audio tape recording and generally not sufficient for acoustic analysis. Copying sound from video tape reduces quality further.
Microphone characteristics Choose a microphone that has appropriate characteristics (i.e., omnidirectional, unidirectional, cardioid, etc.).	Choice of inappropriate characteristics can affect the recording, for instance if a person moves out of range of a unidirectional microphone.
Choose low-impedance microphones, if the microphone is placed more than 10 ft. away from the recorder (if the recorder has to be hidden, etc.).	High-impedance microphones may produce a loss of higher frequencies and hum; cable length cannot exceed 10 feet.
High-quality dynamic or condenser microphone.	Cheap microphones will produce sound distortions and are less sensitive, especially for higher frequencies. Take care when using condenser microphones. They are comparatively fragile, and sound bursts may result in overload.
Lavalier microphones for optimal channel separation and constant speaker-to-microphone distance.	With stationary microphones the speaker-to-microphone distance will vary with speaker movements. The speaker may even move out of the range of a fixed microphone. Variable speaker-to-microphone distance will result in intensity changes, prohibiting comparisons between speakers, e.g., with respect to loudness of the voice.
Recording of stationary speakers with fixed microphone, if recording without the speaker's knowing that you are doing so.	Fixed microphones (if hidden or partly concealed) are less obtrusive than lavalier microphones. Moreover, attaching lavalier microphones may be a problem, and speakers may fiddle with cables, thus producing unwanted noise.
Conditions at recording site Try to isolate against outside sound. If impossible, record during quiet periods. Turn off air conditioners and other equipment with constant mechanical noise.	Background noise will impair sound quality.
Use curtains and other sound-absorbing materials to reduce sound reflections and indirect sound.	Reflections will adulterate the sound signal.

Table 6.3 (*cont.*)

Recommended equipment and procedure	Potential trouble
Conditions at recording site	
Place the microphone on a good solid stand or at least isolate it from floor sounds, etc. by placing it on a felt pad.	Otherwise vibrations, etc. will impair sound quality.
Check amplifiers, cables, etc. for alternating current hum. If necessary use shielding to shut off hum and check connectors for wrong pin wiring.	Otherwise the 50 Hz. (or 60 Hz.) hum will disturb the sound signal.
Use a soundproof chamber to obtain perfect sound quality for sophisticated acoustic analysis.	Acoustic chambers can only be used for some types of experiments. Their obtrusiveness may cause speakers to change their speech; some persons may react with fright or feel uncomfortable in such unfamiliar surroundings.

Source: Wallbott, 1982.

Wallbott, 1982). If one adheres to these recommendations, it is usually possible to do acoustic analysis in compliance with most of the parameters I have described, although the quality may not be as perfect as with speech samples recorded in the laboratory. Even the most careful recording procedure cannot avoid the occurrence of intruding sound, whether it is environmental noises or speech sounds from parents or other people in the room, particularly if natural recording conditions are required. These intrusions have to be carefully edited out before acoustic analysis is attempted, particularly if automatic analysis is used, for otherwise the results become totally uninterpretable (a filter bank or computer cannot differentiate between the voice of a baby and the voice of the mother).

Unfortunately, the vocal signal is much more subject to interference than the visual signal. It is much easier to obtain high-quality video records of facial expression in children, even though much other activity may be going on in the situation, than it is to obtain clean records of vocalizations. Therefore specific precautions have to be taken in research directed at recording emotional vocalization in order to avoid such problems as much as possible. In particular, researchers in this area will have to attempt to use the modern technology available for audio recording, such as the appropriate type of microphone, portable microphones with transmitters permitting free movement of the speaker, and remote control switches, as well as the devices now available to clean the speech signal if recording conditions introduced other noise or problems (band pass and band reject filters, equalizers, etc.). Before high-quality sound recordings can be obtained for acoustic analysis, researchers must stop believing that it is sufficient to set up the microphone and turn on the recorder. Such a procedure may permit the recording of speech samples of purely linguistic interest, for example, to document the learning of grammar, but it will not do for detailed analyses of acoustical properties.

Acoustical measurement apparatus

Details on the equipment and the procedures that make possible objective acoustic analysis are provided in Scherer (1982). In the following survey, I will only give some hints about potentially useful equipment.

For measurements in the time domain, that is, direct measurements on the time signal, it may be sufficient to display the speech wave form on a storage oscillograph and take a photograph of the display. Obviously, this is a very time-consuming procedure, for only very short portions of the acoustic wave form can be examined at a time. It is much more convenient to use a pen recorder to plot the speech wave form. Measurements on the amplitude of the speech wave form are also fairly straightforward, because simple electroacoustic devices can be used to measure changes in the intensity of the signal as recorded. As with the speech wave form, it is convenient to plot the envelope, that is, the integrated signal, continuously on graph paper in order to have a permanent record.

A large number of devices are available to obtain the spectrum of a speech or vocalization wave form. Unfortunately, most of them are quite expensive and difficult to use without lengthy prior experience. The oldest and most established device is the spectrograph, which produces three-dimensional representations of speech spectra with frequency plotted on a vertical axis, time on the horizontal axis and amplitude represented by the degree to which the paper is darkened by the device (Agnello, 1975). Figure 6.6 shows spectrograms of two kinds of infant sounds. Spectrograms like these are frequently used in the analysis of infant vocalizations. For trained analysts, these analog displays of spectral changes in the time dimension provide a convenient and useful summary of the acoustic characteristics of vocalizations. Although some of the analog information contained in a spectrogram can be quantified by appropriate measurement procedures, this is laborious and somewhat imprecise. For quantitative measurements to be used in statistical analysis, it is preferable to use measurement procedures that result in digital values.

Filter banks and spectrum analyzers measure the energy of the signal in particular frequency bands, thus providing spectra of sounds in real time. Most modern spectrum analyzers offer the option of transferring the spectral values to some kind of storage medium for further analysis.

By far the most flexible and at the same time most expensive and demanding analysis is speech analysis via digital computer. Generally, small laboratory

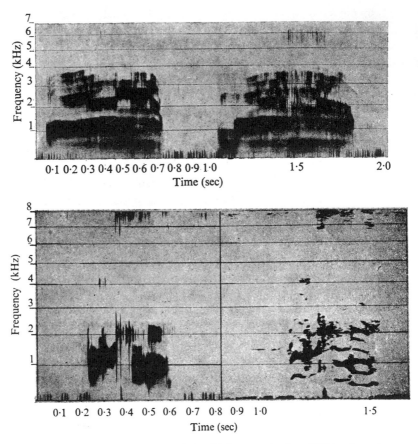

Figure 6.6. Spectrograms for two kinds of infant sounds. *Top:* Wideband spectrogram (450 Hz bandwidth) of two cry segments produced by a normal 2-week-old female infant. A nasal consonant-like element is present in the initial 100 msec portion of the segment on the right. *Bottom:* Wideband (450 Hz bandwidth) and narrowband (45 Hz bandwidth) spectrogram of a comfort sound produced by an 8-week-old female infant. A brief voiceless friction noise is present in its medial portion. *Source:* R. E. Stark, Features of infant sounds: The emergence of cooing, *Journal of Child Language,* 1978, *5,* 384.

computers such as the PDP 11 with analog to digital (A/D) and digital to analog (D/A) conversion periphery are used for such analyses. The details are described in Scherer (1982). Still, if speech signals can be stored on computer tape in a digital form, using A/D conversion on a small computer, it is possible to analyze these tapes on large computers if the appropriate software is available. The digital spectra resulting from this kind of analysis can be used for further statistical analysis. If graphic information is required, a display similar to the spectrograms can be obtained by using appropriate printing or plotting devices (although it is difficult to obtain the same degree of resolution as with a spectrograph) or can be displayed in the form of three-dimensional plots of consecutive spectra (see Figure 6.6). It is to be expected that these techniques will be greatly facilitated by technological advances in the years to come and by the increasing availability of appropriate software. Even if digital speech analysis techniques become more easily available, however, one has to take care when selecting the proper conditions for analysis and be able to detect artifacts that can easily occur with most of these analysis techniques. Consequently, researchers should be warned against the use of highly sophisticated techniques without satisfactory knowledge of the acoustics of speech and the specific bases of the analysis programs used. In addition, the difficulties in preparing speech samples in appropriate form for analysis and the statistical treatment of the data obtained by digital analysis should not be underestimated.

Note

1 Although the terms *amplitude, energy,* and *intensity* are sometimes used interchangeably to denote what is heard as loudness of a sound, there are important differences between the underlying physical phenomena and the appropriate measurement procedures. The complex relationships between these acoustic parameters cannot be discussed in this context (see Small, 1973).

References

Agnello, J. G. Measurements and analysis of visible speech. In S. Singh (Ed.), *Measurement procedures in speech, hearing, and language.* Baltimore, Md.: University Park Press, 1975.

Aldrich, C. A., Sung, C., Knop, C., Stevens, G., & Burchell, M. The crying of newly born babies: 1. The community phase. *Journal of Pediatrics*, 1945, *26*, 313–26.

Bateson, M. Mother–infant exchanges: The epigenesis of conversational interaction. *Annals of the New York Academy of Sciences*, 1975, *263*, 101–13.

Bayley, N. A study of the crying of infants during mental and physical tests. *Journal of Genetic Psychology*, 1932, *40*, 306–29.

Brazelton, T. B., Koslowski, B., & Main, M. The origins of reciprocity: The early mother–infant interaction. In M. Lewis & L. Rosenblum (Eds.), *The effect of the infant on its caregiver.* New York: Wiley, 1974.

Chevalier-Skolnikoff, S. Facial expression of emotion in nonhuman primates. In P. Ekman (Ed.), *Darwin and facial expression.* New York: Academic Press, 1973.

Cicchetti, D., & Sroufe, L. A. An organizational view of affect: Illustration from the study of Down's syndrome infants. In M. Lewis & L. A. Rosenblum (Eds.), *The development of affect.* New York: Plenum Press, 1978.

Crystal, D. Non-segmental phonology in language acquisition: A review of the issues. *Lingua*, 1973, *32*, 1–45.

Crystal, D. The analysis of intonation in young children. In F. D. Minifie & L. L. Lloyd (Eds.), *Communicative and cognitive abilities – Early behavioral assessment.* Baltimore, Md.: University Park Press, 1978.

Crystal, D., & Quirk, R. *Systems of prosodic and paralinguistic features in English.* The Hague, Netherlands: Mouton, 1964.

Darwin, C. *The expression of the emotions in man and animals*. Chicago: University of Chicago Press, 1965. (Originally published, 1872.)

Delack, J. B. & Fowlow, P. J. The ontogenesis of differential vocalization: Development of prosodic contrastivity during the first year of life. In N. Waterson & C. Snow (Eds.), *The development of communication*. New York: Wiley, 1978.

Dittmann, A. T. & Wynne, L. C. Linguistic techniques and the analysis of emotionality in interviews. *Journal of Abnormal and Social Psychology,* 1961, *63,* 201–4.

Duchenne, G. B. A. Mécanisme de la physionomie humaine: ou, Analyse électrophysiologique de l'expression des passions applicable à la pratique des arts plastiques. Paris: Renouard, 1862.

Ekman, P. Universal and cultural differences in facial expressions of emotion. In J. K. Cole (Ed.), *Nebraska Symposium on Motivation* (Vol. 19). Lincoln: University of Nebraska Press, 1972.

Ekman, P., & Oster, H. Facial expressions of emotion. *Annual Review of Psychology,* 1979, *30,* 527–54.

Elias, N. *Ueber den Prozess der Zivilisation* (2nd ed.). Frankfurt: Suhrkamp, 1978.

Emde, R. N., Katz, E. L., & Thorpe, J. K. Emotional expression in infancy: 2. Early deviations in Down's syndrome. In M. Lewis & L. A. Rosenblum (Eds.), *The development of affect*. New York: Plenum Press, 1978.

Fagan, R. M., & Young, D. Y. Temporal patterns of behavior: Durations, intervals, latencies, and sequences. In P. W. Colgan (Ed.), *Quantitative ethology*. New York: Wiley, 1978.

Fairbanks, G. An acoustical study of the pitch of infant hunger wails. *Child Development,* 1942, *13,* 227–32.

Feldstein, S., & Welkowitz, J. A chronography of conversation: In defense of an objective approach. In A. W. Siegman & S. Feldstein (Eds.), *Nonverbal behavior and communication*. Hillsdale, N.J.: Erlbaum, 1978.

Fisichelli, V. R., & Karelitz, S. Frequency spectra of the cries of normal infants and those with Down's syndrome. *Psychonomic Science,* 1966, *6,* 195–6.

Fisichelli, V. R., Karelitz, S., & Haber, A. The course of induced crying activity in the neonate. *Journal of Psychology,* 1969, *73,* 183–9.

Fourcin, A. J. Acoustic patterns and speech acquisition. In N. Waterson & C. Snow (Eds.), *The development of communication*. New York: Wiley, 1978.

Goldman-Eisler, F. *Psycholinguistics: Experiments in spontaneous speech*. New York: Academic Press, 1968.

Green, S. Variation of vocal pattern with social situation in the Japanese monkey (*Macaca fuscata*): A field study. In L. A. Rosenblum (Ed.), *Primate behavior: Developments in field and laboratory research* (Vol. 4). New York: Academic Press, 1975.

Helfrich, H., & Scherer, K. R. Experimental assessment of antidepressant drug effects using spectral analysis of voice. *Journal of the Acoustical Society of America, Supplement 1,* 1977, *62,* 26. (Abstract)

Hetzer, H., & Tudor-Hart, B. Die frühesten Reaktionen auf die menschliche Stimme. *Quellen und Studien zur Jugendkunde* (Vol. 5). 1927.

Irwin, O. C. Research on speech sounds for the first six months of life. *Psychological Bulletin,* 1941, *38,* 277–85.

Irwin, O. C., & Chen, H. P. Speech sounds elements during the first years of life: A review of the literature. *Journal of Speech Disorders,* 1943, *8,* 109–21.

Irwin, O. C., & Weiss, L. The effect of clothing on the general and vocal activity of the newborn infant. *University of Iowa Studies in Child Welfare,* 1943, *9,* 149–62.

Izard, C. E. *The face of emotion*. New York: Appleton-Century-Crofts, 1971.

Izard, C. E. On the ontogenesis of emotions and emotion-cognition relationships in infancy. In M. Lewis & L. A. Rosenblum (Eds.), *The development of affect*. New York: Plenum Press, 1978.

Jürgens, U. Vocalization as an emotional indicator: A neuroethological study in the squirrel monkey. *Behaviour,* 1979, *69,* 88–117.

Kainz, F. *Psychologie der Sprache: Vol. 1. Grundlagen der allgemeinen Sprachpsychologie* (3rd ed.). Stuttgart: Enke, 1962.

Keitel, H. G., Cohn, R., & Harnish, D. Diaper rash, self-inflicted excoriations, and crying in full-term newborn infants kept in the prone or supine position. *Journal of Pediatrics,* 1960, *57,* 884–6.

Ladefoged, P. *Elements of acoustic phonetics.* Chicago: University of Chicago Press, 1962.

Laufer, M. Z., & Horii, Y. Fundamental frequency characteristics of infant non-distress vocalization during the first twenty-four weeks. *Journal of Child Language,* 1977, *4,* 171–84.

Laver, J. *Individual features in voice quality.* Unpublished doctoral dissertation, University of Edinburgh, 1975.

Laver, J. *The phonetic description of voice quality.* Cambridge, England: Cambridge University Press, 1980.

Lehiste, I. (Ed.). *Suprasegmentals.* Cambridge, Mass.: MIT Press, 1970.

Lester, B. M. The organization of crying in the neonate. *Journal of Pediatric Psychology,* 1978, *3,* 122–30.

Lewis, M., & Brooks, J. Self-knowledge and emotional development. In M. Lewis & L. A. Rosenblum (Eds.), *The development of affect.* New York: Plenum Press, 1978.

Leyhausen, P. Biologie von Ausdruck und Eindruck. *Psychologische Forschung,* 1967, *31,* 113–227.

Lieberman, P. *Speech physiology and acoustic phonetics: An introduction.* New York: Macmillan, 1977.

Lieberman, P., Harris, K. S., Wolff, P., & Russell, L. H. Newborn infant cry and nonhuman primate vocalization. *Journal of Speech and Hearing Research,* 1971, *14,* 718–27.

Lind, J., Vuorenkoski, V., Rosberg, G., Partanen, T. J., & Wasz-Höckert, O. Spectrographic analysis of vocal response to pain stimuli in infants with Down's syndrome. *Developmental Medicine and Child Neurology,* 1970, *12,* 478–86.

Mahl, G. F., & Schulze, G. Psychological research in the extralinguistic area. In T. Sebeok, A. S. Hayes, & M. C. Bateson (Eds.), *Approaches to semiotics.* The Hague, Netherlands: Mouton, 1964.

Markel, J. D. & Gray, A. H., Jr. *Linear prediction of speech.* Berlin: Springer, 1976.

Markel, N. N., Meisels, M., & Houck, J. E. Judging personality from voice quality. *Journal of Abnormal and Social Psychology,* 1964, *69,* 458–63.

Marler, P., & Tenaza, R. Signaling behavior of apes with special reference to vocalization. In T. A. Sebeok (Ed.), *How animals communicate.* Bloomington: Indiana University Press, 1977.

Mehler, J., & Bertoncini, J. Infants' perception of speech and other acoustic stimuli. In J. Morton & J. Marshall (Eds.), *Structure and processes.* Psycholinguistic series 2. London: Elek Science Books, 1979.

Mills, M., & Melhuish, E. Recognition of mother's voice in early infancy. *Nature,* 1974, *252,* 123–4.

Minifie, F. D. Speech acoustics. In F. D. Minifie, T. J. Hixon, & F. Williams (Eds.), *Normal aspects of speech, hearing, and language.* Englewood Cliffs, N.J.: Prentice-Hall, 1973.

Müller, E., Hollien, H., & Murry, T. Perceptual responses to infant crying: Identification of cry types. *Journal of Child Language,* 1974, *1,* 89–95.

Ostwald, P. The cry of the human infant. *Scientific American,* 1974, *230,* 84–90.

Partanen, T. J., Wasz-Höckert, O., Vuorenkoski, V., Theorell, K., Valanne, E. H., & Lind, J. Auditory identification of pain cry signals of young infants in pathological conditions and its sound spectrographic basis. *Annales Paediatriae Fenniae,* 1967, *13,* 56–63.

Potter, R. K., Kopp, G. A., & Green, H. C. *Visible speech.* New York: Van Nostrand, 1947.

Prechtl, H. F. R., Theorell, K., Gramsbergen, A., & Lind, J. A statistical analysis of cry patterns in normal and abnormal newborn infants. *Developmental Medicine and Child Neurology,* 1969, *11,* 142–52.

162   K. R. SCHERER

Prescott, R. Infant cry sound: Developmental features. *Journal of the Acoustical Society of America,* 1975, *57,* 1186–91.

Rochester, S. R. The significance of pauses in spontaneous speech. *Journal of Psycholinguistic Research,* 1973, *2,* 51–81.

Schaffer, H. R., Collins, G. M., & Parsons, G. Vocal interchange and visual regard in verbal and pre-verbal children. In H. R. Schaffer (Ed.), *Studies in mother–infant interaction.* London: Academic Press, 1977.

Scherer, K. R. Voice quality analysis of American and German speakers. *Journal of Psycholinguistic Research,* 1974, *3,* 281–90.

Scherer, K. R. Affektlaute und vokale Embleme. In R. Posner & H. P. Reinecke (Eds.), *Zeichenprozesse – Semiotische Forschung in den Einzelwissenschaften.* Wiesbaden: Athenaion, 1977.

Scherer, K. R. Inference rules in personality attribution from voice quality: The loud voice of extraversion. *European Journal of Social Psychology,* 1978; *8,* 467–87.

Scherer, K. R. Non-linguistic vocal indicators of emotion and psychopathology. In C. E. Izard (Ed.), *Emotions in personality and psychopathology.* New York: Plenum Press, 1979. (a)

Scherer, K. R. Personality markers in speech. In K. R. Scherer & H. Giles (Eds.), *Social markers in speech.* Cambridge, England: Cambridge University Press, 1979. (b)

Scherer, K. R. The functions of nonverbal signs in conversation. In R. St. Clair & H. Giles (Eds.), *The social and psychological contexts of language.* Hillsdale, N.J.: Erlbaum, 1980.

Scherer, K. R. Vocal indicators of stress. In J. Darby (Ed.), *The evaluation of speech in psychiatry.* New York: Grune & Stratton, 1981. (a)

Scherer, K. R. Speech and emotional states. In J. Darby (Ed.), *The evaluation of speech in psychiatry.* New York: Grune & Stratton, 1981. (b)

Scherer, K. R. Methods of research on vocal communication: Paradigms and parameters. In K. R. Scherer & P. Ekman (Eds.), *Handbook of methods in nonverbal behavior research.* Cambridge, England: Cambridge University Press, 1982.

Scherer, K. R., Koivumaki, J., & Rosenthal, R. Minimal cues in the vocal communication of affect: Judging emotions from content-masked speech. *Journal of Psycholinguistic Research,* 1972, *1,* 269–85.

Scherer, K. R., & Oshinsky, J. Cue utilization in emotion attribution from auditory stimuli. *Motivation and Emotion,* 1977, *1,* 331–46.

Scherer, K. R., & Tolkmitt, F. The effect of stress and task variation on formant location. *Journal of the Acoustical Society of America, Supplement 1,* 1979, *66,* 512. (Abstract)

Sedlackova, E. *Development of the acoustic pattern of the voice and speech in the newborn and infant.* Prague: Academia, 1967.

Sherman, M. The differentiation of emotional responses in infants: 1. Judgments of emotional responses from motion picture views and from actual observation; 2. The ability of observers to judge emotional characteristics of the crying infants and of the voice of an adult. *Journal of Comparative Psychology,* 1927, *7,* 265–84, 335–51.

Siegman, A. W. The telltale voice: Nonverbal messages of verbal communication. In A. W. Siegman & S. Feldstein (Eds.), *Nonverbal behavior and communication.* Hillsdale, N.J.: Erlbaum, 1978.

Small, A. M. Acoustics. In F. D. Minifie, T. J. Hixon, & F. Williams (Eds.), *Normal aspects of speech, hearing, and language.* Englewood Cliffs, N.J.: Prentice-Hall, 1973.

Sroufe, L. A. Socioemotional development. In J. D. Osofsky (Ed.), *The handbook of infant development.* New York: Wiley, 1979.

Stark, R. E. Features of infant sounds: The emergence of cooing. *Journal of Child Language,* 1978, *5,* 379–90.

Stark, R. E., Rose, S. N., & McLagen, M. Features of infant sounds: The first eight weeks of life. *Journal of Child Language,* 1975, *2,* 205–21.

Stern, D., Jaffe, J., Beebe, B., & Bennett, S. Vocalizing in unison and in alternation: Two modes of communication within the mother–infant dyad. *Annals of the New York Academy of Sciences,* 1975, *263,* 89–100.

Stern, D., & Wassermann, G. A. *Intonation contours as units of information in maternal speech to pre-linguistic infants.* Paper presented at the Society for Research in Child Development, San Francisco, March 1979.

Tembrock, G. *Tierstimmenforschung: Eine Einführung in die Bioakustik* (2nd ed.). Wittenberg Lutherstadt: A. Ziemsen, 1977.

Tischler, H. Schreien, Lallen und erstes Sprechen in der Entwicklung des Säuglings. *Zeitschrift für Psychologie,* 1957, *160,* 210–63.

Tolkmitt, F., Helfrich, H., Standke, R., & Scherer, K. R. Vocal indicators of psychiatric treatment effects in depressives and schizophrenics. *Journal of Communication Disorders,* in press.

Tomkins, S. S. *Affect, imagery, consciousness: Vol. 1. The positive affects.* New York: Springer, 1962.

Tomkins, S. S. *Affect, imagery, consciousness: Vol. 2. The negative affects.* New York: Springer, 1963.

Trager, G. L., & Smith, H. L., Jr. *An outline of English structure.* Washington, D.C.: American Council of Learned Societies, 1957.

Trevarthen, C. Descriptive analyses of infant communicative behaviour. In H. R. Schaffer (Ed.), *Studies in mother–infant interaction.* London: Academic Press, 1977.

Truby, H. M., & Lind, J. Cry sounds of the newborn infant. In J. Lind (Ed.), *Newborn infant cry.* Acta Paediatrica Scandinavica (Suppl.), 1965, *163,* 8–54.

Vuorenkoski, V., Lind, J., Wasz-Höckert, O., & Partanen, T. J. Cry score: A method of evaluating the degree of abnormality in the pain cry response of the newborn and young infant. *Quarterly Progress Status Report.* Stockholm: Department of Speech Communication, Royal Institute of Technology, 1971, 68–75.

Wallbott, H. G. Audiovisual recording: Procedures, equipment, and troubleshooting. In K. R. Scherer & P. Ekman (Eds.), *Handbook of methods in nonverbal behavior research.* Cambridge, England: Cambridge University Press, 1982.

Wasz-Höckert, O., Lind, J., Vuorenkoski, V., Partanen, T. J., & Valanne, E. *The infant cry: A spectrographic and auditory analysis.* Clinics in Developmental Medicine (Vol. 29). London: Spastics International Medical & Heinemann Medical Books, 1968.

Williams, C. E., & Stevens, K. N. Emotions and speech: Some acoustical correlates. *Journal of the Acoustical Society of America,* 1972, *52,* 1238–50.

Wolff, P. H. The natural history of crying and other vocalizations in early infancy. In B. Foss (Ed.), *Determinants of infant behaviour* (Vol. 4). London: Methuen, 1969.

Wundt, W. *Völkerpsychologie* (Vol. 1). Leipzig: Engelmann, 1900.

Zemlin, W. R. *Speech and hearing science: Anatomy and physiology.* Englewood Cliffs, N.J.: Prentice-Hall, 1968.

7 Gaze behavior in infants and children: a tool for the study of emotions?

Ralph V. Exline

Gaze behavior, or social visual attention, has for many years been known to elicit emotional arousal in animals. Chance's observations of rats, blackheaded gulls, great tits, and white boobies led him to postulate that the sight of the other raises aversive drives of flight or aggression at the beginning, or during social encounters, and also that cutoff postures that remove the sight of the other dampen arousal (Chance, 1962). Studies of primates in the field have shown that a mutual glance held between male primates will, for a number of species, trigger mutual threat displays that result in combat unless one member of the dyad looks away and otherwise presents the species-specific deference sign (Hall & DeVore, 1965; Hinde & Rowell, 1962; Jay, 1965; Shaller, 1963). Exline and Yellin (1969) demonstrated the effect across primate genera when they showed that laboratory animals (*Macaca mulatta*) would threaten and even attack a steadily looking human, inhibiting or breaking off the threatening display when the human initially held, then averted, his gaze.

A number of psychologists, for example, Kleinke and Pohlen (1971), Nichols and Champness (1971), and Gale, Lucas, Nissim, and Harpham (1972), have shown increased physiological arousal to be positively related to human exchange of mutual glances in silence, whereas the novelist Mailer presents an eloquent description of the acceleration of hostile feelings he experienced when he found his silent stare being returned by an American neo-Nazi (Mailer, 1968, pp. 160–63).

Gaze-related arousal is claimed to involve positive as well as negative affects. Students of child development early called attention to this in the interaction of mother and infant. Ahrens (1954) suggested that the stimulus of the mother's eyes precedes her mouth in eliciting the smiling response in infants. Rheingold (1961) speculated that "not physical but visual contact is at the basis of human sociability," and Robeson (1967) called attention to the role of eye contact in maternal–infant attachment.

Similarly, social psychologists (e.g., Argyle & Cook, 1976; Argyle & Dean, 1965; Ellsworth & Carlsmith, 1968; Ellsworth, Carlsmith, & Henson, 1972;

164

Exline, 1963; and Exline & Winters, 1965, to name but a few) have demonstrated relationships between mutual gaze and both positive and negative affects in adults. Because the focus of this volume is upon the study of emotions in infants and children, however, results of gaze studies involving adults will be used only as they suggest methods, procedures, or designs that can be adapted to the study of the phenomena in children.

Robeson (1967) agrees that eye-to-eye contact should be added to Bowlby's (1958) list of innate releasers of maternal caretaking responses. Robeson speaks of the "unique peculiarities of (the) visual mode that favor its preeminence as a major vehicle of intrapsychic and interpersonal development" (Robeson 1967, p. 13) and lists from his own work and that of others four reasons to support the above statement. These are that (a) visual fixation and following, contrary to all other neonatal reflexes,[1] do not drop out with maturation but show increasing facility (Greenman, 1963); (b) the pattern associated with fixation and following matures earlier than do other patterns of behavior, by the end of the second month: "It is already in the form it will keep throughout life" (Rheingold, 1961, p. 167); (c) eye control "is among the first acts of the infant that are both intentional and subject to its own control. Vision is the only modality which . . . is constructed as an 'on-off' system that can easily modulate or eliminate sensory input, sometimes at will, within the first few months of life" (Robeson, 1967, pp. 13–14); (d) the eyes are rich stimuli, containing more interesting qualities than do other parts of the body, for example, shininess of globe, mobility, contrast (cornea, iris, pupil configuration), changes size of diameter, variations in width of palprebral fissure.

Though it is difficult to specify precisely the earliest age at which an infant can clearly apprehend another object, Atkinson, Broddick, and Moor (1977) showed that babies as young as 4 weeks old preferred sharply focused pictures of human faces and Fixation is often used as an indication of apprehending attention. White, Castle, and Held (1964) observed the following: (a) 4–6-week-old babies will fixate upon 9-inch distant objects and will follow moving objects jerkily (peripheral pursuit) at 24 inches; (b) at 6 to 8 weeks they will show immediate interest in and accurately swipe at objects; (c) at 10 to 12 weeks they will immediately show fixation and a sharp decrease in activity when a test object is brought as near as 3 inches. These authors claim that 3-month-old infants will show visual accommodation behavior indistinguishable from that of adults.

Haith, Bergman, and Moor (1977) studied visual fixations of equal numbers (eight) of infants aged 3–5 weeks, 7 weeks, and 9–11 weeks who scanned stationary, moving, or talking adult faces. Percentage of visual fixation for all faces increased markedly between 5 to 7 weeks (from 22% to 87%), and talking produced an intensified scanning of the eyes for children in the two older groups.

Maurer and Salapatek (1976) used corneal photography to record eye movements of both 4- and 8-week-old infants faced with their mothers, a strange woman, and a strange man. Four-week-old infants generally looked away from the faces, looked less at the mother than at the strangers and, when fixating the face, fixated on a limited portion of the perimeter. In contrast, the 2-month-old infants generally looked at the faces and looked at more, and more internal, features, especially the eyes.

Kagan and Lewis, however, express doubt that initial fixation is an appropriate indication of attention to an object, believing that fixation alone cannot differentiate an empty stare from "active study or assimilation" (Kagan & Lewis, 1965, p. 95). They suggested that cardiac deceleration be used as an indicator of outward-focused interest and showed that for 24-week-old infants, fixation time correlated positively with cardiac deceleration for highly attentive female infants and for attentive male infants when visual fixations of 9 seconds or more were used. Their data also showed that infants of both sexes fixated longest on colored photographs of female faces 18 in. distant, least on a photograph of a nursing bottle, and for an intermediate period upon a black-and-white picture of a panda bear, a bull's-eye, and a checkerboard. Kagan and Lewis (1965) conclude that in the first 6 months a combination of fixation time and cardiac deceleration best represents attentiveness and that deceleration is brought about by motor and respiratory quieting, which accompany long visual fixations.

From the foregoing it appears that by 2 months, and more certainly by 3 months, we can be relatively confident that observation of the infant's visual and accompanying motor behavior will tell us when the infant attends to an adult interactant. A study by Scaife and Bruner (1975) indicates that by the end of the 1st year infants are capable not only of attending to an adult's face but also of following the direction of an adult's gaze as they turn their heads 90 degrees to right or left of the infant. They reported such following of an adult's gaze to occur, on the average, only 30% at ages 2–4 months, reaching 66% at 8–10 months and 100% for 5 infants aged 11 to 14 months. Thus by age 1 year, infants are not only aware of the other's social attention as represented by the direct gaze at the child but are also capable of following the direction of shifts in such attention. This point will be developed further in the context of a later description of some of my own work concerned with the relevance of gaze direction to the differentiation of affective states displayed by adult stimulus persons.

Studies reported above refer to infant gaze primarily in terms of attention. La Barbera, Izard, Vietz, and Parisi (1976) related attention to emotion when they used the duration of the first visual fixation to slides of an adult face depicting joy, anger, or no emotion. Finding that 4- and 6-month-old children looked significantly more at the joyful face, they suggested that discrimination among various facial expressions of emotion appears earlier than previously thought. Although it would have been desirable for La Barbera et al. to use more than one stimulus face to represent each of the three emotion expressions, their partial confirmation of earlier results reported by Wilcox and Clayton (1968) lends weight to their interpretation. Additional confirmation of this conclusion is provided by Young-Browne, Rosenfeld, and Horowitz (1977), who found that 3-month-old infants discriminated between surprised and happy expressions of males, and by Nelson, Morse, & Leavitt (1979), who found that 7-month-old infants were able to discriminate between photographs of happy and fearful faces of several adults.

Would we expect the same result had the infants seen a three-dimensional live face rather than a two-dimensional slide? Results reported by Kreutzer and Charlesworth (1973) and by Dirks and Gibson (1977) suggested that we would. Although the former used infant's general emotional response rather than their attentive gaze, they found the response to differentiate sad–angry from happy–neutral displays acted out by live models. Dirks and Gibson in a study of 32 5-month-old infants found no difference in fixation time when a live face was followed by its photograph, or by the photograph of a different face with similar hair, eye color, and gender characteristics. Thus it would seem that infants react similarly to emotional expressions whether they are presented by photographs, slides, or live faces; also that infant gaze is a useful indication of discrimination between and among emotional displays on a given face. In these studies the infant's discrimination of one expression of emotion from various others was, with the exception of Kreutzer and Charlesworth (1973), inferred from infant attention, which in turn was inferred from infant gaze. The underlying assumption would seem to be that much less infant gaze is given to stimuli that evoke no interest or arouse unpleasurable sensations.

Such an assumption seems to underlie research that focuses on gaze as a variable of interest in the dyadic interaction of parent and child. Following Robeson's (1967) speculation that a neonate's experiences with a caregiver's more or less skillful use of eye contact while responding to the baby's needs may be the basis for the establishment of trust and even the determinant of the "extent to which older children and adults rely on and use non-verbal forms of communication" (Robeson, 1967, p. 21), one notes a growing interest in the study of the interactive quality of social behavior (Schaffer, 1977; Schaffer & Crook, 1978; Stern, 1974; Zigler & Child, 1973). Schaffer (1977) argues that transactions between child and caregiver must be examined in detail in order to understand better how a child becomes transformed into a social, acculturated being. The appropriate focus of such research would seem to be detailed investigation of contingent mutual behaviors of mother and child, and gaze behavior would seem to lend itself well to such investigation.

Stern's (1974) study of dyadic interaction involving gaze behavior of mothers and infants at play is an excellent example of such mutual interplay. It is particularly interesting for the purpose of this chapter, for it not only demonstrates how one can show gaze to depict the operation of contingent mutuality (Stern develops a state transition matrix and, by an analysis of transitional probabilities, uses it to construct a dyadic state transition diagram that shows—among other outcomes—that the infant's gaze at mother has the effect of reducing the likelihood of her gazing away) but also points to the critically important role of the caregiver in assisting the child to learn how to regulate internal physiological states relevant to arousal and affect. "The infant can reduce his state of arousal by turning away from a stimulus that is too intense, too complicated . . . Similarly, he can turn away from a redundant and boring stimulus to seek a new stimulus, thereby increasing his state of arousal" (Stern, 1974, p. 189).

In the play situation described by Stern, the caregiver's gaze is accompanied by exaggerated facial expression and vocalizations, presumably in an attempt to maintain the infant's attention and pleasurable arousal. He reports that during such mutual interchange, the infant emits signs of increasing excitement and arousal until at some point it appears to become distressed and sharply looks away. At this point the sensitive caregiver, though still watching the infant, will reduce the arousal-eliciting behavior until the baby looks back, at which point the cycle will begin again, repeating itself over and over. Stern suggests that the infant, with the cooperation of a sensitive caregiver, thus learns to extend its optimal range of pleasurable arousal progressively. He also suggests that this activity is relevant to developing the capacity for joy or glee (Stern, 1974, pp. 208–9).

Thus the combination of gaze with facial and vocal expressiveness, appropriately modulated in relation to the infant's signs of pleasurable or distressing arousal, could serve to create in the infant a tie or attachment to the mother's face. Robeson (1967) postulates that: "if the face tie is not established, or if its quality fosters disruption and distress, the infant will experience varying degrees of interference in forming his earliest – and probably future – human relationships. Enduring deviations in eye contact should be concomitants of these attachment disturbances" (Robeson, 1967, p. 22).

That this tie can be more efficiently accomplished if the caregiver keys his or her perceptual inputs to the infant's state of readiness, as suggested by Stern, is also suggested by an investigation by Field (1977) in which mothers were asked either to attempt to keep the infant's attention or to imitate the infant's (gaze and expressive delays). Field's analysis of videotapes of the resulting interactions showed that mothers instructed to keep the infant's attention were themselves more active but obtained less visual attention from the infants. In contrast, those instructed to imitate the infant's behavior were less active but elicited more gaze behavior from the infant. In other words, imitation, which led to greater contingent responsiveness of the mother toward the infant, placed fewer information-processing demands on the infant, with the result that the infant gave more attention to the mother's face.

The foregoing represents only a partial review of the literature concerning gaze behavior between mothers and infants. Nevertheless, it suffices to show that from an initial interest in using gaze as an early indicator of attention, followed by attempts to link it to emotional attachments, many investigators now view gaze behavior, in conjunction with facial, vocal, and other nonverbal acts of both infant and adult, as part of an interactive system that can help to throw light on the processes by which the infant learns to cope more or less well with arousing stimulation controlled by the interacting caregiver. In addition, Campos and Stenberg (1980) suggest that the infant's ability to detect affect information on a human caregiver's face results in the use of the caregiver as a "social reference" by means of which the infant learns, vicariously, to approach or avoid environmental events.

Earlier I stated that the purpose of this chapter was to use gaze studies carried out with adult subjects to suggest methods and procedures that could be used to study the relationship between gaze and emotional behavior in infants and children. There is an important problem to be faced in making this transference, however, that severely limits our ability to generalize adult-relevant procedures to research with infants. The problem is concerned with language. Adults possess it; infants and prelinguistic children do not.

Differences in the linguistic competence of adults and children seriously affect our ability to use the methods of gaze studies of adult subjects to investigate emotional development in infants and children. Exline, Gottheil, Parades, and Winkelmayer (1979), for example, studied the gaze patterns of adults instructed to tell personal experiences of joy, sorrow, and anger to another. This method cannot be used with prelinguistic children and is of dubious value with those children capable of speech but with limited experience of the sort of personal loss that seems necessary to the concept of sorrow as experienced by adults. Again, Ellsworth and Langer (1976), building on earlier work by Ellsworth, Carlsmith, and Henson (1972), have shown that a steady expressionless stare can lead to flight (negative arousal?) or to approach (nonnegative arousal?), depending upon the expectations created in the adult recipient of the gaze by information transmitted in words by a third person (see Kurtz, 1975). Unless subjects are capable of expressing their experiences in speech, or of having expectations created by the ability to comprehend the speech of others, the relationships of their own or others' gaze to states of emotional arousal cannot be investigated by the procedures used by the above-mentioned investigators.

I do not mean to say that the techniques used in the study of gaze of adults are useless in the study of emotional phenomena in children. Once the child is capable of expressing and comprehending thought put into words, one could utilize such procedures with children of varying ages to investigate the earliest age at which the gaze-related phenomena observed for adults make their appearance in children. Let us develop this suggestion. Exline et al. (1979) filmed normal and schizophrenic women telling personal experiences of joy, anger, and sorrow.[2] With the sound eliminated, these films were: (a) viewed by trained coders who recorded the various gaze directions (direct, direct down, direct side, and side down) utilized during the telling of each story; (b) viewed by naive adult judges who then guessed which of the three affects was portrayed in each of the silently presented descriptions. The fidelity of the verbal description to the given affective theme was examined by a blind coding of the verbal protocol for each experience described by each stimulus person. In addition the blind coders rated each protocol for the intensity of the affect as represented in words only.

Normal presenters showed a consistent and different pattern of direct gaze (as compared with down gaze) over the three stories, but only if the verbal protocol of each story was judged to contain intense emotion. Such stimulus persons showed relatively more direct gaze at the listener when recounting happy experiences, least when telling of a sad experience, and an intermediate amount when recalling an angry encounter.[3] Adult judges were more accurate in discriminating among the silently presented stories when the presenter's verbal protocols were (independently) judged to be intense representations of the appropriate theme. Of particular interest was the finding that adult coders were more likely to judge a story as happy, angry, or sad in line with the previously described (i.e., direct relative to down) gaze pattern differences if the gaze pattern differences were themselves clearly distinguishable across the three affective stories of a given presenter. Put another way, if one story showed a very high proportion of direct gazes to down gazes at a listener, another showed the reverse, and the third fell in the middle of the two extremes, then the first presentation would be judged happy, the second sad, and the third angry *regardless of the verbal theme*. That is, a sad story could be judged happy if the presenter looked very directly at but little directly down when describing the sorrowful experience to a listener (Exline et al., 1979).

It would appear that adults both emit and expect others to emit specific gaze patterns when describing an intensely emotional experience to another. Perhaps they relive or act out the emotion as they recall it to another. But we have no such data for children. At what age do the discriminately different gaze patterns appear when children describe such emotions? Does the initial expression as well as the later retelling of these three emotions show the difference in gaze pattern described above? Do children's judgments of such presentations of either adults or other children show the characteristics described above for adults?

We have at present no data bearing on these questions. Once a child is capable of comprehending the instructions and describing such experiences in words, however, it should be possible to film their actions and, subsequently, to code their gaze patterns as they describe such experiences to another. Using such procedures one could film children of various ages, separately analyze the contents of their stories for verbal intensity indicators and, after coding their patterns of gaze directions, compare the data with those already obtained from adults. By such means one could determine the generality of the previous findings over various age groups.

In addition, children of various ages could be shown stimulus films of adults and of other children, obtained as described above, and could then be asked to differentiate among the affects as were the adult judges. Comparison of children's responses to the adult data would be useful to answer questions concerning the age of appearance of accuracy and whether or not the ability increases or decreases with age.

It may well prove to be possible to investigate the interrelationships of gaze direction and specific affect displays in prelanguage children. Though Ekman and Oster (1979) pointed to the uncertainty that exists as to the precise age at which infants produce clearly differentiated facial displays of joy, sorrow, and anger, there is now good evidence that such expressions can be encoded by the end of the 1st year and probably by 9 months of age (Izard et al., 1980). The latter investigators used 10-second segments of videotaped records of behavior spontaneously emitted by 1- to 9-month-old infants. The identification of several 10-second segments of spontaneous affect displays of a given emotion should provide coders with sufficient material to permit investigation of the following questions.

1. Do the spontaneous displays of different basic emotions in preverbal children show different gaze direction patterns according to the emotion displayed? If so, at what age does such differentiation appear?
2. If the answer to the above question is affirmative, is the pattern for each emotion comparable to that accompanying the retelling of intensive emotional experiences by children who are capable of sustained and comprehensible speech? If so, at what age would such comparability manifest itself in prelinguistic children?
3. Assuming affirmative answers to the above questions, is the purity and intensity of the emotional display a necessary condition to the manifestation of the gaze direction pattern, as was the case in adults?[4]

Research need not be limited to the emotions of joy, sorrow, and anger. Fear is another basic emotion that can be studied by the procedures described above. Although at present there is no definitive evidence concerning an adult pattern of gaze direction associated with retelling fearful experiences, one can speculate that deviations to one side or the other would be more characteristic of one retelling an intensely fear-provoking incident – perhaps signifying a desire to escape from such a situation.

Recently my own research, Exline (1978), has called my attention to the phenomenon of blinking during a direct look. In the past the rate of blinking has been found to be positively associated with attention to social stimuli (Ponder & Kennedy, 1927), with increased levels of psychological stress (Wood & Saunders, 1962), and with involvement in cognitive work of increasing difficulty (Peterson & Allison, 1931). It seems reasonable to postulate that one's blink rate increases in proportion to increases in level of psychological tension or arousal (Kanfer, 1960), which suggests yet another line of research involving gaze behavior in relation to emotional behavior in infants and children. Would the rate of blinking, for example, be positively associated with the intensity of emotional arousal? Would the blink rate differ when the emotion is positive rather than negative? Would blink rates of infants and preverbal children differ from those of children capable of expressing their thoughts in words and from those adults?

My own work has been restricted to an examination of blink rates of adult men in very specialized circumstances, namely of presidential candidates Carter and Ford during the three televised debates of the 1976 presidential election campaign. Blinks were recorded only when each man was engaged in the act of speaking, and the data suggest that each candidate's average level of activity during the second and third debates was influenced by his knowledge of how he had fared in the opinion of the public in his confrontation with the other in the previous debate. In the first debate, for example, Carter's overall rate of blinking was significantly lower than Ford's. In the second debate, however (after Ford was judged to have won the previous debate), Carter blinked consistently and significantly more than did Ford. In the second debate Ford made an egregious error concerning the influence Soviet Russia exerted over Eastern Europe. Challenged by a panel member, he persevered in his position, and subsequent opinion polls judged him to have lost the second debate. In the third and final debate Ford's blink rate was recorded as significantly higher than Carter's. Where blink rate was concerned, then, the second debate reversed the results of the first, and the third debate reversed those of the second. It was as if each man's rate of blinking tracked the results of the opinion polls concerning the immediately preceding debate.

Further support for the suggested relationship between psychological stress and rate of blinking can be obtained from a question-by-question analysis of the second debate. During the response period in which Ford misstated the relationship between the Soviet Union and Eastern European nations, his rate of blinking was the lowest recorded for either candidate during the three debates; it was slightly over 12 blinks per minute of speech. Following the panelist's challenge and Ford's reiteration of the suspect position, Ford's blink rate rose over subsequent responses, reaching approximately 48 blinks per minute toward the end of that debate. Never in the remainder of the second and throughout the third debate

did Ford's blink rate return to the low level that had characterized his performance in the opening period of the second debate, the period prior to his challenged assertion concerning Eastern Europe.

What is the relevance of blink rates recorded for grown men in the heat of a
presidential campaign to the investigation of emotional behavior in children and
infants? It has been argued that blink rates of men under psychological stress
could be said to vary directly with their apprehension about their possibly unfa-
vorable comparison with another with whom they were in intense competition.
If a rapid rate of blinking in adults can be taken as an indication of a high level
of emotional distress or discomfort, might not the same be true of children and
even infants? Many years ago Peterson and Allison (1931) suggested that
changes in blinking rate are more significant indicators of emotional states than
is the galvanic skin response. Modern video equipment, which permits tight
closeup shots of good resolution, facilitates the reliable and accurate measurement of blinks by infants as well as by children and adults.

Kagan and Lewis have expressed doubts that initial fixation in infants can
provide a valid indication of attention. How, they ask, does one differentiate an
empty stare from active study (Kagan & Lewis, 1965)? Recording the blink rate
per period of fixation may help to answer the question. One speculates that a
fixation that is characteristic of an empty inattentive stare is accompanied by a
very low rate of blinking, that fixations of interest and positive affect are accompanied by higher rates of blinking, and that very rapid rates of blinking are
associated with eye fixations that occur during, or lead to, accelerated feelings
of emotional distress. In other words the progression from apathy to positive
interest to distress may well be directly related to blink rate.

Earlier in this chapter reference was made to eye engagements between mother
and infant, and it was proposed that infants would avert their gaze to decrease
arousal levels elicited by the steady attention of the mother. If, as suggested,
steady eye engagement does contribute to increasing distress in infants, one
could hypothesize that blinking by the infant would increase as the length of the
eye engagement increased. The highest blink rate during a mutual fixation would
be hypothesized to occur during the period immediately preceding the infant's
gaze aversion.

Ponder and Kennedy in one of the earliest papers published on the blink phenomena provide an interesting lead to how blink rates can be used to identify
incipient or disguised emotional states. They argue that ''a state of mental tension which has no internal or external outlet (e.g., impotent rage, anxiety or
excitement, none of which can be shown or expressed by physical movements)
is accompanied by a rapid blinking rate'' (Ponder & Kennedy, 1927, p. 108).
The direct quotation suggests that the highest rates of blinking will be found in
those children and adults who are *least* expressive (facially, vocally, or gestur-

ally) when emotionally upset. Thus those who inhibit the outward expression of their emotional state may leak evidence of such a state via an increased rate of blinking. This proposition could be tested experimentally with adults and children with language ability by instructing or motivating them to maintain blank, deadpan expressions when placed in stressful or emotion-eliciting situations. An inverse relationship between blinking and the degree to which various other means of conventionally showing emotion are displayed would provide evidence to support the proposition.

The above proposition could also be tested in prelanguage children. The procedures used in a study by Izard et al. (1980) in which the behavior of infants was recorded in situations designed to elicit spontaneous expressive displays of joy, anger, and sorrow are a case in point. Their report suggests that not all of the infants who were filmed could be used to provide stimulus materials representing the appropriate peak emotional display for the affect in question. One wonders if the rate of blinking of infants not used could be shown to be greater than the rates of those whose facial expressions were judged to represent the desired affect best. Should it prove to be possible to verify the Ponder and Kennedy proposition experimentally, infants and children whose interaction with caregivers is of a nature to discourage the easy display of affective states might be supposed nevertheless to signal intense emotional arousal by virtue of accelerated blink rates. There is evidence suggesting that the observation of high blink rates encourages the observer to form derogatory impressions of the blinker (Exline, 1978). The implication is that early identification and correction of socializing practices that encourage the development of this tendency would hold promise of improving the social effectiveness of the developing child.

This chapter has provided a brief review of gaze behavior manifested by infants in the presence of their mothers as a prelude to the consideration of how procedures used in studying the relationships of gaze to emotion expression in adults could be extended to the study of emotion expression in infants and children. I have identified certain problems and suggested how adult-relevant methods could be modified for use with infants and children. Mention was made of the desirability of studying gaze as an interactive aspect of the behavior of mothers with infants and children.[5] In addition I suggested that patterns of gaze direction and of blinking rates might be concomitants, perhaps even indicators, of specific emotional displays. Though it has not been explicitly stated, the reader should understand that gaze in emotional displays is assumed to be but one component in a configuration involving facial expressions, gestures, and tonal qualities of vocalizations. I have, perhaps narrowly, focused on gaze behavior, but I recognize that better understanding of its role in emotion displays rests on investigating gaze in conjunction with other emotion-related expressive signs.

Notes

1 This claim may be overstated. Darwin (1872) argues that facial expressions can be considered to be a complex reflex, and Izard and Buechler (1978, p. 454) provide a summary of their own and others' research strongly suggesting that expressions of interest, disgust, and distress are present at birth. Clearly such expressions do not drop out with maturation.
2 Prior to being filmed, the stimulus persons were given several minutes to think about the experiences they would recount to a sympathetic listener. This was necessary to avoid a facial display that reflected mere cognitive work.
3 The absolute amounts of direct gaze in these patterns are also consistent with amounts reported by Lalljee (1978) in a study in which several actors presented their conceptions of the expressions of joy, rage, and sadness. This was true in spite of the fact that the actors, unaware that their gaze was to be measured, were acting to a camera that represented another person.
4 Research reported by Izard et al. (1980) implies that spontaneous displays of joy, anger, and sorrow can be graded as to the intensity of the display.
5 In this paper scant attention has been given to the details of the procedures used to measure, record, and analyze gaze behavior. Those interested in learning more about such methods and about important methodological issues concerning measurement of the phenomena, will find the following references to be helpful: Exline (1972), Argyle and Cook (1976), Exline and Fehr (1978), and especially Exline and Fehr (in press).

References

Ahrens, R. Beitrag zur Entwicklung der Physiognomie und Mimikerkennen. *Zeitschrift für Experimentalische Angewandte Psychologie,* 1954, *2,* 412–54.
Argyle, M., & Cook, M. *Gaze and mutual gaze.* New York: Cambridge University Press, 1976.
Argyle, M., & Dean, J. Eye contact, distance and affiliation. *Sociometry,* 1965, *28,* 289–304.
Atkinson, J., Broddick, O., & Moor, K. Infants' detection of image defocus. *Vision Research,* 1977, *17,* 1125–6.
Bowlby, J. The nature of the child's tie to its mother. *International Journal of Psychoanalysis,* 1958, *39,* 350–73.
Campos, J. J., & Stenberg, C. R. Perception, appraisal and emotion: The onset of social referencing. In M. Lamb & L. Sherrod (Eds.), *Infant social cognition.* Hillsdale, N.J.: Erlbaum, 1980.
Chance, M. R. A. An interpretation of some agonistic postures: The role of "cut-off" acts and postures. *Symposia of the Zoological Society of London,* 1962, *8,* 71–89.
Darwin, C. R. *The expression of the emotions in man and animals.* London: John Murray, 1872.
Dirks, J., & Gibson, E. Infants' perception of similarity between live people and their photographs. *Child Development,* 1977, *48,* 124–30.
Ekman, P., & Oster, H. Facial expressions of emotion. In M. R. Rosenzweig & L. W. Porter (Eds.), *Annual review of psychology.* Palo Alto, Calif.: Annual Reviews, 1979.
Ellsworth, P. C., & Carlsmith, J. M. Effects of eye contact and verbal content on affective response to a dyadic interaction. *Journal of Personality and Social Psychology,* 1968, *10,* 15–20.
Ellsworth, P. C., Carlsmith, J. M., & Henson, A. The stare as a stimulus to flight in human subjects: A series of field experiments. *Journal of Personality and Social Psychology,* 1972, *21,* 302–11.
Ellsworth, P. C., & Langer, E. J. Staring and approach: An interpretation of the stare as a nonspecific behavior. *Journal of Personality and Social Psychology,* 1976, *33,* 117–22.
Exline, R. V. Explorations in the process of person perception: Visual interaction in relation to competition, sex, and need for affiliation. *Journal of Personality,* 1963, *31,* 1–20.
Exline, R. V. The glances of power and preference. In J. K. Cole (Ed.), *Nebraska Symposium on Motivation* (Vol. 19). Lincoln: University of Nebraska Press, 1972.

Exline, R. V. *Nonverbal behaviors of candidates in the presidential debates of 1976: Possible correlates of perceived competence.* Paper presented at the 2nd National Conference on Body Language, New York, October 18–19, 1978.

Exline, R. V., & Fehr, B. J. Applications of semiosis to the study of visual interaction. In A. W. Siegman & S. Feldstein (Eds.), *Nonverbal behavior and communication.* Hillsdale, N.J.: Erlbaum, 1978.

Exline, R. V., & Fehr, B. J. The assessment of gaze and mutual gaze. In K. Scherer and P. Ekman (Eds.), *Methods of research on nonverbal communication.* New York: Cambridge University Press, in press.

Exline, R., Gottheil, E., Parades, A., & Winkelmayer, R. Gaze patterns of normals and schizophrenics retelling happy, sad, and angry experiences. In C. E. Izard (Ed.), *Emotions in personality and psychopathology.* New York: Plenum Press, 1979.

Exline, R. V., & Winters, L. C. Affective relations and mutual glances in dyads. In S. Tomkins & C. E. Izard (Eds.), *Affect, cognition and personality.* New York: Springer, 1965.

Exline, R. V., & Yellin, A. Eye contact as a sign between man and monkey. *Proceedings of the 19th International Congress of Psychology.* London: Methuen, 1969.

Field, T. M. Effects of early separation, interactive defects, and environmental manipulations on infant–mother face to face interaction. *Child Development,* 1977, *48,* 763–811.

Gale, A., Lucas, B., Nissim, R., & Harpham, B. Some EEG correlates of face to face contact. *British Journal of Social and Clinical Psychology,* 1972, *11,* 326–32.

Greenman, G. W. Visual behavior of newborn infants. In A. Solnit & S. Provence (Eds.), *Modern perspectives in child development.* New York: International Universities Press, 1963.

Haith, M. L., Bergman, T., & Moore, M. J. Eye contact and face scanning in early infancy. *Science,* 1977, *198,* 853–5.

Hall, K. R. L., & Devore, I. Baboon social behavior. In I. Devore (Ed.), *Primate behavior: Field studies of monkeys and apes.* New York: Holt, Rinehart & Winston, 1965.

Hinde, R. A., & Rowell, T. E. Communication by posture and facial expressions in the rhesus monkey (*Macca mulatta*). *Proceedings of the Zoological Society of London,* 1962, *138,* 1–21.

Izard, C. E., & Buechler, S. Emotion expressions and personality integration in infancy. In C. E. Izard (Ed.), *Emotions in personality and psychopathology.* New York: Plenum Press, 1979.

Izard, C. E., Huebner, R., Risser, D., McGinnes, G., & Dougherty, L. M. The young infant's ability to produce discrete emotion expressions. *Developmental Psychology,* 1980, *16,* 132–40.

Jay, P. Field studies. In A. Schrier, H. F. Harlow, & F. Stollnitz (Eds.), *Behavior of nonhuman primates: Modern research trends.* New York: Academic Press, 1965.

Kagan, J., & Lewis, M. Studies of attention in the human infant. *Merrill-Palmer Quarterly,* 1965, *2,* 95–127.

Kanfer, F. H. Verbal rate, eyeblink, and content in structured psychiatric interviews. *Journal of Abnormal and Social Psychology,* 1960, *61* (3), 341–7.

Kleinke, C. L., & Pohlen, P. D. Affective and emotional responses as a function of other person's gaze and cooperativeness in a two-person game. *Journal of Personality and Social Psychology,* 1971, *17,* 308–13.

Kreutzer, M. A., & Charlesworth, W. R. *Infants' reactions to different expressions of emotion.* Paper presented at the meeting of the Society for Research in Child Development, Philadelphia, March 1973.

Kurtz, J. Nonverbal norm sending and territorial defense. (Doctoral dissertation, University of Delaware, 1975). *Dissertation Abstracts International,* 1975, *36,* 1508B. (University Microfilms No. 75–20, 554)

La Barbera, J. D., Izard, C. E., Vietz, P., & Parisi, S. A. Four- and six-month-old infants' visual responses to joy, anger, and neutral expressions. *Child Development,* 1976, *47,* 535–8.

Lalljee, M. The role of gaze in the expression of emotion. *Australian Journal of Psychology,* 1978, *30,* 59–67.

Mailer, N. *The armies of the night.* New York: Signet, 1968.

Maurer, D., & Salapatek, P. Developmental changes in the scanning of faces by young infants. *Child Development,* 1976, *47,* 523–7.

Nelson, C. A., Morse, P. A., & Leavitt, L. A. Recognition of facial expressions by seven-month-old infants. *Child Development,* 1979, *50,* 1239–42.

Nichols, K. A., & Champness, B. G. Eye gaze and the GSR. *Journal of Experimental Social Psychology,* 1971, *7,* 623–6.

Peterson, J., & Allison, L. W. Controls of the eye-wink mechanism. *Journal of Experimental Psychology,* 1931, *14,* 144–54.

Ponder, E., & Kennedy, W. P. On the act of blinking. *Quarterly Journal of Experimental Physiology,* 1927, *18,* 89–110.

Rheingold, H. L. The effect of environmental stimulation upon social and exploratory behavior in the human infant. In B. M. Foss (Ed.), *Determinants of infant behavior* (Vol. 1). New York: Wiley, 1961.

Robeson, K. S. The role of eye to eye contact in maternal–infant attachment. *Journal of Child Psychology and Psychiatry,* 1967, *8,* 13–25.

Scaife, M., & Bruner, J. S. The capacity for joint visual attention in the infant. *Nature,* 1975, *200,* 263–6.

Schaffer, H. R. Early interactive development. In H. R. Schaffer (Ed.), *Studies in mother-infant interaction.* London: Academic Press, 1977.

Schaffer, H. R., & Crook, C. The role of the mother in early social development. In H. McGurk (Ed.), *Issues in childhood social development.* London: Methuen, 1978.

Shaller, G. *The mountain gorilla: Ecology and behavior.* Chicago: University of Chicago Press, 1963.

Stern, D. N. Mother and infant at play: The dyadic interaction involving facial, vocal, and gaze behaviors. In M. Lewis & L. A. Rosenblum (Eds.), *The origins of behavior: Vol. 1. The effects of the infant on its caregiver.* New York: Wiley, 1974.

White, B. L., Castle, P., & Held, R. Observations on the development of visually directed reaching. *Child Development,* 1964, *35,* 349–64.

Wilcox, B. M., & Clayton, F. L. Infant visual fixation on motion pictures of the human face. *Journal of Experimental Child Psychology,* 1968, *6,* 22–32.

Wood, L. A., & Saunders, J. C. Blinking frequency: A neurophysiological measurement of psychological stress. *Diseases of the Nervous System,* 1962, *23* (3), 158–63.

Young-Browne, G., Rosenfeld, H. M., & Horowitz, F. D. Infant discrimination of facial expressions. *Child Development,* 1977, *48,* 555–62.

Zigler, E. F., & Child, I. L. (Eds.). *Socialization and personality development.* Reading, Mass.: Addison-Wesley, 1973.

8   The measurement of emotional state

Michael Lewis and Linda Michalson

The specific problem of measurement to be addressed derives from our interest in the study of emotional development. The particular measurement problem we choose to focus on is how to measure individual differences in emotional state. This particular issue grows out of a common observation, an example of which follows:

G., a house guest for several days, is speaking about her host's two children. She remarks that the two children are quite different: "the first appears to be quite happy and sociable," smiling and moving about and wanting to be near others, while the other looks "a bit fearful," always avoiding new situations and people.

What are we to make of G.'s statements? An analysis reveals that there are three aspects of her remarks that warrant further consideration. First, G. is talking about emotional behavior in her discussion of the children. As we will see, the observation of emotional behavior is usually predicated on a behavior-by-situation analysis. In this example, G. has noticed particular behaviors such as the facial expression of smiling and postural activities that occur in response to particular events, in this case, novel situations and people. Furthermore, her remarks concern behaviors associated with the emotional rather than the cognitive domain.

Second, G. is talking about emotional behavior that is enduring. Rather than referring to the occurrence of a single emotional event, G. is talking about characteristics of the children that apply to many different situations. Whether she has actually observed the children in many different situations or in the same situation on repeated occasions, her remarks allude to enduring attributes of the children as they appear to her, rather than referring to transient emotional states. Consequently, G.'s observations appear to be related to characteristics usually referred to as personality characteristics (see Lewis & Michalson, in press).

The data collection and scale construction were supported in part by grants from the Carnegie Corporation and the Office of Child Development; © 1980 Michael Lewis and Linda Michalson.

The final point in our example stresses the difference between the two children. G.'s observation makes us focus not on how the two children express a particular emotion in a particular context but rather on the degree or amount of a particular emotion expressed over the length of observation. We have little idea whether this observation is limited by the specific context or situations available or by the particular manner in which either child exhibits emotional behavior, yet both factors and more may be a source of individual differences in emotional behavior.

This example and the three points made in our brief discussion are not unique. Students, even at the undergraduate level, experience little difficulty in describing differences in the emotional behaviors of children they observe. They understand what is expected of them, and there is relatively high agreement (especially when we consider that they are untrained observers) concerning individual differences among children, particularly with emotional states such as anger, happiness, and fear.

Because we generally have little difficulty when asked to differentiate among people on the basis of differences in emotional mood, a systematic investigation of individual differences in enduring emotional behavior seems reasonable. Although there has been some discussion of emotional development in the research literature (e.g., Lewis & Rosenblum, 1978; Sroufe, 1979), there is almost no mention of enduring emotions. Moreover, in very few instances has emotional behavior been measured outside the research laboratory. In fact, most studies have used coding systems to identify emotional expressions that involve an elaborate procedure that requires careful observation of facial expressions (Ekman & Ostet, 1979; Izard & Dougherty, this volume). Although such procedures enable us to differentiate among emotional expressions, it cannot be lost on the reader that in our everyday life we are able to perceive and respond to emotional behavior without laboratory procedures and elaborate coding systems. Thus our task was to determine if we could construct a measurement instrument that would: (a) have the capacity to measure several different socioemotional states, specifically, anger, happiness, fear, attachment, and competence; (b) measure these emotions in natural settings related to the everyday activities of children; (c) differentiate among individual children; (d) generate a socioemotional profile for each child; and (e) be appropriate for use with young children between the ages of 3 to 30 months.

Before describing the construction of the socioemotional scales, it is necessary to consider the basic assumptions that underlie our work in the study of emotional development. Two specific topics will be considered: first, a discussion of the terms and concepts related to the study of emotions, and second, the conceptual basis for a measurement system of emotion. Following this discussion, the measurement system itself as well as data relevant to its use will be presented.

Taxonomy of emotional terms

Rather than describing various emotions that have already been portrayed in a number of excellent reviews (e.g., Izard, 1977), we should like to distinguish among some terms more than is usually done in the study of emotions (Lewis & Rosenblum, 1978).

In order for an emotion to occur, some stimulus event must trigger a change in the internal physiological state of the individual. We call this event an elicitor. Emotional elicitors may be either external or internal stimuli. External stimuli can be either nonsocial (e.g., a loud noise) or social (e.g., separation from an appearance of a loved one). On the other hand, internal stimuli may range from specific physiological states (e.g., a drop in blood sugar level) to complex cognitive activities (e.g., failing to assimilate a new experience). Because it is obviously much harder for an experimenter to identify and control an internal elicitor than an external elicitor, most research has focused on external elicitors, with attempts made to determine the specific dimensions of the elicitor that activate the emotion (e.g., Lewis & Brooks, 1974; Skarin, 1977; Sroufe, Waters, & Matas, 1974).

The changes in physiological state produced by the emotional elicitor may be mediated by relatively specific pathways or areas that lie either within the primitive midbrain area or in the neocortex. These pathways or loci are known as emotional receptors. The process by which these emotional receptors acquire their affective function and the type of stimuli capable of activating them may be genetically encoded or acquired through experience. Attempts to trace the neural circuit and to outline the roles played by various neural structures in emotional behavior have been relatively unsuccessful, although the brain-stem reticular formation, the thalamus, the hypothalamus, the limbic system, and the neocortex may be involved to varying degrees in emotion and behavior (Strongman, 1973).

Accompanying the change in the internal physiological state of the individual are observable surface changes in the face, body, voice, and activity level of the individual. The internal response and the surface expression will vary in intensity over time, yet on any one occasion they will endure only for a relatively short period of time. The specific components of the surface expression and their patterning, as well as the constancy with which the expression is linked to a particular internal state, may be influenced by genetic inheritance, individual differences, and cultural roles.

Finally, in order to experience the emotion, it is necessary that individuals be able to perceive the pattern of changes in their physiological state and overt expression and be able to evaluate such changes in relation to the immediate context and past experiences. In addition, individuals must incorporate into their own interpretation the perception and evaluation of these changes by others. This cognitive–evaluative process will be influenced by a vast variety of prior experiences in which other individuals defined the nature of the eliciting event and the appropriateness of particular expressions. In fact, this aspect more than others defines the socialization of emotional behavior [Lewis & Michalson, in press (b)]. This experiential factor is particularly important during infancy, when parents provide a cognitive–evaluative context for the infant's emotional expressions through their words and actions (Brooks-Gunn & Lewis, in press; Lewis & Brooks, 1978; Lewis & Brooks-Gunn, 1979).

Four elements, then, are central to any definition of emotion: (a) an elicited change in the physiological state of the individual, (b) accompanying observable changes in the surface expression, (c) their perception, and (d) their evaluation by the individual (Lewis & Rosenblum, 1978). Given these four aspects, it is possible to define several terms among which the literature on emotion rarely differentiates. Specifically, we wish to differentiate among emotional state, expression, and experience in order to facilitate the construction of theory. As shall become obvious, the continued confusion of terms has obstructed the study of emotional development and the understanding of emotions in general.

Emotional state refers to the internal changes in the physiological activity that are produced when an emotional elicitor triggers an emotional receptor. *Emotional expression,* on the other hand, denotes the observable surface behaviors that accompany the internal response. These may include postural and vocal responses in addition to facial muscular changes. Finally, the perception and evaluation of such changes constitute an *emotional experience*. Although emotional states are defined by physical changes often including external expressions, emotional experiences require cognitive processes. Consequently, until organisms have or utilize the capacity to perceive and evaluate their own behavior – that is, until they are able to self-reflect – it is likely that emotional experiences are restricted. We must therefore restrict our discussion to emotional states. From a developmental perspective, no emotional experience is possible until a concept of self is acquired. In our investigations, this occurs at about 8 months of age or at the time self-permanence emerges (Lewis & Brooks-Gunn, 1979).

As we are interested in measuring differences in emotional behavior, the theoretical distinction between emotional states and experiences is not critical. Even so, such a distinction is important in terms of developmental issues. In fact, because emotional states and experiences are internal activities not open to verification by another, one can never be certain of the internal experience of another. In all our discussion of the development of emotions, this fact must be kept in mind: *Emotional experiences are private acts*. Like all other persons, parents must depend upon empathy and attribution when they state that their infant or child "is frightened" or "is feeling happy or joyful." Emotional experiences are public only insofar as emotional expressions are made available and insofar as the socialization process permits both a correct attribution, that is, an attribution that matches the internal feeling of another person, or an empathic response that is accurate (Lewis, 1980). The implication of these conclusions for a measurement system is important, to wit, any measurement task that requires an observer will involve the same process that observers use in everyday experiences to infer emotional states or experiences. In a word, at this point in the study of emotions we must be satisfied with a measurement system that cannot inform us about internal acts. In our everyday observation of emotions, two classes of events guide both our attributive and empathic behaviors. In order to infer emotional states, we consider *both and at the same time* (a) select vocal, postural, and facial behaviors, and (b) the particular contexts in which these behaviors occur. As we shall see, both behaviors and contexts are necessary to identify specific emotions. The study of emotional behavior must take both the behaviors of the child and the context of those behaviors into account. We will now turn to these factors.

Meaning of behavior

A review of the literature on emotions indicates that for subjects of all ages, no single behavior can act as a necessary and sufficient referent for any single emotion. Even crying, perhaps the most likely candidate, fails to meet this requirement, because crying may signal feelings of anger, sadness, or even joy! Inhibition of action can also be in the service of such different states as thoughtfulness, attention, or fear. A given stimulus may initially evoke smiling and laughter, yet if it is constantly repeated, it may elicit crying. Indeed, some stimuli may at different moments produce a number of patterns in an infant. In this regard, neither approaching nor withdrawing, nor looking toward or away, nor reaching for or holding back, to name a few possibilities, offers us the simple operationally defined distinctions we seek. In a word, there is no one-to-one correspondence between a response and a particular emotion.

From such an analysis, it would appear that a pattern of interrelated responses, not a specific response itself, should be studied. Still, it is not clear that even a complex set of responses can serve as a marker for a particular emotion independent of either the subjective report of the child or the knowledge of the stimulus that elicited that pattern. Nevertheless, patterned responses may offer us the best hope of finding a relationship between behavior and the internal experience we term *emotion*. Toward such an effort, Campos, Emde, Gaensbauer, and Henderson (1975) have suggested the possibility of a relationship between behavioral responses such as facial expressions and the autonomic-nervous-system (ANS) response of heart rate change. In combination these measures may reflect a particular emotion such as fear, although there is still considerable controversy as to whether heart rate response, particularly acceleration, is related to fear (Lewis, Brooks, & Haviland, 1978). To complicate the matter further, the patterns of behavior we observe may differ between groups of individuals, between members of the same group and, to increase the complexity even more, within the same individual at different times. Genetic and ontogenetic factors, cognitive and motor abilities, and cultural experiences as well as immediate antecedent events will all serve to alter the structure of these response patterns in any given individual.

Ontogenetic differences are particularly salient, as the capacities that are critical for the expression of emotions themselves vary with age (Lewis & Starr, 1979). For example, how can physical withdrawal serve as a measure of fear in a child too young to move about? Is eye aversion an index of fear in the infant too young to walk but only an index of distraction or disinterest in the toddler? In short, does a given behavior, or even a set of behaviors, maintain its relationship to the underlying feeling state, or is a more fluid combination of behaviors (those open to transformation with age) required for us to infer a particular emotion?

Because single behavioral responses do not reflect emotional states, some workers have postulated particular emotional systems in the infant that are regarded as uniquely organized sets of responses integrated within the nervous system, each of which is functionally independent of other such systems in terms of the stimuli that elicit it and the neural structures that subsume it. Unfortunately, this systems approach has its own pitfalls, and we may be no better off by the assumption of a system than we are by the selection of a single response measure. In fact, most of the data regarding this issue suggest that no one single system independent of other systems is elicited by a class of events (Bretherton & Ainsworth, 1974; Sroufe et al., 1974). In a study of fear behavior, Haviland and Lewis (1975) found, for example, that the approach of strangers evokes both smiling and prolonged gaze as well as aversion, lip quivering, and even crying.

Another issue related to the measurement of emotions has to do with the problem of assessing the intensity of an emotional state. For example, some children can be said to be more fearful or more happy than others. How can we capture differences in degree or the amount of an emotional state? Although this problem has received almost no attention in the research literature, some of the discussion in studies of fear is relevant. Fear is reserved for intense negative responses, whereas wariness can be used to indicate moderate levels of emotional expression (Rheingold & Eckerman, 1973). Responses such as sobering might reflect even less intensity, an emotional state like that of children paying attention to the events around them. The problem of what to call the behavioral pattern is an example of the type of difficulty that needs to be overcome. It has been widely recognized that the appearance and approach of a novel stimulus or the loss of a familiar one may result in an inhibition of ongoing activity and an increase in attentive behaviors such as eye gaze, heart rate decelerations, and so forth. This is often referred to as a general state of alerting or arousal and has even been referred to as attending or orienting (Lewis, 1975). If one chooses to call this set of behaviors *wariness* or *sobering*, one risks biasing the response as a negative emotional behavior. Because the observer usually knows the context in which the facial–postural responses are obtained, such biasing may be common. In fact, this bias may be exactly what adults use to infer through attribution what the child is feeling.

The specific behaviors or sets of behaviors that we use to reference an emotion include three classes: facial, physiological, and postural, or gestural. Facial expressions of emotion were articulated first by Darwin (1872/1965) and then by Tomkins (1962), Ekman and Friesen (1975), and Izard (1977). We need not spend time discussing their work except to reiterate that most of these systems require an elaborate scoring system before an emotional state can be inferred. Observation of people's behavior in everyday situations indicates that we are capable of making decisions concerning people's internal states without such systems. In the present study of emotions, we rely on these coding systems only to generate a set of facial behaviors to use in our measurement scales.

Because our interest is in the measurement of emotions in naturalistic situations of daily life, we did not consider measurement systems involving physiological behaviors. Nevertheless, we should be alerted to the limitations of such measures and their lack of relationship to other aspects of behavior (Lewis et al., 1978). Although Campos and his associates have shown that heart rate acceleration, a response associated with stress, appears to accompany children's response to fearful events (Campos et al., 1973; Schwartz, Campos, & Baisel, 1973), many explanations for this change are possible. For example, the crying or flight associated with fear may cause general motor arousal, which in turn naturally leads to heart rate increases. In fact, in a recent study, we have shown that heart rate responses do not seem to covary with facial expression except in the case of an *attentive* face. Although attentive faces were highly associated with heart rate deceleration, in this study neither fearful nor happy faces appeared to be related to heart rate change (Lewis et al., 1978). Nevertheless, although others have used heart rate acceleration to reference fear (e.g., Skarin, 1977; Waters, Matas, & Sroufe, 1975), the relationship between physiological indexes and facial expression remains relatively unexplored. It is still widely believed that a covarying set of facial and physiological responses exists, although the search for such sets has yet to prove useful. Besides heart rate, other ANS responses including respiration, galvanic skin responses (GSR), and vasodilation have been used; at this point, none has proved any more reliable in distinguishing among emotional states.

Postural responses in humans have probably received the least attention in empirical studies, a surprising fact, for body movements probably carry considerable information. In fact, at a distance they may have more signal value than facial–muscular changes inasmuch as they are larger and more visible. Postural responses are present in animals with little facial musculature and are used both by humans and conspecifics to signal internal states. We consider wagging of the tail to indicate a dog's pleasure but a cat's displeasure. This example should alert us to two issues: First, postural responses can be used to infer emotions, and second, no response can be considered sufficient for inferring a particular state.

Human postural behavior has not been well studied. Still, we have little trouble distinguishing bodily responses of tension (for example, shaking one's leg or sitting in certain ways) from responses of relaxation (for example, body not held stiffly and muscles not tensed). Movements toward and away from an object are often used to infer emotional states, as are movements such as raising the arms or hitting and throwing. In fact, in a recent study of mothers' use of emotional labels, we have found that mothers of 1-year-olds frequently use postural indicators to infer emotional states. For example, throwing objects and kicking are actions used to infer anger [Lewis & Michalson, in press (b)]. In the absence of facial behavior, postural cues become particularly important for inferring an emotional state. Consider the child who rapidly moves away from the stranger and hides behind its mother. Both facial and physiological responses are unavailable for use by the observer. The postural/movement cues are quite sufficient to label the behavior as fearful or shy, however. Even in conditions where mobility is restricted because the child is either motorically immature or unable to get away (as in a high chair), postural cues are still available. A familiar toy placed on the surface of the high chair in front of the child or a friend approaching often result in children moving themselves as close to the object or person as possible. Proxemics also are used as references for emotions: Consider children who grab their caregivers and hold tightly to them. These behaviors, at least in everyday encounters, are used as indexes of emotional states. Unfortunately, they have been underused in empirical research.

The relationship between facial and postural activity has not been explored, yet facial–postural activities may relate to one another in an additive or substitutive fashion. For example, under intense fear, the child may show both facial and bodily cues that we can reference as fear. On the other hand, the child may use one set rather than another. In fact, it may be the case that the inability to use one set of cues may activate or accentuate the use of another. We have suggested that facial expressions of fear are intensified by preventing the child from fleeing (Lewis, 1980). Those studies in which the child cannot move away from the approaching stranger may produce more facial response than would occur if the child could flee. This seems more than reasonable; part of the fleeing function is to inform the stranger of the internal state of the fleeing organism. If this response is not available, the approaching figure needs to be informed by other means, and facial expression becomes a good alternative. In other words, the inability to express affect through bodily movement may accentuate facial expressions. From a general system's point of view, this would mean that blockage of one set of behaviors from a larger set makes the remaining set of behaviors more intense.

At this point in the research study of emotional expression, many of the issues of measurement remain unanswered. We do not know whether one set of responses better references an emotional state than another. We do not know the relationship between sets of responses, nor do we have any idea of how they change as a function of ontogeny and culture. Clearly, new responses appear as the child develops; in addition, as the child becomes more mature, forms of expressions change. As new responses are added, old ones may become increasingly inappropriate. For instance, in our culture, crying is acceptable in the opening year or two of life, but it is discouraged in the preschool child. Thus the meaning of crying as a referent of emotions changes (Lewis, 1967). Finally, we recognize the possibility of vast individual differences in responses that children use to express emotions. It appears certain to be the case that different children use different responses and combinations of responses. Although the source of these differences is unclear, many have their origins in temperamental differences or different familial patterns of interaction.

Within any discussion of individual differences in response tendencies, we must consider individual differences in the degree of an emotional state. This issue, rather than addressing the topic of transient emotional states, raises the more general topic of enduring states or characteristics of the child. As we mentioned earlier, the difference between fleeting and enduring emotions is of central importance to any theory of development. In the measurement of emotion that we undertook, a variety of facial, postural, and vocal behaviors were used to infer an emotional state. Moreover, we attempted to assess the degree of the emotional state by concentrating on the amount and intensity of emotional expression. If these expressions could be shown to be consistent across a wider number of different situations, we might be able to infer something about enduring states and individual differences in these states.

Stimulus or contextual meaning

We have tried to argue that the referencing of emotions in general and any emotion in particular requires knowledge of the behaviors displayed as well as of the context in which those behaviors occurred (Lewis, 1980; Lewis & Rosenblum, 1978). The matrix, which is made up of behavior and context, provides the means by which all of us are able to reference particular internal states. In fact, it is the case that attribution – a primary means of inferring emotions – is based on both factors. As we have seen, responses and combinations of responses in and of themselves cannot help us in making judgments concerning the particular internal state.

For example, although laughing most of the time reflects a joyous state, knowledge of the context in which this behavior is expressed is critical if a correct inference about the internal state or experience is to be made. To be told whether the context is a good joke or news that one's friend has just died invests any facial or vocal expression with essential meaning. Adults know and children soon learn (exactly how soon has not been systematically studied) that it is important to hide the real feelings and to substitute false cues. An example of this masking of internal states can easily be observed. Laughter at one's boss's joke may mask the true feeling of boredom or even disgust.

Dissociations between facial, postural, and vocal behaviors and internal state are the natural occurrences of socialization and reflect cultural differences. For example, Japanese children are taught early the difference between public and private acts, and this undoubtedly affects the public display of emotion. Dissociations between expression and internal states probably occur more readily for some emotions than others. Happiness and sadness are social emotions to the extent that we use them more readily in social commerce, and we have learned to "put them on" for the sake of others. This is probably less so for fear, because put-on fear is less used socially. Nevertheless, even fear is socialized, as in cases where feeling afraid is inappropriate. In such contexts, not acting afraid is the socially accepted form, and the internal state of fear is hidden behind sets of responses not usually considered fearful. For example, the child or adolescent who does not wish to appear afraid on the roller coaster may laugh instead of crying or moaning. Whatever the expression, the need to understand the context and, more importantly, the interface between behavior and context are vital. Regardless of the measurements or the labels applied, our understanding of the development of any particular emotion and the antecedent conditions depends on our ability to specify the stimulus conditions within which our assessment and evaluations are made.

Even here, in defining the context, there are considerable difficulties. Reliance on the observer/experimenter for the definition of the stimulus is, at best, a risky activity (Pervin & Lewis, 1978), because the definition of the context resides in the subject. Although there may be a relatively high correspondence between what the experimenter intends the context to be and what the subject experiences, it is never perfect. A joyful situation as defined by the experimenter may not be joyful for all the subjects. Thus, to say that all subject responses across an experimenter-defined context are the same is most likely to introduce large amounts of error. Consider the statement, "Today my son was graduated from his school." When asked to describe the feelings evoked by this statement, some people would respond that it is a happy feeling elicited by the achievement of an important goal. Others might respond that the feelings are sad, for now the child will go off to college. Still others might feel a mixture of happiness and sadness. The experimenter who assumes that it is a happy situation for all subjects runs the risk of looking at and summing different contexts and different emotional responses. Parenthetically we could say that this may be one of the reasons why we cannot obtain responses or sets of responses for a particular emotional state with any high degree of reliability; that is, we may be combining different emotional responses.

The issue of stimulus meaning, regardless of who may define the stimulus, raises the problem of measurement. In particular, two aspects of the context have been considered in the research literature: (a) the physical properties of the central stimulus and (b) the contextual cues provided by prior events and current conditions (Lewis, 1980). The physical characteristics of specific stimuli, particularly social stimuli, that influence infants' responses have been studied for only a few emotional states, in particular, fear and happiness. Many studies have explored in detail the social characteristics of people that provoke fear. These include the person's sex, size, age, degree of familiarity, and manner of behaving. It is particularly important to know whether the stimulus is a stranger, a familiar, or an attachment figure.

Furthermore, one must remember that the child's prior experience with the class to which the individual belongs may have an important impact on the child's response even on first exposure to that specific person. Thus, for example, a stranger or even a familiar person wearing a white laboratory coat may provoke an emotional state independent of the person but dependent on the child's past experience with white coats. More generally, on repeated exposure through processes ranging from simple stimulus habituation to complex assimilations to changes in overall levels of arousal, the child shows response changes to the same stimulus. For example, two equally novel toys may evoke very different responses, depending on the state of the child, the state itself being dependent on the history of past events. In one case, the first novel toy presented to the child may evoke arousal, interest, exploration, and pleasure. The second presentation to an already aroused child may provoke upset, however, as the threshold of arousal is raised beyond the pleasurable level and the child is unable to control the arousal. From a more cognitive point of view, a consideration of this temporal sequence of stimuli in terms of both immediate and more remote antecedent events invokes some hypothetical memory capacity that allows children to recognize previously experienced figures and to alter their response configuration accordingly. The development of such cognitive structures, especially in early childhood, is essential in the consideration of past experiences (e.g., familiarity) on the child's emotional state.

In terms of the physical characteristics of specific stimuli, the few studies that exist describe relatively few dimensions. Two that have received some attention are age and sex. In a series of studies in our laboratory, we have shown that children respond more positively to strange children than they do to strange adults (Brooks & Lewis, 1976; Lewis & Brooks, 1974). Sex differences have been reported indicating that male strangers elicit more fear than females (Benjamin, 1961; Greenberg, Hillman, & Grice, 1973; Morgan & Ricciuti, 1969; Shaffran & Décarie, 1973; Skarin, 1977), although there is some reason to believe that height rather than gender may be the important dimension (Feinman, 1980; Weinraub & Putney, 1978).

The broader context in which emotional behavior is observed, however, is perhaps more important than the characteristics of the primary stimulus, yet little attention has been given to the context in the study of infant emotional behavior. In part, one reason for the failure to consider the situation has been the assumption that adults (i.e., the experimenters) know the contexts and therefore know the meaning of the emotional responses we observe. Thus, we create emotion-producing situations such as a visual cliff, a stranger's approach, or a mother–child interaction and assume that the behaviors observed reference fear or joy. Although this may be the case, it must be remembered that the same context for one person may not be the same for another. Even more risky is the danger of circularity in producing a particular emotional context and assuming that the behaviors observed in that context reference a particular emotional state. Haviland and Lewis (1975), in fact, have shown that the approach of a stranger may produce *both* fearful and greeting behaviors. If we are prepared to find only fearful behaviors in fearful contexts, we are apt to err in our interpretation of the meaning of behavior. This may be more than idle speculation and the cause of many discrepancies in the literature on the fear of strangers. The wide-eye gaze and cessation of activity found when the stranger approaches can be found also when infants look at and attend to a visual array of geometric forms. In other words, wide-eye gaze and decreases in activity accompany attending and are not specific to fearfulness. Indeed, as discussed earlier, the use of sobering and other wary behaviors may reflect more of an attentional emotional response than a fearful one.

Although the experimental manipulation of context is often carried out in laboratory studies of emotional responses, the context dimension in the socialization of emotional responses and states in naturalistic circumstances also needs consideration. Independent of the responses that people make, we know that certain contexts are more likely than others to elicit particular emotional states. Funerals are likely to elicit sadness, whereas circuses are likely to elicit joy. Weddings, on the other hand, are more likely to elicit a mixture of emotional states and experiences. Knowledge of the emotional states or experiences likely to be elicited by the context occurs as a consequence of socialization, although there are some models of emotion that ascribe emotional states and experiences to particular unlearned emotional elicitors (Darwin, 1872/1965). Although in fact this may be the case, we hold to the view that emotional states and experiences are elicited for the most part as a consequence of an elaborate process of socialization that includes past experiences, empathy, and the responses of others to our own behaviors, including emotional expressions. In a word, knowledge about which contexts are likely to elicit which emotional states is learned. We would hold that this material is learned as a type of script, similar to that described by Abelson (1976), that informs us prior to the fact that under certain conditions we are more likely to see certain types of emotional responses. In addition to or as part of this socialization process there are two means – attribution and empathy – that we use to decide under which situations we are likely to see which particular emotional states. Whatever the process underlying this knowledge, at some point in development we are able to utilize contextual information in understanding and interpreting emotional behavior.

The development of contextual knowledge is complex and worthy of additional study. One particular way children learn about contextual cues and are influenced by contextual cues is from their observation of others. Lewis and Feiring (1980) have analyzed these effects, describing them as indirect. Study of children's learning through these indirect effects indicates that even young children are capable of using their mother's emotional behavior toward others as a referent in determining the emotional state exhibited by the child toward a third person. Recently, we found that 15-month-old children were considerably less fearful and made friends with a stranger in a shorter amount of time if their mothers showed a positive attitude rather than a neutral attitude toward the stranger upon the stranger's entrance into the room (Feiring, Lewis, & Starr, 1981). These data confirm our view that children's emotional responses can be mediated by their observation of another person's response to these same events. To the extent that the caregiver's presence and behavior constitute part of the context for the child, these variables play an important role in influencing the nature of the emotion that the central stimulus produces. That this appears to be the case in infancy when cognitive faculties are relatively immature suggests that for older children these same factors may play an even more important role in the emotional quality of their interaction with other people and objects.

The construction of socioemotional scales

The measurement instrument that we have constructed derives from the assumption that neither a single behavior (or set of behaviors alone) nor a particular context by itself is sufficient for the understanding of emotional states or experiences. Rather, our inferences concerning states and experiences are based upon the information generated from a matrix composed of contexts and behaviors.[1]

In order to develop an assessment instrument that would meet the requirements of the tasks specified at the beginning of this chapter (which could be used in the context of the daily life of the child and to measure enduring characteristics of individual children), we needed to construct both a behavioral and a situational index. Rather than basing the indexes of behaviors and situations on a laboratory setting, we relied on the observations of children in day-care settings. We chose a day-care setting because it typically contains a wide array of potentially emotional situations. A day-care rather than home environment was chosen also because the socioemotional states that we wished to study required some situations that we felt were more easily obtained in a day-care setting. Moreover, as part of the task was to try to devise an instrument that might be used to evaluate children's emotional status in an intervention program, a day-care setting seemed ideal. It should be noted, however, that the situations we included in the scales can be observed in other contexts, such as the home. Although the instrument was constructed in a day-care context, its use should thus be general.

The methodology of scale construction

Sample. In the construction of the scales, we studied two samples of children. They ranged in age from 3 to 30 months and were from low-income families. Both white and black children were observed, although most of the children were black. In the first sample, there were 34 children (18 male, 16 female); in the second sample, there were 32 children (20 male, 12 female). The children in the sample came from three day-care settings, and the average amount of time they had spent in day care was 4.5 months (ranging from 1 to 19 months). The first sample was used to construct the scales and the second sample to test the replicability of the findings. Data for both samples are available, but we will present here those data representing the combined samples. A complete discussion of the sample and the scale construction appears in Michalson (1980) and Lewis and Michalson [in press (a)], so that in this chapter only the more relevant information will be presented.

Domains. For two reasons it was desirable to study individual differences across a set of emotions rather than on a single emotion. First, we were interested in generating profiles of children's enduring emotional states and second, there is almost no information on the relationships between emotions. To this end and limited by the realities of instrument length and observation time constraints, we chose five socioemotional states: fear, anger, happiness, attachment, [2] and competence. We consider them socioemotional rather than emotional because two states – attachment and competence – do not constitute emotions within the currently used taxonomy (Izard, 1978). The selection of these five states was predicted on the conclusions, gained from reviewing the research literature, that we know more about these than others, that these states are central to development (both social and intellectual), and that they represent both positive and negative emotional states. Furthermore, these states involve a considerable portion of the young child's emotional life.

Situations. In our scale construction, situations are the items on which children's responses are to be scored. Situations were selected as items in a complex manner. To begin with, a thorough review of the literature on the five socioemotional states was undertaken, with special attention paid to the situations that others have used to define and study emotions. We were particularly interested in situations that commonly occur in the everyday environment. Thus although the experiences of both the approach of a stranger and the visual cliff have been used as stimuli designed to evoke fear, only the stranger's approach would be used, because the visual cliff is not likely to be present in an everyday environment.

In addition to the literature review, observations in a day-care setting were made on 12 infants who were not part of the final sample. These observations consisted of detailed descriptions of emotion-inducing situations that occurred at the day-care center along with the infant's responses to the situations. From these sources, lists were made of situations that might evoke each of the five socioemotional states. As we would have assumed, some situations were likely to evoke two or more different states. Our solution for this was to include the particular situation in all of the socioemotional domains that were likely to be associated with it.

The original assessment instrument consisted of 83 items distributed across the five socioemotional domains: fear (13), anger (18), happiness (14), attachment/social affiliation (18), and competence (20) (see Table 8.1). These situations were later reduced to a subset as a consequence of our analysis of the data from Sample 1 and the replication with Sample 2. The end result was a much smaller set of items that totaled 46 (see items marked in Table 8.1). Seven of these items were included in more than one domain. Thus, for example, "peer attacks" was found to elicit both anger and fear. Exactly how these situations were chosen will be explained in the discussion of the results.

Table 8.1. *Situations of the socioemotional scales*

Fear
Arrival
Surprising toy
Toy breaks[a]
Peer cries[a]
Peer attacks[a]
Funny (unusual) sound
Caregiver yells[a]
Caregiver forbids
Caregiver scolds
Unfamiliar room[a]
Stranger (enters room)[a]
Stranger approaches[a]
Strange child (enters room)[a]

Anger
Mother leaves
Wants something peer has[a]
Wants something caregiver has
Wants something unreachable
Difficult toy
Toy breaks[a]
Peer gets attention[a]
Peer grabs toy[a]
Peer attacks[a]
Teased[a]
Hidden object[a]
Caregiver takes toy
Caregiver takes bottle/pacifier
Physical restraint
Caregiver forbids
Caregiver scolds[a]
Obstacle
Mother returns

Happiness
Arrival
Completes task
Surprise toy[a]
Mirror – self[a]
Mirror – other[a]
Peer acts silly
Interaction/special attention[a]
Praise[a]
Peekaboo[a]
Teased[a]
Funny (unusual) sound

Caregiver acts silly[a]
Snack[a]
Music[a]

Attachment/Social Affiliation
Low stress situations
  Caregiver greets[a]
  Another mother and child arrive[a]
  Free play
  Group[a]
  Peer cries
  Interaction/special attention
  Caregiver returns[a]
  Stranger (enters room)
  Strange child (enters room)[a]
  Another mother returns
  Mother returns[a]
High stress situations
  Mother puts child down[a]
  Mother leaves[a]
  Another mother arrives[a]
  Peer gets attention[a]
  Caregiver leaves[a]
  Caregiver puts child down[a]
  Another mother returns

Competence
Arrival
Mother puts child down[a]
Free play[a]
Group
Wants something peer has
Wants something caregiver has[a]
Wants something unreachable[a]
Completes task
Difficult toy
Toy breaks[a]
Mirror – self
Mirror – other
Interaction/special attention
Demonstration[a]
Command
Praise
Hidden object
Caregiver puts child down
Obstacle[a]
Unfamiliar room[a]

[a] Situations in the revised version of the scales.

Behaviors. Five sets of emotional behaviors, one for each socioemotional domain, were obtained from a search of the literature as well as from the observation of infants in day-care programs. Special attention was given to infants' facial, vocal, postural, and motor behaviors that occurred in response to emotion-inducing situations.

Behavioral scaling. Measurement should obviously indicate not simply the presence or absence of an emotion but its level or intensity as well. For example, imagine the following situation, which is likely to elicit fear in infants: An unfamiliar adult enters a room where infants are playing and walks slowly toward them. One child looks up and returns to playing. Another turns his back to the stranger, and a third child screams and runs away. In this example, the third child obviously shows the most fear: Screaming is judged to be a more intense response than either looking away or turning away. In short, by scaling the behaviors of each domain along a dimension of intensity, it becomes possible to compare children according to the level of emotion they exhibit in a variety of circumstances.

The following procedures were conducted for the purpose of scaling the behaviors for each of the five domains. The behaviors of each domain were scaled independently of the behaviors of the other domains, although several behaviors appeared in more than one socioemotional domain. In these instances, the behavior was scaled separately for each state.

Sixteen psychologists having educational degrees ranging from B.A. to Ph.D. were asked to rate the behaviors of each domain on a 5-point scale according to how intense they judged the behaviors to be. The behaviors appropriate for each emotional state were written on index cards, one behavior per card. Five decks of cards and scoring forms were then given individually to the judges, who were given the following information: "This task is part of a project designed to examine the emotions of infants. Each deck of cards contains a group of behaviors that characterize a particular emotion. The task is to rate each behavior on a 5-point scale of intensity (with '1' reflecting low intensity and '5' high intensity) by sorting each deck of cards into five piles. Thus, each pile represents a rank on a 5-point rating scale of emotional intensity. At least one behavior should be in each of the five piles and each deck should be ranked independently of the others." After each deck had been sorted, the judges recorded their behavioral ratings on a special scoring form. Reliabilities of the judges' ratings, computed by an analysis of variance (Winer, 1971), were quite high for all of the socioemotional domains: fear (.96), anger (.96), happiness (.93), attachment (.92), and competence (.92). From the judges' data, mean ratings were computed for each behavior in each domain. In order to distribute the behaviors evenly across the five points, the behaviors – ordered from low to high mean ratings – were assigned ranks by dividing them into five categories. When the number of behaviors within a domain was not divisible by five, the extra behaviors were distributed along the middle ranks (see Table 8.2).

Scoring. The five behavioral ranks became the basis for scoring the items of the scales. The scales were arranged so that each situation and the behaviors corresponding to the emotion the situation might evoke were listed. An observer used these forms to obtain information about the behaviors that occurred in the particular situation. Each situation was scored by using the rank of the most intense behavior observed for that item. Only those behaviors thought to reflect a particular socioemotional domain were scored. For example, if in a fear situation the child smiled but showed no fear behavior, a zero score was given for fear. Similarly, if the child showed an anger response, this was not scored, because the situation aimed specifically to measure fear. Thus items were keyed to measure only those emotions most likely to occur. Scores of zero across many fear situations would reflect a subject low in fearfulness. It was assumed that little fear behavior would be exhibited in other situations that do not usually elicit fear. By summing the item scores for each domain and dividing by the number of items, a mean intensity or total score for each socioemotional state was derived for each subject. If children did not respond to the item, they received a score of zero for that item. Although every attempt was made to observe all items, situations not observed were not scored, nor were they used to calculate the total socioemotional scores.

Observational procedure. The construction of the scales based on the intensity of behavior in response to specific situations generated an instrument that could be used to assess infants and young children in day-care settings. In order to collect data, observers were at the day-care center when the infants and parents (normally mothers) arrived. Each observer watched a different child each day, staying at the center until the mothers returned to take their children home. Observers were instructed to wait for a situation to occur, and when it occurred, the observers would check off the behaviors seen. When it seemed obvious that a situation was not going to occur, the observers were instructed to try to arrange for it to happen. From the original list of 83 items, observations of the first sample were made. Based upon the results of this sample, a revised list of 46 items was obtained. The results based on the entire sample are taken from observations made for the 46 items.

Observer reliability. Two observers collected data on six subjects (three males and three females). Reliabilities were calculated for the behaviors of each emotion by dividing the number of agreements by the number of agreements plus

Table 8.2. *The ranked behaviors*

Domain		Rank			
	1	2	3	4	5
Fear	sober decrease activity tongue hesitate	stare look and avoid lean away suck thumb	pucker frown turn away tense	refuse to look move away whimper tremble	grasp/cling freeze fret/cry scream
Anger	sober look away suck thumbs frown look hard at	pout/pucker increase activity grimace tense hold back tears turn away	move away whimper reach toward shut eyes tightly flail clench fists	refuse to . . . fret/cry tremble move away struggle bang/pound	stomp yell throw objects scream attack
Happiness	relax slight smile	vocalize (pleasant) eyes glow chatter	clasp hands play actively broad smile	flail skip/strut bounce	laugh/giggle act silly squeal with delight
Attachment/ affiliation, low stress	look/glance at lean toward slight smile at	pleasant vocalization watch intently chatter move toward	reach toward touch broad smile at imitate	show/share toy laugh/giggle raise arms call to	follow search for hug/kiss
Attachment/ affiliation, high stress	sober look/glance at suck thumb lean toward	frown pout/pucker tense hold back tears	whimper watch intently touch move/reach toward	tremble raise arms follow call to/for	fret/cry search for grasp/cling yell/scream
Competence	look at alertly vocalize relax mouth object chatter slight smile	eyes glow reach for watch intently broad smile imitate bounce	flail skip/strut manipulate/examine clap hands seek help play actively persist/struggle	squeal with delight call attention to self search for follow instructions join group action show/share toy select alternative activity	refuse help rehearse activity try to fix initiate activity create activity test alternatives

disagreements. Agreement between the observers was highest for the behaviors of the fear domain (91%), followed by anger (90%), competence (90%), attachment (89%), and happiness (85%) domains.

Measurement reliability. Essentially the issue of measurement reliability centers on the problem of whether a single observation provides a sufficient and reliable measure of how a person behaves. This problem can be addressed in two different ways. The more conventional method is to observe individuals twice within a short time period. The consistency of their behavior over time can then be calculated through a correlational analysis. On the other hand, individuals can be observed in multiple situations, each of which is known to be a measure of the same trait or ability. In this context, consistency is established by showing that the multiple situations do, in fact, measure the same thing. Both approaches to measurement reliability were used in constructing the scales. Using the first approach, reliability correlations were obtained that ranged from .93 to .31, with an average correlation of .60. All but the lowest were statistically significant.

Because the behaviors of infants are subject to developmental changes, this method of obtaining reliability must be supplemented with a second method, that of collecting multiple observations of infants' behaviors across a variety of situations. For instance, in the current research, 13 different situations were used to assess fear in the original sample of infants. These situations included events such as "stranger approaches," "unfamiliar room," and "toy breaks." Measurement reliability was then tested by the use of coefficient alpha (Nunnally, 1967), which is a measure of the internal consistency of a group of test items. High coefficient alphas were obtained for the measures of each of the socioemotional domains. Furthermore, these results were replicated with a second sample of infants and, taken together, strongly suggest that the measurements taken in particular situations were not random but reliable across the measurements in other situations.

Consistency of the domain scales

Coefficient alpha can also be regarded as a measure of the homogeneity of the domain or the extent to which the items of the scales were measuring the same emotional state. Because the primary goal of the research was to construct a measurement instrument of *maximum* reliability, an attempt was made to improve the reliability of each domain scale by discarding from it items having a low or negative correlation with the total score. Thus, coefficient alphas were computed for the scales after the items with domain correlations less than .20 were discarded. This constitutes the revised version of the scales.

Results of scale construction

The results of scale construction will be considered in terms of both the internal reliability and external validity of the scales.

Internal reliability of the scales

The alpha coefficients obtained on the first sample for the best items of the scales were .76 for fear, .85 for anger, .77 for competence, .74 for happiness, and .81 for attachment. Whereas the number of items for each state ranged from 13 to 20 in the original scales, the number of items in the shorter, more reliable version of the scales now ranged from 8 to 12. Consequently, the scales were not only more reliable and homogeneous in their revised form but also more efficient to administer, because there were fewer situations to be observed. These revised scales were used to gather data on a second sample of infants to determine whether or not the high reliabilities of the socioemotional scales obtained with the first sample could be replicated. The coefficient alphas based on the data from the second sample were similar to those based on the data of the original sample.

After the reliability and homogeneity of the domain scales had been demonstrated in two different samples of infants, the data from these samples were combined in order to create a larger sample. The reliabilities of the five scales, calculated for the combined sample, were .88 for fear, .80 for anger, .73 for happiness, .82 for attachment, and .87 for competence.

The reliability of the scales as a function of age was also calculated. Three age groups were formed from the original sample: 12 months and younger ($N = 22$), 13 to 18 months ($N = 18$), and 19 months and older ($N = 26$). Coefficient alphas were computed for each socioemotional domain for each age group. The domain scales were found to be reliable for each age group, and the reliabilities compared favorably with those calculated for the combined sample.

These data have bearing on several issues. In the first place, the situations and the individual differences in behaviors measured in the situations are reliable. That is, children who express intense fear in one situation are likely to exhibit intense fear in other situations. This indicates not only that the items making up the scales are reliable but also that the children are consistent in their emotional expressions: A fearful child remains a fearful child across situations. The degree to which the children show consistent behavior across a wide set of situations is the degree to which we can talk about enduring emotional states. It must be noted, however, that high alpha coefficients were obtained by eliminating some situations. Therefore, we must temper our belief that individuals respond in a consistent matter in all situations commonly believed to elicit a particular socio-emotional state. For the moment, the issue of enduring emotional states cannot be settled. Further analysis as to which situations contribute to high coefficient alphas and which do not is necessary in order to explore this question. Nonetheless, that there exists some individual consistency in emotional responses across a set of situations lends support to the view that individuals can be characterized in terms of enduring emotional states.

Independence of socioemotional scales. Another important question concerning the property of the scales was whether or not they were measuring different and distinct emotions or a general emotional dimension such as arousal. That is, were the domain scales independent of each other and were they measuring five different socioemotional states? Product–moment correlations were computed between the domains. Large positive correlations between the domains would indicate that children who rated high on one socioemotional state also rated high on another and that the domain scales might be tapping a single emotional dimension. Small positive or negative correlations, on the other hand, would indicate that the scales were probably independent of one another and were measuring different socioemotional states. Because the aim of these analyses was not to examine the *specific* relationships between pairs of emotions but to determine whether or not the domain scales were tapping a common arousal dimension or measuring independent and distinct emotions, zero-order correlation coefficients were computed rather than partial correlation coefficients. The average correlation for the combined sample was .09, with correlations ranging from $-.23$ to .29. Thus the data indicate that the domains are not highly correlated and therefore offer no support for a general dimension such as arousal. Moreover, no age differences were found.

Having determined that the five domains were not measuring a general characteristic like arousal, we looked at specific relationships between pairs of socioemotional states. The question of interest here was whether, for example, a child who scored high on one domain would score high on any other. In other words, although the relative independence of the five scales as a whole was established, it was not unlikely that some socioemotional states were more related to each other than were others. To explore the specific relationships between any two socioemotional states, the effects of the other extraneous emotions had to be removed from, or partialed out of, the correlation coefficient. This was accomplished statistically through a series of partial correlation analyses. The partial correlations revealed only one significant relationship, that between attachment and fear ($r = .33, p < .01$). Infants who were more attached or showed more social affiliation were also more fearful.

External validity of the scales

The properties of the socioemotional scales give us some confidence that they are capable of measuring emotional behavior and generating reliable data that differentiate among children within the set of socioemotional states we have tried to assess. We now wish to examine the external validity of the scales by considering whether the results obtained using these scales conform to the research findings obtained by other measurement techniques. Specifically, we will examine age and sex differences in socioemotional expression.

Age differences. When the sample of infants was divided into three age groups, the age of the infant proved to be a highly significant effect in emotional expression. The results of a multivariate analysis of variance revealed an overall age effect $[F(10, 108) = 2.93, p < .003]$. To determine for which specific emotions the main effect of age was significant, separate univariate analyses of variance were calculated for each emotion. These individual ANOVAs produced the following results.

The mean *fear* score was 2.03 for the youngest age group, 2.91 for the middle age group, and 2.21 for the oldest age group. These differences were significant $[F(2, 56) = 3.41; p < .04]$. Post hoc Newman–Keuls tests (Winer, 1971) indicated that the middle age group showed significantly more intense expressions of fear than either the youngest or the oldest age groups. The difference between the youngest and oldest age groups was not significant. The research literature on fear supports these results; fearful behavior is greatest between 12 and 18 months (Kagan, 1974; Scarr & Salapatek, 1970).

The mean *anger* scores were 2.56, 2.82, and 3.32 for the youngest, middle, and oldest age groups, respectively. These differences were significant $[F(2, 56) = 3.77; p < .03]$. The more intense expressions of anger by the oldest infants were significantly different from the intensities of anger expressions for either the youngest or middle age groups according to the post hoc tests. The difference between the youngest and middle age groups was not significant. Although there is relatively little research on anger, the increase in anger across age is not inconsistent with other results (Goodenough, 1931, 1932; Main, 1981).

The oldest infants also showed the most intense expressions of *happiness*, with a mean score of 2.65, as compared with mean scores of 2.38 for the youngest age group and 2.33 for the middle age group. These differences were not significant. Izard (1978) has stated that joy is a prime emotion and emerges early. The failure to detect age changes in these data is taken as support for that view.

Expressions of *attachment* or social affiliation were highest in the middle age group, with a mean score of 2.80, as compared with mean scores of 1.95 and

2.05 for the youngest and oldest age groups, respectively. These differences were significant [$F(2, 56) = 4.78; p < .01$]. The differences between the middle age group and each of the other two groups were statistically significant in the post hoc tests. The difference between the youngest and oldest age groups was not significant. The results of these analyses indicate that attachment to various social objects is highest in the 12- to 18-month period, a finding that is also supported by the research literature (Ainsworth et al., 1978). There were no age differences in the expression of *competence,* with mean scores of 3.04, 3.44, and 3.28 for the youngest to oldest age groups, respectively.

In summary, both fear and attachment expressions appear most intensely in the 12- to 18-month period, whereas anger expressions increase in intensity with age. Happiness and competence expressions, on the other hand, do not appear to change over age. These results do not deviate from those reported by others using different measuring instruments and suggest that the scales may be sensitive at least to age differences in emotional expression by situation.

Sex differences. The main effect of the infants' sex did not prove to be significant in the overall expression of socioemotional behavior when we used a multivariate analysis of variance. Univariate analyses showed that sex was a significant factor only in the expression of *fear* [$F(1, 56) = 5.44; p < .03$], with girls showing higher intensities of fear than boys. That girls are observed to express more fearful behavior than boys is consistent with other findings that girls tend to be more fearful than boys (Goulet, 1974; Morgan & Ricciuti, 1969; Schaffer, 1966; Tennes & Lampl, 1964). Girls also tended to show more intense expressions of attachment, anger, and happiness than boys, but the differences between the groups were not statistically significant. Although reports of sex differences in expressions of anger are difficult to interpret (Feiring & Lewis, 1979), we believe that other data confirm our observations that girls tend to be more affable (expressed in measures of happiness and attachment) than boys (e.g., Clarke-Stewart, 1973; Goldberg & Lewis, 1969; Klein & Durfee, 1978; Messer & Lewis, 1972).

Day-care variables. Other characteristics of children in day care were examined, including the child's age at entry into day care and length of time involved in the program. Results from our scales are consistent with what we would expect. For example, competence expressions were greater for children who had spent more time in the day-care centers when they were compared with their peers. These results as well as others that are presented in more detail elsewhere [Lewis & Michalson, in press (a); Michalson, 1980] lead us to believe that the instrument thus far developed can be used to measure socioemotional states in very young children in everyday situations. In the course of these studies, we also came upon

differences between day-care centers. In one day-care center, we found competence scores to be somewhat higher than in another. Investigation of differences
between day-care programs uncovered curriculum differences; one center was
more interested than the second in fostering independence and competence in
children. That our measurement instrument uncovered socioemotional differences that reflect program differences supports our effort to construct an instrument that can be used to examine program differences as well as individual
differences. Although these results are not definitive, they are encouraging.

On the measurement of private acts

The measurement of socioemotional states through an analysis of emotional behaviors in situations has produced an adequate assessment instrument possessing
the internal requirements of scales: observer reliability, measurement consistency, interitem reliability, and differentiation of domains. In terms of validity,
the instrument taps age, sex, and program differences that are in general agreement with a research literature that for the most part has developed from different
measurement systems. On the basis of the results of this measurement system,
we can infer the emotional state of the child, although all we really know is that
certain behaviors are more likely to occur in certain situations. The inference of
emotional states and/or experiences is just that – an inference. No measurement
system currently available can measure internal states and experiences directly.

Although these results bear on several other issues, one in particular deserves
our attention – the enduring nature of emotional states. In most of the research
to date, emotional states are considered as transient events. Although it is not
always made explicit, these transient events must have a certain dynamic characteristic. Because emotional states are a feature of human behavior, it would be
difficult to speak of someone's not having any emotional state. Rather, we en-
vision a flow of states, one leading to another, or an even more complex model
in which combinations of emotions flow, merge, and separate in a continuous
stream of activity. Such a model of emotional states addresses the transient nature of emotions.

Any model of enduring emotional states, however, must address the question
of individual differences. Individual differences can be considered as differences
in emotional states, given the same situation, or as differences in levels or degrees of the same emotional state. In terms of the question posed by this assessment instrument, we are more concerned with the issue of whether some individuals are more happy, angry, or fearful than others. Given a set of similar
situations, is Child A more likely than Child B to express fear, and is Child A
more likely to express more fear than Child B? Such a notion does not necessarily lead us to a trait concept, because emotional assessment is embedded in a

situational analysis. Even so, the issues of individual difference and consistency across situations allow us to consider emotional states as enduring characteristics. Our analysis and scaling procedures have demonstrated individual consistency across situations and as such have provided some support for the notion of enduring emotional states, or at least enduring dispositions to respond similarly to a class of events thought to elicit similar feelings. In exploring these individual characteristics through a cluster analysis technique [described more fully in Lewis & Michalson, in press (a); Michalson, 1980], we have arrived at the conclusion that the profiles of enduring emotional states have much in common with personality profiles.

One further problem needs consideration: the issue of emotional development. Our measurement system is dependent both on specific emotional behaviors and on specific emotional situations. We have used the interface of these two factors to infer emotional states and/or experiences. Nevertheless, we must recognize that our system is limited by the measures used. Nowhere is this limitation more important to remember than in approaching the problem of change or development. Although the measures have appeared to work well enough for children between 3 and 30 months, they are unlikely to work for children much older. In our examination of this problem, our acknowledgment of the private nature of emotions becomes more apparent. Currently we have reason to believe that once an emotional state is achieved, it continues to exist and that major developmental changes occur in (a) those events that contribute to the state or experience, (b) the responses used to reference the state or experience, and (c) the cognitive level of representation. Although we have observed age changes in the intensity of an emotional expression as well as in the differentiation of emotional states, we have no reason to believe that an emotional state is likely to change over age once it has been experienced. Our fearfulness may now have to do with financial ruin rather than with strangers, but the feelings of fear remain the same.

Events that contribute to emotional experiences change as a function of the wide and interconnected cognitive and social capacities that develop concurrently in the child. Thus, before elaborate associations and connections between past events are established, or before standards of social and moral behavior are learned, only a limited set of events contributes to emotional states. Some emotional states appear early in life, and throughout the life cycle people have these same states. The situations that contribute to an emotional state are open to ontogenetic change, however, as well as to individual differences and cultural standards and customs. There may be several types of situations that are capable of contributing to a specific emotional state across the life cycle. For example, Lewis (1980) has listed four situations capable of eliciting fear: (a) past events associated with noxious outcomes; (b) violation of an expectancy coupled with the inability to assimilate and control the event; (c) presentation of the unfamiliar, including objects, events, and people; and (d) violation of the standards of others (although perhaps not in the first $1\frac{1}{2}$ years of life). Although the specific content of these general categories will change over age and will be different for different cultures and in different historical periods, nevertheless these situations may have a high likelihood of eliciting fearful states. In other words, the ontogeny of any emotional state involves a change in the nature of the situation that elicits it (or a change in cognitive ability) rather than a change in state.

Developmental change may also occur in the nature of the responses that reference an emotional state as well as in the elicitors that produce it. As children develop, marked changes in their repertoire of responses occur, in part as a function of maturation and in part as a function of the integration, reorganization, and formation of new skills and abilities. In terms of maturation, the young child confronted by an emotion-eliciting event cannot run until able to do so or cannot call for help until language abilities exist. Thus in some sense what we reference as an emotional expression changes as the abilities of the child change. This holds for individual behaviors as well as the patterns of behavior we use to infer emotional states. Responses change, not only as a function of maturation but also in terms of expected norms, both ontogenetic and cultural. Thus, for example, the fearful behavior referenced by crying becomes less acceptable as the child gets older because crying itself becomes less acceptable as a response, especially within particular subcultures of our society. Crying out in fear is more acceptable for girls than for boys, because boys are expected to be braver, at least in Western society. To the extent that any culture prohibits the expression of emotional behavior, it appears reasonable to assume that emotional responses or expressions may reflect not emotional change per se but only changes in the responses that reference it.

This particular difficulty has led us to conclude that there is, at best, only a limited correspondence between emotional expression and emotional states and/or experiences (Lewis & Rosenblum, 1978). The masking of the face and the inhibition over vocal expression of emotional states seem to occur as a function of the socialization process, be it at a general cultural level or at the level of differences between families. Regardless of the nature of the socialization process or the role of maturation, emotional expression will undergo change. The degree that the behaviors that reference any particular emotion are controlled by cultural norms may be the limit to which we can claim a direct correspondence between an expression and emotional experience. That is, socialization may mask the ''natural'' relationship between emotional states or experiences and emotional expression.

Finally, from an attribution point of view, it may be the case that even if the behaviors that reference emotions remain constant, the culture may redefine the meaning of the responses so that they no longer reference the emotion in the same way that they once did. The reverse seems equally true: A behavior not originally used to reference an emotional state may do so after some point in development. Consequently, although infants' faces have been reported to show many different types of emotions, we usually choose not to believe they have such emotional states (Oster, 1978).

Even within the limitation of development, the study of emotional expression, state, and experience continues. The present system is limited to this culture and the age ranges specified. Still, there is no reason not to assume that a similar analysis could be developed for older children and for different cultures.

Notes

1 The data reported in this section were gathered by Linda Michalson in partial fulfillment of the degree of doctor of philosophy at the Graduate Faculty of Political and Social Science of the New School for Social Research.
2 The attachment domain that we considered is more similar to social affiliation or sociability than to the more traditional concept of attachment. It includes not only attachment to the mother but also behavior toward the caregivers, other children, and even other children's mothers. It also includes high-stress situations such as separation from the mother followed by the approach of a stranger as well as low-stress situations such as free play. In the analysis that will follow, separate behaviors associated with high- and low-stress situations were obtained. The domain will be shown to be single rather than multiple, however.

References

Abelson, R. Script processing in attitude formation and decision making. In J. S. Carroll & J. Payne (Eds.), *Cognition and social behavior*. Hillsdale, N.J.: Erlbaum, 1976.

Ainsworth, M. D. S., Blehar, M., Waters, E., & Wall, S. *Patterns of attachment: A psychological study of the strange situation*. Hillsdale, N.J.; Erlbaum, 1978.

Benjamin, J. D. Some developmental observations relating to the theory of anxiety. *Journal of the American Psychoanalytic Association*, 1961, *9*, 652–68.

Bretherton, I., & Ainsworth, M. D. S. Responses of one-year-olds to a stranger in a strange situation. In M. Lewis and L. A. Rosenblum (Eds.), *The origins of fear*. New York: Wiley, 1974.

Brooks, J., & Lewis, M. Infants' responses to strangers: Midget, adult, and child. *Child Development*, 1976, *47*, 323–32.

Brooks-Gunn, J., & Lewis, M. Affective exchanges between normal and handicapped infants and their mothers. In T. Field & A. Fogel (Eds.), *Emotion and interaction: Normal and high-risk infants*. Hillsdale, N.J.: Erlbaum (in press).

Campos, J. J., Emde, R. N., Gaensbauer, T., & Henderson, C. Cardiac and behavioral interrelationships in the reactions of infants to strangers. *Developmental Psychology*, 1975, *11*, 589–601.

Clarke-Stewart, K. Interactions between mothers and their young children: Characteristics and consequences. *Monographs of the Society for Research in Child Development*, 1973, *38*(6–7, Serial No. 153).

Darwin, C. R. *The expression of the emotions in man and animals*. Chicago: University of Chicago Press, 1965. (Originally published, 1872.)

Ekman, P., & Friesen, W. V. *Unmasking the face*. Englewood Cliffs, N.J.: Prentice-Hall, 1975.

Ekman, P., & Oster, H. Facial expressions of emotion. *Annual Review of Psychology,* 1979, *30,* 527–54.

Feinman, S. Infant response to race, size, proximity, and movement of strangers. *Infant Behavior and Development,* 1980, *3,* 187–204.

Feiring, C., & Lewis, M. Sex and age differences in young children's reactions to frustration: A further look at the Goldberg and Lewis subjects. *Child Development,* 1979, *50,* 848–53.

Feiring, C., Lewis, M., & Starr, M. D. *Indirect and direct effects on children's reactions to unfamiliar adults.* Unpublished manuscript, 1981.

Goldberg, S., & Lewis, M. Play behavior in the year-old infant: Early sex differences. *Child Development,* 1969, *40,* 21–31.

Goodenough, F. L. The expression of the emotions in infancy. *Child Development,* 1931, *2,* 96–101.

Goodenough, F. L. Expression of the emotions in a blind-deaf child. *Journal of Abnormal and Social Psychology,* 1932, *27,* 328–33.

Goulet, J. The infant's conception of causality and his reactions to strangers. In T. Décarie (Ed.), *The infant's reaction to strangers.* New York: International Universities Press, 1974.

Greenberg, D. J., Hillman, D., & Grice, D. Infant and stranger variables related to stranger anxiety in the first year of life. *Developmental Psychology,* 1973, *9,* 207–21.

Haviland, J., & Lewis, M. *Infants' greeting patterns to strangers.* Paper presented at the human ethology session of the Animal Behavior Society, Wilmington, N.C., 1975.

Izard, C. E. *Human emotions.* New York: Plenum Press, 1977.

Izard, C. E. On the development of emotions and emotion-cognitive relationships in infancy. In M. Lewis & L. A. Rosenblum (Eds.), *The development of affect.* New York: Plenum Press, 1978.

Kagan, J. Discrepancy, temperament, and infant distress. In M. Lewis & L. A. Rosenblum (Eds.), *The origins of fear.* New York: Wiley, 1974.

Klein, R. P., & Durfee, J. T. Effects of sex and birth order on infant social behavior. *Infant Behavior and Development,* 1978, *1,* 106–17.

Lewis, M. The meaning of a response, or why researchers in infant behavior should be Oriental metaphysicians. *Merrill-Palmer Quarterly,* 1967, *13,* 7–18.

Lewis, M. Early sex differences in the human: Studies of socioemotional development. In E. A. Rubinstein, R. Green, & E. Brecher (Eds.), *New directions in sex research.* New York: Plenum Press, 1975.

Lewis, M. Issues in the development of fear. In I. L. Kutash & L. B. Schlesinger (Eds.), *Pressure point: Perspectives on stress and anxiety.* San Francisco: Jossey-Bass, 1980.

Lewis, M., & Brooks, J. Self, other, and fear: Infants' reactions to people. In M. Lewis & L. A. Rosenblum (Eds.), *The origins of fear.* New York: Wiley, 1974.

Lewis, M., & Brooks, J. Self knowledge and emotional development. In M. Lewis & L. A. Rosenblum (Eds.), *The development of affect.* New York: Plenum Press, 1978.

Lewis, M., Brooks, J., & Haviland, J. Hearts and faces: A study in the measurement of emotion. In M. Lewis & L. A. Rosenblum (Eds.), *The development of affect.* New York: Plenum Press, 1978.

Lewis, M., & Brooks-Gunn, J. *Social cognition and the acquisition of self.* New York: Plenum, 1979.

Lewis, M., & Feiring, C. Direct and indirect interactions in social relationships. In L. Lipsitt (Ed.), *Advances in infancy research* (Vol. 1). New York: Ablex, 1980.

Lewis, M., & Michalson, L. *Children's emotions and moods: Theory and measurement.* New York: Plenum (in press). (a)

Lewis, M., & Michalson, L. Mothers' labeling of infant affect. In T. Field & A. Vogel (Eds.), *Emotion and Interaction: Normal and High-Risk Infants.* New York: Erlbaum (in press). (b)

Lewis, M., & Rosenblum, L. A. (Eds.) *The development of affect.* New York: Plenum Press, 1978.

Lewis, M., & Starr, M. D. Developmental continuity. In J. D. Osofsky (Ed.), *Handbook of infant development*. New York: Wiley, 1979.

Main, M. Abusive and rejecting infants. In N. Frude (Ed.), *Psychological approaches to child abuse*. Totowa, N.J.: Roman & Littlefield, 1981.

Messer, S. B., & Lewis, M. Social class and sex differences in the attachment and play behavior of the one-year-old infant. *Merrill-Palmer Quarterly*, 1972, *18*, 295–306.

Michalson, L. H. *Measuring emotions in infants*. Unpublished doctoral dissertation, The New School for Social Research, 1980.

Morgan, G. A., & Ricciuti, H. N. Infants' responses to strangers during the first year. In B. M. Foss (Ed.), *Determinants of infant behavior* (Vol. 4). New York: Wiley, 1969.

Nunnally, J. C. *Psychometric theory*. New York: McGraw-Hill, 1967.

Oster, H. Facial expression and affect development. In M. Lewis & L. A. Rosenblum (Eds.), *The development of affect*. New York: Plenum Press, 1978.

Pervin, L., & Lewis, M. Overview of the internal–external issue. In L. Pervin & M. Lewis (Eds.), *Perspectives in interactional psychology*. New York: Plenum Press, 1978.

Rheingold, H. L., & Eckerman, C. O. Fear of the stranger: A critical examination. In H. W. Reese (Ed.), *Advances in child development and behavior* (Vol. 8). New York: Academic Press, 1973.

Scarr, S., & Salapatek, P. Patterns of fear development during infancy. *Merrill-Palmer Quarterly*, 1970, *16*, 53–90.

Schaffer, H. R. The onset of fear of strangers and the incongruity hypothesis. *Journal of Child Psychology and Psychiatry*, 1966, *7*, 95–106.

Schwartz, A., Campos, J., & Baisel, E. The visual cliff: Cardiac and behavioral correlates on the deep and shallow sides at five and nine months of age. *Journal of Experimental Child Psychology*, 1973, *15*, 86–99.

Shaffran, R., & Décarie, T. Short-term stability of infants' responses to strangers. Paper presented at the meeting of the Society for Research in Child Development, Philadelphia, 1973.

Skarin, K. Cognitive and contextual determinants of stranger fear in six- and eleven-month-old infants. *Child Development*, 1977, *48*, 537–44.

Sroufe, L. A. Socioemotional development. In J. D. Osofsky (Ed.), *Handbook of infant development*. New York: Wiley, 1979.

Sroufe, L. A., Waters, E., & Matas, L. Contextual determinants of infant affective response. In M. Lewis & L. A. Rosenblum (Eds.), *The origins of fear*. New York: Wiley, 1974.

Strongman, K. T. *The psychology of emotion*. New York: Wiley, 1973.

Tennes, K. H., & Lampl, E. E. Stranger and separation anxiety in infancy. *Journal of Nervous and Mental Diseases*, 1964, *139*, 247–54.

Tomkins, S. S. *Affect, imagery, consciousness: Vol. 1. The positive affects*. New York: Springer, 1962.

Waters, E., Matas, L., & Sroufe, L. A. Infants' reactions to an approaching stranger: Description, validation, and functional significance of wariness. *Child Development*, 1975, *46*, 348–56.

Weinraub, M., & Putney, E. The effects of height on infants' social responses to unfamiliar persons. *Child Development*, 1978, *49*, 598–603.

Winer, B. *Statistical principles in experimental design* (2nd ed.). New York: McGraw-Hill, 1971.

9 Measuring the development of sensitivity to nonverbal communication

Bella M. DePaulo and Robert Rosenthal

In this chapter we focus not on the experience and expression of one's own emotions but instead on one's sensitivity to the emotions of others. In our own research program, we have been interested primarily in emotions that are expressed nonverbally, although our most recent research paradigms have included both verbal and nonverbal communications. By sensitivity we mean several things. In one sense – the sense in which we have most frequently studied it – sensitivity implies a skill rather than just a reaction or a feeling. Nonverbally sensitive observers are those who can accurately identify the emotions of others. We have also studied sensitivity in the sense of a systematic responsiveness, perceptiveness, or attributional bias. Thus, for example, certain kinds of perceivers may be especially likely to interpret nonverbal displays as hostile and threatening even when all available criteria indicate that those displays contain little or no hostility (Nasby, Hayden, & DePaulo, 1980). Finally, we have studied sensitivity in the sense of a systematic preference for attending to (or weighting) certain kinds of nonverbal cues more than others. For instance, observers may vary in the extent to which they attend to visual cues when those cues conflict with the information simultaneously available from auditory cues (DePaulo, Zuckerman, & Rosenthal, 1980; DePaulo et al., 1978).

These kinds of sensitivities – especially the skill-related sensitivity that is directly linked to an objective criterion of accuracy – are part of the larger set of skills that has been called "social intelligence" (Walker & Foley, 1973). Social intelligence, broadly conceived, might include sensitivity not only to emotions expressed at single points in time but also to systematic situational variations in other persons' affective responses (DePaulo, 1978). Sensitivity to other persons' characteristics such as personality traits, demographic characteristics, and chronic aspects of expressiveness (e.g., demeanor) might also be considered to be aspects of social intelligence. The ability to make all of these kinds of judgments is probably enhanced by skill at judging verbal and contextual cues as

Preparation of this chapter was supported in part by the National Science Foundation. We thank Peter D. Blanck for his helpful comments.

208

well as nonverbal ones; further, the ability to integrate all of these perceptions into a coherent and meaningful impression is likely to be essential.

Such skills are mostly reactive or interpretive. Still, social intelligence includes enactive abilities as well, such as knowing what to express or not express and how and when to express it. Social intelligence, or at least certain aspects of it, presupposes social knowledge – for example, an understanding of how certain types of persons typically respond or of the kinds of reactions characteristically engendered by certain kinds of situations – and perhaps also certain cognitive skills (e.g., role taking).

It is not difficult to enumerate a long list of potential benefits that might conceivably accrue to the socially skillful – even when we limit our discussion to the nonverbally skillful. Thus, for example, we might expect nonverbally sensitive persons to be more effective teachers, clinicians, doctors, leaders, and supervisors – and indeed, there is evidence that this is sometimes so (Rosenthal et al., 1979). In other day-to-day social interactions, too, one might expect the nonverbally sensitive to experience more effective and more gratifying interpersonal transactions. There is evidence to support this hunch, too. Rosenthal et al. (1979), for example, have reported that children and teenagers who are especially skilled at judging nonverbal cues are seen by others as enjoying more popularity. Further, several studies have shown that children who are nonverbally sensitive are especially well adjusted socially (Izard, 1971; Zuckerman & Przewuzman, 1979).

Lest it be implied that nonverbal skill is the royal road to interpersonal success, we hasten to add a few words of caution. First, when considering accuracy of interpersonal perceptions, there may be a sense in which "too good is no good." That is, there may be hazards to knowing too much about other persons' affective states, particularly when those states are being willfully or unconsciously disguised. The developmental implication of this formulation is that we need not expect clear linear age trends in sensitivity to every kind of nonverbal communication. Rather, for certain kinds of affects, such as those defined as off limits either by the communicator or by cultural proscriptions, children may at certain points in the socialization process learn *not* to make (or report) accurate judgments.

Second, even if interpersonal perceivers were to limit themselves to reading those affects that other persons intended to communicate, this accurate reading by itself may still not guarantee a successful interpersonal outcome. Enactive skills (as described above) and the motivation to use those skills in the service of smooth social interchange may be necessary supplements.

The study of social intelligence is not new. It has, however, suffered from the problem that in the aggregate, measures of social intelligence have been shown to be highly related to measures of ordinary intelligence. The prospect for the discriminant validity of measures of social intelligence has, in short, been bleak (Campbell & Fiske, 1959; Keating, 1978; Walker & Foley, 1973).

That component of social intelligence having to do with the decoding of nonverbal cues has also been studied for many years, and its history has been summarized recently (Rosenthal et al., 1979). This area of inquiry has been hampered, however, by the absence of well-standardized, well-validated measures of individual differences in accuracy of decoding nonverbal cues. In addition, much of the earlier work on sensitivity to nonverbal cues employed only a single channel of nonverbal cues – often it was still photographs. This procedure is likely to yield stimulus materials characterized by a low level of ecological validity.

Our research on nonverbal sensitivity extends the earlier work in several ways. Our primary interest has been in individual differences in nonverbal sensitivity – considered both as correlates of other individual difference measures (e.g., traits, abilities, demographic characteristics) and as moderators of various interpersonal outcomes. We felt that this type of focus would be well served by the development of standardized instruments to assess the kinds of sensitivities that interested us most. This standardization step – which of course includes the demonstration of adequate reliability and validity of the instruments as well as the provision of norm groups – is one of the major ways in which our work extends most previous research.

In addition we were interested in assessing sensitivity to different kinds of emotions (e.g., positive ones and negative ones, dominant ones and submissive ones) and to different sources of nonverbal cues (e.g., the face, the body, and the tone of voice). Hence, each of our instruments yields an array of subscores. This design feature lends itself to a more fine-grained study of nonverbal sensitivity; that is, one can study good and bad decoders (judges), or more specifically, one can study good and bad face decoders and/or good and bad decoders of positive affects. It is also possible to study profiles of skills. Thus, for example, we have found that females, as compared with males, tend to be relatively best at judging facial cues, slightly less skilled at judging body cues, and (relatively) worse at judging tone of voice cues (Rosenthal & DePaulo, 1979 a, b). We have also looked at the degree of correspondence between the profiles of the members of an intimate dyad and have compared that to the profile match in nonintimate pairs (Rosenthal et al., 1979).

Finally, from a practical point of view, we wanted our instruments to be easily administered and readily scored. In the next few sections, we describe each of our instruments in more detail.

The Profile of Nonverbal Sensitivity

The Profile of Nonverbal Sensitivity, or PONS test (Rosenthal et al., 1979), measures accuracy in identifying affects communicated by facial expressions,

Table 9.1. *Twenty original PONS scenes arranged in four affective quadrants*

Submissive	Dominant
Positivity: positive	
Helping a customer	talking about one's wedding
Ordering food in a restaurant	leaving on a trip
Expressing gratitude[a]	expressing motherly love
Expressing deep affection[a]	admiring nature[a]
Trying to seduce someone	talking to a lost child[a]
Positivity: negative	
Talking about the death of a friend[a]	criticizing someone for being late[a]
Talking about one's divorce	nagging a child
Returning faulty item to a store	expressing strong dislike
Asking forgiveness[a]	threatening someone
Saying a prayer	expressing jealous anger[a]

Note: PONS = Profile of Nonverbal Sensitivity.
[a] Scenes selected for the Nonverbal Discrepancy Test.
Source: Rosenthal et al., 1979.

body movements, voice tones, and various combinations of these cues. The affects include some of the more classic emotions (e.g., anger) as well as other less commonly studied emotional communications (e.g., admiring nature).

The test itself is a 45-minute black and white 16 millimeter film and soundtrack composed of 220 2-second auditory and visual segments. The 220 segments are a randomized presentation of 20 scenes portrayed by a 24-year-old Caucasian woman, each scene represented in 11 channels of nonverbal communication. The test taker's task is to view the film and for each segment to circle the label that correctly describes the scene enacted in the segment. The test taker makes this choice from two alternative labels printed on an answer sheet containing 220 such pairs of descriptions. Each segment is followed by a pause long enough for the decision to be made and recorded.

Each of the 20 scenes represented in the PONS test involves an affect that is either positive or negative *and* either dominant or submissive. Thus, in all, there are 5 positive–dominant scenes (e.g, talking to a lost child, admiring nature), 5 positive–submissive scenes (e.g., expressing gratitude, expressing deep affection), 5 negative–dominant scenes (e.g., criticizing someone for being late, expressing jealous anger) and 5 negative–submissive scenes (e.g., asking forgiveness, talking about the death of a friend) (see Table 9.1). The 20 scenes were selected from a larger set of 35 situations enacted by the person in the film. The 35 situations were chosen to represent fairly wide variations in intensity and in positivity–negativity of affect; also, a special attempt was made to choose interactive situations and situations likely to be meaningful in many other cultures.

From these 35 situations, the final 20 were selected primarily on their goodness of fit to the four affective quadrants (positive–dominant, PD; positive–submissive, PS; negative–dominant, ND; and negative–submissive, NS), as indexed by judges' ratings; the degree to which the enactments seemed authentic to the encoder (portrayer) and to a group of persons who knew her well was also a major consideration. The scenes were initially judged for intensity as well as positivity and dominance, but because intensity was significantly correlated with both other dimensions, it was not retained as a third classificatory dimension. In order to avoid stereotyped enactments, we selected an encoder of the affective situations who was not a professional actress, and she portrayed the situations without rigid adherence to a script.

The 20 situation descriptions shown in Table 9.1 constitute the response alternatives that appear in the answer booklet for the test. For each of the 220 test items, the test taker chooses between the correct situation label and one other randomly paired incorrect label. A portion of the answer booklet is reproduced in Table 9.2.

The test taker is credited with 1 point for each correct response, 0 points for an incorrect response, and $\frac{1}{2}$ point (chance accuracy, given two response alternatives) for any items left blank. In our use of the tests, individuals have rarely left substantial numbers of items blank. This has been true even with our youngest samples (8- and 9-year olds). Psychiatric groups are occasionally an exception to this rule; interestingly, there were systematic differences in the types of items that these groups left blank, so that the blanks themselves became meaningful dependent variables (Rosenthal et al., 1979).

In addition to a total score (maximum = 220), the PONS test also yields a number of more specific scores; for example, there are separate subscores for the four different affect types (PD, PS, ND, NS) and for the channels. In computing these scores, too, subjects are credited with 1 point, 0 points, or $\frac{1}{2}$ point for their answer to each relevant item.

In the PONS test, each of the 20 situations is represented in each of 11 channels. Five of these channels are pure channels: (a) face alone, no voice, (b) body from neck to knees, no voice, (c) face and body down to thighs (called "face plus body" or "figure"), no voice, (d) electronically filtered voice (called CF for "content filtered"), no picture, and (e) randomized spliced voice (called RS), no picture. The remaining 6 channels are mixed channels, made by combining the pure channels: (f) face plus randomized spliced voice, (g) face plus electronically filtered voice, (h) body plus randomized spliced voice, (i) body plus electronically filtered voice, (j) figure plus randomized spliced voice, and (k) figure plus electronically filtered voice. Table 9.3 displays the 11 channels arranged in a table showing four video levels and three audio levels.

Table 9.2. *Sample items from the PONS test*

Scene	Item
97.	A. expressing jealous anger
	B. asking forgiveness
98.	A. expressing motherly love
	B. criticizing someone for being late
99.	A. talking about one's wedding
	B. talking about the death of a friend
100.	A. expressing strong dislike
	B. asking forgiveness
101.	A. saying a prayer
	B. helping a customer
102	A. nagging a child
	B. leaving on a trip
103.	A. talking about one's divorce
	B. asking forgiveness
104.	A. ordering food in a restaurant
	B. expressing jealous anger
105.	A. criticizing someone for being late
	B. talking about the death of a friend
106.	A. talking about the death of a friend
	B. ordering food in a restaurant
107.	A. leaving on a trip
	B. nagging a child
108.	A. saying a prayer
	B. talking about one's divorce
109.	A. expressing strong dislike
	B. trying to seduce someone
110.	A. ordering food in a restaurant
	B. asking forgiveness
111.	A. talking about one's wedding
	B. leaving on a trip
112.	A. expressing deep affection
	B. admiring nature
113.	A. expressing jealous anger
	B. criticizing someone for being late
114.	A. talking about one's divorce
	B. threatening someone
115.	A. expressing strong dislike
	B. returning faulty item to a store
116.	A. ordering food in a restaurant
	B. threatening someone
117.	A. talking to a lost child
	B. criticizing someone for being late

Source: Rosenthal et al., 1979.

Table 9.3. *The channels of the PONS test*

Audio	Video			
	No cues	Face cues	Body cues	Figure (face + body)
No cues	[c]	20[d]	20	20
RS cues[a]	20	20	20	20
CF cues[b]	20	20	20	20

[a] RS = randomized spliced voice.
[b] CF = electronically content-filtered voice.
[c] Empty cell in design. In statistical analyses, this cell is frequently filled in with a chance-level score for each person in order to allow for a fully crossed repeated-measures analysis.
[d] Numbers refer to the number of test items falling in each cell.
Source: Rosenthal et al., 1979.

This inclusion of both single channels and of multiple channels comprised of the single channels is useful for the developmentalist, for it permits the study of age changes in the decoding of emotional communications that vary systematically in the amount of information that they contain.

Until relatively recently, researchers interested in eliminating the verbal content of utterances had to use a method known as *content standard*. In this method, the speaker would recite (a) standard, meaningless material, such as the alphabet or numbers, or (b) some standard, meaningful, but affectively neutral or ambiguous material, usually a word, a phrase, or a sentence or two. In each of these cases, the speaker would recite the same material over and over (or several speakers would recite the same material once each), varying the mood or voice tone to suit the emotion being sent. The listener can understand the content, but the content does not help the listener to identify the emotion.

Several masking techniques have been developed that seem to be improvements over the content standard method. In these newer methods the speaker is free to use whatever words are appropriate for the emotion or situation; the words are made unintelligible afterward by altering the voice recording in various ways. The advantage of this approach is in increasing the spontaneity and authenticity of the original portrayals. It also allows for the masking of voices recorded unobtrusively – a clear advantage over the content standard method.

The randomized splicing technique (Scherer, 1971) requires the audio tape to be cut into small pieces, reordered randomly, and reassembled. When the spliced tape is played back, the voice sounds natural in many ways, but of course the words cannot be understood because they are scrambled.

The electronic filter used in making the PONS was modeled on the one reported in Rogers, Scherer, and Rosenthal (1971). It removes selected bands of frequencies and clips the audio signal so that the voice sounds muffled and slightly distorted. By carefully adjusting the various controls, the intonation, rhythm, tempo, and loudness of the voice can be retained, but speech intelligibility is lost.

Randomized splicing, then, retains the acoustic properties of the voice while altering the correct sequence of the communication, whereas the electronic filtering does just the reverse: It noticeably changes some acoustic properties of the voice but keeps the sequence intact. In a sense, then, the two methods are complementary.

There are a number of modifications in the PONS testing procedure that can be used to make the test more suitable for children. First, the 45-minute version can be administered in two (or more) separate shorter sessions rather than all at once. Also, short forms of the PONS are available, such as a short video film, which includes only the 20 pure face and 20 pure body items, and an audio tape recording, which includes the 20 CF and 20 RS scenes. Although these two shorter versions of the PONS test assess sensitivity only to pure, single-channel communications, the advantage is that both tests can be administered in full in little more than 15 minutes. A second adaptation for children, often not necessary, allows more time for responding by stopping the film or audiotape momentarily after each scene is played. Also, the tests can be administered individually rather than in group sessions, but this, too, is rarely necessary. Finally, special children's answer booklets are available for each form of the test. For these children's booklets, each of the 20 situation labels has been translated into a simpler wording. For example, "expressing deep affection" was translated as "Judy loves her boyfriend," and "asking forgiveness" was changed to read, "Judy is sorry for what she did." The children's answer booklets are printed in especially large type.

Advantages and disadvantages of the PONS methodology

A persistently troublesome problem in nonverbal communication research involves defining the emotion that is being expressed. A number of researchers have discussed the relative merits of different types of criteria in decoding research (Cook, 1971; Ekman, 1973; Ekman, Friesen, & Ellsworth, 1972; Frijda, 1969; Knapp, 1972). For example, Cook (1971, p. 83) lists five alternative ways of establishing a criterion: (a) face validity (what the encoder intended to send), (b) researcher opinion (the way the researcher labels the emotion); (c) ratings (a panel of judges rate the portrayals); (d) self-description (the encoder evaluates his or her own feelings); and (e) objective or biographical data (independent measures of what the encoder was actually feeling, as in the observation of reactions to experimental or naturally occurring stimuli). In selecting the portrayals for inclusion in the PONS film, we used a total of four of these methods: face validity (what our encoder meant to send); researcher opinion (we evaluated the effectiveness of each portrayal); ratings (a panel of judges rated each portrayal); and self-description (the encoder evaluated her own feelings).

These four methods were the only appropriate procedures, given the design of the PONS film. We did not want to use experimental manipulations to induce real emotions, because only a very restricted range of real emotions could have been ethically produced in this manner. As a result, the PONS encoder was not spontaneously experiencing hate, mourning, jealousy, and the other emotions in the film. The encoder was portraying – but perhaps not really experiencing – the emotions in the film. So Cook's other criterion procedure was inappropriate. It would not have made sense to obtain objective data like physiological measures, for the encoder was not spontaneously experiencing the emotions she portrayed. In summary, the criterion of accuracy in the PONS film is a combination of the emotion that the encoder intended to send and the emotion that the researchers, the encoder, and various judges decided she had in fact sent.

From the standpoint of developmental research in particular, an important consideration is the extent to which the test demands certain cognitive skills of the test taker beyond those relevant to the decoding task itself. Clearly, the PONS test does make some such demands. The decoder needs to have some understanding of the goal of the test and the procedures for taking it. (Usually this information is communicated orally by the person who administers the test.) The test taker must also be able to read the response alternatives in the answer booklet and perhaps also keep the alternatives as well as the nonverbal stimulus itself in mind while deciding upon an answer. The demands for verbal skills can be reduced somewhat by having the answers read out loud to the individual, but even this procedure demands verbal comprehension skill. Encouragingly, the correlation between PONS scores and IQ tends to be near zero despite these cognitive demands; however, the correlation is moderately positive for younger subjects who show low achievement.

As a test designed specifically to measure sensitivity to nonverbal cues, the PONS test does not include any verbal content. It is plausible that an important aspect of nonverbal decoding skill is the ability to integrate verbal and nonverbal information; in many cases (e.g., irony, sarcasm), the meaning of nonverbal cues may be accurately interpretable only in relationship to the accompanying verbal cues. Similarly, the meanings of certain nonverbal cues might be importantly moderated by the presence of particular contextual cues. These possibilities were not overlooked in designing the PONS test; to keep the scope of the test manageable, we intentionally focused on purely nonverbal messages. Even within the nonverbal realm, not every type of communication is represented.

Certain kinds of nonverbal messages (e.g., olfactory cues), of course, simply cannot be sampled using an audio–video methodology. Other kinds of cues (e.g., eye contact, interpersonal distance), though not systematically sampled in the PONS test, could in principle be included in an audiovisual test of nonverbal sensitivity in which two or more persons are filmed while interacting. In fact, Archer and Akert's (1977) Social Interpretations Task (SIT) does include numerous samples of spontaneous social interactions in which such interpersonal nonverbal cues probably play an important role. The SIT test, however, does not vary these cues systematically so as to allow for the assessment of, say, proximity sensitivity. Moreover, the SIT test was not developed primarily as a measure of individual differences.

Clearly, the messages included in the PONS test are posed expressions rather than spontaneously experienced emotions. The latter might have been obtained by filming behavior in natural settings. The potential costs of the more naturalistic procedure include uncertainty over the proper label for the emotion and perhaps even for the psychological context; uneven control over technical quality; and probably abandonment of the goal of filming and audiotaping all the relevant behavior occurring in different channels simultaneously. For researchers interested in pursuing this procedure despite the possible obstacles, Archer and Akert (1977) again provide instructive suggestions. Certain questions that can be asked of the observer of spontaneous social interactions have clear and unambiguous answers, and in certain social settings filming is not particularly problematic. Archer and Akert, for example, filmed an interaction involving two women and a baby and asked the decoder to identify the mother; they also filmed two men right after a basketball game and asked the decoder to identify the winner.

On a priori, though not empirical, grounds, then, we might have preferred spontaneous over posed stimuli because ultimately we want to make inferences about the decoding of everyday nonverbal cues. It would be an error of logic, though a common one, however, to assume that because our ultimate interest is in spontaneous nonverbal cues, a better index of accuracy could be constructed by using such stimuli. Surface similarities between models and things modeled are no guarantee of predictive utility. A model's utility lies in our knowing the relationship between the properties of the model and the thing modeled. At the present time we do not know whether real-life stimuli would, for our purposes of assessing individual differences, be better or worse or not different from the posed stimuli we have employed for the PONS. Moreover, we cannot know for sure how often our ostensibly spontaneous nonverbal cues are in fact carefully chosen and controlled (see Goffman, 1959). What is known, however, that is useful to our understanding of our measure of decoding accuracy is that those people who are good at decoding posed stimuli are also good at decoding spontaneous stimuli $[r(58) = .58, p < .001]$ and that people who send accurately in one mode are also good at sending in the other $[r(57) = .46, p < .001]$ (Zuckerman et al., 1976).

Potentially the most problematic aspect of the PONS test is its use of only a single encoder. There is evidence to suggest that this design feature is not as disastrous as it might have been, however. For instance, one study (Rosenthal, Hall, & Zuckerman, 1978) demonstrates that the use of a single encoder to portray 220 different scenes is no different from the use of 220 different encoders to portray a single scene each, in terms of the homogeneity of responses that the two arrangements elicit. Second, there is evidence that good judges of nonverbal communications tend to be more accurate than poor judges across different encoders (Zuckerman et al., 1975). Thus if one person taking the PONS test is significantly more accurate at judging the PONS sender than is a second person, the first person is likely to be more accurate than the second at judging other persons, too. Further, the large network of validational findings supportive of the PONS as a measure of nonverbal sensitivity probably rules out the possibility that the particular encoder used in the PONS test was extremely idiosyncratic in her nonverbal communications.

Use of a single sender does, of course, rule out certain important research questions. For instance, we cannot learn from the PONS test what kinds of persons might be relatively more skilled at decoding men than women. Developmentally, we might postulate that young children (compared with older children and adults) might be relatively more accurate at decoding women than men because the youngsters interact so much more frequently with their mothers than with their fathers. Further, this relationship might be less characteristic of less traditional families. The study of other kinds of developmental phenomena, however, such as changes with age in skill at judging single versus multiple-modality cues is affected much less by the fact that the test employs only a single sender. In any case, we are currently developing instruments that are amenable to a range of research questions different from that covered by the PONS test (see, e.g., the section "The Person Description Test").

The Nonverbal Discrepancy Test

The PONS test assesses sensitivity to clear, consistent, and intentionally communicated cues. The sender enacted one emotion, and she attempted to convey that same emotion in every channel – her face, her body, and her tone of voice. Many of the messages communicated in everyday life are not nearly so consistent, however. Feelings of ambivalence, attempts at lying and grudging adherences to the norms of etiquette may all lead to the communication of different messages in different channels. It has been suggested that in cases of deception, senders might express the emotions they try to dissimulate through the face, which is the nonverbal channel that people will try hardest to control, but the true affective experiences that they are trying to hide may leak out through the body or tone of voice, which people may not know how to control or simply do not think to control (Ekman & Friesen, 1969, 1974; Ekman, Friesen, & Scherer, 1976; see also Rosenthal & DePaulo, 1979a, b). This conceptualization suggests several different ways to study the decoding of discrepant cues.

First, we might want to learn whether people can accurately determine that a message is or is not discrepant. Then, if it is found that they can, we might want to know which kinds of persons are especially skilled at making these discriminations and which situational or contextual cues facilitate such judgments. Second, we might ask which channel people trust (or weight preferentially) when the information from one channel conflicts with the information that is simultaneously available from another channel. From a purely informational standpoint, we might predict that people will attend preferentially to face cues whenever these conflict with cues supplied by tone of voice, for there is evidence to suggest that the former are generally far more informative (e.g., Dittmann, 1972; Rosenthal et al., 1979). The leakage formulation just described, however, suggests that there may be conditions under which perceivers are relatively less likely to trust facial cues. People who suspect that they are being deceived, for example, may begin to attend relatively more to the less controllable tone of voice cues than to the more readily faked facial cues. Research with the discrepancy test has generated evidence supportive of all of these predictions (DePaulo & Rosenthal, 1979b, c; DePaulo et al., 1978; Zuckerman et al., 1981).

Studying perceptions of discrepant communications in terms of the weighting or discounting of channels is the analytic strategy most frequently employed in the studies reported in the literature on nonverbal cues. Bugental and her colleagues, for example, have shown that children tend to discount visual cues relatively more than adults do – particularly when the visual cue is a woman's smile (Bugental, Kaswan, & Love, 1970).

The Nonverbal Discrepancy Test (NDT) involves the pairing of a visual (face or body) communication with a tone of voice communication which, in terms of its affective content, is very inconsistent, slightly inconsistent, or completely consistent with the face or body message. Subjects are assessed both for their ability accurately to identify the degree of discrepancy in these audiovisual pairings (discrepancy accuracy) and for their tendency to weight the information from the visual channel more heavily than the information from the tone of voice cues (video primacy).

We were particularly interested in relating people's skills and strategies for decoding discrepancies to their social outcomes (e.g., their popularity, the quality of their relationships with the same and the opposite sexes, as perceived by themselves and by others). Whereas in the case of pure and intentionally communicated cues (such as those represented in the PONS test), we might predict that more skilled decoders would enjoy successful social interactions, the prediction may well be just the opposite for skilled judges of discrepancies. People may not want their affective discrepancies to be recognized by other persons; they may prefer the emotions that leak through their body movements or voice tones to slip by unnoticed. A perceiver who is especially adept at recognizing discrepancies, or who tends to attend relatively more than most people to the less controllable audio cues rather than to the more overt visual cues, may know "too much" about other persons' emotions. There is in fact evidence that skill at decoding more covert cues is less beneficial socially than skill at decoding more overt and intentionally communicated cues; there is also suggestive evidence that this tendency to be penalized for knowing too much about other people's affective states is especially characteristic of female decoders (Rosenthal & DePaulo, 1979a, b).

The NDT was developed from the PONS stimulus materials. Two situations were chosen from each of the four affective quadrants, as indicated in Table 9.1.[1] Only the pure single-channel representations of these situations were used – the face, body, RS, and CF portrayals. In each scene of the NDT, one of these situations is portrayed by the face or body, and the same scene or a different one is simultaneously portrayed by a content-filtered or randomized spliced voice. Each of the eight situations is paired with every other situation twice. Hence there are 128 items in the test (8 Situations × 8 Situations × 2 Replications).

Every possible audio–video pairing (face with CF voice, face with RS voice, body with CF voice, body with RS voice) occurs exactly 32 times. For one-quarter of the items, the audio and video segments are from the same affective quadrant; for example, a positive–dominant face might be paired with a positive–dominant voice. These are the consistent scenes. Another quarter of the items consist of audio and video segments from exactly opposite quadrants; for example, a positive–dominant face might be paired with a negative–submissive voice. These are the very discrepant items. The audio and video segments of the remaining items differ on only one of the affective dimensions; for example, a positive–dominant face might be paired with either a positive–submissive or a negative–dominant voice. These are the slightly discrepant scenes. Hence, three-quarters of the items in the NDT involve audio–video pairings that are partially or entirely discrepant.

Subjects taking the discrepancy test record their overall impression of each scene on each of three 9-point rating scales: negative (1) – positive (9); submissive (1) – dominant (9); and not discrepant (1) – discrepant (9). Definitions and examples of positivity, dominance, and discrepancy are given. For younger subjects, these definitions and examples are repeated several times. As with the PONS test, several other adaptations can be made for use with children. For example, the rating pause can be lengthened, and the test can be administered in several sessions. Also, endpoint labels can be changed to sad–happy (instead of negative–positive), weak–bossy (instead of submissive–dominant), and not different–different (instead of not discrepant–discrepant).

Subjects' ratings of the scenes in the discrepancy test yield discrepancy accuracy and video primacy scores, as well as other decoding accuracy scores.

Accuracy and primacy scores

Discrepancy accuracy. Accuracy of decoding discrepancy reflects subjects' ability to recognize the degree of discrepancy between an audio and a visual cue. Accurate judges of discrepancy should rate the scenes that are in fact discrepant as more discrepant than the scenes that are not discrepant. Hence this type of accuracy is computed from subjects' discrepancy ratings by the formula: (discrepancy ratings of the very discrepant scenes $M \times 2$) + (discrepancy ratings of the slightly discrepant scenes M) − (discrepancy ratings of the nondiscrepant scenes $M \times 3$). In this formula, the expected value under the null hypothesis of no accuracy is zero.

Video primacy. Video primacy scores reflect the degree to which any given subject was relatively more influenced by the video than by the audio cues. A subject who is more influenced by the video modality than the audio would rate more positively (a) scenes in which the video cues were positive and the audio cues were negative than (b) scenes in which the audio cues were positive and the video cues were negative. Thus, video primacy scores for positive ratings are computed by subtracting the mean of a subject's positivity ratings of all audio–positive/video–negative scenes from the mean of his or her positivity ratings of all the video–positive/audio–negative scores. Video primacy scores for the dominance ratings are computed in a similar way. Additional video primacy subscores were computed by dividing the test items into items involving the face channel and items involving the body channel. Thus each subject had video primacy subscores for positivity and for dominance ratings, for scenes in which the video cue was a face, and for scenes in which the video cue was a body. The video primacy scores from all of the positivity and dominance ratings were added to produce a net video primacy score.

Positivity and dominance accuracy. Subjects who are accurate at decoding affects should rate scenes in which both the audio and the visual cues are positive as more positive than scenes in which both the audio and visual cues are negative. Similarly, they should rate as more dominant scenes in which both the audio and visual cues are dominant than scenes in which both are submissive. Hence accuracy for positivity ratings is defined as the difference between subject's mean positivity ratings of the positive scenes and their mean ratings of the negative ones. Decoding accuracy scores for dominance are computed in a similar way. Positivity accuracy and dominance accuracy can be added to produce a total decoding accuracy score.

Face, body, and tone accuracy. Decoding accuracy scores can be computed separately (exactly as just described) for only those scenes involving the face (face accuracy) or the body (body accuracy). Because each auditory stimulus in the NDT is also categorized as either positive or negative and either dominant or submissive, accuracy scores for tone of voice can be calculated, too.

We sometimes call these face, body, and tone accuracy scores "mixed" accuracy. Items in the discrepancy test are mixed in several senses; they all involve the simultaneous pairing of audio and visual cues, and each audio and visual cue is either positive or negative *and* either dominant or submissive.

When judging the degree of positivity in a given input, subjects can ignore variations in the degree of dominance in that input; with respect to positivity judgments, variations in dominance are just noise. Similarly, when judging the degree of dominance in a given stimulus, simultaneous variations in positivity are irrelevant to subjects' ratings.

Advantages and disadvantages of the NDT methodology

Because the discrepancy test is derived from the PONS test, it enjoys many of the same advantages and suffers from many of the same limitations. Those have been discussed above and need not be repeated. Here we discuss some of the special problems and promises of the NDT.

The discrepancy test is designed in part to assess people's tendency to weight cues from one channel or modality relatively more than cues from another channel or modality in cases of audio–video cue conflict. With every sample that we have tested, we have found an overall tendency for subjects to weight video cues more than cues given by tone of voice (*video primacy* effect).

In designing the discrepancy test, we made no attempt to equate the level of information contained in the audio and the video stimuli. We did not want to alter the amount of information that a face or a body cue would normally convey in a given time segment in order to make it equal to the amount of information that an audio cue of the same length would convey. We wanted to study subjects' differential attention to naturally occurring chunks of nonverbal information.

There exists in cognitive psychology, however, an extensive series of studies also examining modality primacy, in which the auditory and visual cues do convey the same amount of information. The stimuli used in those studies are very nonsocial, such as tones and lights, and the tasks include perceptual judgments (determining whether a light has been flashed or a tone sounded or whether the tone or light was exposed on the right or on the left) and memory tests (e.g., reproducing a visually produced movement). These studies, too, consistently find that subjects are more influenced by video than by auditory cues (Posner, Nissen, & Klein, 1976).

In any case, our intent is not to suggest that people will always attend more to video cues than to audio cues. The more important goal of a program of research on modality primacy effects is that of determining the dispositional and situational or contextual moderators of this effect. That is, what kinds of persons are especially likely to attend to visual (or auditory) cues? What kinds of judgmental tasks or contextual factors accentuate the effect? Our research has suggested several answers to each of these questions. For example, we have found that females are especially likely to attend preferentially to visual cues, especially when those cues come from the face rather than the body. Males also show stronger video primacy effect for face than for body, but for them the difference is not as pronounced (DePaulo et al., 1978; Rosenthal & DePaulo, 1979b). The nature of the affect being judged also moderates the affect: Subjects show a stronger video primacy effect when judging the degree of positivity in a given stimulus than when judging the degree of dominance (DePaulo & Rosenthal, 1979b; DePaulo et al., 1978). Finally, subjects who are led to expect to see a lot of deception are more likely to discount facial cues than are subjects led to believe that no deception is taking place in the scenarios that they are viewing (Zuckerman et al., 1981).

Although we like to think of our primacy scores as measuring differential *attention,* alternative interpretations are possible. One alternative possibility is that people simply weight more heavily the information from a particular modality (perhaps the one they decode more accurately or the one they believe to convey the more veridical cues), independent of their actual division of attention. Eye-tracking devices, tests of memory for nonverbal stimuli, and complex gadgetry that would allow a subject to sample at will different sources of nonverbal information are all real or fantasized possibilities for zeroing in on subjects' actual distribution of attention to various nonverbal stimuli.

Another potentially problematic feature of the discrepancy test is that the discrepancies are experimentally created rather than naturally occurring. Moreover, our experimental creations are not very like real life. Rarely do we see people "talking to a lost child" with their voices while "expressing jealous rage" with their faces. This problem is very similar to the issue of posed versus spontaneous encodings discussed earlier with respect to the PONS test. For the purposes of measuring individual differences in sensitivity to discrepant nonverbal cues, we cannot know for sure on a priori grounds whether experimentally created discrepancies would be more effective, less effective, or not different from naturally occurring discrepancies. Moreover, the task of finding and defining spontaneously occurring real-life discrepancies is probably even more formidable than that of capturing pure and consistent real-life cues. The experimental approach allows for the creation of discrepancies that can be varied systematically along theoretically meaningful dimensions. In the discrepancy test, we have varied the source of the discrepancy (face–voice vs. body–voice) the nature of the discrepancy (inconsistencies in positivity, in dominance, or in both), and the degree of the discrepancy (three levels). Of course, there are other possibilities as well (e.g., intramodal [verbal/vocal, face/body] rather than intermodal inconsistencies; sequential rather than simultaneously occurring discrepancies).

On a practical level, the discrepancy test is probably a fairly difficult test for a person to take. The stimuli are more complex and unusual than, for example, those in the PONS test, and respondents are required to make three judgments about each scene rather than just one. The test is also more difficult to score than is the PONS test, particularly if a computer is not available.

The person description test

The person description test is our most recently developed measure of sensitivity to emotional communications. Because we have not yet used this instrument in our developmental research, we will not discuss it as extensively as the PONS or the NDT.

In designing this test, we chose a scenario that we regarded as characterized by much ecological validity: people talking about other people. We recruited 40 people – 20 males and 20 females from a college population – and asked them to take 1 minute each to describe (a) someone they liked, (b) someone they disliked, (c) someone they felt ambivalently about, and (d) someone they felt indifferent about. Then we asked them to be deceptive. We instructed them to describe (e) the person they liked as though they disliked him or her ("like as though dislike" condition) and to describe (f) the person they really disliked as though they liked him or her ("dislike as though like" condition). Half of the encoders (randomly selected) described same-sex people, whereas the other half described opposite-sex people. Ambivalence was defined for the subjects as strong feelings of both liking and disliking; indifference was defined as no particularly strong feelings either of liking or disliking.

The videotape derived from these descriptions, which we use as a test of decoding skill, includes the middle 20 seconds of each 1-minute description. Test takers rate each scene on 9-point scales of liking, ambivalence, and deception and occasionally also on scales of disliking, discrepancy, tension, and ambivalence. The full person description task – including all six descriptions from all 40 senders, plus rating pauses after each description – is now 2 hours long, but we are currently developing a short version of the test that lasts 36 minutes.

As in the case of the discrepancy test, difference scores are used to assess accuracy. Thus, for example, *like accuracy* is defined as subjects' mean like rating of the like descriptions minus their mean like rating of the dislike descriptions, and *deception accuracy* is defined as subjects' mean deception rating of the two deceptive descriptions minus their mean deception rating of the two pure (like and dislike) descriptions.

Although, on the face of it, this may appear to be a very verbal task, the structure was such that there were actually no clear linguistic giveaways. First, subjects were asked not to give a broad tip about the kind of person they were describing. That is, they were told not to begin their ambivalence description with the phrase "The person I feel ambivalently about . . ." Second, the kind of person being described was not unambiguously identifiable from the verbal content of the descriptions. If, for example, the encoder was emitting a stream of praise, that encoder might in fact have been describing someone he or she really did like, or he or she might have been describing someone he or she felt ambivalently toward (i.e., liked a lot but also disliked a lot), or the description might have been a deceptive one, in which the encoder was pretending to like someone she or he actually detested.

For the purists in the nonverbal tradition, however, the test can be administered without sound. Alternatively (or in addition) a content-filtered version of the audio tape can be substituted for the undistorted sound track. Varying the kinds of information to be made available to decoders is of interest conceptually as well as methodologically. Such manipulations may be especially interesting to study developmentally. We might find, for example, that children's decoding accuracy is relatively less impaired by the removal of verbal content than is adults' decoding accuracy.

This test has the advantage of involving a large number of encoders, including both males and females, who are talking about males and females. Also, it assesses sensitivity to both pure and mixed communications. The pure messages include positive and negative messages; the mixed messages include communications that are discrepant but not deceptive (i.e., ambivalence) as well as messages that are discrepant and deceptive (the two deceptive descriptions).

The person description test assesses sensitivity to deception in two different ways. First, as just described, the test yields a measure of subjects' ability to distinguish deceptive communications from nondeceptive ones. Accurate decoders of deception by this criterion tend to label deceptive messages as deceptive and pure messages (liking, disliking) as nondeceptive. Alternatively, an accurate detector or deception might be defined as one who sees through to the affect that the liar is trying to hide rather than believing the affect that the liar is attempting to dissimulate (DePaulo & Rosenthal, 1979b; DePaulo, Zuckerman, & Rosenthal, 1980; see also Ekman & Friesen, 1969, 1974). The person description test measures this kind of sensitivity to deception, too (leakage accuracy).

The study of sensitivity to deception – particularly in this second sense of sensitivity to leaked affects – is of special interest because it sheds light on the perceivers' way of dealing with inconsistencies between the experiential and expressive aspect of a sender's emotions. *Leakage accuracy* tells whether a given decoder tends to report the underlying affect that the sender is actually experiencing or the overt dissimulated display that the sender is attempting to express. What this score does not tell, however, is whether a perceiver who reports only the intentionally communicated affects (or vice versa) has actually failed to notice the masked emotions or instead has simply opted politely to ignore them. Conceivably the latter motivationally based response style could turn into the former ability-governed outcome, as the individual who is thoroughly socialized in the ways of decoding decorum eventually comes to suffer an actual deficit in decoding skill. Perhaps the child notices naughty things, the adolescent notices them but pretends she didn't, and the adult finally fails to notice them at all.

Categories versus dimensions

Selecting stimulus materials

In research on the judgment of emotions, as in research on emotional expression, one of the recurrent issues is whether to conceptualize emotions in terms of a number of discrete categories (i.e., happy, sad, angry) or in terms of a number of dimensions (e.g., positivity–negativity, dominance–submissiveness). In developing the stimulus materials for the PONS test and the Nonverbal Discrepancy Test, we began with the two basic dimensions of positivity and dominance and then eventually selected 20 specific affective expressions each of which was clearly located within one of the four affective quadrants. Some of these 20 affects seem quite clearly to be examples of one of the seven emotions that have been postulated as primary affect categories (i.e., happiness, surprise, fear, sadness, anger, disgust, and interest; e.g., Argyle, 1975). Thus, for instance, "expressing jealous rage" would be an example of anger, whereas "talking about the death of a friend" would be an example of sadness. Not all of the 20 scenes fit into one of the seven primary affect categories, and not all of the seven primary affects are represented among the 20 scenarios. It is probably possible to map the seven affects onto the two by two space formed by the crossing of positivity and dominance, however. In fact, in several recent studies of the structure of affective space, it has been shown that most of the commonly discussed affective states can be represented on dimensions of pleasure–displeasure, degree of arousal, and (somewhat less importantly) dominance–submissiveness (Russell, 1978, 1979; Russell & Mehrabian, 1977).

Designing response formats

In developing measures of nonverbal sensitivity, the categories/dimensions issue arises not only in the selection of stimulus materials but also in the design of response formats. In the PONS test, we have used a categorical response format: Subjects choose one of two labels to describe the affective portrayals they observe; in the discrepancy test, we have used a dimensional format: Subjects rate each scene on 9-point scales of positivity, dominance, and discrepancy.

In selecting stimulus materials, a primary concern is often that of achieving a veridical – or at least plausible and workable – representation of affects as they occur in the real world. In designing response formats, there is an analogous veridicality issue and other considerations as well. Roughly, the veridicality issue is this: If it could be conclusively demonstrated that people spontaneously perceive emotions in terms of discrete categories rather than continuous dimensions (or vice versa), then there would be cause to design response formats so as to require categorical judgments (or dimensional ratings). The numerous studies conducted in both traditions compellingly demonstrate that people *can* perform either type of judgmental task; the question of how they do in fact proceed when left to their own perceptual devices is of course a much stickier one. Perhaps this, too, is a developmental question; that is, it is possible that the ability to perceive emotions in terms of categories (versus dimensions) changes with age. From an empirical point of view, a finding reported by Zuckerman and colleagues (Zuckerman et al., 1976) – that accuracy scores computed from dimensional ratings are substantially correlated with accuracy scores computed from categorical judgments – is certainly encouraging, as it suggests that the two approaches are likely to yield similar patterns of results.

Another consideration in selecting response formats is the properties of the dependent variables that they yield. It might be argued, for instance, that accuracy is measured more precisely from dimensional ratings than from categorical ratings. In the case of categorical judgments, the test taker either chooses the appropriate category and is completely right or chooses an inappropriate one and is completely wrong. In making a dimensional rating, on the other hand, the individual can choose from a number of different points on the scale; this judgment, considered along with other judgments that the individual made, is then classified as right or wrong to varying degrees. This precision achieved with dimensional ratings can be approximated in the case of categorical judgments by offering the subject a number of alternatives to choose from in responding to the test items. These alternatives can then be scaled for their similarity to the correct alternative. Subjects are then credited with more points for choosing alternatives that more closely approximate the correct one. This response format has the problem of becoming increasingly cumbersome and time-consuming as the number of response alternatives increases. Also, it may not be the ideal solution for the researcher who wants to remain clearly on the side of the categorists; the scaling of the response alternatives would involve locating those alternatives on one or more dimensions.

In choosing between categorical and dimensional formats, it is also important to consider whether the dependent variable indexes accuracy in a way that is unconfounded with response bias. Take, for instance, the case of an individual who is biased to perceive all nonverbal stimuli as expressions of disapproval. When taking the PONS test, this person might always choose a response alternative that describes a negative affect, regardless of the nature of the affect actually portrayed. Because negative and positive affects occur equally often through the course of the test, this person's total accuracy score will not be unduly inflated by this bias. This person – whose responding does not distinguish at all between negative and positive cues – will receive full credit for choosing a negative label to describe those items that actually are negative and no credit for choosing a negative label to describe those items that are in fact positive. The resulting accuracy score – 50%, indicating a chance level of responding – is exactly the score that she or he deserves.

Still, the PONS test also yields affect subscores – that is, separate scores indicating accuracy at identifying positive, negative, dominant, and submissive affects. When the negative subscore is considered by itself, an individual with a negativity bias would be credited with an inappropriately high score. The design of the PONS test, however, does allow some disentanglement of accuracy and bias, even in this case. One could, for instance, determine whether the percentage of items that subjects answer correctly when the correct answer is negative is greater than the percentage of items that they answer incorrectly when the correct answer is positive. If the answer is yes, then there is evidence of at least some accuracy. One could also test whether subjects respond at a greater than chance level when both response alternatives are negative and when neither is negative; in these cases, a bias to select negative responses cannot affect accuracy rates (see Nasby et al., 1980 for an example of this data analytic procedure).

In the discrepancy test, accuracy is calculated as a difference score based on ratings made on 9-point scales. In contrast to the complex untangling procedures described above for use with categorical response formats, dimensional formats can be employed so as to separate accuracy and bias clearly and straightforwardly. A tendency to rate all (or most) scenes as extremely negative will not bolster the subject's accuracy score, that is, variations in the mean rating on a given scale do not affect the calculation of difference scores based on ratings made on that scale. As long as the subjects rate the positive scenes as more positive than the negative scenes, they will still be credited with some degree of accuracy, regardless of whether their ratings tend to be on the right side or the left side of the rating scale. In the extreme case in which subjects rate all scenes as 1 (the most extremely negative point on the scale), the difference score (rating of the positive scenes minus rating of the negative scenes) will be 0, indicating no accuracy. This, of course, is exactly the score that should be assigned to subjects who make no discriminations at all among the different affects that they perceive.

In a dimensional response format, one type of response is the tendency to give high or low mean ratings on a particular rating scale. In the discrepancy test, the positive label is always next to the right endpoint (the 9 on the 9-point scale) and the negative label is always on the left. Thus, this type of response bias cannot confidently be distinguished from a tendency to circle very low (or very high) numbers. This could be handled quite readily by alternating the positive and negative labels from side to side. Still, this would probably prove quite confusing (and annoying) to subjects. When the labels are consistent on every item, subjects seem to learn to use the scales very quickly; thereafter, they can devote all of their attention and effort to the decoding task rather than to bothersome aspects of the response format.

This issue of ease of responding is still another important consideration in the design of a response format. Adult subjects appear to handle both categorical and dimensional formats quite easily. We suspected that the categorical format would be somewhat easier for children, but even the youngest of the children to whom we have administered the discrepancy test (9-year-olds) have evidenced little or no difficulty with the rating scale tasks.

One of our longer-range plans is to develop measures of children's reactivity to nonverbal cues in a format that requires no verbal skills at all on the part of the children. We are beginning work on measures that require only that the decoder have an intact sensorium. Individual differences in affective discriminations would be measured by exposing very young children (e.g., 18 months) to various nonverbal stimuli (e.g., some of those of Buck, 1976; DePaulo et al., 1978; Rosenthal et al., 1979; Zuckerman et al., 1975, 1976) and observing the resulting facial expressions, body movements, vocalizations, heart rate, and other indexes of responsiveness. Coding of the responses would be primarily on the dimensions of favorableness (or positiveness) and arousal (or interest). Reactivity to nonverbal cues might be defined in part by the consistency and appropriateness of the child's response to the various stimuli. Both between-children consistencies (i.e., most children respond in a particular way to particular stimuli) and within-children consistencies (i.e., a particular child responds in a consistent way to particular kinds of stimuli) would be informative. Probably even younger children can be assessed for their reactivity to nonverbal cues. Young-Browne, Rosenfeld, and Horowitz (1977), for example, have shown that infants are able to discriminate facial expressions at ages as young as 3 months.

In the present section of this chapter we have addressed a number of issues having to do with the use of categories versus dimensions. A more detailed discussion of these and related issues having to do with the conduct of judgment studies is available elsewhere (Rosenthal, in press).

The process of nonverbal decoding

Although a variety of mechanisms have been proposed to characterize the process of nonverbal decoding, well-developed and articulated theories are rare (see, however, Frijda, 1969, for one exception). We do not intend to elaborate such a theory here; rather, our more modest goal is to point to some of the processes or strategies that might be involved in nonverbal decoding and to outline some of the factors that should be considered in a nonverbal decoding theory.

First, the decoder must have some minimal knowledge of the emotion to be decoded. Thus, for example, if a child simply does not know what shame is, she or he probably could not identify it. Also important is a knowledge of the kinds of reactions typically engendered by particular kinds of situations in particular kinds of persons. Specific knowledge about particular persons who are being observed (e.g., knowledge of how they usually express certain emotions) might be useful, too. (In the present discussion we have assumed that the *identification* of emotion is the goal. It should be noted, however, that emotions can probably be *discriminated* with considerably less knowledge of this kind [Young-Browne et al., 1977].)

In terms of specific mechanisms, one that has been proposed is that of projection. The perceiver experiences a certain emotion, then simply projects that feeling onto the person whose emotion is to be decoded. This particular strategy is sometimes discussed as though it were a decoding disease or at best an illegal shortcut to decoding success: If the observer does draw the right inference, he or she has done so without really considering the special characteristics of the person observed. If, however, the decoder's own feelings were in part a reaction to the other person's behaviors and expressions, then the process would not be completely egocentric.

A second mechanism, motor mimicry, has been discussed by Frijda (1969). In this process, the decoder imitates the expressive movements of the encoder or produces a movement that is different from the encoder's specific movement but similar in meaning. Although this strategy might be useful to those who employ it spontaneously, it might not be so effective for people who do not naturally use it. For instance, Frijda has reported that subjects asked to imitate facial expressions sometimes start interpreting first and only then produce facial movements.

A third strategy might be dubbed *dictionary decoding*. The perceiver observes a cue, then looks up its meaning in his or her nonverbal dictionary. This approach to nonverbal decoding would probably not be an accurate description of even the most simpleminded decoder. Any given cue is undoubtedly linked to a variety of meanings, and any one meaning can probably be indexed by a variety of different cues or combinations of cues. Associations between cues and meanings, then, are probably always probabilistic ones. This by no means implies that such associations are therefore unimportant. On the contrary, success at nonverbal decoding is probably incremented considerably by an accurate knowledge of the strength of the real-world associations between cues (or cue combinations) and meanings. Also important is a knowledge of the kinds of dispositional and situational factors that moderate the strength of those associations.

There are other complications, too. In real life, people combine not simply a number of different nonverbal cues, but verbal, situational, and contextual cues, too, as well as the various kinds of prior knowledge described earlier. Further, it is not sufficient to start with a cue (or set of cues) as a given and then study the relation of this cue to meaning. The extraction of the cue is itself problematic, in all or many of the same ways that any kind of categorization is problematic. First, the cue must be noticed. In a multifaceted stimulus array, an observer who is not adept at discerning and focusing in on the most relevant aspects of the display may not even notice certain crucial cues. Second, the cue must be accurately categorized. When, for example, is a smile a smile and not a smirk or a silly grin?

An alternative to this nonverbal features model is a configurational, template, or prototype model. Thus a decoder might have available mental representations of certain emotions to which real-life stimuli might be compared. But what would such representations look like? Would each representation involve a specific person or a kind of person prototype? What if the person to be decoded were very different from the one in the mental representation? Also, does a person need to compare a given stimulus to all possible emotion prototypes to arrive at an accurate identification? Would these comparisons proceed sequentially, or might they all occur simultaneously (parallel processing)? Would either process (sequential or parallel) require more time than nonverbal judgments normally appear to take?

These are all the kinds of issues that cognitive psychologists have long grappled with. Why, then, can't we simply adopt their theories (of pattern recognition, or categorization, etc.) to understand the process of nonverbal decoding? Perhaps we can. Still, we should always be alert to the possibility that there may be something special about this particular kind of skill. The work of Carey and her associates is instructive in this regard: They have documented a developmental course for the recognition of human faces that is different from the developmental progression evidenced for the recognition of houses, landscapes, costumes, stick figures of men, dog's faces, and even inverted human faces (Carey & Diamond, in press).

Moreover, the process of decoding certain nonverbal cues (though perhaps not all) is probably more strongly affected by social and cultural factors than is, for instance, the recognition of the letter A or the identification of random dot patterns. Some of these social and cultural factors might include rules of decoding decorum that are in a sense mirror images of the display rules described in the encoding literature. Thus, for example, from an encoder's perspective, one display rule might be that men are not supposed to express fear; the complementary rule for the decoder might be to pretend not even to notice any such expressions that might actually occur.

In addition to looking for ways to test directly each of the mechanisms just described, one might also glean relevant evidence from other kinds of studies. For example, knowledge of the relative effectiveness of various techniques designed to sharpen nonverbal decoding skills would probably add some constraints to a decoding theory.

Probably there is no one winning way of decoding nonverbal cues. Rather, different strategies are used by different people in different situations and for different purposes. For example Diamond and Carey (1977) in their study of the mechanisms for making unfamiliar faces familiar have shown that children under 10 use more superficial, piecemeal cues than do adults. A similar cue-to-configurational progression might be found to characterize the developmental course of nonverbal decoding. It might also be the case that younger people have a less extensive range of strategies available to them or that they are less adept at switching from one mechanism to another in accordance with situational demands.

Finally, there is evidence that hemispheric effects might also be important in decoding nonverbal cues (Izard, 1977; Rosenthal et al., 1979). Dwyer (1975) found that processing content-filtered items from the PONS test involved greater right hemispheric activity than was the case for more standard verbal material. Similarly, Young (1979) has also shown that the right hemisphere tends to be more involved in the processing of nonverbal cues than of verbal materials. Extending these results, Domangue (1979) reported that subjects whose right hemisphere was relatively dominant tended to be better decoders of content-filtered items of the PONS. Even when nonverbal cues are compared with other nonverbal cues, there are hemispheric effects; in Young's (1979) study, right hemisphere involvement tended to be greater for body than for face cues and greater for content-filtered than for randomized spliced cues. Future cross-sectional and longitudinal studies may show that age changes in lateralization and in hemispheric functioning may be related to age changes in decoding various kinds of nonverbal cues.

Developmental research involving the PONS and discrepancy tests

In our work with the PONS and discrepancy tests, we have been able to study a number of developmental issues. Some of the questions we have addressed include the following: What is the structure of nonverbal decoding skills, and how does this skill structure change with age? In what ways do nonverbal abilities and strategies change developmentally? How do older and younger decoders differ in the ways that they deal with nonverbal stimuli that vary in complexity or informativeness? Are siblings any more similar to each other in their nonverbal sensitivities than randomly paired perceivers? In the following sections, we review our research on each of these questions.

The structure of nonverbal decoding skills

Increasing differentiation. Perhaps one of the most central concepts in developmental psychology is the idea, suggested by both Werner and Piaget, that interpersonal perceptions become more differentiated with age. Werner's orthogenetic principle states: "Whenever development occurs, it proceeds from a state of relative globality and lack of differentiation to a state of increasing differentiation, articulation, and hierarchic integration" (Werner, 1957, p. 126).

To study the Wernerian principle as it applies to the development of nonverbal decoding skills, we obtained the PONS test results of 632 individuals at eight different age levels (age M ranged from 8 to 33 years); then, for each individual, we computed scores indexing accuracy at judging each of the 20 PONS situations. These 20 accuracy scores were intercorrelated separately for each of the eight age levels. For each of these eight correlation matrices, a principal components factor analysis was computed.

We predicted that the factor analyses for the younger age levels would show a simpler factor structure. That is, for younger perceivers more than for older ones, the abilities to decode different types of situations should be strongly related to each other. In factor-analytic terms, the percent of variance attributable to the first factor should be greater for the younger age levels.

The correlation of the mean age at each age level with the percentage of variance attributable to the first principal component of each factor-analytic solution was $-.65$ ($df = 6$, $p < .04$, one-tailed, thus supporting the prediction that nonverbal decoding skills become more differentiated with age [DePaulo & Rosenthal, 1979a]).

The finding of increasing skill differentiation with age is in accord with the results of other more verbally oriented studies of developmental person perception (Brierly, 1966; Olshan, 1970; Scarlett, Press, & Crockett, 1971; Signell, 1966). The interpersonal implications of the degree of differentiation of one's perceptual system have been noted by several researchers studying psychopathology. Reker (1974), for example, showed that disturbed children, compared with normals, used fewer dimensions and less differentiating dimensions in construing social situations; in their perceptions of inanimate objects, on the other hand, the two groups did not differ. In another study of emotionally disturbed boys, Hayden, Nasby, and Davids (1977) showed that those boys who used more differentiated constructs to describe a set of facial photographs responded more adaptively to various interpersonal situations.

Perhaps persons with relatively undifferentiated perceptual structures see many different kinds of affective expressions as essentially equivalent. As Hayden et al. (1977) suggest, a sufficiently differentiated perceptual system may be necessary "for adequately anticipating and predicting the often subtle and diverse demands of social situations" (p. 315).

Increasing leakiness. In our study of skill differentiation, we used only PONS items – all of which involve overt and intentionally communicated cues. Still, we suspected that skill at judging other, more covert communications, such as discrepant messages, might be quite distinct from skill at judging overt cues. To test this, we administered the PONS test and the NDT to a high school and a college sample (DePaulo & Rosenthal, 1979d). We also administered the Brief Exposure PONS, which assesses the ability to decode face and body cues presented at very brief exposures (42 to 1,125 milliseconds). We were interested in the relationships among nine accuracy scores: PONS face, body, and tone; Brief Exposure PONS face and body; and NDT face, body, tone, and discrepancy accuracy.

For the high school sample, the most meaningful of the factor-analytic solutions was a four-factor solution. Factor 1 was defined by the pure face and body variables and by the briefly exposed face and body variables. Factor 2 also tapped skill at judging face and body cues, but the Factor 2 face and body cues were embedded in a mixed stimulus including both audio and video components. Factor 3 was defined by subjects' skill at judging audio cues embedded in a

Table 9.4. *The structure of nonverbal decoding skills: two-by-two interpretation of the four-factor solution (high school students)*

Messages	Modalities	
	Primarily video	Primarily audio
Pure	pure face pure body briefly exposed face briefly exposed body	pure tone
Mixed	mixed face mixed body	mixed tone discrepancy

mixed array, plus their accuracy at identifying the degree of discrepancy in these multimodality stimuli. Factor 4 was a pure tone factor.

These four factors can be conceptualized as a 2×2 matrix that highlights the importance of the number of messages to which subjects are exposed (pure, or single, messages vs. mixed, or multiple, messages) and the modalities to which subjects must attend in order to attain high accuracy scores (see Table 9.4). People who are especially good at judging single-channel, or pure, cues will not necessarily be good at judging multiple-channel, or mixed, cues. Similarly, people who are accurate perceivers when video cues are more relevant to their judgments will not necessarily be accurate perceivers when audio cues must be used.

For the college sample, the factor-analytic solution was different in one important way: The body variables from the Pure Video factor loaded very low on that factor and very high on the Pure Tone factor. The Pure Video factor, then, became a Face-Only factor and the Pure Audio factor became a Tone-Only and Body-Only factor. The Mixed Video and Mixed Audio factors were the same as in the high school sample.

Discrepant cues, briefly exposed cues, voice cues, and body cues have all been hypothesized to be more likely than face cues exposed for normal durations to reveal the feelings that a person may be trying to hide. The voice variables and the discrepancy variables – all ostensibly tapping leakage skills – occur on entirely different factors from the more overt face variables. The distinction between the overt face and the covert body is not borne out by the factor structure except at the college level, when both body variables become detached from the face variables and migrate to the pure tone factor. For the college students, then, the structure of nonverbal decoding skills begins to more clearly resemble a leakage solution: Single-channel face variables are all alone on the first factor, mixed video (and therefore perhaps slightly leaky) variables form another factor, the mixed tone variable and the discrepancy variable form a third factor that is clearly a leakage factor, and the single-channel body and single-channel voice variables define the fourth factor, which is also comprised entirely of ostensibly covert cues.

The development of sensitivity to nonverbal cues

In studies of the development of nonverbal sensitivity involving the PONS test, a linear kind of increasing accuracy with age has repeatedly been reported (Rosenthal et al., 1979). This finding is not surprising; in fact, in view of the previous studies that had already shown that skill at decoding nondiscrepant, intentionally communicated nonverbal cues increases steadily with age (Dimitrovsky, 1964; Gates, 1923; Girgus & Wolf, 1975; Izard, 1971; Kellog & Eagleson, 1931; McCluskey et al., 1975; Zuckerman & Przewuzman, 1979), we would have been very surprised not to find this.

We have also studied age trends in decoding affects by means of the discrepancy test (Blanck et al., 1981). As indicated earlier, the response format of the NDT requires subjects to rate each audiovisual stimulus on separate scales of positivity and dominance. With this test, too, we have found that the ability to judge the degree of positivity and dominance in affective communications grows linearly with age (the age range studied was 9 through 15). There was, however, one suggestive irregularity in an otherwise fairly steadily climbing line: Decoding accuracy decreased somewhat at age 13. Given that the overall linear trend was highly significant and also that this result has not yet been replicated, we usually would not even mention this hint of a developmental dip. We do so here only because of the compelling evidence for a developmental decline at approximately this age in what is perhaps a related area of inquiry. Carey and her associates (Carey & Diamond, in press; Mann, Diamond, & Carey, 1979), in studies of the recognition of unfamiliar faces and voices (the faces and voices themselves rather than the emotions communicated by them) have consistently found a plateau or decline in these abilities between the ages of 12 and 14. Carey suggests that this effect may be attributable to maturational changes (probably in the right hemisphere) associated with the onset of puberty and/or to temporary changes in strategies used to process information.

In contrast to all of these studies revealing overall increases in accuracy in the recognition of faces, voices, and nondiscrepant emotions, our data on the developmental course of accuracy at recognizing discrepancies in nonverbal communications do not provide evidence for a clear linear trend. Although we might expect the cognitive underpinnings of this skill to increase steadily with age, the probable developmental history of the motivational supports for this skill is far less obvious. As we have noted earlier, individuals may at certain times be socialized *not* to notice the discrepancies in other persons' affective communications. The development of cognitive skills, the course of maturation, and the timing of socialization experiences may intertwine in special ways to produce this unusual developmental pattern.

Learning not to look: the development of sex differences in eavesdropping on nonverbal cues

It has been suggested that various types of nonverbal channels or cues can be arranged along a dimension of controllability or overtness. Face cues, for example, are believed to be the most overt of the nonverbal cues that are commonly studied; body cues are thought to be less overt; tone-of-voice cues are believed to be less overt still; and discrepant cues are thought to be the most covert (cf. Rosenthal & DePaulo, 1979a,b). Several series of studies have demonstrated that women, who are usually superior to men in nonverbal decoding, show a systematic decrease in their decoding advantage as the cues that they are judging become more covert or leaky (Rosenthal & DePaulo, 1979a,b). One possible interpretation of these results is that women are more polite or accommodating in their reading of nonverbal cues than are men. That is, they refrain from reading nonverbal cues as those cues become less and less controllable by the sender. The less controllable cues are probably just those cues that senders do not intend to send and do not wish other people to read. Apparently, women politely refrain from this kind of nonverbal eavesdropping.

By testing subjects at several different age levels (pre–high school students, high school students, and college students) on four different kinds of cues varying in overtness, we were able to study the developmental acquisition of females' nonverbal accommodatingness (Blanck et al., 1981). Our analyses showed that as age increased, females lost significantly more and more of their advantage for the more leaky or more covert channels, whereas they gained more and more of their advantage for the less leaky channels. (See Table 9.5.)

Consistent with a learning interpretation, the present findings suggest that females become more nonverbally accommodating as they grow older. Perhaps one of the things that females are learning is that there might be social hazards to being "too good" at understanding certain nonverbal cues.

The developmental priority of the evaluative dimension

In virtually every study that has attempted to chart the fundamental dimensions of a particular psychological domain (e.g., interpersonal behavior, expressions

Table 9.5. *Female superiority in sensitivity to four types of nonverbal cues for three age levels (in σ units)*

| | Age level | | | $r(1)^a$ |
	Pre–high school	High school	College	
Means				
Decoding skill				
Face	−.06	.36	.38	.88
Body	.30	.24	.34	.40
Tone	.28	.32	−.02	−.81
Dis-crepancy	.29	.22	−.28	−.92
$r(2)^b$	.76	−.66	−.96*	
Residuals (interaction)				
Decoding skill				
Face	−.29	.05	.25	.99
Body	.00	−.14	.14	.50
Tone	.08	.04	−.12	−.94
Dis-crepancy	.21	.06	−.26	−.98
$r(2)^b$	.96*	.28	−.99**	

Note: Pre–high school $n = 250$. High school $n = 109$. College $n = 81$.
[a] The correlation of age level with degree of female superiority ($df = 1$).
[b] The correlation of leakiness of channel with degree of female superiority ($df = 2$).
*$p. < .025$, one-tailed. **$p < .005$, one-tailed

of affect, perceptions of persons and objects), an evaluative dimension (positivity–negativity, pleasantness–unpleasantness, hostility–friendliness) has emerged (see DePaulo et al., 1979; Russell, 1979). The significance of this dimension is evidenced not only by its invariable emergence but also by its frequent priority in salience and centrality over other important dimensions such as intensity, dominance–submissiveness, and activity.

Given the importance of the positive–negative dimension in every psychological domain in which a fundamental structure has been sought out, it seems reasonable to expect that dimension to assume developmental priority. That is, children should notice and use this dimension before they notice and use other dimensions. This might be apparent in their ability to make more differentiations along this dimension than along other dimensions – variations in degree of positivity should be relatively more salient to these children than variations in, for example, degree of dominance.

In terms of the NDT stimuli, we expected younger subjects (as compared with older ones) to be relatively more likely to notice discrepancies along the positivity dimension than to notice discrepancies in dominance. As predicted, younger subjects (junior high and high school) were relatively more likely than college students to rate inconsistencies along the positive–negative dimension as highly discrepant (DePaulo et al., 1979).

A similar pattern of results has been reported in a study using accuracy scores (derived from the NDT) as the dependent variable (Zuckerman et al., 1980). The type of accuracy studied was skill at recognizing variations in positivity and dominance; subject ranged in age from 9 to 15. Consistent with the developmental priority hypothesis, younger children, compared with older ones, were relatively more accurate at decoding positive–negative cues. If we were to test even younger children, perhaps we would find that positivity is decoded better than dominance not only in relative terms but also in an absolute sense.

Age changes in sensitivity as a function of the informativeness of the cues

Increases in cognitive processing capacity have been postulated to account for the growth of many cognitive–developmental skills (e.g., Pascual-Leone, 1970; Pascual-Leone & Smith, 1969). If it is in fact the case that younger subjects can integrate less information at any one time than older subjects can, then the relative disadvantage of younger subjects in interpreting nonverbal cues should be particularly marked when a relatively large amount of valid information is available. Although the addition of information relevant to a decoding task should facilitate performance at all age levels, this will be less true for younger subjects, who would be expected to utilize such additional information less effectively.

The structure of the PONS test allows for several different tests of this hypothesis. First, the PONS test includes several single channels (face only, body only, tone only) and several multiple channels (video plus audio). According to the processing capacity argument, younger subjects should do relatively less well at decoding the multiple-channel stimuli than the single-channel cues. In a study of decoders ranging in age from 8 to 33, we found just that (see Table 9.6; DePaulo & Rosenthal, 1978). The same pattern of results was obtained in an analysis that took into account the specific amount of information available in each of the single channels and channel combinations.

We also found evidence for age changes in decoding as function of increasing amounts of information in an analysis of the amount of learning that occurred over the course of the test. Even though subjects do not receive immediate feedback on their responses, they are exposed to more and more of the same general type of information during the course of the PONS film as they repeatedly see

Table 9.6. *Accuracy at decoding single- and multiple-channel nonverbal stimuli*

Age level	Single-channel accuracy (percent)	Multiple-channel accuracy (percent)	Multiple advantage (Multiple minus single)
Third grade	56.60	63.10	6.50
Fourth grade	60.35	66.85	6.50
Fifth grade	63.60	71.70	8.10
Sixth grade	63.10	69.90	6.80
Junior high	70.00	78.80	8.80
High school	72.05	81.15	9.10
College	76.20	85.30	9.10
Adult	74.05	82.65	8.60

and/or hear each channel and each situation. Amount of information, then, inheres in the knowledge subjects are able to accumulate about the nature of the stimuli or about the relative effectiveness of various strategies used to process the stimuli. Subjects should be gathering more and more of this kind of information over the course of the test.

It was hypothesized, and found, that older subjects would be relatively more adept at taking advantage of continual exposure to the same types of nonverbal cues. In short, the accuracy of older subjects increased more than the accuracy of younger subjects over the duration of the test. We think that a growing processing capacity could account for this increasing efficiency in the utilization of nonverbal information. Third graders, for example, simply may not be able to attend actively to all of the information inherent in a stimulus consisting of a face and a body and a tone. Given this limited capacity, these children might either attend to some of the cues and ignore others or divide their attention among all of the available cues. Either strategy is likely to lead to less accuracy than might be possible if all available information could be fully processed.

An alternative interpretation is that the factor that distinguishes between older and younger subjects is not capacity but effort. The following hypotheses suggest two different ways in which effort might mediate differential performance. (a) Younger subjects have the same processing capacity as older ones but simply fail to use it as persistently. Younger subjects are perhaps more easily distracted and more readily fatigued. In the face of a wealth of information, they may attend elsewhere rather than exert additional effort. (b) Younger subjects can process as much information as older ones, but it takes more effort for them to do so. Even if effort were constant across all age levels, then, performance would still be relatively better for the older than for the younger age groups. A third possibility also assumes that older subjects have the same processing ca-

Table 9.7. *Face and body primacy for seven age levels*

| Age level | Channel | | Difference | Overall video primacy M |
	Face	Body		
9	1.25	.23	1.02	.73
10	1.43	.23	1.20	.83
11	1.38	.31	1.07	.84
12	1.63	.36	1.27	1.00
13	1.17	.15	1.02	.66
14	1.72	−.02	1.74	.85
15	1.86	.15	1.71	1.00
M	1.49	.20	1.29	.84

Note: Higher scores indicate greater video primacy.

pacity as younger ones but attributes their greater accuracy to a more effective distribution of attention. It suggests that older subjects might be particularly adept at discerning and focusing on the most relevant aspects of a given stimulus or set of stimuli.

Given the work of Pascual-Leone (1970), Case (1972), and others, it is unlikely that processing capacity remains fixed at successive age levels. It is quite possible, however, that the relative advantage of older subjects in processing large amounts of information is a function not only of a larger processing capacity but also of such variables as greater effort, lower distractibility, greater stamina, and more effective sampling of available cues.

Developmental trends in video primacy effects

For several reasons, we expected the video primacy effect (the tendency for people to be more influenced by video than by audio cues in cases of nonverbal cue conflicts) to increase with age. Research with the PONS test has shown that younger subjects are relatively better at judging tone-of-voice cues than video cues (the dependent variable, of course, was accuracy rather than primacy). Further, Bugental et al. (1970) have also reported that video cues have less impact on young children (relative to adults), an effect that was especially strong for the decoding of women's positive affects.

When we administered the discrepancy test to our sample of 9- to 15-year-olds, however, we found no overall trend for video primacy to increase with age (Zuckerman et al., 1980). (See Table 9.7.) Age did interact significantly with channel (face/body), affective dimension (positivity/dominance), and the degree of discrepancy in the audiovisual pairings (slightly discrepant/very discrepant).

In accordance with previous findings (DePaulo et al., 1978), video primacy was greater for facial expressions than for body cues. More important, however, the results indicated that in comparison with young children, older children showed more video primacy for face but not for body (see Table 9.6). Clearly, the rise of the face as a major source of nonverbal information relative to the voice is, at least to some degree, a developmental phenomenon.

Because the face delivers particularly strong cues of positivity (e.g., the smile) and also accounts for the bulk of the video primacy effect, it was not surprising to find that video primacy was also greater for expressions of positivity than for expressions of dominance. Parallel to the increase of face primacy with age, the superiority of the positivity dimension in video primacy was also greater among older children. Thus, the results indicate that older children showed more video primacy for face and for cues of positivity.

Although the communications in the NDT are not actually deceptive ones, it has been suggested that the discrepant messages in the test – particularly the very discrepant ones – may seem like deceptive communications to a decoder. If this were true, then we might expect perceivers to attend relatively more to the more covert audio cues (which may leak a sender's true underlying affect) as the messages become more discrepant and hence more like deception. Studies with adult subjects have provided some support for this notion: Perceivers did tend to attend relatively more to the audio cues (decreased video primacy effect) when decoding the more discrepant messages (DePaulo et al., 1978). Further, in a study in which subjects were explicitly told that the NDT scenes contained no deception, some deception, or a great deal of deception, those subjects who were led to expect more deception attended relatively more to the tone of voice than to the face cues (Zuckerman et al., 1981). With our sample of 9- to 15-year-olds, we found that the tendency to attend relatively more to the audio cues when judging the more discrepant scenes increased with age (Zuckerman et al., 1980). Although these data by themselves do not warrant the conclusion that children are learning subtle strategies for detecting deception, they are certainly consistent with it. In any case, they suggest that developmental studies of the detection of deception may prove quite illuminating.

Consistent with the research on the structure of decoding skills described earlier, the results of this study also indicate that the profile of nonverbal skills is less differentiated at younger ages. That is, the differences in sensitivity and attention to different channels (face and voice) are less emphasized than they are at an older age. Interestingly, it appears that, in comparison with older children, youngsters are more influenced by leaky and uncontrollable channels such as the body and less influenced by controllable channels such as the face. This means that relatively speaking, children may be influenced less by the information that is sent intentionally (through the face) and more by information that the sender

Table 9.8. *Intraclass correlations for brother–brother pairs and brother–sister pairs*

| | | Type of decoding | | |
| | Decoding accuracy | Discrepancy accuracy | Video primacy | M |
Types of pairs				
Brother–brother	.42*	.30	.35	.36*
Brother–sister	−.24	.55**	.07	.13
M	.09	.43*	.21	.25
Difference	.66*	−.25	.28	.23

Note: Brother–brother $n = 16$. Brother–sister $n = 21$.
*$p < .05$. **$p < .01$.

tries to conceal but that nevertheless leaks out (through the body). In contrast, adults are not only more accurate decoders but are also more likely to be influenced by controllable channels such as the face relative to leaky channels such as the body. It seems almost ironic that because of greater sensitivity to facial expressions, the adult person may lose some of his or her ability to identify more subtle and leaky messages. But, of course, this is what socialization is all about: We may be trained to read the messages that are sent and to ignore the messages that are leaked. If controllable channels are the channels we are supposed to attend to according to the norms of polite interpersonal transactions (cf. Rosenthal & DePaulo, 1979a,b), then it is particularly interesting that the clearest increment in facial attentiveness occurs at ages 14 and 15 – a time when it may be becoming especially important to do the "right" thing in social interaction.

Sibling resemblances in nonverbal skill and style

Our large sample of children who took the NDT included 37 pairs of siblings: 16 brother–brother pairs and 21 brother–sister pairs. This allowed us to investigate whether nonverbal skills might run in families. We studied sibling resemblances in video primacy, discrepancy accuracy, and decoding accuracy (skill at judging positivity and dominance; Blanck et al., 1980).

Intraclass correlations indicating sibling resemblance in nonverbal skills are presented in Table 9.8. Sibling pairs displayed a tendency for family resemblance in nonverbal decoding, suggesting that nonverbal skills may run in families. This resemblance was particularly strong for discrepancy accuracy and weaker for video primacy and decoding accuracy. Overall, brother–brother pairs tended to show more resemblance in nonverbal decoding than did brother–sister pairs, perhaps because same-sex siblings share more common experiences than do opposite-sex siblings (Bowerman & Dobash, 1974). Further, brother–brother pairs may be treated more similarly by other people, especially parents, than brother–sister pairs. This might lead brothers, relative to brother–sister pairs, to develop more similar patterns for making sense out of the nonverbal world.

One last issue for future research

To the infant who cannot yet understand speech, the world is a wholly nonverbal one. At this point in development, content-masked speech is a reality rather than a methodological technique. For the infant, the nonverbal aspects of communication have to be foreground, for the verbal aspects are unintelligible. Yet we know (or strongly suspect) that at some later point in development – and we don't know exactly when this might be – the components flip and the words become the figure, whereas the nonverbals slip quietly into the ground. How this reversal occurs is a question with many parts. Probably one of the parts is an accountability rule: The verbal channel is the one we are assumed to have most control over, and hence it is the one for which we are held most accountable. How and when do children come to learn this rule? Another way to analyze the question is to ask whether the developmental course of verbal foregrounding varies with the type of judgment required or with the nature of the social interaction in which the communication is occurring. Also, when, as adults, do we switch to a strategy of nonverbal foregrounding? Finally, might verbal foregrounding be a universal feature of human communicative systems?

Note

1 The scenes were chosen by the researchers as the most representative of the psychological meaning of each quadrant.
    In addition, each selected scene met the following criteria:
    1. The median accuracy of the face, body, CF, and RS channels of a given scene was greater than 55% among the members of the high school norm group ($N = 480$) used in the validation of the PONS test, where 50% was the expected value under the null hypothesis of no accuracy.
    2. The median correlation of the face, body, CF, and RS versions of each scene with the PONS total score was positive among the members of the high school norm group.

References

Archer, D., & Akert, R. M. Words and everything else: Verbal and nonverbal cues in social interpretation. *Journal of Personality and Social Psychology,* 1977, *35,* 443–49.

Argyle, M. *Bodily communication.* New York: International Universities Press, 1975.

Blanck, P. D., Rosenthal, R., Snodgrass, S. E., DePaulo, B. M., & Zuckerman, M. Sex differences in eavesdropping on nonverbal cues: Developmental changes. *Journal of Personality and Social Psychology,* 1981, *41,* 391–6.

Blanck, P. D., Zuckerman, M., DePaulo, B. M., & Rosenthal, R. Sibling resemblances in nonverbal skill and style. *Journal of Nonverbal Behavior,* 1980, *4,* 219–26.

Bowerman, C. E., & Dobash, R. M. Structural variation in intersibling affect. *Journal of Marriage and the Family*, 1974, *36*, 48–54.

Brierly, D. M. Children's use of personality constructs. *Bulletin of the British Psychological Society*, 1966, *19*, 72.

Buck, R. A test of nonverbal receiving ability: Preliminary studies. *Human Communication Research*, 1976, *2*, 162–71.

Bugental, D. E., Kaswan, J. W., & Love, L. R. Perception of contradictory meanings conveyed by verbal and nonverbal channels. *Journal of Personality and Social Psychology*, 1970, *16*, 647–55.

Campbell, D. T., & Fiske, D. W. Convergent and discriminant validation by the multitrait–multimethod matrix. *Psychological Bulletin*, 1959, *56*, 81–105.

Carey, S., & Diamond, R. Maturational determination of the developmental course of face encoding. In D. Caplan (Ed.), *The biological bases of cognitive processes*. Cambridge, Mass.: MIT Press, in press.

Case, R. Validation of a neo-Piagetian mental capacity construct. *Journal of Experimental Child Psychology*, 1972, *14*, 287–302.

Cook, M. *Interpersonal perception*. Baltimore, Md.: Penguin Books, 1971.

DePaulo, B. M. Accuracy in predicting situational variations in help-seekers' responses. *Personality and Social Psychology Bulletin*, 1978, *4*, 330–33.

DePaulo, B. M., & Rosenthal, R. Age changes in nonverbal decoding as a function of increasing amounts of information. *Journal of Experimental Child Psychology*, 1978, *26*, 280–7.

DePaulo, B. M., & Rosenthal, R. Age changes in nonverbal decoding skills: Evidence for increasing differentiation. *Merrill-Palmer Quarterly*, 1979, *25*, 145–50. (a)

DePaulo, B. M., & Rosenthal, R. Ambivalence, discrepancy, and deception in nonverbal communication. In R. Rosenthal (Ed.), *Skill in nonverbal communication*. Cambridge, Mass.: Oelgeschlager, Gunn, & Hain, 1979. (b)

DePaulo, B. M., & Rosenthal, R. Telling lies. *Journal of Personality and Social Psychology*, 1979, *37*, 1713–22. (c)

DePaulo, B. M., & Rosenthal, R. The structure of nonverbal decoding skills. *Journal of Personality*, 1979, *47*, 506–17. (d)

DePaulo, B. M., Rosenthal, R., Eisenstat, R. A., Rogers, P. L., & Finkelstein, S. Decoding discrepant nonverbal cues. *Journal of Personality and Social Psychology*, 1978, *36*, 313–23.

DePaulo, B. M., Rosenthal, R., Finkelstein, S., & Eisenstat, R. A. The developmental priority of the evaluative dimension in perceptions of nonverbal cues. *Environmental Psychology and Nonverbal Behavior*, 1979, *3*, 164–71.

DePaulo, B. M., Zuckerman, M., & Rosenthal, R. Humans as lie detectors. *Journal of Communication*, 1980, *30*, 129–39.

Diamond, R., & Carey, S. Developmental changes in the representation of faces. *Journal of Experimental Child Psychology*, 1977, *23*, 1–22.

Dimitrovsky, L. The ability to identify the emotional meaning of vocal expressions at successive age levels. In J. R. Davitz (Ed.), *The communication of emotional meaning*. New York: McGraw-Hill, 1964.

Dittmann, A. T. *Interpersonal messages of emotion*. New York: Springer, 1972.

Domangue, B. B. *Hemispheric dominance, cognitive complexity, and nonverbal sensitivity*. Unpublished doctoral dissertation, University of Delaware, 1979.

Dwyer, J. H. *Contextual inferences and the right cerebral hemisphere: Listening with the left ear*. Unpublished doctoral dissertation, University of California, Santa Cruz, 1975.

Ekman, P. Cross-cultural studies of facial expression. In P. Ekman (Ed.), *Darwin and facial expression: A century of research in review*. New York: Academic Press, 1973.

Ekman, P., & Friesen, W. V. Nonverbal leakage and clues to deception. *Psychiatry*, 1969, *32*, 88–106.

Ekman, P., & Friesen, W. V. Detecting deception from the body or face. *Journal of Personality and Social Psychology,* 1974, *29,* 288–98.

Ekman, P., Friesen, W. V., & Ellsworth, P. *Emotion in the human face.* New York: Pergamon Press, 1972.

Ekman, P., Friesen, W. V., & Scherer, K. R. Body movement and voice pitch in deceptive interaction. *Semiotica,* 1976, *16,* 23–7.

Frijda, N. H. Recognition of emotion. In L. Berkowitz (Ed.), *Advances in experimental social psychology* (Vol. 4). New York: Academic Press, 1969.

Gates, G. S. An experimental study of the growth of social perception. *Journal of Educational Psychology,* 1923, *14,* 449–61.

Girgus, J. S., & Wolf, J. Age changes in the ability to encode social cues. *Developmental Psychology,* 1975, *11,* 118.

Goffman, E. The presentation of self in everyday life. Garden City, N.Y.: Doubleday, 1959.

Hayden, B., Nasby, W., & Davids, A. Interpersonal conceptual structures, predictive accuracy, and social adjustment of emotionally disturbed boys. *Journal of Abnormal Psychology,* 1977, *86,* 315–20.

Izard, C. E. *The face of emotion.* New York: Appleton-Century-Crofts, 1971.

Izard, C. E. *Human emotions.* New York: Plenum Press, 1977.

Keating, D. P. A search for social intelligence. *Journal of Educational Psychology,* 1978, *70,* 218–23.

Kellogg, W. N., & Eagleson, B. M. The growth of social perception in different racial groups. *Journal of Educational Psychology,* 1931, *22,* 367–75.

Knapp, M. *Nonverbal communication in human interaction.* New York: Holt, Rinehart & Winston, 1972.

Mann, V. A., Diamond, R., & Carey, S. Development of voice recognition: Parallels with face recognition. *Journal of Experimental Child Psychology,* 1979, *27,* 153–65.

McCluskey, K. W., Albas, D. C., Niemi, R. R., Cuevas, C., & Ferrer, C. A. Cross-cultural differences in the perception of the emotional content of speech: A study of the development of sensitivity in Canadian and Mexican children. *Developmental Psychology,* 1975, *11,* 551–5.

Nasby, W., Hayden, B., & DePaulo, B. M. Attributional bias among aggressive boys to interpret unambiguous social stimuli as hostile displays. *Journal of Abnormal Psychology,* 1980, *89,* 459–68.

Olshan, K. *The multidimensional structure of person perception in children.* Unpublished doctoral dissertation, Rutgers – The State University, 1970.

Pascual-Leone, J. A mathematical model for the transition rule in Piaget's developmental stages. *Acta Psychologica,* 1970, *32,* 301–45.

Pascual-Leone, J., & Smith, J. The encoding and decoding of symbols by children. A new experimental paradigm and a neo-Piagetian model. *Journal of Experimental Child Psychology,* 1969, *8,* 328–55.

Posner, M. I., Nissen, M. J., & Klein, R. M. Visual dominance: An information-processing account of its origins and significance. *Psychological Review,* 1976, *83,* 157–71.

Reker, G. Interpersonal conceptual structure of normal and emotionally disturbed boys. *Journal of Abnormal Psychology,* 1974, *83,* 380–6.

Rogers, P. L., Scherer, K. R., & Rosenthal, R. Content-filtering human speech. *Behavioral Research Methods and Instrumentation,* 1971, *3,* 16–18.

Rosenthal, R. Conducting judgment studies. In K. R. Scherer & P. Ekman (Eds.), *Handbook of methods in nonverbal behavior research.* New York: Cambridge University Press, in press.

Rosenthal, R., & DePaulo, B. M. Sex differences in eavesdropping on nonverbal cues. *Journal of Personality and Social Psychology,* 1979, *37,* 273–85. (a)

Rosenthal, R., & DePaulo, B. M. Sex differences in accommodation in nonverbal communication. In R. Rosenthal (Ed.), *Skill in nonverbal communication.* Cambridge, Mass.: Oelgeschlager, Gunn, & Hain, 1979. (b)

Rosenthal, R., Hall, J. A., DiMatteo, M. R., Rogers, P. L., & Archer, D. *Sensitivity to nonverbal communication: The PONS test.* Baltimore, Md.: Johns Hopkins University Press, 1979.

Rosenthal, R., Hall, J. A., & Zuckerman, M. The relative equivalence of senders in studies of nonverbal encoding and decoding. *Environmental Psychology and Nonverbal Behavior,* 1978, *2,* 161–6.

Russell, J. A. Evidence of convergent validity on the dimensions of affect. *Journal of Personality and Social Psychology,* 1978, *36,* 1152–68.

Russell, J. A. Affective space is bipolar. *Journal of Personality and Social Psychology,* 1979, *37,* 345–56.

Russell, J. A., & Mehrabian, A. Evidence for a three-factor theory of emotions. *Journal of Research in Personality,* 1977, *11,* 273–94.

Scarlett, H. H., Press, A. N., & Crockett, W. H. Children's descriptions of peers: A Wernerian developmental analysis. *Child Development,* 1971, *42,* 439–53.

Scherer, K. R. Randomized-splicing: A note on a simple technique for masking speech content. *Journal of Experimental Research in Personality,* 1971, *5,* 155–9.

Signell, K. Cognitive complexity in person perception and nation perception: A developmental approach. *Journal of Personality,* 1966, *34,* 517–37.

Walker, R. E., & Foley, J. M. Social intelligence: Its history and measurement. *Psychological Reports,* 1973, *33,* 839–64. (Monograph Suppl. 1-V33)

Werner, H. The concept of development from a comparative and organismic point of view. In D. B. Harris (Ed.), *The concept of development.* Minneapolis: University of Minnesota Press, 1937.

Young, L. D. *Differential involvement of the cerebral hemispheres in sensitivity to nonverbal communication: A psychophysiological investigation.* Unpublished doctoral dissertation, Harvard University, 1979.

Young-Browne, G., Rosenfeld, H. M., & Horowitz, F. D. Infant discrimination of facial expressions. *Child Development,* 1977, *48,* 555–62.

Zuckerman, M., Blanck, P. D., DePaulo, B. M., & Rosenthal, R. Developmental changes in decoding discrepant and nondiscrepant nonverbal cues. *Developmental Psychology,* 1980, *3,* 220–8.

Zuckerman, M., Hall, J. A., DeFrank, R. S., & Rosenthal, R. Encoding and decoding of spontaneous and posed facial expressions. *Journal of Personality and Social Psychology,* 1976, *34,* 966–77.

Zuckerman, M., Lipets, M. S., Koivumaki, J. H., & Rosenthal, R. Encoding and decoding nonverbal cues of emotion. *Journal of Personality and Social Psychology,* 1975, *32,* 1068–76.

Zuckerman, M., & Przewuzman, S. J. Decoding and encoding facial expressions in preschool-age children. *Environmental Psychology and Nonverbal Behavior,* 1979, *3,* 147–63.

Zuckerman, M., Spiegel, N. H., DePaulo, B. M., & Rosenthal, R. *Nonverbal strategies for decoding deception.* Manuscript submitted for publication, 1981.

Part IV

Subjective experience, empathy, and attachment

10 The construct validity of the Differential Emotions Scale as adapted for children and adolescents

William E. Kotsch, David W. Gerbing, and
Lynne E. Schwartz

The Differential Emotions Scale as adapted for children and adolescents (DES III) is a brief self-report inventory that assesses 10 fundamental emotions. Izard developed the DES III both from his theory of fundamental emotions (Izard, 1971, 1977) and through extensive empirical research on the adult version of the scale, the Differential Emotions Scale (DES; Izard, 1972; Izard et al., 1974). The aim of the chapter is to present the DES III and to evaluate the underlying measurement model through a series of exploratory and confirmatory factor analyses.

Differential emotions theory

Differential emotions theory (Izard, 1971, 1977) emphasizes discrete emotions as distinct experiential motivational processes. Emotion is defined as a complex process with neurophysiological, neuromuscular, and phenomenological aspects. The theory postulates 10 fundamental emotions: interest, joy, surprise, sadness, anger, disgust, contempt, fear, shame/shyness, and guilt. Each emotion has (a) a specific innately determined neural substrate (b) a characteristic facial display or neuromuscular-expressive pattern and (c) a distinct subjective or phenomenological quality. No one of these three facets constitutes emotion; each is a component of emotion. Thus each fundamental emotion is a system made up of its three components and their interactions. Internal or external events can elicit more than one emotion, and through both innate and learned relationships, one emotion can elicit another. The fundamental emotions are interrelated in dynamic and relatively stable ways. The relatively stable combinations of emotions that occur simultaneously or sequentially are called patterns. In day-to-day human experience it appears that these patterns occur more frequently than do pure emotions.

251

The Differential Emotions Scale

The Differential Emotions Scale (DES) is a self-report instrument designed for use in the assessment of an individual's experience of fundamental emotions or patterns of emotions. The DES was originally conceived as a "state" measure of one's emotions, but variations in the instructions allow the same set of scales to be used in the assessment of emotions experienced over an extended period of time. The frequency with which an emotion is experienced over time may be viewed as an emotion trait. This variation of the DES is labeled the Differential Emotions Scale II.

The DES and DES II both consist of 30 adjectives (items), 3 adjectives for each of the 10 fundamental emotions listed above. The DES items are presented in Table 10.1. The usual DES instructions ask an individual to rate, on a single 5-point intensity scale, the extent to which each word describes the way he or she feels at the present time. The DES II, on the other hand, is composed of a 5-point frequency scale. The DES II instructions ask the individual to consider a specified time period in his or her day-to-day life and to rate the frequency with which he or she experiences each emotion during the time considered. The time may be a specified period in the past (i.e., the past week, month, experiment, or therapy hour) or may refer generally to the individual's entire life (i.e., "how often do you have these feelings in your day-to-day living?").

Development of the scale. The vocabulary in the DES items was derived from an analysis of verbal labels of facial expression. Extensive research has demonstrated that subjects of different ethnic origins, languages, and cultures can differentiate among the facial expressions of the fundamental emotions and label them with a high degree of consensus (Ekman, 1973; Izard, 1971). As part of this research, American, English, French, and Greek subjects were asked to give verbal descriptions of the emotions displayed in a series of cross-culturally standardized facial photographs of the fundamental emotions. This work provided the background for the development of the DES by generating a set of words for each of the emotions that could be viewed as transcultural definitions. Exploratory factor analyses were employed as a guide for the final selection of the 30 DES items.

Validity. Several types of validity studies have been conducted with the DES (Izard, 1971, 1977). The DES has been subjected to repeated exploratory factor-analytic studies that have shown the emotion factors to be highly stable. In all of these analyses, the factors obtained corresponded to the theoretically defined factors.

The DES has also been used in studies of anxiety and depression. Results of

Table 10.1. *The differential emotions scale*

Factor	Item	Item–factor correction
I. Interest (.76)	attentive	.88
	concentrating	.79
	alert	.87
II. Enjoyment (.87)	delighted	.81
	happy	.87
	joyful	.86
III. Surprise (.75)	surprise	.83
	amazed	.85
	astonished	.87
IV. Sadness (.85)	downhearted	.86
	sad	.79
	discouraged	.82
V. Anger (.68)	enraged	.74
	angry	.84
	mad	.86
VI. Disgust (.73)	feeling of distaste	.86
	disgusted	.85
	feeling revulsion	.78
VII. Contempt (.78)	contemptuous	.89
	scornful	.90
	disdainful	.84
VIII. Fear (.68)	scared	.88
	fearful	.90
	afraid	.89
IX. Shame/shyness (.83)	sheepish	.73
	bashful	.87
	shy	.88
X. Guilt (.77)	repentant	.78
	guilty	.83
	blameworthy	.80

Note: Item–factor correlations for state instructions, $N = 259$; test–retest reliabilities for trait instructions given in parentheses, $N = 63$.
Source: Izard, 1977.

these investigations have shown that anxiety and depression can be conceptualized as patterns of the fundamental emotions. One such factor-analytic study investigated the structure of anxiety. Anxiety was operationally defined by both the Spielberger, Gorsuch, and Luchene (1970) State–Trait Anxiety Inventory (STAI) and the fundamental emotions measured by the DES. The two scales were combined and administered to college students who had been instructed to visualize a situation that made them highly anxious. The students used the DES and STAI to describe their emotions and feelings in that situation. An exploratory factor analysis produced eight factors that represented the fundamental emotions. All STAI items that had clear emotional connotation separated and had their primary loading on factors representing four of the fundamental emotions – Fear, Sadness, Guilt, and Joy, the latter factor including negatively weighted STAI items.

A similar factor-analytic study related the fundamental emotions to the concept of depression. Zuckerman's MAACL (Zuckerman, 1960) contributed 19 depression items that were combined with the DES items. An exploratory factor analysis produced eight factors representing the fundamental emotions. Most of the negative MAACL items had their primary factor loadings on the DES factor of Sadness. Several of the positive MAACL items loaded on the DES factor of Interest. These studies show the utility of DES in measuring anxiety and depression and demonstrate that the STAI and MAACL are both multidimensional scales consisting in part of several DES factors.

Mosher and Toedter (1979) used the DES to determine and compare the typical patterns of emotions involved in love and jealousy. College students were asked to describe a situation in which they had experienced love and another in which they had experienced jealousy. The subjects completed the DES while visualizing each situation. The love situation was characterized by interest, joy, sexual arousal, and mild surprise. Disgust, anger, and contempt were rarely experienced. In contrast, the experience of jealousy was characterized by sadness and anger, followed by surprise, contempt, and disgust. In addition, a pretest measure of attitudes toward jealousy added a significant increment of prediction to the occurrence of anger, contempt, and disgust.

Criterion-related validity data has come from a study of the test anxiety situation (Barlett & Izard, 1972). Subjects took the STAI and the DES just prior to taking a major examination in their introductory psychology course. The students were divided into high- and low-anxiety groups on the basis of their STAI scores. High-anxiety subjects had significantly higher DES means for fear, shame/shyness, guilt, sadness, and anger and a significantly lower DES mean for joy.

In a study of the relationship of subjective sexual arousal and emotion, Mosher and O'Grady (1979) showed a sex film to women rated either high or low on the Mosher Forced-Choice Guilt Inventory (Mosher, 1968). The women reported their level of sexual arousal and genital sensations both during and after the film. After the film the women completed the DES and a third measure of sexual arousal. Results showed moderate positive correlations (.48 to .84) between the emotions of interest and joy and the three measures of sexual arousal, and positive correlations between fear and guilt (.65) and between guilt and shame (.72).

Women who rated themselves high on the trait measure of sex guilt reported feeling more guilt, disgust, and fear after viewing the sex film than did women who rated themselves low on sex guilt.

A second type of criterion-related validity data has come from the study of various psychodiagnostic groups (Izard et. al., 1974). The DES II was administered to psychiatric patients of various psychodiagnoses and to normal college students. The instructions for this administration of the DES II asked the patients to rate their emotions as experienced over the "past year or two." Results showed that subjects diagnosed as neurotic reported experiencing less joy and more sadness, fear, and guilt in their daily lives than did normal subjects. Subjects diagnosed with personality disorders reported experiencing less joy than normal subjects. Subjects with adjustment reactions reported more disgust than normals. Schizophrenics reported significantly more disgust and contempt than normal subjects.

The majority of the research on the DES used college students as subjects. Izard (1972) reported a factor-analytic study of depression involving high school students from middle and lower-middle income groups. The factor structure of the DES was similar to that found in an identical study with college students. Still, the magnitude of the factor loadings ranged .2 to .3 below those found in the college sample. The explanation that most likely accounts for this drop in factor loadings is that some of the high school students did not know the meaning of some of the DES adjectives. If some individuals do not understand the meaning of some items, their responses on those items do not contribute to the measurement of the emotion but rather add error. The additional measurement error would attenuate the item–factor correlations. Because this measurement error could be reduced by simplifying the items, a new form of the scale, the DES III, was developed.

The Differential Emotions Scale as adapted for children and adolescents (DES III)

Izard (1979) developed the DES III for use with children and adolescents and with adults having limited education. The DES III was constructed by translating and expanding the single adjectives of the DES into phrases that describe an aspect of the experience of the fundamental emotions. The items of the DES III are presented in Table 10.2. The DES III is scored by summing the scores for the three items that measure each emotion. This results in one score for each of the 10 fundamental emotions. The resulting emotion profile can then be inspected to determine the relative strength (state instructions) or frequency (trait instructions) of individual emotions or emotion patterns. The investigations presented here were aimed at determining the construct validity of the DES III from

Table 10.2. *The differential emotions scale for children and adolescents (DES III)*

Factor	Item
I. Interest	1. Feel like what you're doing or watching is interesting
	2. Feel so interested in what you're doing, caught up in it
	3. Feel alert, curious, kind of excited about something
II. Enjoyment	4. Feel glad about something
	5. Feel happy
	6. Feel joyful, like everything is going your way, everything is rosy
III. Surprise	7. Feel surprised, like when something suddenly happens you had no idea would happen
	8. Feel amazed, like you can't believe what's happened, it was so unusual
	9. Feel like you feel when something unexpected happens
IV. Sadness	10. Feel unhappy, blue, downhearted
	11. Feel sad and gloomy, almost like crying
	12. Feel discouraged, like you can't make it, nothing is going right
V. Anger	13. Feel like screaming at somebody or banging on something
	14. Feel angry, irritated, annoyed
	15. Feel so mad you're about to blow up
VI. Disgust	16. Feel like something stinks, puts a bad taste in your mouth
	17. Feel disgusted, like something is sickening
	18. Feel like things are so rotten they could make you sick
VII. Contempt	19. Feel like somebody is a low-life, not worth the time of day
	20. Feel like somebody is a "good-for-nothing"
	21. Feel like looking down your nose at somebody
VIII. Fear	22. Feel scared, uneasy, like something might harm you
	23. Feel fearful, like you're in danger, very tense
	24. Feel afraid, shaky, and jittery
IX. Shame /shyness	25. Feel ashamed to be seen, like you just want to disappear or get away from people
	26. Feel bashful, embarrassed
	27. Feel shy, like you want to hide
X. Guilt	28. Feel regret, sorry about something you did
	29. Feel like you did something wrong
	30. Feel like you ought to be blamed for something

an analysis of the internal structure of the scale. The investigation of the dimensionality of the DES III consisted of three separate studies. The first study determined whether college-age individuals who are clearly capable of understanding the meaning of the items on the DES and the DES III would interpret the corresponding items similarly. Given the favorable results from the first study, the second and third studies focused on the analysis of the responses to the DES III of children and adolescents. Although we felt that the youngest children in our study were capable of experiencing all 10 emotions, the question remained as to whether these children had the cognitive and verbal ability to report the subjective experiences of all their emotions using a self-report inventory such as the DES.

The model

The a priori measurement model specified by the DES and the DES III defines 10 emotions that are conceptualized as latent variables or factors. Each cluster of observed variables is hypothesized as unidimensional; that is, each of the items within a cluster is specified as an alternate indicator of a single, common underlying emotion. The 10 emotions are specified as distinct entities, although they may be correlated as predicted by the theory.

The equations for this multiple-indicator measurement model are the equations of classical reliability theory. Let

X_j be the j observed variable or item
F_k be the k latent variable or factor
e_j be the error term of the j item
β_j be the regression weight of X_j on F_k.

That is,

$$X_j = \beta_j F_k + e_j$$

In the language of factor analysis, β_j is, by definition, the factor pattern coefficient of item X_j on factor F_k. Because F_k is the only predictor in this equation, by implication, β_j is also the factor loading of X_j on F_k, that is,

$$\beta_j = r_{X_j F_k}$$

The complete 30×10 factor pattern matrix for the model underlying the DES III represents the limiting form of simple structure. Each of the 30 items is a function of only one of the 10 factors, and each factor is represented by a small subset of the 30 items.

The goal of the analysis was to determine the extent to which the items of the DES III conform to the equations of the measurement model. The first analysis primarily investigated the equivalence of the factors measured by the DES and the DES III for college-age subjects. Given this equivalence, the second and third studies addressed the dimensionality of the DES III for children and adolescents.

Analytic technique

Computational analyses

The analysis strategy consisted of a series of exploratory or blind factor analyses followed by a set of conformatory factor analyses. The blind analyses, principal axis with communalities followed by an orthogonal (varimax) or oblique (direct oblimin) rotation, are used to suggest the factorial composition of the observed variables. Still, these blind analyses can only provide crude tests of the hypothesized internal structure of the DES III. As Joreskog (1978) writes:

> That exploratory factor analysis may be quite useful in the early stages of experimentation or test development is widely recognized . . . The results of an exploratory analysis may have heuristic and suggestive value . . . and may generate hypotheses which are capable of more objective testing by other multivariate methods . . . It is highly desirable that a hypothesis which has been suggested by mainly exploratory procedures should subsequently be confirmed, or disproved, by obtaining new data and subjecting these to more rigorous statistical techniques. [Pp. 443, 444]

Thus the confirmatory factor analyses, which provide a direct test of the specified model, were considered primary in determining the construct validity of the DES III. Both the exploratory and confirmatory analyses may be used, in conjunction with the analysis of the item content, to suggest revisions of the model.

Because the a priori model predicts a partitioning of the observed variables into mutually exclusive clusters, the initial confirmatory analysis is provided by a multiple-groups solution in which each group factor is defined by a cluster or group of observed variables. Discussions of this technique are found in Spearman (1904, 1914), Burt (1909, 1917) and Holzinger (1944) and more recently by Nunnally (1978) and Hunter and Gerbing (1979). The analysis computes estimates for (a) the correlations of each item with each of the group factors and (b) the correlations of the group factors with each other. The computations of a multiple-groups analysis can be accomplished with either a centroid factor analysis using a computer program, such as PACKAGE (Hunter & Cohen, 1969; Hunter & Gerbing, 1979), or a full-information maximum-likelihood analysis with LISREL (Joreskog & Sorbom, 1978).

LISREL is the more general program for a confirmatory analysis in the sense that it is not confined to a multiple-groups solution. LISREL accommodates limited multiple-factor models in which some of the observed variables may be expressed as a function of several of the latent variables. The statistical fit of a multiple-groups model may sometimes be improved by permitting some of the items to have multiple antecedents.

Because each item is conceptualized as an imperfect indicator of the underlying emotion, the measurement model for each item contains an error term. According to this model, the emotion is distinct from the error introduced by the measurement process. The appropriate statistical adjustment for this error is to factor the correlations with communalities (e.g., Harmon, 1976). The use of communalities insures that the latent variable F, and not the observed factor or cluster score, is the entity of interest. That is, the use of communalities implies that the computed item–factor and factor–factor correlations are corrected for the attenuation due to the unwanted influence of the error term.

For example, in a centroid multiple-groups analysis, each factor is defined as an unweighted sum of the corresponding items. If the analysis is conducted without communalities, the observed score variances and covariances are analyzed. Thus the computed item–factor and factor–factor correlations are also observed correlations. The problem is that the observed scores contain both true and error score components. Thus the computed correlations are attenuated because of the inclusion of this error in the computations. The error component is removed from the analysis by using communalities (e.g., Harmon, 1976; Hunter & Gerbing, 1979). The resultant item–factor and factor–factor correlations are still defined as the sum of the corresponding items, but they are only estimated, because the factors are now defined as latent variables. These are the correlations of interest, however, for they contain only the true score component. In general, these correlations will be larger than the corresponding observed correlations.

Evaluating the model

The fit of the measurement model to the data is based on the evaluation of the item correlations, that is, the item covariance structure. The model fits if the residuals defined by subtracting the observed correlations from the correlations predicted by the model are zero to within sampling error. Given standardized data, the covariance structure of a multiple-groups model is described by the product rules for internal and external consistency (Hunter & Gerbing, 1979). This covariance structure was first presented by Spearman in 1904 and 1914.

The product rule for internal consistency states that for items X_1 and X_2, which are indicators of the same factor F,

$$r_{X_1 X_2} = r_{X_1 F} r_{X_2 F} = \beta_1 \beta_2$$

The product rule for external consistency states that for factor G and item X, which is an indicator of factor F,

$$r_{XG} = r_{XF} r_{FG}$$

External consistency implies that the correlations of two items within the same cluster are proportional across factors. That is,

$$\frac{r_{X_1 G}}{r_{X_2 G}} = \frac{r_{X_1 F} r_{FG}}{r_{X_2 F} r_{FG}} = \frac{r_{X_1 F}}{r_{X_2 F}}$$

A heuristic test of the fit of the model is based on the size of the residuals, that is, on the number of predicted item correlations not within a specified number of standard errors from the corresponding observed correlations. If this number exceeds the number expected by chance for a given significance level, the model may be rejected.

LISREL also provides a chi-square test of fit of the model under the null hypothesis that the observed covariances conform to the constraints imposed by the model (e.g., the constraints of internal and external consistency). The test, which is based on the likelihood ratio derived from the maximum-likelihood analysis, is a function of the number of cases analyzed and the value of the likelihood function at maximization. The likelihood ratio is a function of the residuals such that the chi-square is zero when the residuals are zero (e.g., Joreskog, 1978).

Joreskog (1978) has warned, however, that "the values of X should be interpreted very cautiously because of the sensitivity of χ^2 to various model assumptions such as linearity, additivity, multinormality, etc., but also [because] . . . if a sufficiently large sample were obtained, the test statistic would, no doubt, indicate that any [proposed] model is untenable" (p. 448). Thus the evaluation of the overall fit of the model is probably best made by a direct examination of the residuals.

LISREL also provides two methods for examining the significance of individual parameters. First, LISREL computes the asymptotic standard errors of each parameter. Second, some of the constraints of a model might be relaxed. "If the drop in χ^2 (between the original and 'relaxed' model) is large compared to the difference in degrees of freedom, this is an indication that the change made in the model represents a real improvement" (Joreskog, 1978, p. 448).

Study 1

A Method

Two-hundred and six college students enrolled in an introductory psychology course at Baylor University completed a combined 60-item DES + DES III immediately following the final examination. The students were instructed to indicate how they felt at the present moment. The 60 items were presented in a random order. All items were measured on the following 5-point Likert scale: very slightly or not at all (0), slightly (1), moderately (2), considerably (3), and very strongly (4).

Results and discussion

Although the primary emphasis is on testing the proposed model with confirmatory factor analyses, most factor-analytic studies have been exploratory. To provide continuity with these exploratory analyses, a traditional exploratory factor analysis is presented before the confirmatory analyses.

Exploratory analysis. The 60×60 item correlation matrix was analyzed with a 10-factor principal-axis factor analysis followed by a varimax rotation. The resulting 10 factor $\times$ 60 item matrix of factor loadings was inspected, and each item was grouped with the factor on which the item had its highest loading. This procedure identified 9 of the 10 emotions. For 5 of the a priori 6-item clusters – interest, joy, surprise, anger, and guilt – all 6 items loaded highest on a single factor. All 12 items of the sadness and fear clusters grouped together on one factor. The shame/shyness cluster was defined by 5 items. The 6th item of the shame/shyness cluster, DES III Item 25, loaded highest on the Guilt factor and had its second highest loading on the Shame/shyness factor. The 3 items of the DES III contempt cluster had reasonably high loadings on a unique factor. Still, 2 items of the DES contempt cluster loaded highest on the Anger factor, and the 3rd item had identical loadings on the Contempt and the Sadness–fear factor. The Disgust factor was defined by 2 items of the DES III and 1 item of the DES. The other 3 items in the disgust clusters had loadings above .3 on this factor.

Confirmatory analysis. The DES + DES III was analyzed in a 20-factor centroid multiple-groups factor analysis provided by PACKAGE. One DES factor and 1 DES III factor were postulated to measure each of the 10 fundamental emotions specified by differential emotions theory: interest, joy, surprise, sadness, anger, disgust, contempt, fear, shame/shyness, and guilt. The loadings of each of the DES III items on the corresponding DES factor and the correlations between the DES and the DES III group factor scores for each emotion are presented in Table 10.3. The factor loadings of the DES III factors indicate that the new DES III items provide a good measure of the fundamental emotions as measured by the DES.

All correlations between corresponding group factors on the DES and DES III were above .92 except interest and contempt, which were .67 and .66, respectively. Examination of the item–factor intercorrelation matrix revealed that the DES III interest cluster is not as strong as the interest cluster of the DES. Specifically, DES III Item 3 shares common variance with the Joy factor. Still, the lower correlations between the DES and DES III contempt clusters result from weakness in the DES items. The contempt items emerge as a strong factor on the DES III.

The results of this study demonstrate that the DES and DES III are equivalent measures of the fundamental emotions for individuals who comprehend the meanings of the DES items.

Table 10.3. *Group factor loadings of the DES III items*

DES and DES III group factors	DES III item numbers	Factor loadings	
		DES	DES III
I. Interest (67)	1	46	68
	2	36	77
	3	55	60
II. Enjoyment (100)	4	74	77
	5	86	86
	6	89	79
III. Surprise (99)	7	63	67
	8	79	72
	9	79	84
IV. Sadness (100)	10	87	84
	11	83	84
	12	86	87
V. Anger (100)	13	65	62
	14	88	88
	15	77	70
VI. Disgust (100)	16	65	58
	17	90	99
	18	82	82
VII. Contempt (100)	19	45	80
	20	50	86
	21	42	41
VIII. Fear (99)	22	76	73
	23	81	85
	24	61	81
IX. Shame/shyness (92)	25	43	46
	26	67	73
	27	73	80
X. Guilt (98)	28	84	83
	29	80	89
	30	84	81

Note: Correlations are corrected for attenuation and multiplied by 100. Correlations between DES factor and corresponding DES III factor are given in parentheses. $N = 206$.

Study 2

Method

Eight hundred and fifty-seven junior and senior high school students ranging in age from 11 years 4 months to 17 years 10 months completed the DES III during a class period 2 days before Christmas vacation. The DES III was administered

Table 10.4. *Instructions for and completion of the scale and sample DES III items*

The DES is a list of words that you can use to show how you feel. Each question asks you about a different feeling. We want you to tell us how often you felt each of these feelings *during the past week*. You can tell us how often you felt each of the feelings on the list by marking one of the letters next to each question.

Here is an example for you to think about. How often did you feel cheerful during the past week?
   If you *rarely or never* felt cheerful during the past week, then you circle the letter A.
   If you *hardly ever* felt cheerful during the past week, then you circle the letter B.
   If you *sometimes* felt cheerful during the past week, then you circle the letter C.
   If you *often* felt cheerful during the past week, then you circle the letter D.
   If you *very often* felt cheerful during the past week, then you circle the letter E.

Now you are ready to read the questions on the list. Read each question and mark your answer. When you are finished check to see that you have answered all thirty questions. It is important that you give an answer to each question.

How often did you	Rarely or never	Hardly ever	Sometimes	Often	Very often
1. Feel regret, sorry about something you did	A	B	C	D	E
2. Feel glad about something	A	B	C	D	E
3. Feel like something stinks, puts a bad taste in your mouth	A	B	C	D	E

Note: The complete DES III can be constructed by randomly ordering the items as they appear in Table 10.2, substituting the revised items 3A, 21A, 24A, and 25A listed at the end of the section "Method."

by the teachers following a demonstration by one of the investigators. Students were asked to indicate how they felt during the previous week after first reflecting on their experiences. They were given no information concerning the meaning of words or phrases on the DES III. Instructions and sample items of the DES III are presented in Table 10.4.

Results and discussion

Exploratory analysis. To provide continuity with the traditional factor-analytic study, the 30 × 30 item correlation matrix was analyzed with a 10-factor principal-axis factor analysis followed by a varimax rotation. The resulting 10 factor × 30 item matrix of factor loadings was inspected, and each item was grouped with the factor on which the item had its highest loading. This procedure identified 9 of the 10 emotions. The 3 items in seven of the a priori clusters defined

Table 10.5. *Exploratory oblique factor pattern of DES III showing items grouped by a priori clusters*

Factors	I			II			III			IV		
	1	2	3	4	5	6	7	8	9	10	11	12
I. Interest	*53*	*61*	*24*	—	16	14	—	—	—	—	—	—
II. Enjoyment	—	—	-24	*-53*	*-67*	*-42*	—	—	—	12	—	—
III. Surprise	—	—	-12	-12	—	-15	*-65*	*-57*	*-41*	—	—	—
IV. Sadness	—	—	—	—	—	-12	—	—	—	*72*	*49*	*39*
V. Anger	—	—	—	—	—	—	—	—	—	—	-12	—
VII. Contempt	—	—	—	—	—	—	—	—	—	—	—	—
VIII. Fear	—	—	—	—	—	—	—	—	—	—	—	—
IX. Shame/shy	—	—	—	—	—	—	—	—	—	—	—	—
X. Guilt	—	—	—	—	—	—	—	—	—	—	—	—

Note: Pattern coefficients between $-.10$ and $.10$ are replaced with a dash. $N = 857$. Cluster VI = disgust. Italics indicate groups.

seven distinct factors. The Interest and Sadness factors were defined by 2 items each. Item 3 in the a priori interest cluster was placed with the items defining the Joy factor, and Item 12 of the a priori sadness cluster was placed with the items defining the Anger factor. The items of the a priori disgust cluster failed to define a single factor. Instead, the items of the disgust cluster loaded moderately on the Anger, Contempt, and Joy factors.

The results of this exploratory factor analysis provided preliminary evidence supporting the measurement model. An orthogonal solution is unnecessarily restricting, however; there is no theoretical reason to expect the underlying emotions to be uncorrelated.

A moderately oblique rotation of the initial principal-axis factor solution did indicate even stronger support for the a priori measurement model. (A direct oblimin rotation with $\delta = 0$ [Harmon, 1976] was used.) For eight of the a priori clusters, all three items loaded highest on a single, unique factor. The six items in the anger and disgust clusters merged to define a single cluster. Thus for each of the three item factors, in no instance did any of the items split apart on separate factors.

Table 10.5 presents the factor pattern matrix of the oblique principal-axis factor solution. The pattern coefficients are the weights that would be assigned to each factor in expressing the item as a linear function of the factors. When these weights are very small, the factor makes a negligible contribution to the variable. Inspection of the table shows that the three items of an a priori cluster are primary in estimating the score on the corresponding factor. This finding provides justification for defining a latent variable as a function of the items in each cluster

V			VI			VII			VIII			IX			X		
13	14	15	16	17	18	19	20	21	22	23	24	25	26	27	28	29	30
—	—	—	—	—	—	—	—	—	—	—	—	−12	—	—	—	—	—
—	—	—	—	22	29	—	—	—	—	—	−14	—	—	—	—	—	—
—	12	—	—	−11	−16	—	—	—	—	—	—	—	—	—	—	—	—
—	—	—	—	—	15	—	—	—	12	—	—	—	—	12	—	—	—
−73	−46	−66	−15	−13	−18	—	—	17	—	—	—	—	—	—	—	−12	—
—	—	—	14	16	17	76	75	31	—	—	—	12	—	—	—	—	—
—	—	—	−14	—	—	—	—	—	−57	−86	−39	−12	—	—	−12	—	—
—	—	—	—	—	—	—	—	—	—	—	−20	−35	−79	−65	—	−11	13
—	—	—	−11	−15	−17	—	—	20	—	—	—	—	—	—	−36	−52	−59

and for performing a multiple groups confirmatory analysis on the 30 × 30 correlation matrix.

Confirmatory analysis. The a priori measurement model specifying 10 factors each consisting of three items was analyzed with the centroid factor multiple-groups factor analysis provided by PACKAGE. The average within-clusters item correlation (excluding self-correlations) equaled .40 (range = .23 to .57). In contrast 26% of the between-clusters item correlations were below .1, 58% were below .2, and 84% were below .3. Only 2% of the between-clusters item correlations exceed the average within-clusters value of .40.

A residual matrix was constructed by subtracting the obtained item–item correlations from the value predicted by the measurement model. A heuristic evaluation of the overall fit of the model can be made by examining the magnitudes of the residuals. A standard error for each observed correlation was computed by using the observed correlation as an estimate of the corresponding population correlation. Of the 435 obtained correlations, 110, or 25%, exceeded their predicted value by more than two standard errors.

An additional test of the model is the evaluation of the parallelism of the 30 items with the 10 group factors. The matrix of factor loadings is presented in Table 10.6. An examination of the columns of Table 10.6 reveals that the item–factor correlations generally conform to the assumption of external consistency. Seventy percent of the italicized loadings exceed .6; the lowest is .37. The relatively large size of the correlations of the items with their own group factor in contrast to the items' correlations with the other group factors provides evidence for the validity of the a priori model.

Table 10.6. *Centroid multiple-groups factor loadings of DES III, showing items grouped by a priori clusters*

Factors	I			II			III			IV		
	1	2	3	4	5	6	7	8	9	10	11	12
I. Interest	*62*	*60*	*44*	48	60	53	27	34	21	−29	−19	−23
II. Enjoyment	41	39	48	*65*	*81*	*65*	28	21	13	−47	−30	−41
III. Surprise	21	26	35	28	22	30	*67*	*56*	*43*	3	9	6
IV. Sadness	−19	−19	−20	−32	−40	−47	−02	02	14	*75*	*69*	*65*
V. Anger	−13	−4	−10	−21	−31	−38	−3	8	11	51	46	58
VI. Disgust	−11	−5	−11	−19	−37	−38	6	17	19	49	41	53
VII. Contempt	−9	0	−7	−15	−25	−20	01	11	13	28	20	31
VIII. Fear	−10	−9	−12	−18	−28	−28	11	14	19	50	52	49
IX. Shame/shy	−6	−9	−12	−17	−30	−28	3	12	17	43	46	46
X. Guilt	−9	−5	0	−11	−17	−21	13	11	20	43	48	42

Note: Correlations have been corrected for attenuation. $N = 857$. Italics indicate groups.

Still, notable exceptions to external consistency are present for Items 3, 22, 27, and 30. In several instances loadings are not parallel with the loadings of the remaining two items in their cluster. For example, in the first italicized group in Table 10.6, the correlation of Item 3 with interest is approximately 70% the size of the correlation of Items 1 and 2 with interest. The correlation of Item 3 with joy should be about 70%, the size of the correlations of Items 1 and 2 with joy, or about .28. The observed value of .48 is much larger than the predicted value.

The a priori multiple-groups model was also analyzed with the full-information maximum-likelihood method of LISREL. The PACKAGE and LISREL solutions agreed fairly well; the largest single difference in the two estimated factor patterns was .17 and only 4 of the 30 estimated pattern coefficients differed by more than .10. The estimated factor–factor correlations in the two solutions were almost identical; the largest discrepancy was only .08.

The overall test to fit of the multiple-groups model was $\chi^2(360) = 965.90$. Because $p > .01$, a literal interpretation of this statistic indicates that the model does not fit the data. A heuristic but more reasonable evaluation of fit is provided by the residuals. The magnitude of the observed correlations varied from .00 to .57. The respective sampling errors of population correlations for these values for 857 subjects are .034 and .028. Using .03 as an average value, a predicted correlation is within two standard errors of the corresponding observed correlation if the magnitude of the residual is no larger than .06. Of the 435 residuals, 70, or 16.1%, were larger than .06, and the largest residual was .160.

Thus both the centroid and full-information maximum-likelihood analyses of the multiple-groups model suggests that the fit of the model could be improved

V			VI			VII			VIII			IX			X		
13	14	15	16	17	18	19	20	21	22	23	24	25	26	27	28	29	30
−13	−14	−7	−1	−5	−21	−9	−1	−9	−9	−9	−22	−24	−5	−4	−6	−9	1
−29	−37	−25	−12	−24	−39	−19	18	−17	−22	−27	−24	−33	−15	−22	−12	−18	−9
6	−3	17	11	15	16	3	14	13	24	21	11	7	18	13	14	13	19
50	55	51	23	36	57	20	24	27	51	47	54	57	33	41	39	41	31
71	62	77	30	39	57	37	41	42	37	40	38	44	23	27	29	34	18
48	56	55	37	63	69	43	47	46	41	44	40	43	34	36	31	35	33
41	45	46	30	38	50	68	83	42	26	29	23	34	15	20	11	19	22
35	40	41	30	26	44	18	27	27	72	79	59	55	37	44	38	40	31
30	35	33	24	33	41	20	24	23	42	42	58	55	74	71	33	42	32
32	35	33	24	29	43	11	19	28	46	40	49	43	40	37	52	72	49

statistically. To improve the statistical fit of the model, it is necessary to generalize the multiple-groups model to a multiple-factor model in which some of the items are linked to more than a single factor. A variety of respecified models were analyzed, with each respecification based on the information provided by the residuals. The factor pattern for the final analysis is presented in Table 10.7. Although the chi-square test of fit was negative ($\chi^2(329) = 571.49, p > .01$), the analysis of the residuals indicated that the fit of the model was quite good. Only 15 of 435, or 3.4%, of the residuals were larger than the approximate two standard errors of .06. Moreover, the magnitude of the largest residual was only .086.

The statistical importance of the additional factor pattern coefficients in the revised model, which is a multiple-factor generalization of the original multiple-groups model, is evaluated in two different ways. First, the difference in the chi-square values for the original and revised models was 394.42. This large drop in the chi-square value relative to the loss of 31 degrees of freedom indicates the significance of the additional pattern coefficients as a set. Second, the magnitudes of all but four of the estimated pattern coefficients were larger than twice their standard errors. The smallest ratio of a parameter estimate to its standard error was 1.61.

Despite the improved fit obtained with the revised model, the original multiple-groups model remains valid. The size of most of the pattern coefficients that were not part of the original model is small. Item 3 is the only item for which a pattern coefficient off the diagonal block is larger than the corresponding diagonal block coefficient. And only for Items 3, 21, 24, and 25 does the size of an

Table 10.7. *Factor pattern from the confirmatory multiple-factor analysis, showing items grouped by a priori clusters*

	I			II			III			IV		
Factors	1	2	3	4	5	6	7	8	9	10	11	12
I. Interest	*57*	*64*	*23*	0	0	0	0	16	0	0	0	0
II. Enjoyment	0	0	*31*	*70*	*80*	*61*	0	0	0	0	20	0
III. Surprise	0	0	15	0	0	16	*71*	*52*	*48*	0	0	0
IV. Sadness	0	0	0	0	0	−22	0	0	0	*73*	*74*	*53*
V. Anger	0	0	0	0	0	−8	0	0	0	0	0	22
VI. Disgust	0	0	0	11	0	0	−16	0	0	0	0	0
VII. Contempt	0	0	0	0	0	0	13	0	0	0	0	0
VIII. Fear	0	0	0	0	0	0	0	0	0	0	0	0
IX. Shame/shy	0	0	0	0	0	0	−10	0	0	0	0	0
X. Guilt	0	0	0	0	0	0	0	0	0	0	11	0

Note: $N = 857$. Italics indicate groups.

off-diagonal block coefficient approach the size of the coefficient on a diagonal block.

A second indication of the utility of the original multiple-groups model is derived from an analysis of factor scores. Although a set of differential weights for computing factor scores could be derived from a multiple-groups analysis, the simplest method is to define each factor score as the unweighted sum of the items that define the group. In the multiple-factor model, each factor score is computed as a weighted linear composite of all 30 items. The weighting reflects the size of the pattern coefficients as well as the correlations among factors.

The correlations between the factor scores computed by unit weighting and from the factor score regression weights derived from the multiple-factor confirmatory analysis are presented in Table 10.8. The magnitude of these correlations provides strong evidence for the validity of the original multiple-groups model. The 10 latent variables defined by the more sophisticated multiple-factor model are almost identical to the 10 latent variables defined by the a priori model.

A separate confirmatory factor analysis using data from the youngest group of children (11.4 to 13.11) was performed to determine if the measurement model would show signs of failure. Both the factor loadings from the centroid multiple-groups analysis and the factor pattern from the confirmatory multiple-factor analysis were very similar to the solutions presented in Tables 10.6 and 10.7. The analysis of the residuals from the multiple-factor model indicated that 3.8% of the residuals exceeded their predicted values by two standard deviations, which

V			VI			VII			VIII			IX			X		
13	14	15	16	17	18	19	20	21	22	23	24	25	26	27	28	29	30
0	0	0	0	0	−13	−8	0	0	0	0	−10	−16	0	0	0	0	0
0	−11	0	0	0	0	0	0	0	0	0	0	0	0	0	0	0	0
0	0	12	0	0	0	0	0	0	0	0	0	0	0	0	0	0	0
0	0	0	0	0	0	0	0	0	0	0	0	0	−19	0	0	0	0
70	65	71	0	0	0	0	0	16	0	0	0	12	0	0	0	0	−20
0	0	0	28	56	76	0	0	0	0	0	0	0	0	0	0	0	0
0	0	0	0	0	0	73	80	34	0	0	0	09	0	0	0	0	16
0	0	0	15	0	0	−9	0	0	74	77	39	13	0	0	0	0	0
0	0	0	0	0	0	0	0	0	0	0	26	47	86	68	0	0	0
0	0	0	0	0	0	0	0	13	0	0	11	0	0	0	54	65	60

Table 10.8. *Correlation between factors derived from the multiple-groups and multiple-factor solutions*

Factor	Correlation
I. Interest	92
II. Enjoyment	96
III. Surprise	92
IV. Sadness	91
V. Anger	97
VI. Disgust	87
VII. Contempt	95
VIII. Fear	97
IX. Shame/shyness	97
X. Guilt	91

is less than the 5% predicted by chance. Thus the measurement model provides a uniform fit across the age range represented in this study.

The correlations among factors derived from the centroid multiple-groups solution are presented in Table 10.9. Factor means for each of the emotions were computed as an unweighted composite of the corresponding three DES III items. These means for subgroups of the sample are presented in Table 10.10. Inspection of the table shows that the emotion profiles are similar across both age and sex.

Table 10.9. *Intercorrelation of the 10 emotions measured by the DES III*

Factor	Interest	Enjoyment	Surprise	Sadness	Anger	Disgust	Contempt	Fear	Shame/shy	Guilt
I. Interest	100	50	28	-22	-11	-9	-6	-12	-11	-5
II. Enjoyment	76	100	25	-42	-32	-30	-20	-26	-26	-15
III. Surprise	49	38	100	05	06	14	09	17	12	16
IV. Sadness	-34	-57	08	100	55	45	27	54	47	43
V. Anger	-16	-43	10	74	100	50	45	41	34	32
VI. Disgust	-16	-45	25	69	75	100	45	39	38	34
VII. Contempt	-09	-28	15	37	62	70	100	27	24	19
VIII. Fear	-19	-35	26	72	55	59	37	100	49	43
IX. Shame/shyness	-17	-36	19	65	47	58	35	68	100	41
X. Guilt	-08	-23	27	64	47	57	30	64	62	100

Note: Correlations below the diagonal have been corrected for attenuation. $N = 857$.

Table 10.10. *DES-III emotion profiles: means (standard deviations)*

Factor	Males				Females				Total
	YNG	MID	OLD	Total	YNG	MID	OLD	Total	
I. Interest	7.9	7.7	7.7	7.7	7.6	7.7	7.5	7.6	7.7
	(2.2)	(2.1)	(2.2)	(2.2)	(2.3)	(2.0)	(2.3)	(2.2)	(2.2)
II. Enjoyment	8.3	8.1	7.9	8.1	8.6	8.7	8.6	8.6	8.4
	(2.1)	(2.1)	(2.1)	(2.3)	(2.1)	(2.2)	(2.5)	(2.3)	(2.3)
III. Surprise	5.1	5.6	5.1	5.3	5.5	6.0	5.5	5.7	5.5
	(2.4)	(2.3)	(2.3)	(2.4)	(2.4)	(2.1)	(2.4)	(2.3)	(2.3)
IV. Sadness	4.1	4.7	4.5	4.5	5.3	6.0	5.7	5.7	5.1
	(2.5)	(2.3)	(2.6)	(2.5)	(2.7)	(3.0)	(2.4)	(2.3)	(2.3)
V. Anger	5.7	6.3	5.9	6.0	5.4	6.2	5.9	5.9	6.0
	(2.8)	(2.8)	(3.0)	(2.8)	(2.8)	(2.9)	(2.8)	(2.8)	(2.7)
VI. Disgust	4.2	5.0	4.5	4.6	3.8	4.5	4.1	4.2	4.4
	(2.5)	(2.6)	(2.6)	(2.6)	(2.3)	(2.1)	(2.1)	(2.2)	(2.4)
VII. Contempt	3.5	4.8	4.5	4.4	3.3	4.0	3.6	3.7	4.0
	(2.6)	(2.7)	(2.6)	(2.7)	(2.5)	(2.7)	(2.7)	(2.6)	(2.6)
VIII. Fear	3.4	3.9	2.7	3.4	4.0	4.3	3.8	3.1	3.7
	(2.4)	(2.4)	(2.2)	(2.4)	(2.8)	(3.0)	(2.6)	(2.8)	(2.6)
IX. Shame/shy	3.5	4.7	3.9	4.1	4.2	5.0	4.4	4.6	4.4
	(2.8)	(2.7)	(2.7)	(2.8)	(2.6)	(2.7)	(2.3)	(2.6)	(2.7)
X. Guilt	4.8	5.0	4.5	4.8	4.8	5.2	5.2	5.1	5.0
	(2.2)	(2.1)	(1.9)	(2.1)	(2.1)	(2.1)	(2.4)	(2.2)	(2.1)

Note: YNG = youngest group, ages 11.4–13.11. Male *n* = 119. Female *n* = 116. MID = middle group, ages 14.0–15.11. Male *n* = 178. Female *n* = 199. OLD = oldest group, ages 16.0–17.10. Male *n* = 106. Female *n* = 116. Male *n* = 413. Female *n* = 441. Total *n* = 854. Range = 0–12.

Table 10.11. *Centroid multiple-groups factor loadings of DES III, showing items grouped by a priori clusters*

Factor	I			II			III			IV		
	1	2	3A	4	5	6	7	8	9	10	11	12
I. Interest	*54*	*53*	*44*	32	42	47	19	31	18	−25	−12	−17
II. Enjoyment	35	32	29	*64*	*68*	*58*	24	32	14	−49	−18	−29
III. Surprise	9	31	20	23	32	25	*71*	*57*	*41*	−1	13	14
IV. Sadness	−12	−18	−16	−32	−35	−38	−2	12	14	*67*	*61*	*47*
V. Anger	−2	2	−7	−30	−30	−27	6	9	14	52	42	49
VI. Disgust	−14	1	−3	−24	−21	−22	21	25	18	38	46	46
VII. Contempt	3	4	−8	−24	−10	−6	13	16	2	37	18	26
VIII. Fear	1	1	1	−14	−15	−16	4	15	18	32	42	34
IX. Shame/shy	−7	−7	1	−14	−7	−13	19	23	21	39	54	34
X. Guilt	3	3	−3	−5	8	−2	24	32	26	36	44	33

Note: Correlations have been corrected for attenuation. $N = 456$.

Study 3

The purpose of this study was twofold: (a) to determine if the measurement model would fit the responses of children between the ages of 8 and 12 and (b) to determine if the DES III can be improved through revision of the weakest items.

Method

The subjects were 457 elementary school children ranging in age from 8.1 to 12.2. Except for the scale modifications listed below, this study was identical to Study 2. The instructions and the DES III scale were modified accordingly: (a) The sample item, "Feel cheerful," which appeared in the instructions of the previous study (Table 10.4) was printed on the DES III form. This allowed the children to complete the sample item. This item, which was not scored, appeared as Example A on the form. (b) Four revised items of the scale were:

Item 3A: Feel alert, kind of curious about something
Item 21A: Feel like you are better than somebody
Item 24A: Feel afraid
Item 25A: Feel ashamed, like you want to disappear.

Results and discussion

An exploratory nine factor principal-axis factor analysis followed by an oblique rotation revealed seven factors that accounted for nine of the a priori clusters.

V			VI			VII			VIII			IX			X		
13	14	15	16	17	18	19	20	21A	22	23	24A	25A	26	27	28	29	30
0	-3	-6	-6	0	-11	-2	-10	11	-5	7	0	-17	17	2	5	-2	6
-31	-31	-31	-15	-6	-33	-16	-23	6	-24	-13	-13	-19	-2	-9	2	-8	7
16	13	6	23	23	13	8	7	14	18	20	13	21	22	21	19	34	32
44	66	55	33	25	55	29	45	-1	52	44	49	59	26	37	32	53	28
63	*59*	*79*	25	29	56	30	47	18	43	41	34	39	20	29	19	45	26
51	48	45	*39*	*52*	*62*	39	35	22	44	39	37	52	31	33	25	41	23
47	40	33	25	26	42	*64*	*64*	*31*	21	28	10	30	24	25	17	22	17
34	36	30	27	20	31	17	18	5	*81*	*77*	*79*	37	26	21	23	36	19
34	40	32	24	42	39	25	35	13	42	35	42	*29*	*58*	*32*	30	52	36
36	31	37	17	30	30	15	25	11	31	35	39	62	26	26	*55*	*70*	*51*

The interest and joy clusters merged to define one factor, as did the anger and sadness clusters. The fear, surprise, guilt, shame/shyness, and contempt clusters each defined a unique factor. The disgust items failed to define a factor.

The a priori measurement model was analyzed with the confirmatory centroid multiple-groups analysis. The average within-clusters item correlation (excluding self-correlations) equaled .35 (range = .16 to .64). Only 1.2% of the between-clusters item correlations exceeded the average within-clusters value.

The matrix of factor loadings is presented in Table 10.11. Both the relatively large size of the correlations with their own group factor and the parallelism of clustered items across factors provide evidence for the validity of the a priori model. Table 10.11 shows that the revised items 3A, 21A, and 24A are good indicators of their respective latent factors. Still, the size of the factor loading of Item 21A is less than optimal. Item 25A is a poor indicator of shame/shyness for this sample.

An examination of the residual matrix showed that 16.5% of the observed correlations exceeded their predicted value by more than two standard errors. Many of these high residuals involve Item 25A. The multiple-groups solution was computed omitting Item 25, which resulted in a two-item shame/shyness cluster. In this analysis, the number of observed correlations exceeding their predicted value by two standard deviations fell to 8.5%, indicating a good fit of the model.

The confirmatory multiple-groups factor analysis of the 30 items using the maximum-likelihood solution yielded $\chi^2(360) = 671.9 p > .01$. Six percent of the observed correlations exceeded their predicted value by more than two standard errors. An analysis using a multiple-factor model similar to the one presented in Study 2 yielded $\chi^2(321) = p > .01$. Only 2 of the 435 observed correlations ex-

Table 10.12. *DES III emotion profiles: means (standard deviations)*

	Males		Females		
Factor	Ages 8–9	Ages 10–11	Ages 8–9	Ages 10–11	Total
I. Interest	7.79	8.16	7.27	8.15	7.91
	(2.47)	(2.31)	(2.64)	(2.19)	(2.39)
II. Enjoyment	7.54	7.88	8.28	8.70	8.13
	(2.50)	(2.81)	(2.56)	(2.14)	(2.54)
III. Surprise	5.89	5.79	6.05	5.95	2.91
	(2.74)	(2.68)	(2.98)	(2.50)	(2.69)
IV. Sadness	4.98	5.04	4.99	5.08	5.03
	(2.50)	(2.84)	(2.65)	(2.70)	(2.69)
V. Anger	6.46	6.22	5.33	6.29	6.11
	(3.29)	(3.10)	(2.94)	(2.89)	(3.04)
VI. Disgust	5.10	4.55	4.87	4.52	4.71
	(2.74)	(2.64)	(2.93)	(2.33)	(2.63)
VII. Contempt	4.09	3.96	3.28	3.77	3.79
	(2.72)	(2.49)	(2.81)	(2.45)	(2.60)
VIII. Fear	4.12	4.14	4.18	4.96	4.40
	(3.38)	(3.24)	(3.36)	(2.98)	(3.23)
IX. Shame/shyness	4.17	3.73	4.07	4.46	4.10
	(2.85)	(2.57)	(2.40)	(2.79)	(2.67)
X. Guilt	5.71	5.45	4.78	4.98	5.23
	(2.80)	(2.52)	(2.43)	(2.18)	(2.48)

Note: Males: ages 8–9 $n = 90$. Ages 10–11 $n = 139$. Females: ages 8–9 $n = 90$. Ages 10–11 $n = 130$. Range = 0–12.

ceeded their predicted value by more than two standard errors. The means and standard deviations of the 10 factors are presented in Table 10.12. The correlations among the factors are presented in Table 10.13.

This study provided additional support for the measurement model. First, the analysis of the model in Study 2 was cross-validated in Study 3. Second, it was shown that the DES III can be used to measure the 10 fundamental emotions experienced by children as young as 8 years. In addition, the revised Items 3A, 21A, and 24A are better indicators of their respective latent factors than the original items. These revised items should replace the original items in the DES III.

Summary and conclusions

The DES III is a 30-item self-report scale that measures the fundamental emotions defined by differential emotions theory. The scale can be administered to children above the age of 8 years. Groups of three items are summed to obtain

Table 10.13. *Intercorrelations of the 10 emotions measured by the DES III*

Factor	Interest	Enjoyment	Surprise	Sadness	Anger	Disgust	Contempt	Fear	Shame/shy	Guilt
I. Interest	100	37	22	-17	-3	-6	0	0	0	3
II. Enjoyment	63	100	26	-35	-32	-21	-13	-17	-11	0
III. Surprise	40	42	100	9	11	21	20	15	22	29
IV. Sadness	-31	-55	15	100	54	42	27	44	44	39
V. Anger	-4	-46	17	82	100	44	37	38	34	34
VI. Disgust	-11	-36	38	74	72	100	32	33	38	28
VII. Contempt	0	-21	18	46	59	61	100	17	27	19
VIII. Fear	1	-23	22	61	50	51	25	100	36	32
IX. Shame/shyness	1	-18	38	72	52	68	46	50	100	41
X. Guilt	5	1	49	64	51	50	32	44	67	100

Note: Correlations below the diagonal have been corrected for attenuation. $N = 456$.

scores on 10 emotions: interest, joy, surprise, sadness, anger, disgust, contempt, fear, shame/shyness, and guilt.

The construct validity of the model was assessed with exploratory factor analyses and with two multiple-groups confirmatory factor analyses, using both centroid and the full-information maximum-likelihood methods. The exploratory analyses, especially the factor pattern from the oblique rotation of Study 2, suggested that the a priori model was appropriate for these data sets. The a priori model was directly tested with the confirmatory multiple-groups analyses. Both multiple-groups analyses of the DES III provided reasonable support for the measurement model derived from differential emotions theory, which asserts that the experience of emotion can be divided into 10 discrete categories of emotion.

A multiple-factor analysis, which permitted more causal links from the factors to the items, indicated that the modification of the a priori model improved the statistical fit of the model. In a statistical sense, the adjustments to the factor pattern of the common factor model provided by the full-information maximum-likelihood analysis resulted in a slightly better fit than the fit of the a priori theoretical solution provided by the multiple-groups factor analysis. We conclude, however, that the a priori model is superior in a substantive sense because (a) the a priori model is theoretically based and thus is more likely to cross-validate; (b) most of the additional factor pattern coefficients in the multiple-factor model were small in size; and (c) the factor scores obtained from unit weighting correlate very highly with the factor scores from the improved multiple-factor solution.

There is, however, an important characteristic shared by both the multiple-groups and multiple-factor models. Both models provide evidence for the construct validity of the DES III, for both models retain 10 distinct emotions as the underlying factors. The difference is that because the items of the multiple-groups model are each an indicator of only a single factor, the analysis with the multiple-groups model is easier to score and interpret.

Analysis of the factor loadings from the centroid multiple-groups analysis or the confirmatory multiple-factor solution of Study 2 did indicate that it may be desirable to modify some of the items that serve as indicators of the underlying emotions. Our analysis showed that Items 3, 21, 24, and 25 of the DES III could be rewritten to improve the multiple-groups model. These improved alternatives are listed and analyzed in Study 3.

Initially we suspected that the measurement model would begin to fail, as the age of the respondent decreased, because of lack of comprehension of the task or of specific items. This failure did not occur for the children as young as 8 in our sample, however. The similarity between the item–factor correlations from Study 2 and Study 3 suggests that the psychological meaning of the items was essentially the same for our 8-year-olds as it was for our 17-year-olds. Thus we did not reach the lower age limit of the DES III in the population in question. Although the factorial composition of the scale is relatively invariant across the age range under study, the interrelationship among the factors could vary as a function not only of age but also of sex and other variables such as the particular set of circumstances associated with a given administration of the test. The existence of stable patterns or profiles can be explored in detail through Q factor analysis. This is a logical next step in our work on the DES III.

Given the cumulative evidence from the orthogonal and oblique exploratory analyses and from the confirmatory factor analyses with both centroid multiple groups and full-information maximum likelihood, the validity of the 10 distinct emotions that are measured by the 10 corresponding groups of DES III items has been supported for three different data sets represented by college-age adults, adolescents, and children above the age of 8. The examination of the construct validity of these 10 emotions must ultimately extend beyond the realm of paper and pencil measures, and the present study encourages such future validation studies. The DES III is now ready for research and other applications that will ultimately determine its scientific and clinical utility.

References

Bartlett, E. S., & Izard, C. E. A dimensional and discrete emotions investigation of the subjective experience of emotion. In C. E. Izard (Ed.), *Patterns of emotions: A new analysis of anxiety and depression.* New York: Academic Press, 1972.

Burt, C. Experimental test of general intelligence. *British Journal of Psychology,* 1909, *3,* 94–177.

Burt, C. *The distribution and relations of educational abilities.* London: P. S. King, 1917.

Ekman, P. *Darwin and facial expression.* New York: Academic Press, 1973.

Harmon, H. H. *Modern factor analysis* (3rd ed.). Chicago: University of Chicago Press, 1976.

Holzinger, K. J. A simple method of factor analysis. *Psychometrika,* 1944, *9,* 257–62.

Hunter, J. E., & Cohen, S. H. Package: A system of computer routines for the analysis of correlational data. *Educational and Psychological Measurement,* 1969, *29,* 697–700.

Hunter, T. E., & Gerbing, D. W. *Unidimensional measurement and confirmatory factor analysis* (Occasional Paper No. 20). East Lansing: Michigan State University, Institute for Research on Teaching, 1979.

Izard, C. E. *The face of emotion.* New York: Appleton-Century-Crofts, 1971.

Izard, C. E. *Patterns of emotions: A new analysis of anxiety and depression.* New York: Academic Press, 1972.

Izard, C. E. *Human emotions.* New York: Plenum Press, 1977.

Izard, C. E. *The differential emotions scale for children (DES-III).* Unpublished manuscript, University of Delaware, 1979.

Izard, C. E., Dougherty, F. E., Bloxom, B. M., & Kotsch, W. E. *The Differential Emotions Scale: A method of measuring the subjective experience of discrete emotions.* Unpublished manuscript, Vanderbilt University, 1974.

Joreskog, K. G. Some contributions of maximum likelihood factor analysis. *Psychometrika,* 1967, *32,* 443–82.

Joreskog, K. G. Structural analysis of covariance and correlation matrices. *Psychometrika,* 1978, *43,* 443–77.

Joreskog, K. G., & Sorbom, D. *LISREL IV – A general computer program for estimation of a linear structural equation system by maximum likelihood methods.* Chicago: National Educational Resources, 1978.

Mosher, D. L. Measurement of guilt in females by self-report inventories. *Journal of Consulting and Clinical Psychology,* 1968, *32,* 690–95.

Mosher, D. L., & O'Grady, K. E. Sex guilt, trait anxiety, and females' subjective sexual arousal to erotica. *Motivation and Emotion,* 1979, *3,* 235–49.

Mosher, D. L., & Toedter, L. *Jealousy in differential emotions theory.* Unpublished manuscript, University of Connecticut, 1979.

Nunnally, J. *Psychometric theory.* New York: McGraw-Hill, 1978.

Spearman, C. General intelligence, objectively determined and measured. *American Journal of Psychology,* 1904, *15,* 201–93.

Spearman, C. The theory of two factors. *Psychological Review,* 1914, *21,* 101–15.

Spielberger, C. P., Gorsuch, R. R., & Lushene, R. E. *State–trait anxiety inventory test manual for form X.* Palo Alto, Calif.: Consulting Psychologists Press, 1970.

Zuckerman, M. The development of an affect adjective check list for the measurement of anxiety. *Journal of Consulting Psychology,* 1960, *24,* 457–62.

11   The measurement of empathy

Martin L. Hoffman

Empathy has long interested social philosophers and social scientists who see it as one of the basic human attributes supportive of social life. Over the years the term has been defined in many ways, most of which fit into two broad rubrics. One pertains to the awareness of another person's feelings, thoughts, intentions, self-evaluations, and the like. This cognitive conception of empathy has inspired considerable research, under such headings as person perception, role taking, recognition of affect in others, and social cognition.

Our concern here of course is with the second conception, empathy as a vicarious affective response to others. The two types of empathy interact; as we shall see, the ability to respond vicariously often depends on the extent to which one can cognitively infer another's affective state. Conversely, vicariously aroused affect supplies inner cues to the observer that may add meaning to the affect that he or she infers in another. Thus cognitive considerations cannot be ignored, and they will be discussed here in detail, but the main focus of attention will be on the affective dimension of empathy which until recently has been neglected by researchers.

Despite the paucity of empirical research, the interest in empathy as vicarious affective arousal does have a long history, going back at least 2 centuries. Writers such as Hume, Rousseau, Shelley, and Adam Smith viewed empathy as the essential connecting link between people that makes social life possible. Early psychological theorists such as Stern, Scheler, and McDougall advanced the view that empathy provides the motivational base for specific prosocial acts like helping and comforting others, taking turns, cooperating, and sharing. Serious research on empathy, however, has only recently begun (see review by Hoffman, 1978), and as in the case of direct affect, empathy researchers have found the measurement problem formidable.

Before we can seriously discuss the measurement of any human attribute, it is necessary to know what we are measuring. Empathy has perhaps been more elusive than most concepts in the literature, and problems of definition abound. This chapter will thus have two parts. In the first part, certain important definitional issues will be raised, and the attempt will be made to clarify and resolve them. To do this adequately it will be necessary to provide a summary of the various mechanisms of vicarious affect arousal, a discussion of how vicarious affect may be transformed by social cognitive processes, and a brief description of the developmental levels of empathic experience that should theoretically result. The second part of the chapter will consist of a critical review of the various physiological and verbal indexes of empathy that have been used.

Definitional issues

Two important issues of definition can be found in the literature on empathy. The first issue pertains to the degree of veridicality of the observer's response. To what extent must the affect aroused in the observer match the affect aroused in the person directly exposed to the stimulus event? Most writers believe there must be a match, but they differ as to the degree of match required. Some apply rather strict criteria and insist on an exact match (e.g., Feshbach & Roe, 1968), whereas others require only that there be general agreement, for example, agreement as to positive or negative emotional tone (e.g., Stotland, 1969). Requiring an exact match would seem to simplify the scoring of empathy, for the presence or absence of an exact match can be readily ascertained. I have argued, however, that using an exact match as the criterion would lead us to discard many empathic responses, especially by children. Furthermore, because the achievement of an exact match requires a high level of perceptual and cognitive development, to insist on one is to end with an operational definition that confounds affective and cognitive processes (Hoffman, 1977).

A second issue pertains to the nature of the cues or stimuli that evoke an empathic response. For a response to be labeled empathic, must the observer respond to the expressive (e.g., facial) cues reflecting the model's affective experience, or is the designation still appropriate if the response is made to situational cues alone? Most writers ignore this issue, although some (e.g., Iannotti & Meacham, 1974) suggest that we use the facial cue as the essential criterion. Thus if the observer responds affectively to the model's situation but not to the expressive cues from the model, Iannotti and Meacham would not call the response empathy. I have argued that this is an unwise, arbitrary restriction because it rules out many instances in which we respond vicariously to people's verbal or written communication about their feelings or to information that we may receive about them in their absence (Hoffman, 1977).

The two issues – degree of match and nature of the eliciting cue – may at times come together. Imagine a child, for example, who is having a good time laughing and playing and does not know that he is mentally retarded or has a terminal illness. Is an observer who feels sad because he knows the child's condition any less empathic than an unknowing observer who feels vicarious joy? And what about an observer who feels vicarious joy even though he knows the child's fate?

To resolve these dilemmas we must go back to the basic definition of empathy, examine the complexities of empathic arousal and the experience of empathic affect, and do this with a developmental perspective. The variables that need to be considered in measuring empathy should follow from such an examination.

The arousal and experience of empathy

The basic distinction between direct and empathic affect is a simple one: When a person responds with direct affect, the stimulus event is impinging on him; when a person responds with empathic affect, the stimulus event is impinging on someone else. It follows that empathy may best be defined in terms of the arousal of affect in the observer that is appropriate to someone else's situation rather than his own. The focus of the definition is then on the *process* of affect arousal rather than on the accuracy of the match or the type of cue to which the observer responds. The degree to which the observer's affect matches the model's affect, then, may be an important variable to be studied, for example developmentally, rather than a part of the definition of empathy. The same is true of the type of cue that elicits empathy in the observer. Responding to expressive cues from the model is only one class of arousal mechanism, not the only one. Indeed, at least five mechanisms of empathic arousal can be identified (Hoffman, 1977), which I will now summarize briefly.

1. *Classical conditioning*. The first mode of empathic affect arousal is the direct conditioning of empathy that results when one observes expressive cues of affect from another person at the same time that one is having a direct experience of a similar affect. The result is that expressive cues from others become conditioned stimuli that evoke the affect in the self. Aronfreed and Paskal (1965) demonstrated this kind of empathic conditioning with schoolchildren in the laboratory. It often occurs in real life, too, as when the mother's affective state is transferred to the infant through physical handling. For example, if the mother feels anxious or tense, her body may stiffen, with the result that the child may also feel distress at the same time. Later on, the distress cues from the mother, that is, her facial or verbal expressions that accompanied her distress, can serve as conditioned stimuli that evoke distress in the child even when there is no physical contact between them. Furthermore, through stimulus generalization, similar facial and verbal expressions by other persons may evoke distress feelings in the child.

2. *Direct association*. A second type of empathic conditioning was described some time ago by Humphrey (1922). When we observe someone experiencing

an emotion, his facial expression, voice, posture, or any other cue from him or from the situation that reminds us of past situations in which we experienced that emotion may evoke a similar emotion in us. (The usual example cited is the boy who sees another child cut himself and cry. The sight of the blood, the sound of the cry, or any other distress cue from the victim or anything about the situation that reminds the boy of his own past experiences with pain may evoke an empathic distress response.) This arousal mode does not depend on physical handling, nor does it require the co-occurrence of directly experienced affect in the self and expressive cues of the affect from others. The only requirement is that the observer has had *past* affective experiences that were associated with cues having something in common with the expressive cues from the model or with cues in the situation. It thus provides the basis for a variety of affective experiences with which children, and adults as well, may empathize.

3. *Mimicry.* The third mode was proposed by Lipps (1906), who viewed empathy as an isomorphic, unlearned response to another person's expression of emotion. There are two steps: The observer first automatically imitates the other with slight movements in facial expression and posture (*motor mimicry*). This then creates kinesthetic cues within the observer that contribute (through afferent feedback) to the observer's understanding and feeling of the same emotion. This conception of empathy has been neglected, but there is recent research, which I have reviewed elsewhere (Hoffman, 1977), suggesting its plausibility.

4. *Symbolic association.* The fourth mode, like the second, is based on the association between cues of affect from the model or the situation and the observer's past experiences of the affect. In this case, though, the cues from the model evoke empathic affect in the observer not because of their physical or expressive properties but because they symbolically indicate the model's feelings. For example, one can respond empathically to someone by reading a letter from him or hearing someone else describe what has happened to him. This is obviously a relatively advanced mode of empathic arousal, because it requires language. It is still largely involuntary, however, and the language serves mainly as a mediator between the model's affective cues and the observer's empathic response.

5. *Role taking.* The fifth mode is different in that it usually involves a deliberate cognitive act of imagining oneself in another's place. More specifically, the research suggests that empathic affect is most likely to be generated when we try to imagine how we would feel if the stimuli impinging on the other person were impinging on us (Stotland, 1969). Why should this happen? I would suggest that associative connections are made between the stimuli impinging on the model and similar stimulus events in the observer's own past. That is, imagining oneself in the other's place may produce an empathic response because it has the

power to evoke associations with real events in one's own past in which one actually experienced the emotion in question. The process may thus have something in common with the associative modes discussed previously. The important difference is that in this case the evoking stimulus is the mental representation of oneself in the other's situation. That is, the arousal is triggered by a cognitive transformation of events (what is happening to the other is viewed as happening to the self) and is thus more subject to conscious control.

These five modes of empathic arousal do not form a developmental stage sequence in the sense that each mode encompasses and replaces the preceding one. The last, role-taking mode, being deliberate, is probably infrequent – used, for example, at times by certain parents and psychotherapists. The first four modes, involving conditioning, direct and symbolic association, and mimicry, however, enter in at different points in development and may continue to operate through life for most people. The important point for present purposes is that if empathy can be aroused in these five ways, only one of which (mimicry) may require expressive cues from the model, then the definition of empathy cannot be confined to responses to expressive cues from the model.

Besides an affect-arousal component, empathy also has a cognitive component. Thus, regardless of the arousal mode, the mature empathizer knows, among other things, that his arousal is due to a stimulus event impinging on someone else, and he has some idea of what the other person is feeling. Young children who lack the distinction between self and other may be empathically aroused without these cognitions. In other words, how people experience empathy depends on the level at which they cognize others. This suggests that the development of empathic responsiveness must correspond at least partly to the development of a cognitive sense of the other person. The cognitive sense of the other undergoes dramatic changes developmentally and thus provides a conceptual basis for a developmental scheme for empathy. I have reviewed the literature and pieced together four social-cognitive stages (Hoffman, 1975). Briefly, (a) for the most of the 1st year children apparently experience a fusion of self and other. (b) By about 10 months, they attain *person permanence* and become aware of others as physical entities distinct from the self. (c) By 2 or 3 years, they acquire a rudimentary sense of others as having inner states (thoughts, perceptions, intentions, feelings) that are independent of their own, although at first they cannot discern what the other's inner states are. This is the initial step in role taking. Later they become able to discern the other's inner states, progressing from simple to complex states. (d) By late childhood, they become aware of others as having personal identities and life experiences beyond the immediate situation.

Empathy may thus be viewed as having an effective component that is experienced differently as the child progresses through these four social-cognitive stages. I will now describe four levels of empathic response that may result from the coalescence of empathic affect and the cognitive sense of the other.

1. *Global empathy.* For most of the first year, before the child has achieved *person permanence,* expressive cues reflecting another person's affective experience may elicit a global empathic affective response – a fusion of feelings and stimuli that come from the infant's own body, from the dimly perceived *other,* and from the situation. Because infants cannot yet differentiate themselves from others, they must often be unclear as to who is experiencing the affect, and they may at times act as if what is happening to the other were happening to them. An example is an 11-month-old girl who saw another child fall and cry. She first stared at the victim, looking as though she were about to cry herself, and then put her thumb in her mouth and buried her head in her mother's lap, just as she does when *she* is hurt.

The transition to the second level begins as the child approaches person permanence. At first, children are probably only vaguely and momentarily aware of the other person as distinct from the self, and the mental image of the other, being transitory, may often slip in and out of focus. Consequently, children at this intermediate stage probably react to another's affect as though the dimly perceived self and the dimly perceived other were somehow simultaneously, or alternately, experiencing the affect. This is a difficult concept; and an example may help. A child I know whose typical response to his own distress, beginning late in the 1st year, was to suck his thumb with one hand and pull his ear with the other also did this when he saw someone else in distress, which is an example of the first level of empathic functioning. Something new happened at 12 months. Seeing a sad look on his father's face, he proceeded to look sad and suck his thumb while pulling on his *father's* ear! In a similar example, Zahn-Waxler, Radke-Yarrow, and King (1979) describe a child whose first positive overture to someone in distress, at 12 months, involved alternating between gently touching the victim and gently touching himself. In other words, these children were beginning to recognize the difference between self in distress and other in distress, but the distinction was not yet clear.

2. *"Egocentric" empathy.* The second level of empathic response is clearly established when the child is fully aware of the self and other as distinct physical entities and is thus able for the first time to be empathically aroused while also being aware that another person, and not the self, is having the direct emotional experience. The child cannot yet fully distinguish between his own and the other person's inner states, however, and is apt to confuse them with his own, as illustrated by his efforts to help others, which consist chiefly of giving the other person what he himself finds most comforting. Examples are a 13-month-old who responded with a distressed look to an adult who looked sad and then of-

fered the adult his beloved doll; and another who ran to fetch his *own* mother to comfort a crying friend, even though the friend's mother was equally available. (In labeling this empathic level, I used quotation marks because the term *egocentric* is not entirely accurate. Although the child's attempts to help indicate a confusion between what comforts him and what comforts others, these same acts together with his facial responses also indicate that he is responding with the appropriate empathic affect.)

3. *Empathy for another's feelings.* With the beginning of role taking, the child becomes aware that other people's feelings are independent of his own and are based on their own needs and interpretation of events. Consequently, he tries to be more responsive to cues about what other people are feeling. By 3 years, even in artificial situations, children can recognize and respond empathically to happiness or sadness in others in simple situations. And with the development of language, which enables children for the first time to derive meaning from symbolic cues of affect, not just its facial and other somatic expressions, they can begin to empathize with a wide range of emotions. They can even be aroused empathically by information pertinent to someone's feelings in that person's absence. This leads to the fourth empathic level.

4. *Empathy for someone's general life condition.* By late childhood, owing to the emerging conception of self and other as continuous persons with separate histories and identities, one is aware that others have feelings and experiences beyond the immediate situation. Consequently, for example, though one may continue to be empathically aroused by another's immediate distress, one's empathic concern is intensified when one knows that the other's distress is not transitory but chronic. This fourth level, then, consists of empathically aroused affect combined with an image of another's general level of distress or well-being, an image that may at times contradict situational or expressive cues. When this contradiction occurs, as in the example of the retarded or terminally ill child mentioned earlier, the immediate situational or expressive cues lose much of their force because the observer knows that they only reflect a transitory state. The image of the other's general condition may thus be more compelling and at times may override contradictory situational or expressive cues.

To summarize, empathy is the coalescence of vicariously aroused affect and a mental representation of the other, at whatever level the observer is capable of experiencing. Individuals who progress through the four stages become capable of a high level of empathic responsiveness. They can process various types of information – that gained from their own vicarious affective reaction, from the immediate situational cues, and from their general knowledge about the other's life. They can act out in their minds the emotions and experiences suggested by this information and can introspect on all of this. They may thus gain an understanding and respond affectively in terms of the circumstances, feelings, and wishes of the other while maintaining the sense that this person is separate from themselves.

This analysis of the role of social cognition in the development and experience of empathy should make it clear that a perfect match between the observer's affect and the model's affect can only be attained through age and experience and, furthermore, that it is only in early infancy that a person responds solely in terms of surface, expressive cues from the model. From about 2 years on, children are aware that others have inner states, and they are increasingly capable of inferring what these inner states are from a knowledge of the other's situation as well as from associative connections between the other's situation and their own past experience.

The methodological implications of the foregoing analysis may be summarized as follows: (a) To insist on a high degree of match between the observer's and the model's affect may not only confound affective and cognitive processes but may also obscure certain fundamental issues in the development of empathy, such as the fact that the veridicality of empathic responses, as well as the range of affects with which the child can empathize, increases with age owing to the child's cognitive development and the increasing variety of affects that he experiences directly. (b) Because empathy is a response either to expressive cues from the model or to situational cues, or more likely, to a combination of the two, the measurement of empathy should not be based on responses to one type of cue, to the exclusion of the other. To insist that the observer respond to expressive cues from the model would rule out instances in which people respond empathically on the basis of their knowledge about the model's immediate situational context or the life events preceding the model's current state.

These considerations argue against the use of a stringent operational criterion for empathy. Stotland's suggestion that there need only be a match as to positive or negative emotional tone may be appropriate in most instances. It would not be appropriate, however, when a discrepancy exists between the model's expressed affect and his general life circumstances, as in the example of the retarded child cited earlier. I would suggest the following, more generally applicable criterion, which follows more directly from the definition of empathy and also takes into account the observer's developmental level: The observer's affect must be more like that called for by the model's circumstances, as known to the observer, than like that called for by the observer's own circumstance. This criterion is admittedly broad and may serve as only a general guideline for measurement. Until more is known about empathy, however, the most effective way to proceed may be for the investigator to start with this general guideline and to work out specific measures of empathy that fit the age group and the particular affect under study. We now turn to a consideration of specific techniques of measurement.

Measurement of empathy

The discussion thus far indicates the need for measuring instruments that provide assurance both that affect is aroused in the observer and that the affect is more appropriate to the model's situation than to the observer's. It follows that an ideal index of empathy may require a verbal report of some kind to make sure the observer's affect was empathically rather than directly aroused. To tap the observer's empathic affect independently of his conscious experience, however, may ordinarily require a physiological index. Let us examine the physiological – autonomic and somatic – as well as the verbal measures currently in use.

Autonomic indexes

Autonomic indexes of empathy, which have been used with adults, appear to be ideal for providing evidence as to whether or not affect has been aroused in the observer and for indicating the level of intensity of the affect aroused. Autonomic indexes lack precision, however, and if used alone provide little evidence as to the quality and direction of the affect. An increase in skin conductance, for example, when one is observing someone being exposed to a highly noxious stimulus may usually signify an empathic reaction. It has been suggested by Berger (1962) and others, however, that some subjects may be enjoying the other person's pain (e.g., "I was rather embarrassed to see that I was grinning when my partner got shocked" [Bandura & Rosenthal, 1966, p. 60]). The response may also reflect a startle reaction to the victim's bodily movements, a direct response to the noxious stimulus or to the sound of the victim's scream, or even the fear that what happened to the victim might happen to the self. In the latter case the victim's response serves merely as a source of information about the observer's own probable fate. Examples of these pseudovicarious affects are the young boy who responds with fear to the sound of someone's cry or to the sight of a sibling being spanked for no apparent reason or the boy who feels sad when his mother is sad because past experience tells him that when she is sad she is not likely to satisfy his needs. Finally, an autonomic response when observing someone engaged in a pleasurable activity may reflect annoyance that someone else, and not the self, is experiencing pleasure (Stotland, 1969).

Thus although autonomic measures may indicate degree of emotional arousal, to measure vicarious arousal or empathy with confidence requires instituting certain controls that enable the investigator to rule out spurious causes of the affect aroused. This may be done in different ways. Craig & Weinstein (1965), for example, simply told their subjects that the model was being shocked, and the model, a confederate, made no sudden movement that might produce a startle response in the observer. Also, to avoid a fear response, the subjects were told that they would serve only as observers and not as models. Krebs (1975) used an interesting procedure to rule out startle effects. In one experimental condition it was necessary for the model to jerk his arm in response to an apparent shock; to offset the observer's reaction to this gesture, a control group was included in which the model jerked his arm as part of a "reaction-time experiment" which did not include a shock. One may also supplement the autonomic index with a verbal report to make sure that the autonomic arousal reflects an empathic response (Krebs, 1975; Stotland, 1969).

The discussion thus far has been confined to skin conductance, because this has been the most frequent autonomic index used. What about other indexes, such as heart rate? There is evidence that infants as young as 8 or 9 months of age show an increase in heart rate just before crying, which suggests that heart rate acceleration is indicative of negative affect or stress (Vaughn & Sroufe, 1979). As noted by Kagan in Chapter 3, school-age children, as well as adults, generally show a slowing of the heart rate when they are attending to an external event but a speeding of the heart rate when they are in distress or when they are asked to perform difficult cognitive operations like remembering or reasoning. The question we may ask is: When a person observes someone in distress, will the observer's heart rate increase due to his (empathic) distress or will it decrease because he is attending to an event that is external to himself? In other words, which has primacy, the elicited empathic affect or the cognitive–attentional dimension of empathy? One possibility is that the answer depends on the level of intensity of the empathic affect. If the intensity is low, we may expect the cognitive dimension to predominate and the heart rate, therefore, to decelerate. If the intensity is very high, however, the observer's experience may be so aversive that although the affect originated through vicarious arousal mechanisms, the observer's experience is that of a high degree of stress to the self (Hoffman, 1977). In that case we might expect the heart rate to accelerate.

Another possibility, consistent with the first, is that, given a low level of intensity, whether the heart rate accelerates or decelerates depends on the predominant mode of empathic arousal. The five arousal modes discussed earlier vary in the degree to which cognition plays a central role. If the most highly cognitive mode were involved, the one in which empathic affect is generated by imagining oneself in the other's situation, we might expect the heart rate to decrease. The earlier, more primitive arousal modes, on the other hand, might be expected to produce an increase in heart rate. Following the same line of reasoning, we might in general expect more heart rate acceleration in child empathizers and more heart rate deceleration in adult empathizers. (Some findings pertinent to the direction of heart rate shift accompanying empathic arousal will be presented later.)

It is also possible that for all practical purposes the direction of change in the heart rate makes no difference, as evidenced by the finding that any deviation in the heart rate, whether an increase or a decrease, was associated with the tendency of adult observers to help someone who was ostensibly in danger (Gaertner & Dovidio, 1977).

Perhaps the biggest problem in using autonomic indexes of empathy is that suggested in a study by Buck, Savin, Miller, and Caul (1972). Subjects who were called senders watched a series of slides designed to elicit various affects. Other subjects watched the senders' faces over closed-circuit television and made judgments about the nature and intensity of their affect. Skin conductance and heart rate data were recorded for the senders. The main finding of interest here was a negative relationship between the senders' skin conductance and the accuracy with which their facial expressions communicated affect to the observer. In other words, people who expressed affect through changes in skin conductance tended not to express affect through their facial expressions; those who expressed affect through facial expressions tended not to do so physiologically. Buck et al. cite other research, some of it with children, supporting the same conclusion. They also discuss possible theoretical explanations; for example, children who are discouraged from expressing emotions may eventually stop doing so publicly (through facial expressions) but continue to do so privately (physiologically). None of these studies or theories deals with empathy, but they do collectively suggest that there may be a fundamental problem in relying exclusively on autonomic indexes of any emotion, whether directly or empathically aroused.

With all the problems, we may ask whether there is any evidence for the validity of autonomic indexes of empathy. Intuitively, and on evolutionary grounds (Hoffman, 1981), a physiological response to another's distress should be more likely to reflect an empathic than a sadistic or other negative reaction, and there is some evidence for this view. First, the investigators report that sadistic responses are infrequent. Second, there is evidence that watching someone being shocked not only raises one's skin conductance but also makes one feel consciously distressed (Craig & Lowery, 1969). Third, in an experiment by Krebs (1975), subjects in the condition designed to produce the most empathy did show an increase in skin conductance and also stated that they identified with the victim, to a greater degree than subjects in other conditions. Fourth, the increases in skin conductance appear to be associated with a general tendency to put oneself in the other person's place: Subjects who obtained high scores on a questionnaire measure of the tendency to put oneself in the place of characters in plays, novels, and movies showed greater skin conductance increases when observing someone in physical pain (though not when observing someone in a neutral situation) than did people who obtained low scores on the questionnaire (Stotland, 1969).

Perhaps the most impressive evidence for the validity of certain autonomic indexes can be found in the studies showing that people who respond autonomically when observing someone under stress are also predisposed to help the victim (see review by Hoffman, 1977). I will now summarize two of the best designed studies in this group, done by Krebs (1975) and by Gaertner and Dovidio (1977). Krebs employed a skin conductance index of empathy, introspective reports about the extent to which the subjects identified with a model undergoing shock, and an altruistic index that required subjects to choose between helping the other at a cost to themselves or helping themselves at a cost to the other. The opportunity for altruism followed the empathy trials. There were two experimental conditions, and the one in which the subjects showed more empathy, both physiologically and verbally, was the same one in which they showed more altruistic behavior. In that experimental condition, then, an increase in skin conductance preceded the altruistic act. Gaertner and Dovidio's design was quite different, and the findings are perhaps more convincing. The subjects, female undergraduate students, observed (through earphones) a situation in which a confederate left an experimental task in order to straighten out a stack of chairs that she thought was about to topple over on her. A moment later the confederate screamed that the chairs were falling on her, and then was silent. The main finding was that the greater the subject's cardiac responsiveness (as indexed by heart rate acceleration), the more quickly she intervened. Furthermore, the autonomic arousal was not merely the artifactual result of the subject rising from her chair, because the arousal preceded the rising: The heart rate acceleration score was based on data obtained during the 10-second period immediately following the confederate's scream, whereas the median latency for rising was 40 seconds. Thus the speed of intervention was systematically related to the magnitude of the heart rate acceleration just prior to the intervention.

The evidence, then, is that an autonomic response to another person's distress – an increase in skin conductance and either an increase or a decrease in heart rate – may indeed be a valid indicator of the observer's empathic arousal. Whether this is true of other affects remains to be seen.

Somatic indexes

Somatic indexes such as facial expression, posture, and gaze have the advantages that autonomic indexes have, of being nonverbal and, at least in natural settings, spontaneous and thus potentially free of a bias in the area of social desirability. Somatic indexes also have the additional advantage of allowing the subject freedom of movement and may thus be uniquely adapted for use in natural settings. Last but not least, whereas autonomic indexes may signify empathic arousal and level of intensity of arousal, it has long been known that they cannot discriminate between different emotions. Somatic indexes apparently can do this to some extent. The facial expression of emotion, at least, can provide accurate information about the occurrence of pleasant or unpleasant emotional states. Many experiments have replicated this finding. Hamilton (1973), for example, rated children's facial expressions as they watched a film depicting people in happy and sad situations. Empathy scores were based on the subjects' facial expressions as they watched the film, and a high degree of accuracy was obtained. A high degree of accuracy has also been reported in adults (Zuckerman et al., 1976). In another study, children who looked happy rather than sad when watching television violence subsequently showed more aggressive behavior than altruistic behavior (Ekman et al., 1972). And more recently, children who looked sad when watching a videotaped recording of a young adult who was unhappy about losing a valued possession were more likely to make a small sacrifice in order to help the victim than were children who did not look sad when watching the film (Lieman, 1978). The last two findings mentioned are especially important because they indicate that the subject's facial response is not merely due to imitation of the model. If the subjects were merely imitating, there would be no reason to expect them to act subsequently the way they did. Thus although systematic research on the use of facial expression as an empathy index has yet to be done, the findings thus far are encouraging. It must be noted, however, that the findings have not been extended to the possible distinctions among *particular* positive or negative emotions.

Another potentially more important limitation of facial expression has already been mentioned, namely, the evidence that suggests an inverse relationship between autonomic response and facial expression. As noted, these findings may reflect the fact that facial expression is public and can be controlled. It may therefore be influenced by punishments and rewards for various types of emotional behavior, especially during the socialization process. The same thing may also be true of other somatic indexes.

Verbal indexes

The only empathy measure of note that has been used with children, and the only one used to assess individual differences in empathic tendency, is that devised by Feshbach and Roe (1968). It consists of a series of slide sequences in which children the same age and sex as the subject are shown in different affect-eliciting situations (e.g., the child has lost a pet dog). Accompanying each sequence is a short narration, which includes no affective labels, describing the events depicted in the slides. After presenting a slide sequence, the child is asked, "How do you feel?" The responses are recorded verbatim and are later assigned empathy scores based on their accuracy, that is, on the extent to which they approximate the investigators' judgment of the affect conveyed in the story. There are four story sequences in all, each one depicting a different emotion: happiness, sadness, anger, and fear. The subject's empathy score is the sum of the scores obtained for the four stories.

This measure appears to have several limitations, and its use raises a number of general questions that are worth mentioning for the help they may provide in devising improved measures for future use. One problem is that the measure provides no information about the intensity of empathic affect that may be aroused. Second, it seems unlikely that a subject's emotions can be so easily manipulated as to shift rapidly from story to story. Third, relying on verbal responses makes the measure vulnerable to the effects of social desirability. Fourth, some of the stories represent more than the one designated emotion. In a story intended to elicit anger, for example, a child is playing with a friend. The friend breaks a window and then, when the principal comes out, blames it on the first child. To receive full credit for an empathic response subjects must say they feel angry, although fear would also seem appropriate for this story. Finally, as I noted earlier, there is a question of just how accurate the response should be in order to be fully credited as an empathic response. Are young children who say they feel sad in response to slides depicting another's fear any less empathic than children who say they feel afraid? I think that under most conditions the answer is no, because the children who say they feel sad are as likely as the others to be responding to the model's situation and not their own, although they may lack the cognitive and linguistic discrimination skills needed to differentiate between fear and sadness. Giving credit for accuracy may thus confound empathy with the child's level of cognitive development. If we are interested in empathy as an affective response, all that may be necessary, as suggested earlier, is a rough correspondence between the subject's affect and the model's affect.

A related issue is raised by Iannotti and Meacham's (1974) modification of the Feshbach and Roe technique. Illustrated stories are presented in which the facial response of the child in the story is inappropriate to the situation; for example, a boy is frowning at his birthday party. High empathy scores are assigned responses that fit the emotion indicated by the story child's facial expression but not the emotion appropriate to his situation. This approach has several problems. First, previous research shows that children under 5 years are often confused cognitively when personal and situational cues are contradictory (Burns & Cavey, 1957; Deutsch, 1974). Iannotti and Meacham's method, like Feshbach and Roe's, may therefore confound subjects' empathic affect with their cognitive level. Second, the method may not be ecologically valid, for in real life both personal and situational cues are generally congruent, and situational cues are often necessary to give meaning to personal cues. It appears, then, that although Iannotti and Meacham's measure may (as it was designed to do) prevent the subject from obtaining a high empathy score by projecting his or her own probable feelings in the situation, it may also serve to mask the young child's empathic responsiveness in everyday life.

A final problem with the Feshbach and Roe measure is that the scoring procedure assumes that empathy is unidimensional: Scores for the four emotions depicted in the stories are added to obtain an overall empathy score. It may seem reasonable to assume that people who empathize with someone experiencing one emotion will be more likely than others to empathize with someone experiencing another emotion. There is some evidence, however, at least in children, that this may not be true. Sawin (1979) found no relationship between Feshbach and Roe empathy scores and helping behavior. Significant positive correlations were obtained, however, between helping behavior and the subscore for empathic sadness. That is, children who showed empathic sadness were more apt to help than children who did not show empathic sadness, which is also in keeping with the already noted frequent finding that arousal of empathic distress leads to helping behavior. These findings suggest that researchers using the Feshbach and Roe measure should give thought to the particular use to which they intend to put the measure.

The findings also raise the general questions, pertinent to all of the indexes discussed, of whether empathy is unidimensional and whether the degree of unidimensionality varies as a function of age. On the one hand, we might expect an increase in unidimensionality with age, as part of the general increase in personality consistency that occurs with age. On the other hand, the general increase in consistency with age may be reflected in an increased tendency to express certain affects and not to express others – whether directly or empathically aroused – rather than an increased tendency to respond or not respond empathically to all affects. A person who is prone to direct anger but not to sadness, for example, may empathize with someone who is angry but not with someone who is sad. The need for research on the unidimensionality issue, and the relevance of such research to empathy measurement, are clear. Until that research is done, investigators would probably be well advised to assume specificity rather than unidimensionality and to tailor the empathy measures they use to the needs of the particular affective variables under investigation.

Another verbal measure of empathic tendency is the Mehrabian and Epstein (1972) inventory. I will only comment briefly on this measure because it is appropriate only for adults. Furthermore, although the measure has the virtue of easy administration, its validity is to be questioned. Though some of the 30 items in the scale clearly pertain to empathy (e.g., "Seeing people cry upsets me"), others do not (e.g., "Sometimes the words of a song can move me deeply"; "I would rather be a social worker than work in a job training center"). If one wanted a simple paper-and-pencil index of empathy, one might consider Stot-

land's three-item fantasy–empathy scale, which has been found to predict helping behavior at about the same level of confidence as the Mehrabian–Epstein
inventory (Hammersla, 1973).

The difference between empathic affect and direct affect

It seems clear from the foregoing that the arousal mechanisms and cognitive
processes are very different for empathic and direct affect. In thinking about the
differences, and the similarities, several interesting issues come to mind. One
pertains to the use of nonverbal measures of empathy. Can we assume that a
good physiological index of direct affect is also a good index of empathic affect?
Consider the fact that the three most prevalent empathic arousal modes described
earlier all involve associative mechanisms. When these mechanisms underlie an
empathic response, the person is actually responding vicariously to cues in someone else's situation that resemble cues to which he has responded with direct
affect in the past. Now, this may not be all that different from the case in which
a person responds directly to an event impinging on him; here, too, he may be
responding in part to cues that resemble cues to which he has responded with
direct affect in the past. That is, the cues in any event impinging directly on a
person may not all be experienced for the first time; some may be associated
with affect-eliciting situations in his past. We may thus speak of an associative
component even in a person's direct affective response to events. A possible
similarity therefore exists between direct and empathic affective responses – they
both may have an associative component. Consequently, we might expect little
difference between the physiological response to cues in someone else's and in
one's own, situation. In other words, a good physiological index of direct affect
may sometimes also be a good index of empathic affect. This is not true, of
course, as we shall see, when the affect-eliciting event is a powerful physical
stimulus such as an electric shock.

As people grow older, fewer of the cues to which they respond either directly
or empathically are apt to be experienced for the first time. That is, their affective responses will include an increasingly greater associative component. To the
extent that they do, the difference between empathic and direct affect might be
expected to diminish with age.

On the other hand, the two most advanced modes of empathic arousal, which
depend less exclusively on associative mechanisms and more on language and
cognition, may be presumed to underlie more of the individual's empathic responses as he grows older. And of course, the actor's cognitive sense of others
also increases with age. For these reasons, we would expect a sharper differentiation between direct and empathic affect with age, hence an increasing difference between physiological indexes of direct and empathic affect.

The only pertinent research to date says nothing about age difference, but it does indicate that there may be measurable physiological differences between empathic and direct affect, at least in adults and when the affect-eliciting event is a powerful physical stimulus. The main finding was that the direct experience of electric shock produced a rise in skin conductance along with an increase in the heart rate, which suggests high stress. Observing someone else receive the shock, on the other hand, resulted in a rise in skin conductance, along with a decrease in the heart rate, which suggests an attentional component in empathy (Craig & Lowery, 1969). Further research is needed along these lines, with children as well as adults and on affect-eliciting events that are not physical. Similar research also needs to be done with the somatic indexes of empathy. The issues are similar, but there may also be differences due to the fact that autonomic and somatic response patterns may be implicated differently in the arousal of empathy. The somatic responses are prominent in the mimicry-and-feedback mechanism, which requires, at least in young children, that the model be present and visible to the observer. The autonomic responses are more likely to be implicated in the various conditioning and association mechanisms, in which situational cues, physical or symbolic, are required but expressive cues from the model are not.

Conclusions

Though empathy has received increased attention as a research topic, systematic research on how to measure it has not yet been undertaken. All things considered, it would appear that until the research needed to resolve the above issues has been completed, investigators would be well advised, where possible, to consider using one type of index to tap intensity and another to tap direction of arousal. As for the most promising single approach, at this juncture it would appear to be an index of facial expression. Despite the problems mentioned earlier, this is the only index so far that appears to respond quickly to changes in affect and to be capable of tapping, to some degree, both the intensity and direction of affect.

References

Aronfreed, J., & Paskal, V. *Altruism, empathy, and the conditioning of positive affect.* Unpublished manuscript, University of Pennsylvania, 1965.

Bandura, H., & Rosenthal, L. Vicarious classical conditioning as a function of arousal level. *Journal of Personality and Social Psychology,* 1966, *3,* 54–62.

Berger, S. M. Conditioning through vicarious instigation. *Psychological Review,* 1962, *69,* 450–66.

Buck, R. W., Savin, V. J., Miller, R. E., & Caul, W. F. Communication of affect through facial expressions in humans. *Journal of Personality and Social Psychology,* 1972, *23,* 362–71.

Burns, N., & Cavey, L. Age differences in empathic ability among children. *Canadian Journal of Psychology*, 1957, *11*, 227–30.

Craig, K. D., & Lowery, J. H. Heart rate components of conditioned vicarious autonomic responses, *Journal of Personality and Social Psychology*, 1969, *11*, 381–87.

Craig, K. D., & Weinstein, M. S. Conditioning vicarious affective arousal. *Psychological Reports*, 1965, *17*, 955–63.

Deutsch, F. Female preschoolers' perceptions of affective responses and interpersonal behavior in videotaped episodes. *Developmental Psychology*, 1974, *10*, 733–40.

Ekman, P., Liebert, R. M., Frieson, W. V., Harrison, R. A., Zlatchin, C., Malmstrom, E. J., & Baron, R. A. Facial expressions of emotion while watching televised violence as predictors of subsequent aggression. In G. A. Comstock, E. A. Rubenstein, and J. P. Murray (Eds.), *Television and social behavior* (Vol. 5). Technical Report. Washington, D.C.: Government Printing Office, 1972.

Feshbach, N. D., & Roe, K. Empathy in six- and seven-year olds. *Child Development*, 1968, *39*, 133–45.

Gaertner, S. L., & Dovidio, J. F. The subtlety of white racism, arousal, and helping behavior. *Journal of Personality and Social Psychology*, 1977, *35*, 691–707.

Hamilton, M. L. Imitative behavior and expressive ability in facial expression of emotion. *Developmental Psychology*, 1973, *8*, 138.

Hammersla, J. F. *Spontaneous helping behavior.* Unpublished doctoral dissertation, University of Washington, 1973.

Hoffman, M. L. Developmental synthesis of affect and cognition and its implications for altruistic motivation. *Developmental Psychology*, 1975, *11*, 607–22.

Hoffman, M. L. Empathy, its development and prosocial implications. In H. E. Howe, Jr., & C. B. Keasey (Eds.), *Nebraska Symposium on Motivation* (Vol. 25). Lincoln: University of Nebraska Press, 1978.

Hoffman, M. L. Is altruism part of human nature? *Journal of Personality and Social Psychology*, 1981, *40*, 121–37.

Humphrey, G. The conditioned reflex and the elementary social reaction. *Journal of Abnormal and Social Psychology*, 1922, *17*, 113–9.

Iannotti, R. J., & Meacham, J. A. *The nature, measurement and development of empathy.* Paper presented at the meeting of the Eastern Psychological Association, Philadelphia, April 1974.

Krebs, D. Empathy and altruism. *Journal of Personality and Social Psychology*, 1975, *32*, 1124–46.

Kurdek, L. A., & Rodgo, M. M. Perceptual, cognitive, and affective perspective-taking in kindergarten through sixth-grade children. *Developmental Psychology*, 1975, *11*, 643–50.

Lieman, B. *Affective empathy and subsequent altruism in kindergartners and first graders.* Paper presented at the meeting of the American Psychological Association, Toronto, September 1978.

Lipps, T. Das Wissen von fremden Ichen. *Psychologische Untersuchungen*, 1906, *1*, 694–722.

Mehrabian, A., & Epstein, N. A measure of emotional empathy. *Journal of Personality*, 1972, *40*, 525–43.

Sawin, D. B. *Assessing empathy in children: A search for an elusive construct.* Paper presented at the meeting of the Society for Research in Child Development, San Francisco, March 1979.

Stotland, E. Exploratory investigations of empathy. In L. Berkowitz (Ed.), *Advances in experimental social psychology* (Vol. 4). New York: Academic Press, 1969.

Vaughn, B., & Sroufe, L. A. The temporal relationship between infant heart-rate acceleration and crying in an aversive situation. *Child Development*, 1979, *50*, 565–7.

Zahn-Waxler, C., Radke-Yarrow, M., & King, R. M. Childrearing and children's prosocial initiations toward victims of distress. *Child Development*, 1979, *50*, 319–30.

Zuckerman, M., DeFrank, R., Hall, J., & Rosenthal, R. Encoding and decoding of spontaneous and posed facial expressions. *Journal of Personality and Social Psychology*, 1976, *34*, 966–77.

Part V

Commentary

12   Emotion and the cardiovascular system: a critical perspective

Paul A. Obrist, Kathleen C. Light, and Janice L. Hastrup

There has been a considerable effort over the years to study behavioral processes such as emotion through the measurement of cardiovascular activity. It is undeniable that experimental procedures that alter affective states also modify cardiovascular activity. Still, considerable evidence now accumulating indicates that cardiovascular events may not provide much insight into affective processes such as the quality or intensity of an emotional experience. The purpose of this chapter is to review some of this evidence, commenting primarily on the results of our own research. Only two aspects of cardiovascular function will be discussed, namely heart rate (HR) and blood pressure (BP). Our observations will serve as an example of the problems involved in trying to interpret either the HR or the BP as some simple index of affective processes. The chapter will close in a more positive vein, however, by presenting some evidence suggesting that a behavioral–biological strategy may make a significant contribution to the role of the organism–environment interaction in the etiology of cardiovascular pathophysiology, specifically in essential hypertension, and that a developmental strategy, among others, may shed light on this issue.

Phasic heart rate effects

Approximately 25 years ago, there appeared in the literature reports that HR decelerates in anticipation of signaled aversive stimuli. These HR changes are short-term or phasic effects associated with discrete experimental stimuli such as a conditioned stimulus. Besides having a brief duration (e.g., 5–6 seconds), they

The research cited in this paper and performed by the authors was supported by the following research grants and awards: MH 07995, National Institute of Mental Health; HL 18976 and HL 23718, National Heart, Lung, and Blood Institute; National Service Awards F–32–HL 05531 to Kathleen C. Light and F–32–HL 05671 to Janice L. Hastrup, National Heart, Lung, and Blood Institute.

299

are small in magnitude (5–6 beats per minute: Obrist, Wood, & Perez-Reyes, 1965). Because these HR decreases occurred in anticipation of an apparently emotional instigating event, we can consider the anticipatory HR changes as a reflection of some sort of an anticipatory emotional state. At least, some investigators did so when they referred to it as an example of experimental anxiety (Notterman, Schonfeld, & Bersh, 1952). Still, several considerations cast doubt on such an interpretation. For one thing, although the anticipatory response is an HR deceleration, the unconditioned response is an acceleration of HR – hence a reversal of the anticipatory response. This result is somewhat unprecedented in the classical conditioning of other autonomically mediated responses. Also, this directional difference implies that the anticipatory emotional experience is different from the emotional experience evoked by the aversive stimulus. That conclusion may not be unreasonable, in that we may become momentarily anxious awaiting a painful experience. On the other hand, dogs, which also demonstrate an acceleration of HR to the aversive unconditioned stimulus, demonstrate an acceleratory anticipatory HR response (Obrist & Webb, 1967). Does this mean that dogs have a different emotional experience than humans when anticipating an aversive event? To complicate matters further, cats are like humans – the anticipatory HR response is a deceleration (Howard et al., 1974). Finally, humans also show a similar anticipatory deceleration of HR during procedures that do not involve aversive stimuli but have some emotional or motivational significance for the individual. These procedures include signaled reaction time tasks (Obrist, Webb, & Sutterer, 1969), exercise, conceptual activities, and viewing pictures of seminude women (Wood & Obrist, 1968). What kinds of anticipatory emotional state do these HR changes reflect? If we stick by the contention that any HR deceleration reflects a momentary increase in anxiety, then we have to conclude that all these events evoke anxiety – a conclusion that does not seem logically compelling.

A second line of evidence that casts doubt on the meaning of the anticipatory HR response emerges from classical conditioning studies attempting to delineate the biological basis, that is, mechanisms, of these HR changes. Under these experimental conditions, one might expect diffuse sympathetic excitation because of observations such as Cannon's (1929). In fact, we do observe such sympathetic effects in regard to sweat gland and vasomotor activity. But instead of an increase in HR, reflecting sympathetic activation of the myocardium, we observe HR deceleration due to an increase in vagal or parasympathetic excitation. Such a vagal influence is indicated by the results of pharmacological blockade.[1] Under such conditions, the anticipatory deceleration is no longer seen. Rather, there is now an anticipatory HR acceleration (Obrist et al., 1965) (see Figure 12.1). Thus there is sympathetic excitation, but it is masked by vagal excitation. Such observations force us to qualify our concept of the diffuse nature

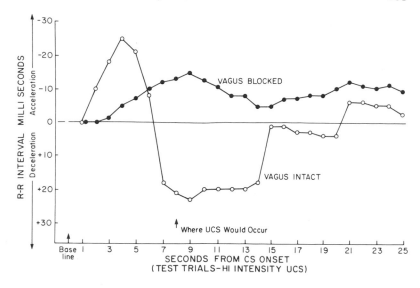

Figure 12.1. Second-by-second heart rate changes on nonreinforced test trials during classical aversive conditioning with the vagal (parasympathetic) innervation of the heart intact and blocked. *Source:* Obrist, Wood, & Perez-Reyes (1965).

of sympathetic excitation, and any view that relegates parasympathetic effects to vegetative and other states of relaxation and tranquillity.

Another line of evidence from both the classical conditioning and signaled reaction time (RT) paradigm is that simultaneous with the phasic decrease in HR is a phasic decrease in somatomotor, or striate, muscular activity (for reviews, see Obrist, Howard, Lawler, Galosy, Meyers, & Gaebelein, 1974; Obrist et al., 1970a). This takes the form of a momentary decrease in rather subtle somatic events such as mouth and tongue movements, eye blinks and movements, a momentary suspension of respiration, the inhibition of more gross somatic acts, for example, postural adjustments (Obrist, 1968; Obrist et al., 1969; Obrist et al., 1970b; Obrist et al., 1973) and, in the cat (Howard et al., 1974), a decrease in electrical activity in the pyramidal tract. On the other hand, dogs, which accelerate their HR, typically demonstrate an increase in somatomotor activity such as struggling (Obrist & Webb, 1967). Such effects suggest that these phasic HR changes, both decreases and increases, are integrated in the central nervous system by mechanisms similar to those involved when one exercises or inhibits or initiates any type of somatomotor activity. The evidence for this possibility is reasonably compelling (Obrist et al., 1979). If so, then we must view the HR changes not simply as a reflection of any affective state but as indicative of whether the organism resorts to inactivity or activity when faced with inescapable aversive events. Some species, including man, under such conditions might be referred to as behavioral freezers. This does not mean that they demonstrate increased muscle tension. There is no evidence that they do (Hofer, 1970; Obrist, 1968). Rather, they become immobile. In the case when no aversive stimuli are used, such as the signaled RT task, such immobility could function to facilitate performance on the task, as the types of somatomotor activity that are inhibited are usually task irrelevant.

A final observation to note is that by changing the experimental paradigm using aversive stimuli from classical conditioning to a shock-avoidance task, we were finally able to demonstrate a sympathetic influence[2] on HR that was also independent of concurrent somatomotor activity (Obrist, Lawler, Howard, Smithson, Martin, & Manning, 1974). This new task was a signaled RT task in which shock avoidance was made contingent on the adequacy of performance. The sympathetic effect was actually not evidenced during the 8-second fore period of the RT task. Here only vagal influences on HR were seen that were again directionally related to concurrent somatomotor activity. The sympathetic influence was observed following response execution commencing toward the end of the 8-second period between response execution and the point in time when the aversive stimulus would occur. Somatomotor activity at this point in time was directionally opposite to the accelerated HR, that is, it was returning to baseline. The principal difference in the experimental paradigms is that with classical conditioning, the individual has no control over the aversive events, whereas with shock avoidance some control is possible. These observations have led us to hypothesize that sympathetic influences can be evoked once the subject is given some opportunity to cope actively with the aversive events; vagal influences, on the other hand, dominate when the individual can only passively cope with these events. A couple of follow-up studies lend further support to this hypothesis, particularly in regard to sympathetic effects (Obrist et al., 1978; Light & Obrist, 1980a). In any case, this evidence proves to be another embarrassment to using HR as an affect meter, because the direction of the anticipatory HR change associated with aversive stimuli is a function not of a particular affective state that one would assume is common to both conditions but of whether the organism can act to control the receipt of these stimuli. This fact suggests an important role for a cognitive variable that interacts with or even overrides any influence an affective state may have on HR. In all fairness, it should be pointed out that affective processes probably influence HR in these paradigms. This is indicated by the observation that sympathetic influences on the HR are potentiated by not giving individuals any experience with the aversive stimulus until the first time their reaction time does not meet criterion (Light & Obrist, 1980a). This is in contrast to familiarizing the individual with the aversive stimulus prior to the onset of the reaction time task. These effects are not sustained, however.

Before summarizing this section, we should note that the phasic anticipatory

HR changes observed in the reaction time paradigm have been viewed not so much as indexes of affective states but as indexes of attentional processes. There is evidence that phasic HR changes might be viewed in this manner, because HR is found to covary with performance. For example, from our studies, we found across a group of 48 subjects a correlation [$r(46) = .31$] between speed of performance and the magnitude of the phasic HR changes associated with responses' execution (Obrist et al., 1969). We also observed, using a within-subjects analysis, that performance time was significantly faster on trials evidencing the greatest phasic HR decrease (Obrist et al., 1970b). This is not too surprising in light of the relationship between these phasic HR changes and the inhibition of task-irrelevant somatomotor activities. That is to say, the relationship between HR and performance time may be due to the relationship between HR and somatomotor activity. We do in fact find that the inhibition of task-irrelevant somatomotor activity related to performance time in a similar and somewhat more pronounced manner than HR.

Even though such data suggest that HR does index attentional processes, the effects are not pronounced, and there are two other lines of evidence, again from our own studies, that question the sensitivity of the phasic HR changes to alterations in attentional states. One study evaluated phasic HR changes in four age groups of normal healthy children – 4-, 5-, 8-, and 10-year-olds and young adults during a signaled reaction time task. We used these five age groups because we thought that the facility to attend would improve with age and that this would be reflected in the phasic HR changes. In essence, we sought a naturalistic way to manipulate attentional processes. The manipulation worked with respect to performance. The median reaction time decreased with each age group, the range being a median of 611 milliseconds with 4-year-olds to a median of 231 milliseconds with young adults. There were no differences among age groups with regard to the phasic HR changes, however. They were of a similar magnitude with each age group. Interestingly, some of the somatomotor measures did evidence an age effect consistent with performance (Obrist et al., 1973). In a second study using 10-year-olds and young adults, we manipulated attentional processes through incentives. Again using a signaled RT task, we observed an appreciable improvement in performance time in both age groups under high incentive, but again this was not reflected in the phasic HR decreases (Lawler, Obrist, & Lawler, 1976). Such data may thus be seen to call into question the particular sensitivity of HR to alterations in attentional processses. At times, we seem to see a certain sensitivity, whereas at other times there is no degree of sensitivity. The whole issue of sensitivity has in large part been neglected, and we believe that until it is addressed and resolved, the demonstration of a phasic decrease in HR in conjunction with momentary increases in attention will not shed much light on still another behavioral process.

In summary, there are several lines of evidence that question the use of phasic HR changes as reflections of some anticipatory affective state. In classical conditioning, the phasic anticipatory HR response in humans is a deceleration, even though the unconditioned response is an acceleration. This deceleration is vagally mediated and covaries directly with phasic changes in somatomotor activity. When the experimental paradigm is modified, giving the individual some control in avoiding aversive stimuli, sympathetic effects are observed. It would appear, then, that the neural control of the heart is appreciably influenced by cognitive processes associated with our experimental manipulations and is not consistently related to affective states.

Tonic heart rate effects

Tonic levels of HR, that is, heart rate values averaged over blocks of time (e.g., minutes), have been evaluated in some behavioral paradigms in the expectation that HR would reflect various affective states (see Elliott, 1974, for brief review). We have recently modified our method of data quantification from evaluating phasic HR effects to evaluating such tonic effects. This is because changes in tonic levels of HR from some pretask baseline are in general more pronounced and sustained than phasic effects, changes that are superimposed upon these tonic levels of activity. Also, these tonic level effects appear more relevant to issues such as the role of behavioral factors in pathophysiological conditions of the cardiovascular system. We should note just one observation relevant to the current discussion.

Pronounced individual differences in HR reactivity as evaluated tonically that have been observed are a reasonably stable characteristic of the individual in that they extend over several conditions. For example, one group of 56 subjects was exposed to three experimental procedures that differ in their affective impact both quantitatively and qualitatively. These were: submerging the foot in ice water for 90 seconds; viewing an erotic movie that depicted explicitly sexual behavior; and performing an unsignaled reaction time task in which shock avoidance was made contingent on the adequacy of performance. Also, HR was evaluated under two baseline conditions. One, occurring just prior to exposure to the above three experimental procedures, is the pretask baseline. A second, relaxation baseline, obtained some 1 to 2 weeks later, involved having the subjects return to the laboratory on two separate occasions and relax for 15 minutes in the experimental chamber, knowing that they would not be exposed to any other experimental procedure. The average HR during each baseline and the three experimental procedures are depicted in Table 12.1 and as a function of HR reactivity to the shock-avoidance task. The latter involved dividing subjects into

Table 12.1. *Mean heart rate during two types of baselines and three experimental tasks*

Relaxation baseline	Pretask baseline	Change (%)	Heart rate reactivity					
			Cold pressor	Change (%)	Film	Change (%)	Shock avoidance	Change (%)
63	80	26	96	51	86	35	120	90
65	78	20	92	40	80	23	103	57
68	75	75	88	29	80	18	93	37
67[a]	66[b]	-2	80[c]	19	72[d]	7	76[e]	13

Note: Mean heart rate has been quartiled on bases of HR reactivity during shock avoidance using the relaxation baseline as the reference point. $N = 56$.

The mean HR values given for the relaxation baseline represent the average of the first 4 and last 3 minutes of each of the two 15-minute rest periods. Mean HR for the pretask baselines is the average HR in the last 3 minutes of a 5-minute instructed rest period. The cold pressor HR level represents the average HR for the entire 90 seconds of that event. For both the film and shock-avoidance task, the mean HR values are averages of the first 2 minutes of each procedure. Data are presented in descending order of HR reactivity.

[a] $M = 66$.
[b] $M = 75$.
[c] $M = 89$.
[d] $M = 79$.
[e] $M = 98$.

quartiles on the basis of the difference between their average HR during the relaxation baseline and the first 2 minutes of the shock-avoidance task.

The shock-avoidance task evoked overall the largest changes in HR and the most pronounced individual differences. The latter ranged from a -11 beats per minutes to a 103 beats-per-minute change. Nine of the subjects demonstrated HR increases in excess of 50 beats per minute, whereas another seven demonstrated changes of less than 10 beats per minute. What is also apparent in Table 12.1 is that the more reactive subjects with respect to the shock-avoidance task are also more reactive to the two other experimental procedures as well as to the pretask baseline. The least reactive subjects, on the other hand, remain unreactive under all conditions. The stability of these individual differences was also revealed by positive and significant correlations between change scores for any pair of experimental procedures. The correlation between the change from the relaxation baseline for the cold pressor and film was .58, whereas for the cold pressor and shock-avoidance task and film and shock-avoidance task, it was .53 in both instances.

We have detailed these individual differences because we do not have much insight into their basis and meaning. In turn, this should caution us about using tonic HR as a reflection of some behavioral state or process, affective or otherwise. A couple of points are noteworthy. First, consider the magnitude of difference in response shown by the two extreme quartiles on the shock-avoidance task. The one extreme demonstrates on the average a 90% increase above the relaxation baseline, whereas the other extreme on the average demonstrates a 13% increase – a sevenfold difference. One might conclude that the reactors become more engaged in the task, but can we put any kind of quantitative value on this engagement? Are the reactors seven times more engaged? We have observed in a more recent study (Light & Obrist, 1980b) that when a sample of 60 subjects was dichotomized into the 30 most and 30 least reactive HR subjects, the more reactive subjects were 27 milliseconds faster on the average using a similar shock-avoidance task. This is a significant difference. Yet it is quantitatively small, reflecting approximately a 10% difference between mean values, not a 700% difference such as we observed between the extreme quartiles in Table 12.1. Second, such an interpretation generates another questionable conclusion. Because the hyperreactors demonstrate hyperreactivity to the pretask baseline as well as cold pressor and film, does this mean that they are more apprehensive or anxious as they rest just prior to the first experimental procedure, that they experience the cold pressor as more painful, and that they are more sexually aroused? This possibility does not strike us as very likely.

We do need to explore the basis of these individual differences. We have evidence, to be presented in the last part of this chapter, that they relate to a parental history of hypertension, but whether they reflect some overall difference in emotionality that generalizes to any novel and arousing situation is unknown. It is known, however, that these individual differences are probably not due to any differences in such characteristics as age, sex, and general intellectual ability. For example, our subjects are quite homogeneous with regard to age and sex. They are 18–20-year-old males. Also, they were typically recruited from the introductory psychology course from the Chapel Hill campus of the University of North Carolina. Because admission standards are reasonably robust, our subjects probably do not noticeably differ with regard to scholastic aptitude or having career aspirations that might influence their perception of the situation. We have also evaluated some of the subjects on such personality dimensions as the ego strength scale, which is reported to assess coping ability (Roessler, 1973), the Jenkins activity survey (Jenkins, 1967), which assesses type A–B coronary-prone behavior, and the Rotter internal–external locus-of-control scale (Rotter, 1966). Until now, none of these scales has related to reactivity.

Tonic blood-pressure effects

Blood pressure has not been as commonly used as HR to assess behavioral processes, probably because it is more difficult to measure. Nonetheless, we would like to describe briefly some blood-pressure data collected in conjunction with tonic HR levels, under the conditions previously described. These blood-pressure data deserve mention for two reasons. First, these data, like the HR data, indicate the impropriety of treating these cardiovascular events in too simplistic a manner. Second, they point to a new direction in which our research is moving and one that we believe will make a more positive contribution to our understanding of the human condition than research that has focused on assessing affective states and cardiovascular activity.

The two components of the blood pressure, the systolic (SBP) and diastolic (DBP), will be discussed separately, because they have demonstrated some interesting differences during our various experimental procedures. With the SBP, there are similarities to the HR effects. First, there are again the appreciable individual differences. Using the relaxation baseline as the reference point, the differences observed at the onset of the shock-avoidance task range from -2 to 75 millimeters of mercury. Second, the magnitude of change in HR and SBP tends to be appreciably related in that subjects who show the greater HR reactivity demonstrate greater SBP reactivity. Third, individuals who demonstrate the greatest SBP reactivity to the shock-avoidance task also demonstrate greater reactivity to the pretask rest, the cold pressor, and the film, but not to the relaxation baseline. These observations are straightforward and very similar to the previously described HR effects; thus the comments made regarding HR also apply to these SBP changes.

With the DBP, however, the consistency in cardiovascular change is no longer seen. First, the individual differences are less pronounced, and the DBP tends to covary less consistently with HR. Second, the experimental condition, that is, shock-avoidance task, which evokes the largest HR and SBP change, evokes the smallest DBP change as compared with the cold pressor and film. Third, when one blocks the sympathetic innervations of the heart with an agent that does not impair the sympathetic innervations involved with vasoconstriction, DBP increases more than with an intact innervation. In contrast, SBP and HR increase less following such a pharmacological intervention. On the other hand, blockade had little effect on the DBP and SBP changes during the cold pressor and film. Finally, the DBP differences between the two types of baseline were minimal and nonsignificant.

These differences among the blood-pressure effects create problems for anyone attempting to link the BP to emotional arousal. For example, suppose our primary concern was to determine which of the experimental tasks was the most arousing or evoked the most intense emotional experience as indexed by the BP. If we had measured only the SBP, we would have concluded that it was the shock-avoidance task. When we measure both the SBP and DBP, the answer is equivocal. Even worse, suppose we had measured just the DBP. Then we would have been forced to conclude that it was the cold pressor. Next, suppose our experimental aims to identify the individuals who were the highest in reactivity to the shock-avoidance task. In the light of the observation that the SBP and DBP are marginally but negatively correlated during this condition, we would again find an uninterpretable situation because our SBP reactors tend to be our DBP nonreactors and vice versa. This is not the case with the cold pressor and film. Attempting to designate which individuals had the greatest emotional arousal is thus a function of which aspect of the BP is measured and also of the conditions under which it was measured. Finally, when we view the blood pressure as an index of emotionality, how can we explain the observation that blocking the neurogenic influence of the heart results during the shock-avoidance task is an attenuation of the SBP but a potentiation of the DBP change? Meanwhile, such blockade has minimal influence on both aspects of the blood pressure during the other two events, the cold pressor and film.

There is no way to explain such blood-pressure effects with behavioral concepts such as fear and hostility (Ax, 1953). Still, these effects are explainable with an understanding of neurogenic influences on blood-pressure control. Even at the behavioral level, they are somewhat understandable by recourse to the concept of flight and fight. For example, in the active coping task such as the shock-avoidance task, the cardiovascular adjustment is somewhat comparable to an exercise response and can be viewed as anticipatory or preparatory for action. On the other hand, during those procedures, particularly the classical conditioning paradigm, where the individual has little or no control but is instead passive or helpless, the cardiovascular adjustment is more consistent with a state of immobilization. Still, preparation for flight or fight may not seem to be an appropriate description of the cardiovascular adjustments seen during shock avoidance; our subjects are probably not planning some intense effort such as flight. But the mobilization response is only pronounced in some individuals and may represent a legacy of our more primitive ancestors for whom flight or fight might have been the natural outcomes of such challenging events.

Another perspective on the cardiovascular system

Our current research focuses on the issue of the role of organism–environment interactions in the etiology of essential hypertension. This issue is hardly resolved, and the position that the etiology of hypertension has a significant behavioral component is still a matter more of faith than of fact. It is our position, however, that a behavioral–biological strategy can make a significant contribution with regard to this issue that will overshadow anything we can add to an understanding of emotional development per se. This position reflects our modification of our research strategies such that we no longer view the blood pressure as exclusively a symptom but delineate the mechanisms by which the blood pressure is controlled and the means by which these mechanisms are influenced by the organism–environmental interactions. To illustrate this point, it is necessary first to review briefly the literature on blood-pressure control in hypertension and one of our more recent studies.

Observations from long-term clinical investigations suggest that a marginally elevated BP, or borderline hypertension, seen in individuals in the 20–30 age range may in some instances be a precursor of a more elevated and sustained hypertension (Julius, 1977; Julius & Schork, 1971). In a significant number of these individuals, the elevated pressure is due to an elevated cardiac output in association with an elevated heart rate and myocardial force resulting from excessive sympathetic drive on the heart (Julius, 1977). This statement contrasts with the hemodynamic picture in older individuals with a more elevated pressure, in whom increased vascular resistance is the primary controller of the BP (Lund-Johansen, 1967, 1979). Such observations of an excessive neurogenic drive on the myocardium were made under conditions that did not permit determination of whether these neurogenic influences are evoked by the organism–environmental interaction. Our recent data on behaviorally induced neurogenic elevations on HR, indirect measures of cardiac force, and SBP come closer to such a definitive demonstration.

That we observe such appreciable individual differences in myocardial reactivity is a necessary observation if we are to implicate behavioral factors in the etiological process, because this raises the question of whether such behaviorally initiated myocardial hyperreactivity is one of the early precursors of hypertensive disease. The relationship must be ascertained if we are to implicate behavioral factors in the etiology and undertake preventive procedures. Answers to this question cannot be obtained, however, until reasonably long-term longitudinal studies are under way. Such studies should not only evaluate the eventual consequences of excessive sympathetic drive on the heart but also delineate other events that might influence the BP in this deleterious manner, which too may be triggered by behavioral influences. In order to justify the cost and energy of such a longitudinal effort, we are evaluating several questions with respect to our young adult population that if answered in the affirmative would encourage us to undertake such an effort. One such study has recently been completed with encouraging results (Hastrup, Light, & Obrist, 1980).

Hypertension has been demonstrated to be familial (Paul, 1977). That is to say, a given person is more apt to develop hypertension if one parent is hypertensive than if neither parent is hypertensive. The probability of developing hypertension is even greater if both parents are hypertensive. These findings suggested that if excessive sympathetic drive on the myocardium is an early precursor of a later hypertension, then the incidence of hypertension in the parents of our more reactive subjects should be greater than in our less reactive subjects. In order to evaluate this possibility, we obtained a usable health history from both parents of 104 of our subjects. Of these 208 parents, 34 were classified as hypertensive on the basis of information they provided. When the incidence of parental hypertension was examined in relationship to the son's HR and SBP, a reasonably consistent picture emerged. In particular, parental hypertension was found to be strongly related to the absolute level of HR during the first 2 minutes in the shock-avoidance task. Eighteen of the 34 hypertensive parents had sons whose average HR was in the upper quartile of the distribution, whereas 12 others had sons in the next highest quartile. Thus, 30 of these 34 hypertensive parents had sons who were in the upper half of the HR distribution during shock avoidance. Similar but not quite as pronounced effects were seen with HR reactivity difference scores. With SBP, similar effects were seen with both absolute levels of pressure and difference scores during shock avoidance. Also, the SBP level during the pretask rest related to parental history, where the median split was 24–9 (SBP was not available for 1 subject, which eliminated one hypertensive parent).

These relationships between parental history and the son's cardiovascular responsiveness can be seen in another and somewhat more dramatic way. This demonstration involves comparing average values of HR and SBP during the relaxation baseline, pretask baseline, and onset of the shock-avoidance task among subjects with two hypertensive parents ($N = 9$), one hypertensive parent

Table 12.2. *Mean systolic blood pressure (millimeters of mercury) during two baselines and a shock-avoidance task as a function of hypertension in the parents*

History	Relaxation baseline	Pretask baseline	Shock avoidance
No parent hypertensive[a]	120	129	143
One parent hypertensive[b]	124	132	150
Both parents hypertensive[c]	125	138	164

[a] $N = 79$.
[b] $N = 15$.
[c] $N = 9$.

($N = 15$), and no hypertensive parent ($N = 79$). Such a comparison involving SBP levels is illustrated in Table 12.2. With the relaxation baseline, there are but small differences between the subgroups; these differences begin to widen during pretest baseline and become even greater during shock avoidance, with markedly higher SBP levels seen in sons of the hypertensive parents. This finding indicates an interaction between behavioral influences and the familial trend in hypertension and whatever genetic and/or environmental contribution it reflects.

We are currently extending our family history data base. Also, we are about to initiate studies that will evaluate in preadolescents as well as in 1–2-year-olds, first, whether individual differences in reactivity can be seen, and then, whether such differences are related to reactivity differences in the parents, determining as well any relationship reactivity differences bear to hypertension in the parents and grandparents. Such a developmental strategy will at least permit us to ascertain at what ages reactivity differences are seen and whether behaviorally evoked hyperreactivity is a reasonably long-standing characteristic. If it is, we would argue further for its significance in the etiological process.

Summary

This chapter has provided evidence largely from our own research, which has gradually led us to the judgment that cardiovascular events such as HR and blood pressure will not provide particularly useful information about affective processes and their development. We do not mean to imply that the affective component of any given situation is of no significance in evoking cardiovascular changes. Still, we do not believe, in the light of our evolving understanding of the cardiovascular system, that this component can be used in a quantitative manner to mirror affective states.

We are not alone in our skepticism about the use of cardiovascular events, particularly HR, to index behavioral states and processes. In reviewing the literature on the use of HR to index the conditioned emotional response in the context of two-factor learning theory, Rescorla and Solomon (1967) conclude: "To expect simple heart-rate changes, which are only a small portion of this system, to mirror adequately a state such as 'fear' is to oversimplify hopelessly the operation of the cardiovascular system" (p. 168). In another context and with respect to using HR to index social and emotional arousal, Elliott (1974) concludes "that there is no obvious mandate in evidence for using HR to measure complex variables in social psychology and personality" (p. 527). Finally, Clifton (1978) ends a recent article on cardiac responses in infants as follows:

In conclusion, we must continue to remind ourselves that the heart is influenced by a multitude of neural commands from many different sources. The resulting HR is always an integrated response reflecting the different demands from both the autonomic and central nervous systems. Those of us who would infer psychological meaning from HR changes must be ever aware that we are dealing with a major life-sustaining organ in the body, subject to many controls. [P. 91]

Addendum

Although this chapter casts doubt on the value of heart rate (HR) to index behavioral states, Profs. Carroll Izard and Jerome Kagan, after reading it, raised the question of whether phasic HR decreases in anticipation of or in response to sensory stimuli do not indicate states such as interest or surprise or orienting. There is a substantial literature indicating that such HR changes can be viewed in the way they suggest. Thus the presence of phasic HR deceleration conveys some meaning about a behavioral state. But we have some reservations about the uncritical use of HR for these purposes.

First, it is not clear whether the absence of an HR response indicates a lack of interest and so forth or whether a response to a given stimulus in the opposite direction (HR acceleration) indicates a different behavioral state. Such HR effects could come about not because the subjects failed to be interested but because they responded somatically (see Clifton, 1978; Obrist, 1968). In the light of our experience investigating phasic HR effects, we suggest that it is necessary when using HR for these purposes to measure somatic activity simultaneously, particularly movements in and around the mouth (chin electromyograph, or EMG) and ocular activity. This conclusion is also reached by Clifton (1978), who found in newborns that spontaneous sucking on a pacifier washed out any HR effects associated with sensory stimuli.

Second, evidence is insufficient to permit use of such phasic HR decreases in a quantitative manner. That is to say, HR does not appear sufficiently sensitive to depict the intensity of interest or surprise. If, for example, we found that one individual manifested a greater phasic HR deceleration in response to a stimulus than another did, we would not feel very able on the basis of available data to conclude that the discrepancy reflected differences in how much interest either had in the stimulus. Our reservations on this matter are further strengthened by reports like that of Iacono and Lykken (1978). Theirs is one of the most extensive and systematic evaluations of HR as an index of attention. Although the results demonstrated an influence of the level of attention on performance and the commonly reported preparatory HR deceleration, the magnitude of the deceleration was not influenced by the manipulation of attention (it was of a similar amplitude across conditions). Furthermore, the HR deceleration was minimally related to performance either between or within subjects.

Third, we would recommend that investigators who wish to assess behavioral states focus their efforts on measures more directly concerned with that state than is HR. For example, if one were interested in determining whether an individual oriented toward a stimulus, eye movements should prove informative. They are not so very difficult to measure, and we have had uniformly good luck in obtaining clean records. Facial expression is another area with which Professor Izard is concerned. Although EMG measures are not as simple as eye movement, they might facilitate identification of emotion states (see Schwartz et al., 1980). One should keep in mind that the heart is much more distally involved in such behavioral processes than are the eyes and face. We contend that evolution does not require the heart to be particularly sensitive to behavioral states; the opposite view might be argued, if one considers that the heart is critically involved in life-sustaining functions. Might it not be placing too much responsibility on the cardiovascular system, which must supply the tissues with oxygen and nutrients, remove metabolic waste products, maintain kidney function, and keep the body temperature within narrow limits, to require that system also to be particularly sensitive to behavioral states?

Finally, our attitude might be better understood by briefly describing where our research efforts began and where they are going. Some of our earlier studies involved the use of HR to index arousal or attention. The results were not overly encouraging. Later, as we became involved with assessing neurohumoral mechanisms in the control of the heart, particularly sympathetic effects, our focus began to change. Our data necessitated some adjustment. In comparison with our earlier work, much more pronounced changes in myocardial activity were observed. The changes were more plausibly relevant to pathophysiology than as an index of some underlying behavioral process. The pronounced individual differences described earlier in this chapter further reinforced our attitude. We do not wish to imply that the myocardial changes that are now the subject of our attention, and the individual differences, are unrelated to some aspect of the individual's behavior. Active coping appears important, but the individual differences remain a mystery. In any case, when one finds oneself able to interpret a phenomenon (cardiovascular, in our case) more productively in one manner than in another, not surprisingly one's focus and attitudes change.

Notes

1 This is a procedure whereby parasympathetic or vagal influences on HR are prevented by the intravenous administration of the pharmacological blocking agent atropine. When sympathetic influences on the heart are evaluated, the procedure is similar except that the pharmacological agent is propranolol. In both cases, the agent selectively blocks the influence of one or the other innervation. Whatever HR response remains is attributed to the influence of the remaining intact innervation.
2 As a matter of clarification: This sympathetic influence is seen with both innervations intact. That this HR acceleration is in fact sympathetic in origin was determined by pharmacological blockade of the sympathetic innervations.

References

Ax, A. F. The physiological differentiations between fear and anger in humans. *Psychosomatic Medicine*, 1953, *15*, 433–42.

Cannon, W. D. *Bodily changes in pain, hunger, fear and rage*. New York: Appleton, 1929.

Clifton, R. K. The relation of infant cardiac responding to behavioral state and motor activity. In W. A. Collins (Ed.), *Minnesota Symposia on Child Psychology* (Vol. 11). Hillsdale, N.J.: Erlbaum, 1978.

Elliott, R. The motivational significance of heart rate. In P. A. Obrist, A. H. Black, J. Brener, & L. V. DiCara (Eds.), *Cardiovascular psychophysiology: Current issues in response mechanisms, biofeedback, and methodology*. Chicago: Aldine, 1974, 505–37.

Hastrup, J. L., Light, K. C., & Obrist, P. A. *Parental history of hypertension in relationship to sympathetic response to stress*. Manuscript submitted for publication, 1980.

Hofer, M. A. Cardiac and respiratory function during sudden prolonged immobility in wild rodents. *Psychosomatic Medicine*, 1970, *32*, 633–47.

Howard, J. L., Obrist, P. A., Gaebelein, C. J., & Galosy, R. A. Multiple somatic measures and heart rate during classical aversive conditioning in the cat. *Journal of Comparative and Physiological Psychology*, 1974, *87*, 228–36.

Iacono, W. G., & Lykken, D. T. Within-subject covariation of reaction time and foreperiod deceleration: Effect of respiration and imperative stimulus intensity. *Biological Psychology*, 1978, *7*, 287–302.

Jenkins, C. D. Recent evidence supporting psychologic and social risk factors for coronary disease. *New England Journal of Medicine*, 1976, *294*, 987–94; 1033–8.

Julius, S. Borderline hypertension: Epidemiologic and clinical implications. In J. Genest, E. Koiw, & O. Kuchel (Eds.), *Hypertension: Physiopathology and treatment*. New York: McGraw-Hill, 1977.

Julius, S. & Schork, M. A. Borderline hypertension: A critical review. *Journal of Chronic Disease*, 1971, *23*, 723–54.

Lawler, K. A., Obrist, P. A., & Lawler, J. E. Cardiac and somatic response patterns during a reaction time task in children and adults. *Psychophysiology*, 1976, *13*, 448–55.

Light, K. C., & Obrist, P. A. Cardiovascular response to stress: Effects of opportunity to avoid shock experience and performance feedback. *Psychophysiology*, 1980, *17*, 243–52. (a)

Light, K. C., & Obrist, P. A. Cardiovascular reactivity to behavioral stress in young males with normal and mildly elevated systolic pressures: A comparison of clinic, home and laboratory measures. *Hypertension*, 1980, *2*, 802–8. (b)

Lund-Johansen, P. Hemodynamics in early essential hypertension. *Acta Medica Scandinavica*, 1967, Suppl. 842.

Lund-Johansen, P. Spontaneous changes in central hemodynamics in essential hypertension – a 10 year follow up study. In G. Onesti & C. R. Klimt (Eds.), *Hypertension – determinants, complications and intervention*. New York: Grune & Stratton, 1979.

Notterman, J. M., Schonfeld, W. N., & Bersh, P. J. Conditioned heart rate responses in human beings during experimental anxiety. *Journal of Comparative and Physiological Psychology*, 1952, *45*, 1–8.

Obrist, P. A. Heart rate and somatic-motor coupling during classical aversive conditioning in humans. *Journal of Experimental Psychology*, 1968, *77*, 180–93.

Obrist, P. A., Gaebelein, C. J., Teller, E. S., Langer, A. W., Grignolo, A., Light, K. C., & McCubbin, J. A. The relationship among heart rate, carotid dP/dt and blood pressure in humans as a function of the type of stress. *Psychophysiology*, 1978, *15*, 102–15.

Obrist, P. A., Howard, J. L., Lawler, J. E., Galosy, R. A., Meyers, K. A. & Gaebelein, C. J. The cardiac somatic interaction. In P. A. Obrist, A. H. Black, J. Brener, & L. V. DiCara (Eds.), *Cardiovascular psychophysiology: Current issues in response mechanisms, biofeedback and methodology*. Chicago: Aldine, 1974.

Obrist, P. A., Howard, J. L., Sutterer, J. R., Hennis, R. S., & Murrell, D. J. Cardiac-somatic changes during a simple reaction time task: A developmental study. *Journal of Experimental Child Psychology*, 1973, *16*, 346–62.

Obrist, P. A., Langer, A. W., Light, K. C., Grignolo, A., & McCubbin, J. A. Myocardial performance and stress: Implications for basic and clinical research. In H. D. Kimmel, E. H. Van Olst, & J. F. Orleveke (Eds.), *The Orienting Reflex in Humans*. New York: Erlbaum, 1979.

Obrist, P. A., Lawler, J. E., Howard, J. L., Smithson, K. W., Martin, P. L., & Manning, J. Sympathetic influences on cardiac rate and contractility during acute stress in humans. *Psychophysiology*, 1974, *11*, 405–27.

Obrist, P. A., & Webb, R. A. Heart rate during conditioning in dogs: Relationship to somatic-motor activity. *Psychophysiology*, 1967, *4*, 7–34.

Obrist, P. A., Webb, R. A. & Sutterer, J. R. Heart rate and somatic changes during aversive conditioning and a simple reaction time task. *Psychophysiology*, 1969, *5*, 696–723.

Obrist, P. A., Webb, R. A., Sutterer, J. R., & Howard, J. L. The cardiac-somatic relationship: Some reformulations. *Psychophysiology*, 1970, *6*, 569–87. (a)

Obrist, P. A., Webb, R. A., Sutterer, J. R., & Howard, J. L. Cardiac deceleration and reaction time: An evaluation of two hypotheses. *Psychophysiology*, 1970, *6*, 695–706. (b)

Obrist, P. A., Wood, D. M., & Perez-Reyes, M. Heart rate during conditioning in humans: Effects of UCS intensity, vagal blockade and adrenergic block of vasomotor activity. *Journal of Experimental Psychology*, 1965, *70*, 32–42.

Paul, O. Epidemiology of hypertension. In J. Genest, E. Koiw, & O. Kuchel (Eds.), *Hypertension: Physiopathology and treatment*. New York: McGraw-Hill, 1977.

Rescorla, R. A., & Solomon, R. L. Two process learning theory: Relationships between Pavlovian conditioning and instrumental learning. *Psychological Review*, 1967, *74*, 151–82.

Roessler, R. R. Personality, psychophysiology and performance. *Psychophysiology*, 1973, *10*, 315–27.

Rotter, J. B. Generalized expectancies for internal versus external control of reinforcement. *Psychological Monographs*, 1966, *80*(1, Whole No. 609).

Schwartz, G. E., Brown, S. L., & Ahern, G. L., Facial muscle patterning and subject experience during affective imagery: Sex differences. *Psychophysiology*, 1980, *17*, 75–82.

Wood, D. M., & Obrist, P. A. Minimal and maximal sensory intake and exercise as unconditioned stimuli in human heart rate conditioning. *Journal of Experimental Psychology*, 1968, *76*, 254–62.

13   An ethological approach to research on facial expressions

William R. Charlesworth

Most of us share two commonsense beliefs about facial expressions: One is that outward changes in facial muscle movement are frequently associated with inward changes in emotional state; the other is that changes in facial muscle movement frequently serve as signals to others, thereby changing their behavior. Both beliefs are represented in scientific research. The former (the expressive aspect) has been a major concern of psychologists interested primarily in emotional states, how various body systems, including the facial nerves and related musculature, express these states, and how these states are recognized by others. The latter (the regulative aspect)[1] has been a major concern of a diverse group of researchers, including among them ethologists, anthropologists, primatologists, and some psychologists who are primarily interested in investigating the behavioral effect of facial muscle movements upon the individuals perceiving them and who wish to determine the socially adaptive function such movements may have for the individual making them. Psychologists and ethologists, of course, have been well aware of both aspects. Historically, though, psychologists have conducted a relatively vast amount of research on emotions in general, the bulk of which has been oriented toward the expressive aspect. (For treatments of this topic, see Ekman, Friesen, & Ellsworth, 1972; Izard, 1971; Knapp, 1963; Plutchik, 1962; and Tomkins, 1962, 1963). Ethologists, in contrast, have conducted a much smaller amount of research on facial expressions, and this little has been oriented more toward the regulative aspect than toward the expressive (Eibl-Eibesfeldt, 1975; Ploog, 1970).

In the present discussion, I will concentrate on the ethological approach to facial expressions. By *ethological* I mean an approach that has developed historically from the early work of Heinroth, Whitman, and Craig, to the later work of Lorenz, von Frisch, von Holst, Tinbergen, Baerends, Kortlandt, Hinde, and oth-

Special thanks go to Prof. Detlev Ploog, Max Planck Institute for Psychiatry, Munich, Germany, for providing the basic concept underlying this chapter and the encouragement by his good example to write it. Additional thanks go to Peter LaFreniere, Edward Reed, and Carroll Izard for their helpful comments on this chapter.

ers, all of whom have been influenced to one degree or another by what animals do every day in their natural habitats, by Darwin's work in particular, and by evolutionary theory in general. For those unfamiliar with ethology, I recommend starting with *Grzimek's Encyclopedia of Ethology* (Immelmann, 1977). Also, the present discussion includes some notions currently employed in sociobiology and evolutionary biology.[2]

The expressive/regulative distinction can be illustrated by a commonplace expression – the smile. People smile when they are pleased or happy, or even, as has been observed in infants, when they are sleeping. They also smile in social situations when they want to express their pleasure to others or to ward off hostile behavior. In the first instance we are interested in what the smile signifies, what measures of internal state are correlated with it, when it first occurs, whether it is cross-culturally recognizable, and so forth. Studying the expressive aspects of smiling poses relatively easier research tasks than studying its regulative aspects. Observing and describing the social conditions under which smiling occurs, the immediate effects it has on the observer (as well as on the individual smiling), and its adaptive function present in general no easy research task. This may be one reason why the expressive aspect has historically received much more emphasis than the regulative aspect.

A good example of this historical difference in emphasis can be found in Charles Darwin's classic *The Expression of Emotions in Man and Animals* (1872/1896). As the title suggests, Darwin placed almost exclusive emphasis in the book on the expressive aspect of emotions. In this respect he was more in anticipation of the psychologists' approach to facial expression than the ethologists'. Darwin was, however, aware of the regulative aspect. For example, he saw expressions as "the first means of communication between the mother and her infant" (p. 365) and noted that "the language of the emotions, as it has sometimes been called, is certainly of importance for the welfare of mankind" (p. 367). Such comments, however, appear to have had a negligible effect on most subsequent research on emotions. The impetus to focus on the regulative aspect of emotional expressions seems to have come primarily from animal watchers intrigued by the often strange antics of animal social behavior.

The animal watchers included ethologists, and as far as I can determine, they developed the idea that emotional behaviors had social significance. Historically ethologists have focused heavily upon reproductive behavior in animals, which by definition includes most if not all social behavior. Ethologists have also traditionally been interested in physical and social stimuli that release behavior. The notion of the sign stimulus evolved from this interest. Stimuli that originate in the behavior of Animal A and change the probability of behavior in Animal B came to be called social releasers, that is, signals communicating various kinds of information about the sender – subject information, such as age, sexual identity, and species membership, as well as behavioral or psychological information concerning the sender's readiness to attack, flee, mate, submit, and so forth. An introduction to the concept of social releaser can be found in Eibl-Eibesfeldt's (1975) chapters on releasers and their role in communication. The concept of the releaser seems to have developed from field observations of animal displays used in intraspecific communication. As Klopfer and Hailman (1972) note, displays have been the "favorite behavior patterns among ethologists," appearing in the modern ethological literature in the classic work of Lorenz (1941/1971), Daanje (1950), Morris (1956), and Tinbergen (1959). These ethologists, like those after them, were interested not only in the immediate function of displays in social situations but also in their evolutionary history. It is generally assumed that displays emerged from behavior patterns that originally possessed no communicative value (a process called *ritualization*). Such patterns include thermoregulatory behavior (feather fluffing in birds), defecation and urination, intention movements (beginning movements of attack or retreat), and displacement activities generated by conflict situations involving the simultaneous occurrence of approach and avoidance tendencies (yawning, scratching, and pecking – all out-of-context behaviors). These patterns appear in the animal's repertoire, possessing little or no communicative value, and only over evolutionary time do they acquire signal value for conspecifics. What an animal does as an isolated expression of a personal need, for example, may come to acquire communicative significance for others and may thereby assume a socially regulative function. Human facial expressions and gestures as well as other nonverbal behaviors can be viewed the same way, although they have not been given the same treatment by ethologists until quite recently.

Two good examples of such ethological work can be found in Zivin's (1977) study of how children use facial expressions in dominance relationships and in the Lockard et al. (1978) study of postural signals terminating social interactions. Using videotape records of children in naturalistic interactions, Zivin discovered that in winning and losing kinds of social encounters, high-ranking children (by peers' hierarchy rankings) make more facial expressions, similar to nonhuman primate dominance-related threat stares, than do low-ranking children. The simultaneous presence of raised brows and chin and a direct stare toward the other person's eyes (a display quite similar topologically to that of some species of monkey and ape) appears to be used instrumentally to control interactions in subtle and not-so-subtle ways by high-ranking children. In the Lockard et al. study, significant changes in posture were observed prior to ending a social interaction. Such changes were interpreted as signals of departure readiness, preparing the persons involved for a social transition. The transition can be viewed as facilitating "the continuance of affiliative ties while initiating a change in the social situation." As the authors point out, behavioral patterns other than postural changes, such as breaking eye contact, could also function as "intention signals to depart" (p. 223).

Why we should consider adopting the ethological position that emphasizes the regulative aspect of expressive behavior is a question we can answer in two ways. One stresses the limits of the approach taken by many psychologists, and the other provides both theoretical and empirical reasons why the ethological approach has the potential for stimulating new research in the area. Before investigating these two answers, I should make clear that distinguishing the expressive from the regulative aspect of emotional expressions is attempted in order to stimulate additional research, not to divide what cannot be divided.

One of the problems with a psychological term such as *emotion* is that it is a singular noun, which gives the impression that it refers to a single entity. This entity is usually defined in dictionaries as an affective state of which one is conscious. Psychologists frequently give the impression that the main purpose of their research is to discover the true nature of this state. One could, however, argue that *emotion* is not solely a name for an affective state but a relational term referring to a number of diverse events, internal and external, that occur simultaneously and sequentially in a more or less consistent way. Such diverse events include cognitive and external physical events as well as conscious affective states, none of which alone constitutes the emotion and none of which occurs the same way twice.

Surprise research provides an example. After collecting many cinematographic samples of individuals in surprise situations, it became clear that the facial expressions immediately following the onset of what we thought were surprise stimuli varied greatly in form across individuals and often quite frequently within individuals. We were initially puzzled by this, for we were expecting the "real" expression of surprise to reveal itself. It did not, not even after more than a hundred hours of close inspection of 16 millimeter film records. We began to realize that such an expectation was unreasonable and began paying attention to the surprise stimulus itself and to the cognitive state of the subject. We were subsequently led to conclude that conceptualizing about surprise required simultaneous cognizance of sets of variables, not just a particular facial expression or verbal report of surprise. These variables included: the stimulus supposedly causing the surprise reaction, the subject's expectation of the stimulus, and the subject's reaction to the stimulus after it was perceived. These three sets of variables were by necessity linked, suggesting that *surprise* had best be considered as a relational term – one that only made sense when it was used to connect perceptual/cognitive, external stimulus, and motor expressive variables (along with verbal reports, if the researcher desired). The matter became complicated, however, when we became aware of the commonplace observation that some people can produce an authentic facial expression of surprise. Conscious intention thus entered the picture, and with it the idea that expressions (even the so-called cognitive emotions like surprise) can be used to regulate social behavior.

Two substantive conclusions resulted from this surprise research: (a) Surprise is a multivariate phenomenon, not a psychological entity that expresses itself behaviorally in a standard way – it is instead a label for a complex network of measurable emotional and cognitive events, external stimuli, observable behaviors, and phenomenological as well as social consequences, and (b) surprise can be productively viewed as multifunctional response, serving expressive functions as well as playing a role in cognitive development (Charlesworth, 1969). If this were true for surprise, why not for other emotions? In attempting to answer this question we found ourselves raising the issue of the conceptual paradigm used by psychologists. By viewing emotions as covert unitary entities that could be made accessible with increasingly better neurophysiological probes and microscopic analysis of facial muscle movements, psychologists may have excluded many important variables from emotion research.

The surprise research also resulted in another conclusion – a methodological one, namely that the standard research on surprise may have relied too heavily upon an experimental approach (including assessment). Experimentation has been without question the most esteemed methodology of modern scientific psychology. In his 1962 *Encyclopaedia Britannica* article on emotion, Landis expressed a well-established view among psychologists that elevated the experimental method above others in establishing scientific evidence of a phenomenon: "There does not exist a sufficient experimentally determined evidence upon which to formulate a complete or satisfactory explanation of the psychological experience of emotion. Our knowledge of the topic of emotion is much less complete than our knowledge of most of the other basic topics in the field of psychology." This view, accompanied by improvements in techniques for recording and analyzing expressions of emotions, may have prematurely narrowed our research approach to emotion as well as limiting its conceptual basis. A more observational, descriptive approach with attention paid to the wide variations of emotional expression in everyday life and the effects such expressions have on others could have led us more rapidly to other aspects of expressions such as the regulative function observed by animal observers.

Sixteen years after Landis's article, Grastyan in *The New Encyclopaedia Britannica* defined emotion as "verbally expressible subjective experiences; concomitant internal changes, and observable motor behavior (e.g., facial expression, gesture, posture)." This was presumably not an idiosyncratic definition: Grastyan's bibliography includes such major authorities on emotions as Young, Arnold, Hebb, Gellhorn and Loofbourrow, and Candland. Grastyan's definition accounts for emotions in terms of three major factors – subjective, autonomic, and motor expressive, all three also covered in Landis's article. The definition does not include the regulative or communicative aspect of emotion, nor its relationship to instrumental behavior in general. These aspects, however, were not unknown to psychologists at the time.

Fifteen years before Grastyan's article, Knapp (1963) edited the results of a symposium paying tribute to Darwin's pioneering efforts in developing a theory of emotional expression. In this volume, entitled *Expressions of Emotions in Man*, researchers from a number of different disciplines presented their views on emotion. Birdwhistell, an anthropologist, made a case for studying "those patterned and learned aspects of body motion which can be demonstrated to have communicational value" (p. 125). Birdwhistell's now well known work in kinetics represents a major effort in the direction he suggested, but it was not pursued as it deserved to be. Bateson, arguing for a social scientist's point of view, felt that emotion researchers should take Pribram's use of the term *signals of state* as a starting point of social research experiments. Representing psychiatry and an evolutionary point of view, Hamburg carried the communicative aspect of emotion expressions into the scheme of human evolution by emphasizing the survival need for communication in establishing stable bonds between infants and parents and between adult group members in general. In his concluding remarks on the symposium, Knapp noted that the communicative aspect of emotion expression was "most emphasized and for that reason requiring least comment." He added: "From the start of life emotions signalize needs, attitudes, anticipations, and impulses toward action. They are socially adaptive" (p. 332).

In short, the notion that expressive behavior should be studied in terms of adaptive communication (regulation) was clearly available to psychologists, but it was not heeded in any significant way. After Knapp's volume appeared, Bowlby (1969) and Spitz (1965), both within the ethological tradition, were, to my knowledge, among the first to stress the important adaptive function of infant expressive behavior as signaling needs and facilitating the bonding process. More recently, Izard (1979) touched upon the socially adaptive value of expressive behavior in a general discussion of an evolutionary–developmental perspective of emotions, and Ekman (1979) developed the notion of emotional and nonverbal conversational signals, noting the neglect of the latter in the research literature and emphasizing the importance of such signals in communicating social and personal information to others. In spite of the insights of such writers (and undoubtedly because of the relatively recent appearance of their work), the implications of the evolutionary point of view have still not been taken seriously, at least not by those doing empirical studies. Traditionally most psychologists structure their research activities around experimental situations of relatively short duration that take place in settings of little if any ecological validity and with primary focus upon the manipulation of a small number of preselected stimuli. Procedures for documenting dependent variables usually consist of closely observing changes in facial expression, measuring autonomic activity, or interviewing or testing subjects on points of facial expression recognition. All of these are, obviously, valuable activities. But the interesting question of whether expressive behaviors engaged in spontaneously in everyday life situations play an instrumental role in regulating social behavior has not been pursued. And the even more interesting question of whether the effects of regulating social behavior actually have any consequences for the individual's adaptation or even survival has hardly been addressed by anyone. This, then, I see as a limit of the traditional psychological view of emotion expressions. The question of whether the ethological approach can proceed beyond this limit remains to be answered.

The crux of the ethological approach to emotions and their expressions has its roots in early formulations of instinct theory. In an essay on affect and emotion, Peters (1963) described Darwin's position as one in which emotions constitute the "feeling or awareness side of instincts." Because instincts by definition involve innate behavior patterns that usually serve adaptive functions, emotions are by necessity implicated in adaptive instrumental behavior. McDougall's theory of instinct established significant links between perceptions, motives, emotions, and actions – all operated together because all were functionally aimed at achieving the same adaptive goal. According to Peters, "The modern comparative ethologist school has improved on this theoretical view by introducing the concept of the inner releasing mechanism which is activated by stimuli . . . and which triggers modifiable behavior patterns" (p. 439). Peters further maintained that such an approach was fruitful in studying innate behavior in animals but had not been applied to human beings, and had the effect of making emotion recede "into the forest of behavior." The emphasis of ethology upon behavior has undoubtedly diminished the research importance of unobservable internal states. The crucial historical point here is that the notion that actions and emotions are linked together became part of the ethologist's thinking quite early. Fletcher (1966) in *Instinct in Man* described in detail how numerous writers (McDougall, Freud, Drever, and others) viewed emotion as playing a dominant role in man's instinctual life by reinforcing impulse, interest, persistence, *and* behavior. An updated representation of this view can be found in Izard's (1978) discussion of the facilitative role of emotions during early ontogenesis. According to Izard, one of the major functions of emotions is to facilitate various aspects of cognitive development as well as interactions with the environment, the result being the gradual formation over ontogenesis of multiple links between emotions and basic behavioral survival processes. This view is similar in many ways to that taken here.

Darwin's more specific point that facial expressions themselves could be socially adaptive, nonadaptive, or even maladaptive (all depending) becomes a special directive to ethologists because it emphasizes not only the communicative aspect of emotions but how the social effects of such communication become part of the evolutionary process. In an updated reinforcement of Darwin's view, Ghiselin (1974) noted that "it makes nonetheless a great deal of sense that emotional conditions would play a major role in determining how organisms communicate and how their means of communication will evolve" (p. 261). Ghiselin also noted that present-day successors to Darwin "tend to presuppose that emotional expressions are there for the sake of communication, ignoring Darwin's view that some have a communicative function but others do not" (p. 255). Obviously, the only way to test the hypothesis that emotions have regulative functions is to study facial expressions in naturalistic social conditions and observe what happens.

As noted in the beginning of this discussion, the connection between emotional expression and instrumental acts related to survival was realized early by ethologists and was studied under the rubric of displays that evolved by the process of ritualization of behaviors originally having no communicative value. The conceptual bond between emotion expression and instrumental behavior is, however, even stronger than that formed by the notion of ritualization. Darwin's first general principle of emotions, the principle of "serviceable associated habits," attempted to show how instrumental behaviors in the service of some body need could, in some abbreviated or slightly variant form, come to acquire signal value. Horses accustomed to pulling carriages (and to being rewarded afterward for doing so) may come to paw the ground when left hitched to the carriage too long. Their pawing is interpreted as a sign of their eagerness to pull the carriage. The point here is that not only can expressive behaviors come to have instrumental value, but instrumental behaviors can come to have expressive value that communicates information about internal states – another good reason to view expressive behavior within the context of adaptive social behavior.

When we connect instrumental and expressive behavior in this way we are inevitably led to pay close attention to the consequences of behavior. In his article "Emotion" for *The New Encyclopaedia Britannica,* Grastyan was aware of this and maintained (apparently with some hesitation), that "a definition of emotion would have to qualify the relevant phenomena, to note conditions that bring them about, and perhaps to specify their consequences." Grastyan did not have to qualify his insight with "perhaps." The key notion in the communicative approach to expressions is precisely that of consequences. We need to ask what happens socially as a result of a facial expression and whether what happens is positive, neutral, or negative for the persons involved. When we ask these questions we are presupposing that the consequences of expressive behavior serve some vital function in the sense that they enable the persons involved to get a life job done (no matter how small or large).

From the ethological view, behavioral consequences play a paramount role in helping us understand the proximal mechanisms that give rise to and control behavior and shed some light on the ultimate reasons for the behavior's presence in the animal (species). Animals engage in most behaviors, we can assume, because their consequences are valuable. For the individual this includes all behaviors, instrumental (conscious, voluntary) and expressive (unconscious, involuntary).

In either case, the theory of evolution by natural (and sexual) selection is relevant. Selection operates upon behaviors as well as upon other phenotypic features of the organism. The consequences of doing, or failing to do, something can be viewed as biologically relevant in the sense that the reproductive fitness of an individual, relative to others, is increased, reduced, or destroyed by specific behavioral acts.[3] The extent to which a particular behavior contributes to fitness can range from very minimal to drastic or could conceivably (though theoretically improbably) be neutral. What is of interest to ethologists (and, of course, sociobiologists) is how the consequences of everyday behavior per se affect the level of individual adaptation in both the short run and the long run. The long run may include the number of offspring the individual leaves to future generations as well as the individual's general health and welfare.

Much of human and nonhuman primate adaptation is achieved by social behavior. Nonsocial behavior (usually labeled *maintenance behavior*) includes such things as sleeping, resting, locomoting, caring for the body's surface, ingesting, seeking food, building shelter, acquiring relevant adaptive skills, and so forth. Both classes are not unconnected, although social behavior, by definition, is carried out in all the interaction with other members of the same species that takes place from birth to death.

When we consider a human's total life span, at least two major life tasks involving social behavior become apparent. Early in life it is vitally important for the infant to attach itself to an adult and to insure that the adult is attached to it. Without a caring adult the infant would perish. Later on in life it is vitally important for the individual to establish a working relationship with members of its own group, both male and female. Without these relationships the individual would not have adequate access to vital space, food, shelter, and other resources and also would not reproduce. In most cases, primate isolates barely survive if at all. During this second phase (i.e., after the individual is more or less weaned from its parents) at least two major classes of behavior (with peers or other adults) are necessary – cooperative behavior and competitive behavior. According to the orthodox sociobiological view, both classes of behaviors serve the same ultimate purpose – to insure that the individual survives and reproduces his/her genes, often at cost to others (v. Dawkins, 1976). It is also recognized by sociobiologists that competition is widespread in animal species but not universal and that there are no data to assert that competition is a universally inevitable human behavior when vital resources are in short supply. Nevertheless, competition is a very common human behavior and may be more widespread than originally believed if other behaviors, such as deception, are subsumed under it. Whether or not the sociobological view in general is totally justified when applied to human behavior is an empirical matter. So far it has raised some interesting questions. If individuals are basically selfish, and outright aggression (as ethologists and sociobiologists are wont to believe) is uneconomical and dangerous for all involved, how do individuals compete and why and when do they cooperate (or appear to cooperate)?

One answer of primary interest here is that in order to cooperate and still serve one's own needs successfully, individuals must master the various prosocial skills required by the group. These skills include instrumental behaviors recognized as consciously intended acts toward others that maintain social harmony. Individuals must also master certain expressive skills that have the effect of making impressions upon others and consequently influence their behavior. Because expressive behavior is usually considered unintentional (spontaneous and unreflective), it is frequently viewed as more revealing of the individual's true feelings, ideas, and attitudes than is instrumental behavior. Expressive behavior, however, can also be considered as intentional. An individual may intentionally smile in order to reduce uneasiness in others, even when that person is not even remotely happy or feeling friendly at the moment. Acting out emotional behaviors in order to regulate the behavior of others, in other words, can be a very common phenomenon. Also, individuals can conceal from others their motives, feelings, and plans, as well as their selfish or antisocial actions. In addition, individuals can detect deception in others; without at least some rudiments of this ability, most individuals would conceivably be at a great disadvantage. Acquiring deception skills might be one of the most important parts of the human socialization process. Alexander (1979) suggested that the function of teaching children games conceivably is to get children to follow rules as well as to learn how to cheat in acceptable ways without getting caught. Games could thus serve a number of societal functions – bonding individuals to each other and to the group, teaching socially acceptable rules and cooperation, and also showing how deception is possible and perhaps necessary in certain situations in order to satisfy one's own needs fully. It should be quickly pointed out that from an evolutionary point of view, prosocial behavior and honesty are without question necessary for the individual; without them reproductive success would be virtually impossible. Nevertheless, we should recognize that antisocial behavior and deception are widespread human strategies because of the competition inherent in virtually every human group, including the family. One who can cooperate and who on occasion can appear to be cooperating when in fact competing is at a decidedly greater advantage in most human groups than one who does not have these skills. Apropos of animal behavior, there is a growing body of literature suggesting that animal signals may be more socially manipulative than is currently thought (Dawkins & Krebs, 1978). Honesty about intentions and emotional states in the form of clear-cut behavioral displays may be only one social strategy among animals; another strategy includes such behavior as various forms of deception.

It is reasonable to assume that the ability to engage in deceptive behavior and to detect such behavior is acquired during normal development. As far as I can determine, systematic research on the process of this acquisition in humans has not yet been carried out. Perhaps the first instance of it is in the young infant's discovery that crying (a reflex, or respondent) brings positive results; sometime later, crying becomes an operant employed on increasing number of occasions in order to repeat the original positive results. As the child grows older he or she learns how to act the part of an imaginary friend, how to keep a straight face when telling a fib, how to act overjoyed in the presence of a person who just gave a nice gift with the promise of giving more, how to flatter a friend into giving more candy or a bully into stop pushing. The child also comes to know that someone is "just kidding" or is telling a lie, and, alas, in adulthood the person can become seriously involved in various forms of deception, some so subtle as to deceive well-trained custom officials, loved ones, supervisors and employees and, as Alexander and Noonan (1979) point out, even oneself. Furthermore, deception can become formalized in the sense that some professions, legitimate and otherwise, are built upon people's abilities to feign certain emotions and other people's ability to judge them as sincere.

The face, from what we know of it, is one of the most sensitive areas for display of human emotion and intention, possibly even more so than voice and posture. There is a wealth of information on this topic that need not be mentioned here. As intimated earlier, however, most of this information has been obtained in experimental (assessment) situations. These situations may or may not reflect what is going on in the outside world as far as everyday use and recognition of facial expression are concerned. Definitely not revealed by the experimental approach are: (a) the frequency with which and situational contexts in which theoretically interesting and relatively easily discriminable facial expressions are used in social situations, (b) the nature of the immediate effect that the expressions have on the social relationship, and (c) the long-term effect, if any, that certain expressions have on the individual's adaptation and reproductive success. The latter is obviously a rather stringent requirement (somewhat ludicrous at first glance) to place on any study. It is not an impossible requirement to meet, however. For example, the effects of greeting and flirting behavior must certainly be related to human social adaptation and reproduction, as Eibl-Eibesfeldt (1979) shows in his cross-cultural studies. And as Savitsky and Eby (1979) have pointed out on the basis of a review of many studies, joyful people (presumably those who smile a lot) are seen as very likable and hence most probably have a social, and consequently a reproductive, advantage over those who are not. Also, people who show distress generally managed to weather aggressive attacks better than those who do not show distress – appeasement behaviors such as crying, moaning, and complaining most probably aid survival in a significant way. Examples of such findings can also be found in Ann Landers's column or in a good novel. More scientific knowledge of them as they occur in everyday situations is still badly needed, however. Obtaining such knowledge requires a particular kind of research strategy, one that ethology is in a good position to supply. Four major features of the strategy will be discussed here.

1. The research focus is upon everyday life situations in which social interaction has an indeterminate outcome because individual skills rather than social rules regulate the interaction and hence determine its outcome. For example, we would not focus on paying for an article in most stores in the United States because the outcome is regulated from the beginning. Paying for an article in stores in countries where striking the best bargain is expected could be the focus of our attention, however, because the outcome is dependent upon individual skills, part of which are expressive behaviors. In such life situations at least one member of the interaction needs the goods, service, recognition, permission, and so forth from the other. Some examples of such situations may be found in the Lockhard et al. (1976) study of panhandling. Others include times when drivers are stopped by police for a traffic violation; when a subordinate asks a superordinate for a salary or wage increase; when there is conflict between two children in a schoolyard; when children go to the principal's office for violations; when adults are interviewed by the Internal Revenue Service; when lone encounters take place between same-age, different-sex individuals on elevators; and when a supervisor is compelled to induce subordinates to work harder and enjoy it. In such situations asymmetries in needs and abilities lead to social interactions in which the individuals involved must regulate the behavior of the other in such a way as to maximize the chances of their own success. Although competition and cooperation can be mixed in complex ways, thus complicating data collection and evaluation, outcomes are usually simple to determine – Participant A succeeds, or B succeeds, or neither succeeds. Trichotomizing the outcomes of social interactions in this manner is a widespread research strategy, ranging from studies of children's behavior (Furman & Masters, 1978) to a biobehavioral approach to politics (Wiegele, 1979). What is important to emphasize here is that such asymmetrical situations are not constructed by the researcher (as part of an experimental or assessment setting) but are allowed to occur spontaneously (hence unpredictably) in everyday contexts where the outcome is of direct personal sig-

nificance to the participants involved. Only then can the behavior released by such situations be connected in any meaningful way to adaptation or reproductive success. The connection may be remote, minuscule, or even impossible to establish for a particular individual, but sampling many similar situations involving different individuals will eventually shed light on the general nature of the adaptation problems themselves, their outcomes and, conceivably, the evolutionary origins of the behaviors involved. Research on the fear grin in primates involved in agonistic encounters is a good example of this (Chevalier-Skolnikoff, 1973).

2. Once the research focus has been selected, at least three aspects of the situations subsumed under it should be documented – the conditions surrounding and immediately leading up to them, the behaviors involved, which include the expressive behaviors (the primary target); the associated overt instrumental behaviors (smiling is an example of the expressive; giving flowers to the hostess of a dinner party is an example of the instrumental); and the immediate consequences of the behaviors for both the actor and receiver (the hostess smiles and says, "Thank you," the giver nods and smiles, "You're welcome") and the accompanying subjective (cognitive/affective) consequences for both, as determined afterward by short interviews (the giver reports feeling successful or pleased that he has made the hostess happy or achieved a small gain; the hostess reports a positive feeling mixed with a bit of uneasiness because a debt may have been incurred or the act may not have been totally sincere). All three aspects are viewed as integral parts of the encounter, each deriving a portion of its significance from the other two. That the overt instrumental behavior is recorded along with the expressive, even though the main emphasis is upon the latter, is very important because such a combination is the only grounds upon which the function of the act of giving flowers and smiling can be adequately ascertained. A field experiment in which smiling is replaced by a neutral face or look of seriousness can be conducted at a subsequent date to determine the exact role the smile plays. The possible long-term consequences of such an act may be estimated on the basis of knowing more about the relationship between giver and hostess, the customs of the time, and so forth. Shoring up a weakening relationship, strengthening an already strong relationship, starting a new relationship – each possibility can be viewed in terms of the wider contribution of the relationship to each participant's life. Jobs may be involved, social contacts important to obtain other services, positive recommendations for one's children, and so forth. Although such behavior may be coolly calculated or warmly spontaneous, it is important to keep in mind that despite its relatively infrequent and rapid occurrence, its relative simplicity, and cultural expectedness, it makes a contribution to the social relationships of both participants and hence may have a significant effect on the participant's overall adaptation.

3. Selecting those aspects of facial expression as primary targets is part of the

major strategy. It is not necessarily a difficult job. Smiling and visual attention (looking at, staring at, gazing at) are, as many psychological studies have demonstrated, important behaviors to record, including their variations – smiling nervously, glancing instead of looking for a predictable period of time, and so forth. A fine-grained analysis of expressive behaviors (especially the details of the variations) filmed at high speed may be unnecessary, even during an exploratory study, to determine which categories will be useful. Only behaviors that make a difference to the participants need be recorded. It is conceivable that a large number of discrete facial movements are socially irrelevant in everyday situations in the sense that they play no role in regulating behavior. Simple questionnaire responses by a hundred or so adults to a number of filmed instances (from television or motion pictures) may be sufficient to identify and categorize a significantly large number of socially regulative facial expressions. More complex or less stereotyped responses may have to be identified, described, and documented for observer training on the basis of detailed analysis of films or videotapes. One could, however, take another tack and ask the participants what they experienced during the interchange and how they would interpret or explain it. In such situations a mixture of behavioristic and phenomenalistic approaches is perhaps the most fruitful. In any case, a sensitivity to comparable situations in other species can also be helpful, along with an awareness of the broader evolutionary implications of similar situations for the evolution of primate species.

Apropos of the question of evolutionary significance and the issue of what expressions to focus upon we might consider Mayr's (1974) notion of closed and open behavioral programs. The former is a "genetic program that does not allow appreciable modifications during the process of translation in the phenotype"; it is one in which "nothing can be inserted in it through experience" (p. 651). An open program is a "genetic program that allows for additional input during the lifespan of its owner" (ibid.). These terms, which represent Mayr's way of dealing with the historical controversy about innate versus learned behavior, are not simply new labels for old phenomena. Mayr goes an interesting step further by arguing that closed programs could be adaptive in environments where the relevant releasing stimulus conditions were relatively constant across generations. Each new generation of a particular species would not have to learn anew the important dimensions of life-relevant stimuli if the stimuli never changed and each member of the generation had a closed program for recognizing the stimuli and producing them when it was appropriate to do so. An open program, conversely, enables each generation to learn during ontogeny the characteristics of life-relevant stimuli that are variable across, and even within, generations. For example, the stimulus characteristics of the animal's physical habitat may change significantly season by season, perhaps even daily, hence the animal must be able to explore and learn (insert new experiences into the program) in order to respond appropriately to the environment. The novel point that Mayr makes is that the invariant stimuli for most animals usually come from the physical and behavioral characteristics of conspecifics. Conspecifics maintain their identity across generations, thereby making recognition of them possible for reproductive purposes. On this basis, then, we could plan our strategy on the assumption that an important class of human social behaviors, such as facial expressions, may well be sufficiently stereotyped to allow more or less immediate recognition (such as the smile), and there may be a relatively small number of such expressions, each with a better than chance likelihood of being associated with certain types of competitive/cooperative social situations. The same would also be true for response mechanisms that make such facial expressions fairly standard across species members. Eibl-Eibesfeldt (1979) and Ekman (1972) have contributed empirical data to support this notion. The main point here, then, is that a relatively small number of facial expressions may well regulate many kinds of human social encounters. These expressions are known by most, if not all, adults and are relatively simple to detect, describe, and consciously manipulate once they are recognized as important. Hence field studies of such expressions most probably can be carried out without permanent recording devices and concern for high-speed photography of microanalysis of nuances. All that may be needed is an alert observer (participant observer when appropriate). What an average adult (and child for that matter) cannot pick up in a significant social situation could conceivably have little or no significant communicative value and hence could serve no socially regulatory function. This approach, of course, would recognize large individual differences in recognition and production of socially regulative facial expressions.

4. The last feature of an ethological research strategy for studying expressive behavior has to do with the individual and the characteristic circumstances associated with his or her life that lie outside the situations of social interaction in which the expressive behaviors occur. This feature is perhaps at first glance the most impractical for researchers, for it requires putting the individual's behavior into a much broader life framework than has ever been used in facial expression work. Still, it is not as unrealistic as it appears, if one considers the use to which good clinicians put information about their patients' past problems and life circumstances when they interpret current behavior, instrumental as well as expressive. The Savitsky and Eby (1979) study is a step in this direction as far as particular expressions are concerned. The main point here is that expressive behavior cannot be viewed in isolation. Information about life context, especially that involving individual survival and reproductive behavior, can serve as valuable material for interpreting the meaning and subsequent significance of expressive behaviors occurring in social encounters. When such encounters are viewed as instances in which cooperative and competitive behaviors between individuals

are played out in all their complexity, we have made an important step toward understanding the significance of facial expressions in regulating social interaction.

In summary, then, the ethological approach has a unique and somewhat complicating contribution to make to the study of facial expressions. It emphasizes the role that expressions play in regulating everyday social behavior; it focuses upon the adaptive nature of such behavior that makes a significant difference to the individuals engaged in it; it emphasizes the importance of looking at such behavior in terms of the competitive/cooperative nature of social interaction, thereby bringing the study of human behavior into a comparative and evolutionary framework; it sharpens our attention to the widespread use of deception in social interaction and gives a rationale for why deception strategy is closely tied with expressive behavior; and it puts expressive behaviors into the widest context possible – the survival of the individual and the species.

Notes

1 The term *regulative* is used here to stress the necessity for studying the behavioral consequences of emotional behavior for the observer of the behavior. *Communicative* is often used by psychologists and occasionally by ethologists and could be used in contradistinction to *expressive*, but I feel it is not strong enough. A particular facial expression could communicate a particular emotion to an observer but have no effect on his or her behavior. *Regulative* suggests that the observer's behavior is visibly affected and hence can be studied objectively along with its consequences. Izard (1980) suggests that specific reference should be made to the fact that *social* regulation is meant here, not *internal* or *self-regulation,* which is viewed by Gelhorn, Izard, and others as an important function of emotion expression. This suggestion is well taken. Hereafter, *regulative* will be used to refer specifically to social regulation.

2 The labels *ethology, sociobiology,* and *evolutionary biology* currently share a number of connotations. The last named, often viewed as subsuming the former two, covers a much wider range of phenomena, of which behavior and its adaptive significance are only a part. Sociobiology deals mostly with social groups and their relationship to reproductive fitness of individuals. Ethology, in contrast, focuses more upon individuals and their social as well as nonsocial adaptations. Because of significant refinements of evolutionary theory within the past decade or so, biologists have grown more convinced that the evolution of traits took place at the individual level, not at the group level (species, breeding populations, or social groups). The research implications of this statement are that the process of individual adaptation must be studied in greater detail as well as longitudinally. Ethology has more conceptual and methodological tools for the operationalization of evolutionary concepts at the individual behavioral level than does sociobiology, which heretofore has relied heavily upon population statistics or behavioral consequences rather than on the behavioral process of adaptation itself. For this reason I feel that ethology is presently the more qualified discipline for addressing specific issues of behavior adaptations and their role in evolution, especially when humans are involved, whose behavioral processes must be observed in action. Actually, the issue of how to label the present approach to the study of the function of facial expressions involves questions more of semantics and economy than of substance. Many sociobiologists use the same methods as ethologists, and some of the important concepts in the present approach have been directly taken from sociobiology.

3 *Reproductive success* refers to the extent to which an individual contributes his or her genes to subsequent generations, relative to other individuals. The contribution can be in terms of number of surviving offspring (children) and their offspring (grandchildren) as well as in terms of the offspring of genetic relatives. In humans, reproductive behavior can be defined functionally in terms of the extent to which a particular behavior contributes to reproductive success. This means that a wide range of behavior (whatever the environment requires) can be defined as being reproductive to one degree or another. Included in this range are such obvious behaviors as: flirting, bonding, copulating, carrying and delivering offspring, caring for offspring during infancy, supporting offspring physically and emotionally later on in life, insuring them a proper education, and safeguarding their security when they are adults as well as the security and welfare of their own offspring.

References

Alexander, R. *Dominance and human affairs*. Seattle: University of Washington Press, 1979.

Alexander, R. D., & Noonon, K. M. Concealment of ovulation, parental care and human social evolution. In N. A. Chagnon & W. Irons (Eds.), *Evolutionary biology and human social behavior: An anthropological perspective*. North Scituate, Mass.: Duxbury Press, 1979.

Bowlby, J. *Attachment and loss* (Vol. 1). New York: Basic Books, 1969.

Charlesworth, W. R. The role of surprise in cognitive development. In D. Elkind & J. Flavell (Eds.), *Studies in cognitive development: Essays in honor of Jean Piaget*. New York: Oxford University Press, 1969.

Chevalier-Skolnikoff, S. Facial expression of emotion in nonhuman primates. In P. Ekman (Ed.), *Darwin and facial expression: A century of research in review*. New York: Academic Press, 1973.

Daanje, A. On locomotory movements in birds and the intention movements derived from them. *Behaviour*, 1950, *3*, 49–98.

Darwin, C. *The expressions of the emotions in man and animals*. New York: Appleton, 1896. (Originally published, 1872.)

Dawkins, R. *The selfish gene*. New York: Oxford University Press, 1976.

Dawkins, R., & Krebs, J. R. Animal signals: Information or manipulation? In Krebs, F. R., & Davies, N. B. (Eds.), *Behavioural ecology: An evolutionary approach*. Sunderland, Mass.: Sinauer, 1978, 282–309.

Eibl-Eibesfeldt, I. *Ethology: The biology of behavior* (2nd ed.). New York: Holt, Rinehart & Winston, 1975.

Eibl-Eibesfeldt, I. Human ethology: Concepts and implications for the science of man. *The behavioral and brain sciences*, 1979, *2*, 1–57.

Ekman, P. Universals and cultural differences in facial expressions of emotion. In J. K. Cole (Ed.), *Nebraska Symposium on Motivation* (Vol. 19). Lincoln: University of Nebraska Press, 1972.

Ekman, P. About brows: Emotional and conversational signals. In M. von Cranach, K. Foppa, W. Lepenies, & D. Ploog (Eds.), *Human ethology: Claims and limits of a new discipline*. Cambridge, England: Cambridge University Press, 1979.

Ekman, P., Friesen, W. V., & Ellsworth, P. *Emotion in the human face*. New York: Pergamon Press, 1972.

Fletcher, R. *Instinct in Man*. New York: Schocken, 1966.

Furman, W., & Masters, J. C. *An observational system for coding reinforcing, neutral and punitive interactions among children*. Minneapolis, Minn.: Institute of Child Development, 1978.

Ghiselin, M. T. *The economy of nature and the evolution of sex*. Berkeley: University of California Press, 1974.

Immelmann, K. (Ed.). *Grzimek's encyclopedia of ethology*. New York: Van Nostrand Reinhold, 1977.

Izard, C. E. *The face of emotions*. New York: Appleton-Century-Crofts, 1971.

Izard, C. E. On the development of emotions and emotion-cognition relationships in infancy. In M. Lewis & L. A. Rosenblum (Eds.), *The development of affect*. New York: Plenum Press, 1978.

Izard, C. E. Emotions as motivations: An evolutionary-developmental projective. In H. E. Howe & R. Dienstbier (Eds.), *Nebraska Symposium on Motivation* (Vol. 26). Lincoln: University of Nebraska Press, 1979.

Izard, C. E. Personal communication, July 1980.

Klopfer, D. H., & Hailman, J. P. (Eds.). *Function and evolution of behavior: An historical sample from the pens of ethologists*. Reading, Mass.: Addison-Wesley, 1972.

Knapp, P. H. (Ed.). *Expression of the emotions in man*. New York: International Universities Press, 1963.

Lockard, J. S., Allen, D. J., Schiele, B. J., & Wiemar, M. J. Human posture signals: Stance, right shifts, and social distance as intention movements to depart. *Animal Behaviour*, 1978, *26*, 219–24.

Lockard, J. S., McDonald, L. L., Clifford, D. A., & Martinex, R. Panhandling: Sharing of resources. *Science*, 1976, *191*, 406–8.

Lorenz, K. Comparative studies of the motor patterns of *Anatinae*. In Lorenz, K., *Studies in animal and human behaviour* (Vol. 2). Cambridge, Mass.: Harvard University Press, 1971. (Paper originally published, 1941.)

Mayr, E. Behavior programs and evolutionary strategies. *American Scientist*, 1974, *62*, 650–9.

Morris, D. The feather postures of birds and the problem of the origin of social signals. *Behaviour*, 1956, *9*, 75–113.

Peters, H. N. Affect and emotion. In M. Marx, (Ed.), *Theories in contemporary psychology*. New York: Macmillan, 1963.

Ploog, D. Social communication among animals. In F. O. Schmitt (Ed.), *The neurosciences: Second study program*. New York: Rockefeller University Press, 1970.

Plutchik, R. *The emotions: Facts, theories and a new model*. New York: Random House, 1962.

Savitsky, J. C., & Eby, T. Emotion awareness and antisocial behavior. In C. E. Izard (Ed.), *Emotions in personality and psychopathology*. New York: Plenum Press, 1979.

Spitz, R. A. *The first year of life*. New York: International Universities Press, 1965.

Tinbergen, N. Comparative studies of the behavior of gulls (*Laridae*): A progress report. *Behaviour*, 1959, *15*, 1–70.

Tomkins, S. S. *Affect, imagery, consciousness: Vol 1. The positive affects*. New York: Springer, 1962.

Tomkins, S. S. *Affect, imagery, consciousness: Vol. 2. The negative affects*. New York: Springer, 1963.

Wiegele, T. C. *Biopolitics: Search for a more human political science*. Boulder, Colo.: Westview Press, 1979.

Zivin, G. On becoming subtle: Age and social rank changes in the use of facial gestures. *Child Development*, 1977, *48*, 1314–21.

14   The construction of emotion in the child

George Mandler

My comments are informed by a long interest in the origin of emotional experience and behavior and a very recent and brief acquaintance with problems of emotional development per se. I welcome the opportunity to comment on such problems from a point of view that has had relatively little attention in the developmental field. At the same time I must emphasize that I claim no expertise in that field; rather, I want to raise questions that arise from my particular theoretical orientation. My view on problems of emotion has been presented extensively elsewhere, and I will, in particular, draw on three recent publications: my 1975 book *Mind and Emotion* and two recent chapters, one a brief statement of the theoretical position, the other a theoretical extension that addressed problems of stress (1979a, 1980).

My major intent is to describe a theoretical orientation that focuses on the generation or production of emotional experience. Rather than accepting emotional feelings as elementary givens, my concern is with the specification of the conditions and variables that produce the kinds of states that the common language labels *emotions*. The approach is anchored in modern work (e.g., that of Schachter) as well in 19th-century conflict theories of emotion (e.g., Dewey, Paulhan; and see Mandler, 1979b, for discussion).

A point of view

My position is closely identified with modern cognitive psychology, also known as the human-information-processing approach. By *cognition* (knowledge) we mean all the processes, mechanisms, and structures that are ascribed to the human organism in order to make thought and action comprehensible, predictable, and manipulable. In a sense *cognition* has achieved a range of intent that is nearly coextensive with the concept of mind. We arrive therefore at a theory-rich psychology whose practitioners are loosely united by a concern with structures, mental organizations, relational (rather than associationistic) processes, and – at times – computational and neurological metaphors. We are not primarily concerned with the contents of consciousness (or with the categories of the common language); rather, we attempt to specify those theoretical mechanisms that are responsible for the contents of consciousness, as well as for the usual common categories of human behavior, such as motivation, thought, and emotion.

If it is the case that the visible, audible, and experienced aspects of human thought and behavior are to be analyzed in terms of their causal antecedents, then clearly so-called emotional behaviors and experiences become prime targets for such a cognitive analysis. Like other workers in the same tradition, I have undertaken exactly such analysis. Briefly, I assume that emotional experiences are the holistic outcome of two separable but not necessarily independent processes and mechanisms. One is global autonomic (visceral) arousal; the other is cognitive evaluation. The former determines the intensity, the latter the quality, of emotional experience.

Conventional wisdom about the emotions rejects, or is at least uncomfortable with, this basic assumption. The available evidence is interpretable in a variety of ways, but the position does have the advantage of testability. Intensity of experienced emotion is assigned (in most cases) to measurable autonomic reactions, and its quality must be related to evaluative cognitions.

The impact of autonomic arousal is mediated by autonomic perception, including autonomic imagery in the absence of physical arousal. Arousal itself is, in the majority if not in all of the cases, the consequence of cognitive, perceptual, behavioral interruption. I use the term *interruption* in a neutral sense; it does not imply an aversive event. For example, receiving a larger salary than expected may be just as interrupting as receiving a smaller one. Interruptions occur whenever any initiated train of thought or behavior cannot be completed, whenever a cognitive or perceptual schema is violated by either external or internal events.

Cognitive evaluation is really another term for the cognitive, pervasive, and continuing process whereby the human mental system perceives, categorizes, constructs, and evaluates its internal and external environment. With respect to the emotional complex the stress is on evaluation because it best describes the particular cognitions that interact with arousal to generate emotional states. Arousal with a cognition equivalent to a statement such as "That's a park and a horse carriage" produces no noticeable emotional states; but "That's a bridle path and a horse is bearing down on me" will generate an emotional state because of the particular (explicit or implicit) evaluative cognition that says that it is bad to be in the path of a galloping horse. Many writers in the emotional field have posited some fundamental judgment of good or bad as the basis for human evaluation or appraisal. Here again I insist on a psychological analysis. What are the mechanisms that produce the phenomenal experience of good/bad evaluations? I have suggested several, among them the quality of the structure involved in cognizing the event; if accommodation/assimilation proceeds smoothly and without difficulty, we tend toward the positive; when such structural change or use becomes difficult or impossible (as when encountering an unacceptable novel event), we sometimes tend toward the bad evaluation. Another basis for the good/bad dimension can be found in the association with innately aversive events (such as tissue injury, loss of support, some smells, and so forth). Finally, much of the good/bad distinction is acquired as part of our cultural/social context and is accepted without further analysis in the process of socialization.

It should be clear from the above that I reject as inadequate those explanatory systems of emotional states that require an innate, unlearned, fundamental emotional repertory, though there are innately aversive and pleasurable events or states that contribute to the construction of the emotional state. Nor do I believe that facial expressions *express* some underlying fundamental emotion. I do accept some degree of universality of facial expression, but I believe both emotional theory and evolutionary arguments are served better by seeing them as primitive communication devices. They are nonverbal signals that communicate evaluations about external and internal states. They do not, of course, communicate evaluations as soon as they appear (as in the newborn), any more than the phonemic productions of the very young child function as communicative language. As soon as cognitive development achieves evaluative knowledge, however, these expressions can be used to communicate such judgments. Because facial expressions are primarily evaluative, they form (but only in conjunction with visceral arousal) an important component of emotional displays and experiences. Similar arguments can be made about the adaptive and evolutionary history of defensive aggression (hostility), sexuality (lust), and humor. These action systems do not express emotions but form an important part of them.

A final introductory word about consciousness. I assume, together with most cognitive psychologists, that consciousness is best viewed as a limited capacity system. We assume that in contrast to older views of cognition, the products and not the processes of mental life are generally (but not always) available in consciousness.

Cognitive and emotional development: an artificial separation

The brief survey of my position on emotional life should make obvious my choice of topic in this essay: The emotions of the child (and the adult) are constructed in the process of development. The construction will to a large extent depend on the individual's cognitive development, on the way he or she learns to construct the world, the individual reality. There are some primitive emotional reactions that can appear prior to extensive cognitive development. Fearlike reactions may be constructed out of autonomic reactions and unlearned responses to the environment. Still, these primitive emotions during early stages of development are often dissimilar from the adult emotion. For example, in the adult the category of emotions classified as fear usually has some quite specific cognitive content. In any case, I shall concentrate in these pages on the acquired rather than the innate aspects of emotional experience. Thus I shall assume that in many, if not most, cases, emotional development depends on the particular cognitive development of the individual. Although there are issues in the development of visceral responsivity to which I shall return later, we will see that even these depend in many instances on cognitive evaluative processes.

I consider the distinction between cognitive and emotional development an artificial separation, because from my point of view emotional development (if it is to be considered separately at all) is a function of cognitive development. It is of course the case that much of the work on cognitive development has dealt with issues of intellective, problem-solving, and language functioning, and many of the insights gained from a knowledge of those processes have relatively little bearing on emotional functioning. Still, the development of the evaluative perception of the world, the construction of the social world, and the acquisition of evaluative categories all presumably proceed in a fashion similar to the development of spatio/temporal perception, the construction of physical objects, and the acquisition of semantic categories in the narrow sense. One of the consequences of arguing my position involves recognizing that the differentiation of complex emotional states should go hand in hand with cognitive development and differentiation.

In the rest of this chapter I will raise questions about cognitive/evaluative development on the one hand and autonomic/visceral development on the other. I will focus on those aspects of development that are directly relevant to the construction of emotion. Because it is not my intention to review the existing literature on these topics, the following discussion in no way implies that some (or all) of these questions have not been previously addressed; many of them have. My intent, however, is to point out those areas of investigation and potential knowledge that are specifically relevant to the point of view expressed here.

The development of cognitive/evaluative processes

Consciousness

If, as I have argued elsewhere, the limited-capacity consciousness system is the arena for emotional experience, then one of the first questions that arises concerns the change in conscious capacity with age – if any change in fact occurs. Currently there are two major theoretical contenders, one that capacity changes over ontogeny and the other that the apparent developmental changes are a function of the increasing ability of the organism to organize and structure mental products (and pari passu the representation of the external world). If – as I tend to believe – the latter interpretation is correct, then the organization of autonomic perception and evaluative cognitions, as well as actions, will significantly change conscious contents during the course of development. At least the anecdotal evidence suggests that adults can think about, or keep in mind, more disparate events at any one time than the young child can. The apparent lack of continuing attentiveness on the part of some children may be one symptom of the relative capacity of conscious attention. Better packaging (chunking) of information seems to be one result of cognitive growth, but increased skill in time sharing may also be involved. The issue is of particular importance to problems of emotion and stress because experienced emotion requires some share of conscious capacity. How well that capacity is used in general will determine the extent to which these emotional states interfere, for example, with other ongoing thought and action.

What is the relative importance of automatic versus capacity-demanding perceptions and actions? We know that certain perceptual processes require little or no conscious capacity; they are automatic. On the other hand, there is evidence that these automatic reactions develop from attentive repetitions of nonautomatic ones. Similarly, some actions require conscious capacity (learning to ride a bicycle), whereas others do not (bicycle riding by the accomplished rider). It is also possible that the distinction between voluntary and involuntary actions in the common language in part involves the automatic/conscious continuum. The development of automatic perceptions and skills not only has pure cognitive import for development but also addresses the development of emotions. Some emotions seem to be more automatic (involuntary?) than others. I am addressing here of course only those cognitions, perceptions, and skills that develop automaticity in the course of human growth. Some automatic/involuntary reactions are clearly "built into" the organism. Predominant among these is the noncognitive autonomic response to interruption (as seen in the newborn in the response to loss of support, for example). In addition, there are perceptual, cognitive, and action structures (such as scanning and sucking) that are the basis of further cognitive development. Given some built-in automatic structures and the vast array of cognitive structures still to be developed, the important question to be asked is: What characteristics of the child and of the environment determine the growth of automaticity, the utilization of limited capacity consciousness, and – consequently – the development of emotional experience?

Values, cultural and individual

The cognitive evaluation of the world is an important determiner not only of the kinds of complex emotions that the individual can and will experience but also of the specific emotions that any particular event is likely to elicit. Yet there are many emotions that seem to occur cross-culturally and transsocially. All human beings apparently experience fear, anxiety, grief, and joy. I cannot repeat in detail the arguments I have given for the basis of these generalities. Briefly, there appear to be general cognitive conditions that seem to be concomitant with these emotions. For example, joy is often related to the occurrence of an unanticipated positively valued event, grief to the absence of an important and structurally central object (usually but not always human), anxiety to helplessness – the unavailability of appropriate coping mechanisms. Still, it is well known that there are important individual as well as cultural differences in the experience of and the occasions for these emotions. Emotional labels are convenient categorical language devices that facilitate communication, but they do not – by definition – accommodate the nuances of emotional experience.

One of the central cultural influences on the pervasive, as well as the individual, emotions concerns the frequency with which certain emotions are encountered in a culture or society, as well as the distribution of their intensities. The values, categories, and schemata that encode a particular societal structure (culture) will determine in part how and when anxiety, grief, depression, and fear will be experienced. Developmental studies of how the problem of helplessness is handled, of how people deal with the absence of significant others, of the cognitive manipulation of pain, and of the expression of feeling in the presence of the unexpected address problems of the noxious emotions. Similar questions about the context of early problem solving, of the categorization of parent figures, of play and the interactions with peers, of giving and receiving comfort, and of attitudes toward sexual stimulation will enlighten us about the development of the positive emotions.

In order to understand the development of the emotions, we need to know how the child comes to construct systems of values. How does the categorization of values develop? To what extent are the categories of the common language accepted during socialization without conflict, and when does conflict between value structures and the message of the common language arise? How do variations in the semantic, syntactic, and pragmatic aspects of the home language affect values and the categories imposed on the world? More generally, we must become more alert to the evaluative structures imposed on the emotional life of the child (and the adult) by the prevailing value structures of the society in which people construct their emotions. A competitive society will encourage competitive and often hostile evaluations and therefor hostile emotions; a cooperative society will encourage positive reactions to arousing situations. The anthropological literature abounds with instances of such generalizations, and an anthropology of our own culture can alert us to the influence of pervasive cultural values on emotional development. For example, television viewing of violence in a violent culture should have emotional consequences quite different from those to be expected in a cooperative nonviolent culture.

The development of autonomic/visceral functions

The perception of arousal

Central to the role of peripheral autonomic responses in the framework outlined here is the implication that global arousal must be perceived in order to become effective. Conscious emotional experience depends on the registration of visceral arousal. It is in fact the perceived rather than the actual level of arousal that affects the intensity of emotional experience. Thus, the notion of unconscious emotions is a contradiction in terms, but what others have meant to index by such a concept may well be the occurrence of unregistered, unperceived visceral arousal.

The perception of internal autonomic events, just like the perception of spatio/temporal events in the environment, depends on the acquisition of perceptual structures that govern what is perceived and what is perceivable. At the present time we know very little about the early development of the perception of autonomic events. We know that the autonomic activity of the newborn is immensely variable. That variation often occurs independently of external events. It seems reasonable to assume that the first steps toward building stable perceptual structures occur during this period. Of particular interest would be the development of individual thresholds for the perception of visceral arousal. I have argued elsewhere that high and low thresholds for such perception may be one of the bases for the development of sociopathic and anxiety-neurotic response patterns, respectively.

Functions of the autonomic nervous system

I view the functions of the autonomic nervous system as more broadly adaptive than is indicated by the classical position on homeostasis. Recent evidence has shown that various autonomic reactions alert the organism for potential action, direct and focus attentional mechanisms, and often serve as an auxiliary alerting mechanism. These functions seem to be particularly important with respect to the interruption/arousal conjunction. One result of such a position is that rather than seeing emotional arousal as a remnant of our presapient past, I consider it a central process in adaptive coping with the environment.

If such an argument is correct, then the interaction of visceral regulatory systems with early cognitive (and emotional) development deserves serious attention. There is some evidence that in the very young child (as sometimes in the adult), attention to arousing events is delayed until the autonomic nervous system has reacted (with a latency of 1–2 seconds or more). Detailed studies of the time course of this reaction and its development toward the generally much quicker adult response seem most important for an understanding of the development of emotional reactions in children. More generally, how do children learn to take advantage of the alerting function of the visceral system?

Related questions address the problem of the sympathetic–parasympathetic balance and the source of temperamental differences. Individuals differ in the relative balance between reactions of the sympathetic and parasympathetic nervous systems. Are these differences preset, or are they influenced by environmental events during development? Are they related to temperamental differences, which seem to be relatively innate in origin? Specifically, are differences in temperament (speed, attention, reactivity) related to physiological activity, to differences in differential attention and scanning of the world, or to both? What is their developmental course?

In the course of exploring the developmental consequences of a constructivist position on emotion, I have alluded to a number of already well-established research areas, including socialization and moral development. I want to stress again that my attempt should not be seen as an assessment of the state of the art. My purpose is to illustrate the kinds of questions that need to be answered. We have information on some of them, but more is needed.

Concluding comments

I will conclude with some more general questions about the developmental construction of emotion. First, I have omitted the fascinating problem of emotional inhibitors. William Kessen and I suggested some years ago (Kessen & Mandler, 1961) that distress and anxiety in the infant can usefully be analyzed in terms of inhibitions of a fundamental state of arousal. We contrasted such an analysis with the traditional approach to distress and anxiety that invokes elicitors and arousing occasions. Some of the potent inhibitors (stroking, rocking, sucking) not only deserve more attention by investigators but are also of special interest because their effectiveness seems to decline over ontogeny.

Second, we need to reexamine our use of the concept of stress. In particular, psychologists are probably more likely to break out of the definitional circle that defines as a stressor any event that produces certain stress symptoms. Some suggestions that point toward an independent, psychological definition of a stressor in terms of cognitive and arousal functions already exist, but such a definition needs to be refined and theoretically based. It seems unlikely that we will gain much insight into the question of how children learn to perceive and cope with stress unless we start with some reasonable theoretical framework that will at least generate the appropriate queries. Related to such an enterprise would be the abandonment of definitions that depend on enumeration, as the notion of *noxious stimulus* so obviously does.

Finally, it is well known in both psychology and the real world that any prior emotional state makes an individual more susceptible to subsequent emotional events. The prior states color the subsequent emotion and also frequently potentiate its intensity. What is the developmental course of this effect? I find the effect itself easily explicable in terms of my position; a high level of prior arousal should potentiate a subsequent emotional event, and the prior cognitive/evaluative state should influence subsequent ones. How does this emotional priming affect the very young child?

To conclude: The emotions of the child, as of the adult, are constructed from a variety of events, including cognitive and visceral ones, from acquired and innate structures, and from cultural and idiosyncratic signals. Just as the constructive approach has enlivened the contemporary study of language, memory, and perception, so might the constructive approach to emotion open new insights to the development of the child.

References

Kessen, W., & Mandler, G. Anxiety, pain, and the inhibition of distress. *Psychological Review,* 1961, *68,* 396–404.

Mandler, G. *Mind and emotion.* New York: Wiley, 1975.

Mandler, G. Thought processes, consciousness, and stress. In V. Hamilton & D. M. Warburton (Eds.), *Human stress and cognition: An information processing approach.* London: Wiley, 1979.(a)

Mandler, G. Emotion. In E. Hearst (Ed.), *The first century of experimental psychology.* Hillsdale, N.J.: Erlbaum, 1979.(b)

Mandler, G. The generation of emotion: A psychological theory. In R. Plutchik & H. Kellerman (Eds.), *Theories of emotion.* New York: Academic Press, 1980.

Index

Acoustic cues, 130
Acoustic parameters, 132–4, 144, 149
Acoustical measurement apparatus, 157
Acquisition of language, 151
Activation, 130
Adaptation, 327, 329
  individual, 325
Adaptive communication (regulation), 322, 337
Affect
  definitions of, 98
  direct, 281
  empathic, 294
  management of, 128
Affectograms, 118
  dyadic, 119
  group, 124
  individual, 119
Affex (System for Identifying Affect Expressions by Holistic Judgments), 114
  reliability of, 115–16
  validity of, 116–17
Affiliation, 192
Age differences, 200
Aggression, 33
Androgens, 33
Anger, 130, 169, 192
Anger–fear, 82
Anxiety, 130, 252
Arousal, 38, 129, 134, 137, 148, 199, 312
Assessment, 187
Attachment, 30, 192
Attention, 50, 166
  social–visual, 164
Attentional processes, 303
Attribution, 180
Autonomic nervous system, 341–2
  patterns of activity in, 80
Autonomic/visceral functions, development of, 341–2

Babbling, 151
Baseline
  pretask, 305
  relaxation, 305
Behavior
  antisocial, 326
  competitive, 325
  cooperative, 325
  prosocial, 326
  reproductive, 331
Behavioral pattern, 183
Behavioral programs
  closed, 330
  open, 330
Behavioral scaling, 194
Bias, 208
Blink rates, 172
Blinking, 172
Blood pressure, 82, 299, 307, 309

Call system in animals, 128
Cardiovascular functions, 299
  changes in, 80
Carotid sinus, 39
Circadian pattern, 27
Circadian rhythm, 24, 26
Classical conditioning, 281
Cognition, 335
Cognitive/evaluative processes
  development of, 338–40
Competence, 192
Competition, 328
Confirmatory factor analyses, 258
Consciousness, 336–7
Content-masking techniques, 212
Contingent mutuality, 168
Control, 302
Cooperation, 328
Coping, 27, 29, 302

Cortisol, 24, 26
Crying, 131, 149

Darwin, 318
Day care, 191
Deception, 326
Defense, 29
Denial, 29
Depression, 79, 85, 252
Development of contextual knowledge, 190
Differential emotions theory, 97, 98, 251
Discrepancy, 39
Dishabituation, 51
Dissociation, 86
Distress, 43, 149, 153

Ecological validity, 322
Ego strength scale, 307
Emergent property, 68
Emotion(s), 128, 299, 320
    characteristics of, 8–11
    complexity of, 97
    components of, 98
    construction of, 338
    definition of, 1,8,9
    in development, 101
    differentiation of, 148
    discreteness of, 131, 150
    experience of, 180
    expression of, 180
    indexes of, 9
    and personality, 97, 98
    universality of, 97
- Emotion and cognition, 6
Emotion systems, 183
Emotional behavior, 178
Emotional blends, 70, 79–80
Emotional development, 203, 335–8
Emotional elicitors, 180
Emotional expressions, 85
Emotional receptors, 180
Emotionality, 32
Empathic arousal, mechanisms of, 281–3
Empathic response, levels of, 284
Empathy, 180
    for another's feelings, 285
    definition of, 286
    definitional issues, 286
    egocentric, 284
    facial expression as index of, 291
    global, 284
    indexes of, 288–92
    for someone's general life condition, 285
Enduring states, 186
Energy distribution in the voice spectrum, 139,
    145

Ethological approach, 317
Ethological position, 320
Ethology, 332
Evaluations, 187
Evolution, theory of, 325
Evolutionary biology, 318
Evolutionary–developmental perspective, 322
Expressive displays, 174
Eye movements, 313

Facial behavior, measurement of, 101–24
Facial expression, 129, 131, 132, 148, 150–2,
    180, 184, 252, 337
    adaptive nature of, 317
    expressive aspect of, 317
    regulative aspect of, 317, 321, 324
Fear, 40, 171, 192, 312
Feshbach and Roe technique, 292
Fixation
    initial, 166
    time, 51
    visual, 165
Fretting, 50
Fundamental frequency, 129, 136, 143, 147

Gaze behavior, 164
    patterns of, 165–70
Grief, 130
Growth hormone, 32

Habituation, 50
Happiness, 192
Heart rate, 82, 288, 299, 312
    acceleration, 38, 40, 300
    deceleration, 38, 166, 300
    variability of, 40, 50
    see also cardiovascular functions
Hemispheric asymmetry, 87
Hemophiliac, 29
Hormones, 21
Hospitalization, 28

Individual differences, 27, 179, 305
Inhibition, 41
Instincts, 323
Interest, 167
    in infants, 312
Interruption, 336
Intonation contours, 137
Intraindividual differences, 31
Intraspecific communication, 319

Jenkins activity survey, 307
Joy, 169

LISREL, 258
Locus-of-control, 307

Long-term spectra, 141
Loudness, 130, 144

Max (Maximally Discriminative Facial Movement Coding System), 105–7
 reliability of, 107–10
 validity of, 110–14
Measurement, 175, 178
Measurement model, 257
Mimicry, 282
Moods, 130
Mother–child relationship, 30
Mother–infant attachment, 150
Multiple-factor models, 258
Muscle activity, 76

Natural (and sexual) selection, 325
Naturalistic social conditions, 324
Noncry vocalizations, 151
Nonverbal channels, 214
Nonverbal communication, 167, 214
 deception in, 225
 decoding, 208–9, 230–3
 leakage, 234–6
Nonverbal decoding strategies, 230–3
Nonverbal Discrepancy Test, 218
Nonverbal sensitivity, 209–10
 age changes in, 236–43
 development of, 236–7
 sex differences in, 237, 238
Novelty, 26

Orienting, 312

PACKAGE, 258
Parasympathetic system, 40, 300
Patterning, 67
Person Description Test, 224–6
Pitch, *see* fundamental frequency
PONS Test, 210–18
Postural responses, 185
Prosocial skills, 326
Psychophysiology, 67

Reaction time, 300
Reliability Theory, 257
Repression, 86
Reproductive success, 327, 329
Respiration, 40
Reticular formation, 39
Ritualization, 319
Role taking, 282

Sadness, 130
Schema, 39
Separation, 30, 43

Separation anxiety, 44
Sex differences, 78–9, 201
Sexual arousal, 252
Shock avoidance, 302
Sign stimulus, 318
Sinus arrhythmia, 40
Situational analysis, 203
Situations, 192
Social intelligence, 208–10
Socialization, 187
Sociobiology, 318
Socioemotional domains, 192
Socioemotional scales, 191
Somatomotor, 39, 301
Sorrow, 169
Sound/silence events, 135, 136
Stability, 39, 53
State transition matrix, 168
Steroids
 corticosteroid, 23, 27, 31
 in the newborn, 24
Stimulus meaning, 188
Stress, 22, 27–9, 86, 172
Subjective experience, 70
Surgery, 27, 28
Surprise, 312, 320
Sweat gland, 300
Symbolic association, 282
Sympathetic excitation, 300

Tempo, 130
Threat displays, 164
Timidity, 40
Trait, 202
Transitional probabilities, 168
Two-factor learning theory, 312

Uncertainty, 44
U-shaped function, 52

Vagal, 39, 40, 300
Vascular resistance, 309
Vasomotor activity, 300
Video primacy
 developmental tendency in, 241
 in nonverbal communication, 221
Vocal expression, 128
Vocal tract, 133, 134, 141, 147
Vocalization
 in emotion, 128
 of infant, 131, 146
Voice
 parameters of, 129
 production of, 133, 134
 quality of, 145
Vulnerability, 45